THE DEVILS OF LOUDUN

*the text of this book is printed
on 100% recycled paper*

ÆT. 37.
1627.

VRBANVS GRANDERIVS
IVLIODVNENSIS ECCLESIÆ
RECTOR. MDCXXVII.

E. Grasset d.

THE
DEVILS
OF
LOUDUN

BY
ALDOUS HUXLEY

HARPER COLOPHON BOOKS

HARPER & ROW, PUBLISHERS

NEW YORK, HAGERSTOWN, SAN FRANCISCO, LONDON

THE DEVILS OF LOUDUN. Copyright, 1952, by Aldous Huxley.
Printed in the United States of America.

"I am gall, I am heartburn" from poems of Gerard Manley Hopkins,
copyright, 1948, by Oxford University Press, Inc.

First HARPER COLOPHON edition published 1965 by
Harper & Row, Publishers, Incorporated, New York.

ISBN: 0-06-090210-8

Library of Congress catalog card number: 66-15223

79 80 81 82 83 10 9 8 7 6 5

THE DEVILS OF LOUDUN

CHAPTER ONE

IT WAS in 1605 that Joseph Hall, the satirist and future bishop, made his first visit to Flanders. "Along our way how many churches saw we demolished, nothing left but rude heaps to tell the passenger, there hath been both devotion and hostility. Oh, the miserable footsteps of war! . . . But (which I wondered at) churches fall, and Jesuits' colleges rise everywhere. There is no city where these are not rearing or built. Whence cometh this? Is it for that devotion is not so necessary as policy? These men (as we say of the fox) fare best when they are most cursed. None so much spited of their own; none so hated of all; none so opposed of by ours; and yet these ill weeds grow."

They grew for a very simple and sufficient reason: the public wanted them. For the Jesuits themselves, "policy," as Hall and his whole generation knew very well, was the first consideration. The schools had been called into existence for the purpose of strengthening the Roman Church against its enemies, the "libertines" and the Protestants. The good fathers hoped, by their teaching, to create a class of educated laymen totally devoted to the interests of the Church. In the words of Cerutti—words which drove the indignant Michelet almost to frenzy—"as we swathe the limbs of an infant in the cradle to give them a right proportion, so it is necessary from his earliest youth to swathe, so to speak, his will, that it may preserve through his life a happy and salutary suppleness." The spirit of domination was willing enough, but the flesh of propagandist method was weak. In spite of the swaddling of their wills, some of the Jesuits' best pupils left school to become free thinkers or even, like Jean Labadie, Protestants. So far as "policy" was concerned, the system was never as efficient as its creators had hoped. But the public was not interested in policy; the public was interested in good schools, where their boys could learn all that a gentleman ought to know. Better than most other purveyors of education, the Jesuits supplied the demand. "What did I observe during the seven years I passed under the Jesuits' roof? A life full of moderation, diligence and order. They devoted every hour of the day to our education, or to the strict fulfillment of their vows. As evidence of this, I appeal to the testimony of the thousands who, like myself, were educated by them." So wrote Voltaire. His words bear witness to the excellence of the Jesuits' teaching methods. At the same time, and yet more emphatically, his entire career bears witness to the failure of that "policy," which the teaching methods were intended to serve.

When Voltaire went to school, the Jesuit colleges were familiar features of the educational scene. A century earlier their merits had seemed positively revolutionary. In an age when most pedagogues were amateurs in everything except the handling of the birch, their disciplinary methods were relatively humane and their professors carefully chosen and systematically trained. They taught a peculiarly elegant Latin and the very latest in optics, geography and mathematics, together with "dramatics" (their end-of-term theatricals were famous), good manners, respect for the Church and (in France, at least, and after Henri IV's conversion) obedience to the royal authority. For all these reasons the Jesuit colleges recommended themselves to every member of the typical upper-class family—to the tender-hearted mother, who could not bear to think of her darling undergoing the tortures of an old-fashioned education; to the learned ecclesiastical uncle, with his concern for sound doctrine and a Ciceronian style; and finally to the father who, as a patriotic official, approved of monarchical principles and, as a prudent bourgeois, counted on the Company's backstairs influence to help their pupil to a job, a place at court, an ecclesiastical sinecure. Here, for example, is a very substantial couple—M. Corneille of Rouen, *Avocat du Roy à la Table de Marbre du Palais*, and his wife, Marthe le Pesant. Their son, Pierre, is such a promising boy that they decide to send him to the Jesuits. Here is M. Joachim Descartes, Counselor of the Parlement of Rennes. In 1604 he takes his youngest—a bright little fellow of eight, called René—to the recently founded and royally endowed Jesuit College of La Flèche. And here too, at about the same date, is the learned Canon Grandier of Saintes. He has a nephew, son of another lawyer not quite so rich and aristocratic as M. Descartes or M. Corneille, but still eminently respectable. The boy, called Urbain, is now fourteen years old and wonderfully clever. He deserves to be given the best of educations, and in the neighborhood of Saintes the best education available is to be had at the Jesuit College of Bordeaux.

This celebrated seat of learning comprised a high school for boys, a liberal arts college, a seminary, and a School of Advanced Studies for ordained postgraduates. Here the precociously brilliant Urbain Grandier spent more than ten years, first as schoolboy, and later as undergraduate, theological student and, after his ordination in 1615, as Jesuit novice. Not that he intended to enter the Company; for he felt no vocation to subject himself to so rigid a discipline. No, his career was to be made, not in a religious order, but as a secular priest. In that profession a man of his native abilities, pushed and protected by the most powerful organization within the Church, could hope to go far. There might be a chaplaincy to some great noble, the tutorship of some future marshal of France, some cardinal in the bud. There might be invitations to display his remarkable eloquence before bishops, before princesses of the blood, even before the Queen herself. There might be diplomatic missions, appointments of high administrative posts, rich sinecures, juicy pluralities. There might—though this was unlikely, considering that he was not of noble birth—but there conceivably might be some princely bishopric to gild and gladden his declining years.

At the outset of his career circumstances seemed to authorize the most sanguine of these expectations. For at twenty-seven, after two years of advanced theology and philosophy, young Father Grandier received his reward for so many long semesters of diligence and good behavior. By the Company of Jesus, in whose gift it lay, he was presented to the important living of Saint-Pierre du Marché at Loudun. At the same time, and thanks to the same benefactors, he was made a canon of the collegial church of the Holy Cross. His foot was on the ladder; all he now had to do was to climb.

Loudun, as its new parson rode slowly toward his destination, revealed itself as a little city on a hill, dominated by two tall towers—the spire of St. Peter's and the medieval keep of the great castle. As a symbol, as a sociological hieroglyph, Loudun's skyline was somewhat out of date. That spire still threw its Gothic shadow across the town; but a good part of the townspeople were Huguenots who abhorred the Church to which it belonged. That huge donjon, built by the Counts of Poitiers, was still a place of formidable strength; but Richelieu would soon be in power and the days of local autonomy and provincial fortresses were numbered. All unknowing the parson was riding into the last act of a sectarian war, into the prologue to a nationalist revolution.

At the city gates a corpse or two hung, moldering, from the municipal gallows. Within the walls, there were the usual dirty streets, the customary gamut of smells, from wood smoke to excrement, from geese to incense, from baking bread to horses, swine and unwashed humanity.

Peasants, and artisans, journeymen, and domestics—the poor were a negligible and anonymous majority of the city's fourteen thousand inhabitants. A little above them the shopkeepers, the master craftsmen, the small officials clustered precariously on the lowest rung of bourgeois respectability. Above these again—totally dependent upon their inferiors, but enjoying unquestioned privileges and ruling them by a divine right—were the rich merchants, the professional men, the people of quality in their hierarchical order: the petty gentry and the larger landowners, the feudal magnates and the lordly prelates. Here and there one could find

4

a few small oases of culture and disinterested intelligence. Outside these oases the mental atmosphere was suffocatingly provincial. Among the rich, the concern with money and property, with rights and privileges, was passionate and chronic. For the two or three thousand, at the most, who could afford litigation or needed professional legal advice, there were, at Loudun, no less than twenty barristers, eighteen solicitors, eighteen bailiffs and eight notaries.

Such time and energy as were left over from the preoccupation with possessions were devoted to the cozy little monotonies, the recurrent joys and agonies of family life; to gossip about the neighbors; to the formalities of religion and, since Loudun was a city divided against itself, to the inexhaustible acerbities of theological controversy. Of the existence at Loudun, during the parson's incumbency, of any genuinely spiritual religion there is no evidence. Widespread concern with the spiritual life arises only in the neighborhood of exceptional individuals who know by direct experience that God is a Spirit and must be worshiped in spirit. Along with a good supply of scoundrels, Loudun had its share of the upright and the well-intentioned, the pious and even the devout. But it had no saints, no man or woman whose mere presence is the self-validating proof of a deeper insight into the eternal reality, a closer unison with the divine ground of all being. Not until sixty years later did such a person appear within the city walls. When, after the most harrowing physical and spiritual adventures, Louise du Tronchay came at last to work in the hospital of Loudun, she at once became the center of an intense and eager spiritual life. People of all ages and of every class came flocking to ask her about God, to beg for her advice and help. "They love us too much here," Louise wrote to her old confessor in Paris. "I feel quite ashamed of it; for when I speak of God, people are so much moved that they start crying. I am afraid of contributing to the good opinion they have of me." She longed to run away and hide; but she was the prisoner of a city's devotion. When she prayed, the sick were often healed. To her shame and mortification, Louise was held responsible for their recovery. "If I ever did a miracle," she wrote, "I should think myself damned." After a few years she was ordered by her directors to move away from Loudun. For the people there was now no longer any living window through which the Light might shine. In a little while the fervor cooled; the interest in the life of the spirit died down. Loudun returned to its normal state—the state it had been in when, two generations earlier, Urbain Grandier rode into town.

From the first, public sentiment in regard to the new parson was sharply divided. Most of the devouter sex approved of him. The late Curé had been a doddering nonentity. His successor was a man in the prime of youth, tall, athletic, with an air of grave authority, even (according to one contemporary) of majesty. He had large dark eyes and, under his biretta, an abundance of crinkly black hair. His forehead was high, his nose aquiline, his lips red, full and mobile. An elegant Van Dyck beard adorned his chin, and on his upper lip he wore a narrow mustache sedulously trained and pomaded so that its curling ends confronted one another, on either side of the nose, like a pair of coquettish question marks. To post-Faustian eyes his portrait suggests a fleshier, not unamiable and only slightly less intelligent Mephistopheles in clerical fancy dress.

To this seductive appearance Grandier added the social virtues of good manners and lively conversation. He could turn a compliment with easy grace, and the look with which he accompanied his words was more flattering, if the lady happened to be at all presentable, than the words themselves. The new parson, it was only too obvious, took an interest in his female parishioners that was more than merely pastoral.

Grandier lived in the gray dawn of what may be called the Era of Respectability. Throughout the Middle Ages and during the earlier part of the modern period the gulf between official Catholic theory and the actual practice of individual ecclesiastics had been enormous, unbridged and seemingly unbridgeable. It is difficult to find any medieval or Renaissance writer who does not take it for granted that, from highest prelate to humblest friar, the majority of clergymen are thoroughly disreputable. Ecclesiastical corruption begot the Reformation, and in its turn the Reformation produced the Counter Reformation. After the Council of Trent scandalous

Popes became less and less common, until finally, by the middle of the seventeenth century, the breed died out completely. Even some of the bishops, whose only qualification for preferment was the fact that they were the younger sons of noblemen, now made a certain effort to behave themselves. Among the lower clergy abuses were checked from above by a more vigilant and efficient ecclesiastical administration, and from within, by the zeal radiating from such organizations as the Society of Jesus and the Congregation of the Oratory. In France, where the monarchy was making use of the Church as an instrument for increasing the central power at the expense of the Protestants, the great nobles and the traditions of provincial autonomy, clerical respectability was a matter of royal concern. The masses will not revere a Church whose ministers are guilty of scandalous conduct. But in a country where not only *l'Etat*, but also *l'Eglise*, *c'est Moi*, disrespect for the Church is disrespect for the King. "I remember," writes Bayle in one of the interminable footnotes of his great *Dictionary*, "I remember that I one day asked a Gentleman who was relating to me numberless Irregularities of the Venetian Clergy, how it came to pass that the Senate suffered such a thing, so little to the Honour of Religion and the State. He replied, that the public Good obliged the Sovereign to use this Indulgence; and, to explain this Riddle, he added that the Senate was well pleased that the Priests and Monks were held in the utmost contempt by the People, since, for that reason, they would be less capable of causing an Insurrection among them. One of the Reasons, says he, why the Jesuits there are disagreeable to the Prince is because they preserve the Decorum of their Character; and thus, being the more respected by the inferior People, are more capable of raising a Sedition." In France, during the whole of the seventeenth century, state policy toward clerical irregularities was the exact opposite of that pursued by the Venetian Senate. Because it was afraid of ecclesiastical encroachment, the latter liked to see its clergymen conducting themselves like pigs and disliked the respectable Jesuits. Politically powerful and strongly Gallican, the French monarchy had no reason to fear the Pope, and found the Church very useful

7

as a machine for governing. For this reason it favored the Jesuits and discouraged priestly incontinence, or at least priestly indiscretion.* The new parson had embarked on his career at a time when clerical scandals, though still frequent, were becoming increasingly distasteful to those in authority.

In his autobiographical account of a seventeenth-century boyhood and youth, Grandier's younger contemporary, Jean-Jacques Bouchard, has left us a document so clinically objective, so completely free from all expressions of regret, from any kind of moral judgment, that nineteenth-century scholars could publish it only for private circulation and with emphatic comments on the author's unspeakable depravity. For a generation brought up on Havelock Ellis and Krafft-Ebing, on Hirschfeld and Kinsey, Bouchard's book no longer seems outrageous. But though it has ceased to shock, it must still astonish. For how startling it is to find a subject of Louis XIII writing of the less creditable forms of sexual activity in the flat, matter-of-fact style of a modern college girl answering an

* The following extracts are taken from H. C. Lea's summary of conditions in the French Church after the Council of Trent. In the earlier part of our period "the influence of the Tridentine canons had been unsatisfactory. In a royal council held in 1560 . . . Charles de Marillac, Bishop of Vienne, declared that ecclesiastical discipline was almost obsolete, and that no previous time had seen scandals so frequent, or the life of the clergy so reprehensible. . . . The French prelates, like the Germans, were in the habit of collecting the 'cullagium' from all their priests, and informing those who did not keep concubines that they might do so if they liked, but must pay the license-money whether or no." "It is evident from all this that the standard of ecclesiastical morals had not been raised by the efforts of the Tridentine fathers, and yet a study of the records of church discipline shows that with the increasing decency and refinement of society during the seventeenth and eighteenth centuries the open and cynical manifestations of license among the clergy became gradually rarer." The avoidance of scandal became a matter of paramount importance. If concubines were kept, they were kept "under the guise of sisters and nieces." By a code of regulations issued in 1668 it was decreed that friars of the Order of Minims should not be excommunicated if, "when about to yield to the temptations of the flesh, or to commit theft, they prudently laid aside the monastic habit." (Henry C. Lea, *History of Sacerdotal Celibacy*, Chapter XXIX. "The Post-Tridentine Church.")

All this time spasmodic efforts were being made to enforce respectability. In 1624, for example, the Reverend René Sophier was found guilty of committing adultery in a church with the wife of a magistrate. The *Lieutenant Criminel* of le Mans condemned him to the gallows. The case was appealed to the Parlement of Paris which sentenced him, instead, to be burnt alive.

anthropologist's questionnaire, or a psychiatrist recording a case history! Descartes was ten years his senior; but long before the philosopher had started to vivisect those writhing automata, to which the vulgar attach the names of dog and cat, Bouchard was conducting a series of psycho-chemico-physiological experiments on his mother's chambermaid. The girl, when he first took notice of her, was pious and almost aggressively virtuous. With the patience and acumen of a Pavlov, Bouchard reconditioned this product of implicit faith so that she became at last a devotee of Natural Philosophy, as ready to be observed and experimented upon as to undertake researches on her own account. On the table next to Jean-Jacques' bed were piled half a dozen folio volumes on anatomy and medicine. Between two assignations, or even between two experimental caresses, this odd forerunner of Ploss and Bartels would open his *De Generatione*, his Fernelius or his Ferandus and consult the relevant chapter, subsection and paragraph. But, unlike most of his contemporaries, he would accept nothing on authority. Lemnius and Rodericus a Castro might say what they liked about the strange and alarming properties of menstrual blood; Jean-Jacques was determined to see for himself whether it really did all the things it was reputed to do. Seconded by the now willing chambermaid, he made a succession of trials, only to find that, from time immemorial, the doctors, the philosophers and the theologians had been talking through their mortarboards and birettas. Menstrual blood did not kill grass, did not tarnish mirrors, did not blast the buds of the vine, did not dissolve asphalt and did not produce ineradicable spots of rust on the blade of a knife. Biological science lost one of its most promising investigators when, in order to get out of marrying his collaborator and *corpus vile*, Bouchard precipitately left Paris in order to seek his fortune at the papal court. All he wanted was a bishopric *in partibus*, or even, at a pinch, in Brittany— some unpretentious little benefice of six or seven thousand livres a year; that was all. (Six thousand five hundred livres was the income derived by Descartes from the judicious investment of his patrimony. It was not princely; but at least it permitted a philosopher to live like a gentleman.) Poor Bouchard was never

9

beneficed. Known to his contemporaries only as the ridiculous author of a *Panglossia*, or collection of verses in forty-six languages, including Coptic, Peruvian and Japanese, he died before he was forty.

Loudun's new parson was too normal and had too hearty an appetite to think of turning his bed into a laboratory. But, like Bouchard, Grandier was the scion of a respectable bourgeois family; like Bouchard, he had been educated at an ecclesiastical boarding school; like Bouchard, he was clever, learned and an enthusiastic humanist; and like Bouchard, he hoped to make a brilliant career in the Church. Socially and culturally, if not temperamentally, the two men had much in common. Consequently what Bouchard has to say of his childhood, his school days and his holiday diversions at home may be regarded as being indirectly evidential in regard to Grandier.

The world revealed by the *Confessions* is very like the world revealed to us by modern sexologists—but, if anything, a little more so. We see the small fry indulging in sexual play—indulging in it freely and frequently; for there seems to be singularly little adult interference with their activities. At school, under the good Fathers, there are no strenuous games, and the boys' superfluous energy can find no vent except in incessant masturbation and the practice, on half-holidays, of homosexuality. Pep talks and pulpit eloquence, confession and devotional exercises are to some slight extent restraining influences. Bouchard records that, at the four great feasts of the Church, he would refrain from his customary sexual practices for as long as eight or ten days at a stretch. But, try as he might, he never succeeded in prolonging these interims of chastity to a full fortnight, *quoy que la dévotion le gourmandast assez*—despite the fact that he was not a little checked and chided by devotion. In any given set of circumstances our actual behavior is represented by the diagonal of a parallelogram of forces having appetite or interest as its base and, as its upright, our ethical or religious ideals. In Bouchard's case and, we may suppose, in the case of the other boys whom he names as his companions in pleasure, the devotional upright was so short that the angle between the long base and the diagonal of manifest behavior was of only a very few degrees.

When he was at home for the holidays Bouchard's parents assigned him sleeping quarters in the same room with an adolescent chambermaid. This girl was all virtue while she was awake, but could not, it was obvious, be responsible for what happened while she was asleep. And according to her private system of casuistry, it made no difference whether she was really asleep or merely pretending. Later on, when Jean-Jacques's school days were over, there was a little peasant girl who minded the cows in the orchard. For a halfpenny, she was ready to grant any favors her young master might demand. Yet another maid, who had left because Bouchard's half brother, the Prior of Cassan, had tried to seduce her, now re-entered the family's service and soon became Jean-Jacques's guinea pig and co-worker in the sexual experimentation described in the second half of the *Confessions*.

Between Bouchard and the heir to the throne of France the gulf was wide and deep. And yet the moral atmosphere in which the future Louis XIII was brought up is similar in many respects to that breathed by his humbler contemporary. In the *Journal* of Dr. Jean Héroard, the little prince's physician, we possess a long and detailed record of a seventeenth-century childhood. True, the Dauphin was a very exceptional child—the first son born to a King of France in more than eighty years. But the very preciousness of this unique infant throws into yet sharper relief certain, to us, most extraordinary features of his upbringing. If this sort of thing was good enough for a child, for whom, by definition, nothing was good enough, then what, we may ask ourselves, was good enough for ordinary children? To start with, the Dauphin was brought up with a whole flock of his father's illegitimate children by three or four different mothers. Some of these left-handed brothers and sisters were older than himself, some younger. By the age of three—and perhaps earlier—he knew very clearly what bastards were and in what manner they were fabricated. The language in which this information was communicated was so consistently coarse that the child was often shocked by it. "*Fi donc!*"

he would say of his *Gouvernante*, Mme. de Montglat, "how nasty she is!"

Henry IV was very partial to dirty songs, and his courtiers and servants knew large numbers of them, which they were forever singing as they went about their business in the palace. And when they were not vocalizing their smut, the Prince's attendants, male and female, liked to joke obscenely with the child about his father's bastards and his own future wife (for he was already as good as betrothed), the Infanta, Anne of Austria. Moreover, the Dauphin's sexual education was not merely verbal. At night the child would often be taken into the beds of his waiting women—beds which they shared (without nightdresses or pajamas) either with other women or their husbands. It seems likely enough that, by the time he was four or five, the little boy knew all the facts of life, and knew them not merely by hearsay, but by inspection. This seems all the more probable since a seventeenth-century palace was totally without privacy. Architects had not yet invented the corridor. To get from one part of the building to another, one simply walked through a succession of other people's rooms, in which literally anything might be going on. And there was also the matter of etiquette. Less fortunate in this respect than his or her inferiors, a royal personage was never permitted to be alone. If one's blood were blue, one was born in a crowd, one died in a crowd, one even relieved nature in a crowd and on occasion one had to make love in a crowd. And the character of the circumambient architecture was such that one could scarcely avoid the spectacle of others being born, dying, relieving nature and making love. In later life Louis XIII displayed a decided aversion for women, a decided, though probably platonic, inclination for men, and a decided repugnance for all kinds of physical deformity and disease. The behavior of Mme. de Montglat and the other ladies of the court may easily have accounted for the first and also, by a natural reaction, for the second of these two traits; as for the third—who knows what repulsive squalors the child may not have stumbled upon in the all too public bedchambers of Saint-Germain-en-Laye?

Such, then, was the kind of world in which the new parson had been brought up—a world in which the traditional sexual taboos lay very lightly on the ignorant and poverty-stricken majority and not too heavily upon their betters; a world where duchesses joked like Juliet's nurse and the conversation of great ladies was a nastier and stupider echo of the Wife of Bath's; where a man of means and good social standing could (if he were not too squeamish in the matter of dirt and lice) satisfy his appetites almost *ad libitum*; and where, even among the cultivated and the thoughtful, the teachings of religion were taken for the most part in a rather Pickwickian sense, so that the gulf between theory and overt behavior, though a little narrower than in the medieval Ages of Faith, was yet sufficiently enormous. A product of this world, Urbain Grandier went to his parish with every intention of making the best both of it and of the other, the heavenly universe beyond the abhorred chasm. Ronsard was his favorite poet, and Ronsard had written certain *Stanzas* which perfectly expressed the young parson's point of view.

> *Quand au temple nous serons,*
> *Agenouillés nous ferons*
> *Les dévots selon la guise*
> *De ceux qui, pour louer Dieu,*
> *Humbles se courbent au lieu*
> *Le plus secret de l'Eglise.*

> *Mais quand au lit nous serons,*
> *Entrelacés nous ferons*
> *Les lascifs selon les guises*
> *Des amants qui librement*
> *Pratiquent folâtrement*
> *Dans les draps cent mignardises.**

It was a description of "the well-rounded life," and a well-rounded life was what this healthy young humanist was resolved to lead. But a priest's life is not supposed to be well-rounded; it is

* When we are in the temple, kneeling, we shall act the part of the devout, in the manner of those who, to praise God, humbly bow themselves in the most secret corner of the Church. But when we are in bed, intertwined, we shall act the part of wantons, in the manner of those lovers who, free and frolicsome, practice a hundred fondling arts.

supposed to be one-pointed—a compass, not a weathercock. In order to keep his life one-pointed, the priest assumes certain obligations, makes certain promises. In Grandier's case the obligations had been assumed and the vows pronounced with a mental restriction, which he was to make public—and then only for a single reader—in a little treatise on the celibacy of the clergy, written some ten years after his first coming to Loudun.

Against celibacy Grandier makes use of two main arguments. The first may be summed up in the following syllogism. "A promise to perform the impossible is not binding. For the young male, continence is impossible. Therefore no vow involving such continence is binding." And if this does not suffice, here is a second argument based on the universally accepted maxim that we are not bound by promises extorted under duress. "The priest does not embrace celibacy for the love of celibacy, but solely that he may be admitted to holy orders." His vow "does not proceed from his will, but is imposed upon him by the Church, which compels him, willy-nilly, to accept this hard condition, without which he may not practice the sacerdotal profession." The upshot of all this was that Grandier felt himself at perfect liberty ultimately to marry and, meanwhile, to lead the well-rounded life with any pretty woman who was ready to be co-operative.

To the prudes in his congregation the new parson's amorous propensities seemed the most horrible of scandals; but the prudes were in a minority. To the rest, even to those who had every intention of remaining virtuous, there was something pleasantly exciting in the situation created by the incumbency of a man of Grandier's appearance, habits and reputation. Sex mingles easily with religion, and their blending has one of those slightly repulsive and yet exquisite and poignant flavors, which startle the palate like a revelation—of what? That, precisely, is the question.

Grandier's popularity with the women was enough, of itself, to make him extremely unpopular among the men. From the first, the husbands and fathers of his female parishioners were deeply suspicious of this clever young dandy with his fine manners and his gift of the gab. And even if the new parson had been a saint, why

14

should such a plum as the living of St. Peter's go to a foreigner? What was wrong with the local boys? Loudun's tithes should go to Loudun's own sons. And, to make matters worse, the foreigner had not come alone. He had brought with him a mother, three brothers and a sister. For one of those brothers he had already found a job in the office of the town's chief magistrate. Another, who was a priest, had been appointed chief vicar of St. Peter's. The third, also in orders, had no official position, but prowled around hungrily on the lookout for clerical odd jobs. It was an invasion.

Even the grumblers had to admit, however, that M. Grandier could preach a thundering good sermon, and was a very able priest, full of sound doctrine and even of secular learning. But his very merits told against him. Because he was a man of wit and wide reading, Grandier was from the first received by the most aristo-cratic and cultivated personages in the town. Doors which had always remained closed to the rich bumpkins, the uncouth officials, the louts of gentle birth, who constituted the high, but not the highest, society of Loudun, were immediately opened to this young whippersnapper from another province. Bitter was the resentment of the excluded notables, when they heard of his intimacy, first with Jean d'Armagnac, the newly appointed Governor of the town and castle, and then with Loudun's most famous citizen, the aged Scévole de Sainte-Marthe, eminent alike as jurisconsult and states-man, as historian and poet. D'Armagnac thought so highly of the parson's abilities and discretion that, during his absences at court, he entrusted to Grandier the entire management of his affairs. To Sainte-Marthe the Curé recommended himself, above all, as a human-ist who knew the classics and could therefore appreciate at its true worth the old gentleman's Virgilian masterpiece, *Paediotrophiae Libri Tres*—a didactic poem on the care and feeding of infants, so popular that no less than ten editions were called for during the author's lifetime, and at the same time so elegant, so correct, that Ronsard could say that "he preferred the author of these verses to all the poets of our age, and would maintain it however great the displeasure he might thereby give to Bembo, to Navagero and the divine Fracastoro." Alas, how transitory is fame, how absolute

15

the vanity of human pretensions! For us, Cardinal Bembo is hardly more than a name, Andrea Navagero rather less, and such immortality as is enjoyed by the divine Fracastoro belongs to him solely in virtue of the fact that he gave a politer nickname to the pox by writing, in flawless Latin, a medical eclogue about the unhappy Prince Syphilus who, after many sufferings, was relieved of the *morbus Gallicus* by copious draughts of a decoction of guaiacum. The dead languages grow ever deader, and the three books of *Paediotrophia* treat of a less dramatic phase of the sexual cycle than the *libri tres* of the *Syphilid*. Once read by everyone, once reckoned as diviner than the divine, Scévole de Sainte-Marthe has now vanished into the darkness. But at the time when Grandier made his acquaintance, he was still in his sunset glory, the grandest of Grand Old Men, a kind of National Monument. To be received into his intimacy was like dining with Notre Dame de Paris or dropping in for a chat with the Pont du Gard. In the splendid house to which this Elder Statesman and Dean of Humaner Letters had now retired Grandier talked familiarly with the great man and his hardly less distinguished sons and grandsons. And there were visiting celebrities—the Prince of Wales, *incognito*; Théophraste Renaudot, unorthodox physician, philanthropist and father of French journalism; Ismaël Boulliau, the future author of the monumental *Astronomia Philolaica* and the first observer to determine with precision the periodicity of a variable star. To these were joined such local lights as Guillaume de Cerisay, the *Bailli*, or Chief Magistrate of Loudun, and Louis Trincant, the Public Prosecutor, a pious and learned man who had been a schoolfellow of Abel de Sainte-Marthe and who shared the family's taste for literature and antiquarian research.

Hardly less gratifying than the friendship of these choice spirits was the enmity displayed by all the others, the outsiders. To be mistrusted by the stupid because he was so clever, to be envied by the inept because he had made good, to be loathed by the dull for his wit, by the boors for his breeding and by the unattractive for his success with women—what a tribute to his universal superiority! And the hatred was not one-sided. Grandier detested his enemies as heartily as they detested him. " 'Damn' braces, 'bless' relaxes." There are many people for whom hate and rage pay a higher dividend of immediate satisfaction than love. Congenitally aggressive, they soon become adrenalin addicts, deliberately indulging their ugliest passions for the sake of the 'kick' they derive from their psychically stimulated endocrines. Knowing that one self-assertion always ends by evoking other and hostile self-assertions, they sedulously cultivate their truculence. And, sure enough, very soon they find themselves in the thick of a fight. But a fight is what they most enjoy; for it is while they are fighting that their blood chemistry makes them feel most intensely themselves. 'Feeling good,' they naturally assume that they *are* good. Adrenalin addiction is rationalized as Righteous Indignation and finally, like the prophet Jonah, they are convinced, unshakably, that they do well to be angry.

Almost from the first moment of his arrival at Loudun, Grandier was involved in a series of unseemly but, so far as he was concerned, thoroughly enjoyable quarrels. One gentleman actually drew his sword against the parson. With another, the *Lieutenant Criminel*, who headed the local police force, he indulged in a public slanging match, which soon degenerated into physical violence. Outnumbered, the parson and his acolytes had to barricade themselves in the chapel of the castle. Next day Grandier complained to the ecclesiastical court and the *Lieutenant Criminel* was duly reprimanded for his part in the scandalous affair. For the Curé it was a triumph—but at a price. An influential man who had merely felt an unreasoned dislike for him was now his mortal and inveterate enemy, on the watch for any opportunity to be revenged.

As a matter of elementary prudence no less than of Christian principle, the parson should have done his utmost to conciliate the enmities by which he was surrounded. But in spite of all those years with the Jesuits, Grandier was still very far from being a Christian; and in spite of all the good advice he received from d'Armagnac and his other friends, he was incapable, where his passions were involved, of acting with prudence. A long religious training had not abolished or even mitigated his self-love; it had

17

served only to provide the ego with a theological alibi. The un-tutored egotist merely wants what he wants. Give him a religious education, and it becomes obvious to him, it becomes axiomatic, that what *he* wants is what God wants, that *his* cause is the cause of whatever he may happen to regard as the True Church and that any compromise is a metaphysical Munich, an appeasement of Radical Evil. "Agree with thine adversary while thou art in the way with him." To men like Grandier, Christ's advice seems like a blasphemous invitation to make a pact with Beelzebub. Instead of trying to come to terms with his enemies, the parson set to work to exacerbate their hostility by every means in his power. And his power, in this respect, amounted almost to genius.

The Good Fairy, who visits the cradles of the privileged, is often the Bad Fairy in a luminous disguise. She comes loaded with presents; but her bounty, all too often, is fatal. To Urbain Grandier, for example, the Good Fairy had brought, along with solid talents, the most dazzling of all gifts, and the most dangerous—eloquence. Spoken by a good actor—and every great preacher, every success-ful advocate and politician is, among other things, a consummate actor—words can exercise an almost magical power over their hearers. Because of the essential irrationality of this power, even the best-intentioned of public speakers probably do more harm than good. When an orator, by the mere magic of words and a golden voice, persuades his audience of the rightness of a bad cause, we are very properly shocked. We ought to feel the same dismay when-ever we find the same irrelevant tricks being used to persuade people of the rightness of a good cause. The belief engendered may be desirable, but the grounds for it are intrinsically wrong, and those who use the devices of oratory for instilling even right beliefs are guilty of pandering to the least creditable elements in human nature. By exercising their disastrous gift of the gab, they deepen the quasi-hypnotic trance in which most human beings live and from which it is the aim and purpose of all true philosophy, all genuinely spirit-ual religion to deliver them. Moreover, there cannot be effective oratory without oversimplification. But you cannot oversimplify without distorting the facts. Even when he is doing his best to tell the truth, the successful orator is *ipso facto* a liar. And most successful orators, it is hardly necessary to add, are not even trying to tell the truth; they are trying to evoke sympathy for their friends and antipathy for their opponents. Grandier, alas, was one of the majority. Sunday after Sunday, in the pulpit of St. Peter's, he gave his celebrated imitations of Jeremiah and Ezekiel, of Demosthenes, of Savonarola, even of Rabelais—for he was as good at derision as at righteous indignation, at irony as at apocalyptic thunder.

Nature abhors a vacuum, even in the mind. Today the aching void of boredom is filled and perpetually renewed by movies and radio, television and the comic strips. More fortunate than we, or else less fortunate (who knows?), our ancestors depended, for the assuagement of their ennui, on the weekly performances of their parish priest, supplemented from time to time by the discourses of visiting Capuchins or traveling Jesuits. Preaching is an art, and in this, as in all other arts, the bad performers far outnumber the good. The parishioners of St. Peter's in the Market could congratulate themselves on possessing, in the Reverend Grandier, a superb virtuoso, ready and able to improvise entertainingly on the sublimest Christian mystery as well as on the most touchy, the most delicate and scabrous of parochial issues. How roundly he denounced abuses, how fearlessly he reproved even those in high places! The chronically bored majority were delighted. Their applause merely served to increase the fury of those who had been made the victims of the parson's eloquence.

Among these victims were the monks of the various orders which had, since the cessation of open hostilities between Huguenots and Catholics, established houses in the once Protestant city. Grandier's prime reason for disliking the monks was the fact that he himself was a secular priest and as loyal to his caste as the good soldier is loyal to his regiment, the good undergraduate to his school, the good Communist or Nazi to his party. Loyalty to organization A always entails some degree of suspicion, contempt or downright loathing of organizations, B, C, D and all the rest. And this is true even of component groups within a larger, superordinated whole. Ecclesiastical history exhibits a hierarchy of hatreds, descending by orderly degrees from the Church's official and ecumenical hatred of heretics and infidels to the particular hatreds of Order for Order, school for school, province for province and theologian for theologian.

"It would be good," St. Francis de Sales wrote in 1612, "it would be good, through the intervention of pious and prudent prelates, to bring about union and mutual understanding between the Sorbonne and the Jesuit Fathers. If in France the bishops, the Sorbonne and the Orders were thoroughly united, in ten years it would be all up with heresy." (*Œuvres* XV, 188) It would be all up with heresy because, as the saint says in another place, "Whoever preaches with love preaches sufficiently against heresy, though he may never utter a controversial word." (*Œuvres* VI, 309) A Church divided by intestine hatreds cannot systematically practice love and cannot, without manifest hypocrisy, preach it. But instead of union there was continued dissension; instead of love there was the *odium theologicum* and the aggressive patriotism of caste and school and order. To the feud between the Jesuits and the Sorbonne was soon added the feud between the Jansenists and an alliance of Jesuits and Salesians. And after that came the long-drawn battle over Quietism and Disinterested Love. In the end the Gallican Church's quarrels, internal and external, were settled, not by love or persuasion, but by authoritarian ukase. For the heretics there were the *dragonnades* and finally the Revocation of the Edict of Nantes. For the squabbling ecclesiastics there were papal bulls and threats of excommunication. Order was restored, but in the most unedifying way possible, by means the most coarsely unspiritual, the least religious and humane.

Partisan loyalty is socially disastrous; but for individuals it can be richly rewarding—more rewarding, in many ways, than even concupiscence or avarice. Whoremongers and money-grubbers find it hard to feel very proud of their activities. But partisanship is a complex passion which permits those who indulge in it to make the best of both worlds. Because they do these things for the sake of a group which is, by definition, good and even sacred, they can admire themselves and loathe their neighbors, they can seek power and money, can enjoy the pleasures of aggression and cruelty, not merely without feeling guilty, but with a positive glow of conscious virtue. Loyalty to their group transforms these pleasant vices into acts of heroism. Partisans are aware of themselves, not as sinners or criminals, but as altruists and idealists. And with certain qualifications, this is in fact what they are. The only trouble is that their altruism is merely egotism at one remove, and that the ideal, for which they are ready in many cases to lay down their lives, is nothing but the rationalization of corporate interests and party passions.

When Grandier criticized the monks of Loudun, it was, we may be sure, with a sense of righteous zeal, a consciousness of doing God's work. For God, it went without saying, was on the side of the secular clergy and of Grandier's good friends, the Jesuits. Carmelites and Capuchins were all very well within the walls of their monasteries, or conducting missions in out-of-the-way villages. But they had no business to poke their noses into the affairs of an urban bourgeoisie. God had decreed that the rich and respectable should be guided by the secular clergy, with a little assistance perhaps from the good fathers of the Company of Jesus. One of the new parson's first acts was to announce from the pulpit that the faithful were under an obligation to make confession to their parish priest, not to any outsider. The women, who did most of the confessing, were only too ready to obey. Their parish priest was now a clean, good-looking young scholar, with the manners of a gentleman. One could not say as much of the average Capuchin or Carmelite director. Almost overnight the monks lost most of their fair penitents and, along with them, most of their influence in the town. Grandier followed up this first broadside with a succession of uncomplimentary references to the Carmelites' principal source of income—a miracle-working image called Notre-Dame de Recouvrance. There had been a time when a whole quarter of the city was filled with inns and boardinghouses for the accommodation of the pilgrims who came to beg the image for health or a husband, for an heir or better luck. But now Notre-Dame de Recouvrance had a formidable rival in Notre-Dame des Ardilliers, whose church was at Saumur only a few leagues from

Loudun. There are fashions in saints, just as there are fashions in medical treatment and women's hats. Every great church has its history of upstart images, of parvenu relics ruthlessly displacing the older wonder-workers, only to be elbowed out of public favor, in their turn, by some newer and momentarily more attractive thaumaturge. Why did Notre-Dame des Ardilliers come to seem, almost suddenly, so vastly superior to Notre-Dame de Recouvrance? The most obvious of the doubtless very numerous reasons was that Notre-Dame des Ardilliers was in charge of the Oratorians and, as Grandier's first biographer, Aubin, remarks, "All the world agrees that the Priests of the Oratory are able men and more cunning than the Carmelites." The Oratorians, it should be recalled, were secular priests. Perhaps this helps to explain Grandier's skeptical coolness toward Notre-Dame de Recouvrance. Loyalty to his caste impelled him to work for the profit and glory of the secular clergy and for the discredit and ruin of the monks. Notre-Dame de Recouvrance would certainly have sunk into oblivion, even if Grandier had never come to Loudun. But the Carmelites preferred to have another opinion. To think about events realistically, in terms of multiple causations, is hard and emotionally unrewarding. How much easier, how much more agreeable to trace each effect to a single and, if possible, a personal cause! To the illusion of understanding will be joined, in this case, the pleasure of hero worship, if the circumstances are favorable, and the equal, or even greater pleasure, if they should be unfavorable, of persecuting a scapegoat.

To these petty enemies Grandier soon added another capable of doing him immeasurably greater harm. Early in 1618, at a religious convention attended by all the ecclesiastical dignitaries of the neighborhood, Grandier went out of his way to offend the Prior of Coussay by rudely claiming precedence over him in a solemn procession through the streets of Loudun. Technically the parson's position was unassailable. In a procession originating in his own church, a Canon of Sainte-Croix had a right to walk in front of the Prior of Coussay. And this right held good even when, as was here the case, the Prior was at the same time a Bishop. But there is such a thing as courtesy; and there is also such a thing as circumspection. The Prior of Cous-

22

say was the Bishop of Luçon, and the Bishop of Luçon was Armand-Jean du Plessis de Richelieu.

At the moment—and this was an additional reason for behaving with magnanimous politeness—Richelieu was out of favor. In 1617 his patron, the Italian gangster, Concini, had been assassinated. This *coup d'état* was engineered by Luynes and approved by the young King. Richelieu was excluded from power and unceremoniously driven from the court. But was there any reason for supposing that this exile would be perpetual? There was no reason at all. And, in effect, a year later, after a brief banishment to Avignon, the indispensable Bishop of Luçon was recalled to Paris. By 1622 he was the King's First Minister and a Cardinal.

Gratuitously, for the mere pleasure of asserting himself, Grandier had offended a man who was very soon to become the absolute ruler of France. Later, the parson would have reason to regret his incivility. Meanwhile the thought of his exploit filled him with a childish satisfaction. A commoner, an obscure parish priest, he had lowered the pride of a Queen's favorite, a bishop, an aristocrat. He felt the elation of a small boy who has made a long nose at the teacher and "got away with it" unpunished.

Richelieu himself, in later years, derived an identical pleasure from behaving toward princes of the blood exactly as Urbain Grandier had behaved toward him. "To think," said his old uncle, as he watched the Cardinal calmly taking precedence of the Duke of Savoy, "to think that I should have lived to see the grandson of lawyer Laporte walking into a room before the grandson of Charles V!" Another horrid little boy had triumphantly got away with it.

The pattern of Grandier's life at Loudun was now set. He fulfilled his clerical duties and in the intervals discreetly frequented the prettier widows, spent convivial evenings in the houses of his intellectual friends and quarreled with an ever widening circle of enemies. It was a thoroughly agreeable existence, satisfying alike to head and heart, to the gonads and the adrenals, to the social persona and his private self. There had as yet been no gross or manifest misfortune in his life. He could still imagine that his amusements were gratuitous, that he could desire with impunity and abhor without effect.

In fact, of course, destiny had already begun to render its account, but unobtrusively. He had suffered no hurt that he could feel, only an imperceptible coarsening and hardening, only a progressive darkening of the inner light, a gradual narrowing of the soul's window on the side of eternity. To a man of Grandier's temperament—the sanguine-choleric, according to the Constitutional Medicine of his day—it still seemed obvious that all was right with the world. And if all was right with the world, then God must be in His Heaven. The parson was happy. Or, to put it a little more precisely, in the alternation of his moods, it was the manic that still predominated.

In the spring of 1623, full of years and honors, Scévole de Sainte-Marthe died and was buried with all due pomp in the church of St. Pierre du Marché. Six months later, at a memorial service attended by all the notables of Loudun and Châtellerault, of Chinon and Poitiers, Grandier spoke the great man's *oraison funèbre*. It was a long and splendid oration in the manner (not yet old-fashioned, for the first edition of Balzac's stylistically revolutionary letters did not appear until the following year) of the "devout humanists." The elaborate sentences glittered with quotations from the classics and the Bible. A showy and superfluous erudition exhibited itself complacently at every turn. The periods rumbled with an artificial thunder. For those who liked this sort of thing—and in 1623 who did not?—this, most decidedly, was the sort of thing they would like. Grandier's oration was received with general applause. Abel de Sainte-Marthe was so much moved by the parson's eloquence that he penned and published a Latin epigram on the subject. No less flattering were the lines which M. Trincant, the public prosecutor, wrote in the vernacular.

> Ce n'est pas sans grande raison
> Qu'on a choisi ce personnage
> Pour entreprendre l'oraison
> Du plus grand homme de son âge;
> Il fallait véritablement
> Une éloquence sans faconde
> Pour louer celuy dignement
> Qui n'eut point de second au monde.

Poor M. Trincant! His passion for the Muses was genuine but hopeless. He loved them, but they, it is evident, did not love him. But if he could not write poetry, he could at least talk about it. After 1623 the Public Prosecutor's drawing room became the center of Loudun's intellectual life. It was a pretty feeble life, now that Sainte-Marthe was gone. Trincant himself was a well-read man; but most of his friends and relatives were not. Excluded from the Hotel Sainte-Marthe, these people had, unfortunately, a prescriptive right to an invitation from the Public Prosecutor. But when they came in at the door, learning and good conversation flew out of the window. How could it be otherwise with those bevies of cackling women; those lawyers who knew about nothing except statutes and procedure; those country squires whose only interests were dogs and horses? And finally there were M. Adam, the apothecary, and M. Mannoury the surgeon—Adam, the long-nosed, Mannoury, the moon-faced and pot-bellied. With all the gravity of doctors of the Sorbonne, they held forth on the virtues of antimony and blood-letting, on the value of soap in clysters and the cautery in the treatment of gunshot wounds. Then, lowering their voices, they would speak (always, of course, in strictest confidence) of the Marquis's pox, of the King's Counsel's wife's second miscarriage, of the Bailiff's sister's young daughter's green sickness. At once absurd and pretentious, solemn and grotesque, the apothecary and the surgeon were predestined butts. They invited sarcasm, they solicited the shafts of derision. With the merciless ferocity of a clever man who will go to any lengths for the sake of a laugh, the parson gave them what they asked for. In a very little while he had two new enemies.

And meanwhile another was in the making. The Public Prosecutor was a middle-aged widower with two marriageable daughters, of whom the elder, Philippe, was so remarkably pretty that, throughout the winter of 1623, the parson found himself looking more and more frequently in her direction.

Watching the girl as she moved among her father's guests, he compared her appraisingly with his mental image of that spritely young widow whom he was now consoling, every Tuesday afternoon, for the untimely death of her poor dear husband, the vintner. Ninon was unschooled, could hardly sign her own name. But under the inconsolable sable of her weeds, the full-blown flesh was only just beginning to lose its firmness. There were treasures there of warmth and whiteness; there was an inexhaustible fund of sensuality, at once frenzied and scientific, violent and yet admirably docile and well-trained. And, thank God, there had been no barriers of prudery to be laboriously demolished, no wearisome preliminaries of Platonic idealization and Petrarchian courtship to be gone through! At their third meeting, he had ventured to quote the opening lines of one of his favorite poems.

> Souvent j'ai menti les ébats
> Des nuits, t'ayant entre mes bras
> Folâtre toute nue;
> Mais telle jouissance, hélas!
> Encor m'est inconnue.

There had been no protest, only the frankest laughter and a look out of the corner of the eye, very brief but unequivocal. At the end of his fifth visit, he had been in a position to quote Tahureau again.

> Adieu, ma petite maîtresse,
> Adieu, ma gorgettte et mon sein,
> Adieu, ma délicate main,
> Adieu, donc, mon téton d'albâtre,
> Adieu, ma cuissette folâtre,
> Adieu, mon oeil, adieu, mon cœur,
> Adieu, ma friande douceur!
> Mais avant que je me départe,
> Avant que plus loin je m'écarte,
> Que je tâte encore ce flanc
> Et le rond de ce marbre blanc

Good-by, but only until the day after tomorrow, when she would come to St. Peter's for her weekly confession—he was a stickler for weekly confessions—and the usual penance. And between then and next Tuesday he would have preached the sermon he was now preparing for the feast of the Purification of the Blessed Virgin—the finest thing he had done since M. de Sainte-Marthe's funeral oration. What eloquence, what choice and profound learning, what subtle, but eminently sound theology! Applause, felicitations! The *Lieuten-ant Criminel* would be furious, the friars green with envy. "M. le Curé, you have surpassed yourself. Your Reverence is incompar-able." He would go to his next assignation in a blaze of glory, and for a victor's crown she would give him her encircling arms, for guerdon those kisses of hers, those caresses, that ultimate deification in the heaven of her embrace. Let the Carmelites talk of their ec-stasies, their celestial touches, their extraordinary graces and spiritual nuptials! He had his Ninon, and Ninon was enough. But looking again at Philippe he wondered whether, after all, she was enough. Widows were a great consolation, and he saw no reason for giving up his Tuesdays; but widows were most emphatically not virgins, widows knew too much, widows were beginning to run to fat. Whereas Philippe still had the thin bony arms of a little girl, the apple-round breasts and smooth columnar neck of an adolescent. And how ravishing was this mixture of youthful grace and youthful awkwardness! How touching and at the same time how provocative and exciting were these transitions from a bold, almost foolhardy coquetry to sudden panic! Overacting the part of Cleopatra, she in-vited every man to constitute himself an Antony. But let any man show signs of accepting the invitation, and the Queen of Egypt van-ished; only a frightened child remained, begging for mercy. And then, as soon as mercy had been granted, back came the Siren, chant-ing allurements, dangling forbidden fruits with an effrontery of which only the totally depraved and the totally innocent are capable. Innocence, purity—what a glorious peroration he had composed upon that sublimest of themes! Women would weep when he pro-nounced it—now thunderously, now in the tenderest whisper—from the pulpit of his church. Even the men would be touched. The purity of the dew-dabbled lily, the innocence of lambs and little chil-dren. Yes, the friars would be green with envy. But, except in ser-mons and in heaven, all lilies fester sooner or later into rottenness; the ewe lamb is predestined, first to the indefatigably lustful ram, then to the butcher; and in Hell the damned walk on a living pave-ment, tessellated with the tiny carcasses of unbaptized babies. Since the Fall, total innocence has been identical, for all practical purposes, with total depravity. Every young girl is potentially the most knowing of widows and, thanks to Original Sin, every potential impurity is already, even in the most innocent, more than half actualized. To help it to complete actualization, to watch the still virginal bud unfold into the rank and blowzy flower—this would be a pleasure not only of the senses, but also of the reflective intellect and will. It would be a moral and, so to say, a metaphysical sensuality.

And Philippe was not merely young and virginal. She was also of good family, piously brought up and highly accomplished. Pretty as paint, but knew her catechism; played the lute, but went regularly to church; had the manners of a fine lady, but liked reading and even knew some Latin. The capture of such a prey would tickle the hunter's self-esteem and be regarded, by all who knew of it, as a great and memorable exploit.

In the aristocratic world of a few years later, "women," according to Bussy-Rabutin, "gained as much esteem for men as arms." The conquest of a celebrated beauty was equivalent, very nearly, to the conquest of a province. For their triumphs in the boudoir and the bed, such men as Marsillac and Nemours and the Chevalier de Grammont enjoyed a fame almost equal, while it lasted, to that of Gustavus Adolphus or Wallenstein. In the fashionable slang of the time, one "embarked" on one of these glorious affairs, embarked deliberately and self-consciously for the express purpose of cutting a more considerable figure in the world. Sex can be used either for self-affirmation or for self-transcendence—either to intensify the ego and consolidate the social persona by some kind of conspicuous "embarkation" and heroic conquest, or else to annihilate the persona and transcend the ego in an obscure rapture of sensuality, a frenzy of romantic passion or, more creditably, in the mutual charity of the perfect marriage. With his peasant girls and his middle-class widows of little scruple and large appetite, the parson could get all the self-transcendence he wanted. Philippe Trincant now offered an occasion for the most agreeable and modish kind of self-affirmation— with a hoped-for sequel, when the conquest had been consummated, of some peculiarly rare and precious kind of sensual self-transcendence.

Delicious dream! But a most troublesome obstacle stood in the way of its fulfillment. Philippe's father was Louis Trincant, and Louis Trincant was the parson's best friend, his staunchest and most resolute ally against the monks, the *Lieutenant Criminel* and the rest of his adversaries. Louis Trincant trusted him, trusted him so completely that he had made his daughters give up their old confessor so that they might become Grandier's penitents. And would the Curé be good enough to read them an occasional lecture on filial duty and maidenly modesty? Didn't he agree that Guillaume Rogier was not quite good enough for Philippe, but would make a very suitable match for Françoise? And surely Philippe ought to keep up her Latin. Could he possibly find time to give her an occasional lesson? To abuse such trust would be the blackest of crimes. And yet its very blackness was a reason for committing it. On all the levels of our being, from the muscular and sensational to the moral and the intellectual, every tendency generates its own opposite. We look at something red, and visual induction intensifies our perception of green and even, in certain circumstances, causes us to see a green halo round the red object, a green afterimage when the object has been removed. We will a movement; one set of muscles is stimulated and, automatically, by spinal induction, the opposing muscles are inhibited. The same principle holds good on the higher levels of consciousness. Every yes begets a corresponding no. "There is more faith in honest doubt, believe me, than in all the creeds." And there is (as Butler pointed out long since, and as we shall have occasion to observe on many occasions during the course of this history), there is more doubt in honest faith, believe me, than in all the Bradlaughs and all the Marxist textbooks. In moral education induction poses a peculiarly difficult problem. If every yes tends automatically to evoke its corresponding no, how can we inculcate right conduct without at the same time inductively inculcating the wrong conduct which is its opposite? Methods for circumventing induction exist; but that they are not always well applied is sufficiently proved by the existence of vast numbers of stubborn and "contrary" children, of adolescents who are consistently "agin the government," of perverse and antinomian adults. Even the well-balanced and the self-controlled are sometimes aware of a paradoxical temptation to do the exact opposite of what they know they ought to do. It is a temptation, very often, to an evil without point or profit, to a gratuitous and, so to say, disinterested outrage against common sense and common decency. Most of these inductive temptations are successfully resisted—most, but by no means all. Every now and then sensible and fundamentally decent people will embark, all of a sudden, on courses of which they themselves are the first to disapprove. In these cases the evil-doer acts as though he were possessed by some entity different from and malignantly hostile to his ordinary self. In fact, he is the victim of a neutral mechanism, which (as not uncommonly happens with machines) has got out of hand and, from being the servant of its possessor, has become his master. Philippe was exceedingly attractive and "the strongest oaths are straw to the fire in the blood." But as well as fire in the blood there is induction in the brain. Trincant was the parson's best friend. The very act of recognizing that such a thing would be monstrous created in Grandier's mind a perverse desire to betray him. Instead of making a supreme effort to resist the temptation the parson tried to find reasons for yielding. He kept telling himself that the father of such a delicious morsel as Philippe had no right to behave so trustfully. It was sheer folly—no, worse than folly; it was a crime that deserved condign punishment. Latin lessons, indeed! It was the story all over again of Héloise and Abelard, with the Public Prosecutor as Uncle Fulbert, inviting the ravisher to make himself at home. Only one thing was lacking—the privilege, so freely accorded to Héloise's tutor, of using the birch. And perhaps if he asked for it, the imbecile Trincant would grant him even that. . . .

Time passed. The widow continued to enjoy her Tuesdays; but on most of the other days of the week Grandier was to be found at the Public Prosecutor's. Françoise was already married; but Philippe was still at home and making excellent progress with her Latin.

> *Omne adeo genus in terris hominumque ferarum*
> *et genus aequoreum, pecudes, pictaeque volucres*
> *in furias, ignesque ruunt; amor omnibus idem.**

* Thus every race on earth of men and beasts, the creatures of the sea, the herds, the birds of brilliant hue, are swept with fiery passions; love is the same for all.

And even the vegetables feel the tender passion.

> *Nutant et mutua palmae*
> *foedera, populeo suspirat populus ictu,*
> *et platano platanus, alnoque assibilat alnus.**

Laboriously Philippe translated for him the tenderer passages in the poets, the more scabrous episodes in mythology. With a self-denial which his widow made it rather easy for him to practice, the parson refrained from anything like an assault upon his pupil's honor, from anything that might even be interpreted as a declaration or a proposition. He merely made himself charming and interesting, told the girl two or three times a week that she was the most intelligent woman he had ever known and occasionally looked at her in a way that made Philippe drop her eyes and blush. It was all rather a waste of time, but not unamusing. And luckily there was always Ninon; luckily, too, the girl could not read his thoughts.

They sat in the same room, but not in the same universe. No longer a child, but not yet a woman, Philippe was the inhabitant of that rosy limbo of phantasy which lies between innocence and experience. Her home was not at Loudun, not among these frumps and bores and boors, but with a god in a private Elysium, transfigured by the radiance of dawning love and imaginary sex. Those dark eyes of his, those mustaches, those white and well-kept hands—they haunted her like a guilty conscience. And what wit he had, what profundity of knowledge! An archangel, as wise as he was beautiful and as kind as he was wise. And he thought her clever, he praised her diligence; above all he had a certain way of looking at her. Was it possible that he . . . ? But no, no, it was sacrilegious even to think such thoughts, it was a sin. But how could she ever confess it—to *him*?

She concentrated all her attention on the Latin.

> *Turpe senex miles, turpe selinis amor.†*

But a moment later she was overwhelmed by a vague but violent longing. In her imagination memories of inchoate pleasures found

---

* In mutual bond the palm trees sway, the poplars sigh in harmony together, together sigh the plane trees, the alder whispers to the other alder.
† An old man's soldiering is foulness, and foulness an old man's love.

themselves suddenly associated with those all-seeing eyes, those white yet hairy hands. The printed page swam before her eyes; she hesitated, stammered. "The filthy old soldier," she brought out at last. He gave her a little rap over the knuckles with his ruler and told her she was lucky not to be a boy; for if a boy had made that kind of blunder, he would have felt obliged to take decidedly sterner measures. He flourished the ruler. Most decidedly sterner. She looked at him, then quickly turned away. The blood rushed into her cheeks.

Already firmly established in the prosaic and disillusioned contentment of a happy marriage, Françoise brought back to her sister firsthand reports from the matrimonial front. Philippe listened with interest, but knew that, where she herself was concerned, everything would always be quite different. The daydream prolonged itself, was elaborated into greater and ever greater detail. At one moment she was living at the parsonage as his housekeeper. At another he had been elevated to the see of Poitiers and there was an underground passage between the episcopal palace and her house in the suburbs. Alternatively she had inherited a hundred thousand crowns, whereupon he left the Church and they passed their time between the court and their estate in the country.

But always, sooner or later, she had to wake up again to the dismal realization that she was Philippe Trincant and he, M. le Curé; that even if he loved her (and she had no reason for supposing that he did) he could never say so; and that even if he were to say so, it would always be her duty to stop her ears. But meanwhile what happiness it was, over her seam, her book, her embroidery frame, to imagine the impossible! And then the excruciating joy of hearing his knock, his step, his voice! The delicious ordeal, the heavenly purgatory of sitting with him in her father's library, translating Ovid, deliberately making mistakes so that he would threaten to whip her, listening to that rich sonorous voice as it talked of the Cardinal, of the rebellious Protestants, of the war in Germany, of the Jesuits' position on prevenient Grace, of his own prospects for preferment. If only matters could go on like this forever! But it was like asking (just because the end of a madrigal is so beautiful, just because the evening light turns everything it touches into something else, something incomparably lovelier) it was like asking for a lifetime of summer sunsets, for dying falls in perpetuity. With a part of her mind she knew that she was deceiving herself; but for a few blissful weeks she was able, by closing the eyes of her reason, to believe that life had come to a halt in Paradise and would never resume its march. It was as though the gulf between fantasy and the actual had been abolished. Real life and her daydreams were momentarily the same. Her imaginings were no longer the consoling denial of the facts; the facts had identified themselves with her imaginings. It was a bliss, she felt, without sin, because so eventless, so completely inward; a bliss like that of Heaven, a bliss to which she could give herself wholeheartedly, without fear or self-reproach. And the more completely she abandoned herself to it, the intenser it became until at last she found it impossible to keep it to herself. One day she spoke of it in the confessional—guardedly, of course, without hinting, as she imagined, that it was the confessor himself who was the cause of these emotions.

Confession succeeded confession. The parson listened attentively, and every now and then put a question which proved to her how far he was from suspecting the truth, how completely he had been taken in by her innocent deception. Gaining courage, Philippe told him everything, everything in the most intimate detail. Her happiness at this time seemed to have passed the limits of the possible and was a kind of enduring paroxysm, an exquisite frenzy which she could renew at will, could go on renewing forever. Forever, forever. And then the day came when she made her slip of the tongue, when, instead of "him," she said "you," and then tried to withdraw the word, became confused and, under his questioning, burst into tears and confessed the truth.

"At last," Grandier said to himself, "at last!"

And now it was all plain sailing—just a matter of carefully graduated words and gestures, of a tenderness modulating by insensible degrees from the professionally Christian to the Petrarchian, and from the Petrarchian to the all too human and the self-transcendently animal. Descent is always easy, and in this case there would be plenty of casuistry to lubricate the slide, and, after the bottom had been reached, all the absolution a girl could ask for.

A few months later there was an embarkation in form. Frankly, it was a little disappointing. Why couldn't he have been content with the widow?

For Philippe, meanwhile, eventless and inner bliss had given place to the frightening reality of passion avowed and reciprocated, to the long-drawn torments of moral struggle, to prayers for strength, to vows that she would never yield, and at last, in a kind of despair, as though she were throwing herself over a cliff, to surrender. Surrender had brought with it none of the things she had imagined it would bring. Instead, it had brought the revelation, in her archangel, of a demented brute and the discovery, in the depths of her own mind and body, at first of the predestined victim, the suffering and therefore happy martyr, and then, suddenly, apocalyptically, of an alien no less unlike herself than that ferocious embodiment of passion had been unlike the eloquent preacher, the witty and exquisitely polished humanist with whom originally she had fallen in love. But falling in love, as she now perceived, was not the same as loving. It was as an imagination that one fell in love, and what one fell in love with was only an abstraction. When one loved, one loved a complete existence and loved it with one's whole being, with the soul and every fiber of the body, with the self and this other, this new-found alien beneath, beyond and within the self. She was all love and only love. Nothing but love existed—nothing.

Nothing? With an almost audible snigger, Fate sprung the trap she had been preparing for herself. And there she was, pinned helplessly between physiology and the social order—pregnant but unmarried, dishonored beyond redemption. The inconceivable had become the actual; that which had been out of the question was now a fact. The moon waxed, hung for a glorious night or two in its full splendor, then waned, like the last hope, and disappeared. There was nothing for it but to die in his arms—to die, or if that were impossible, at least forget for a little and be someone else.

Alarmed by so much violence, such a recklessness of self-abandonment, the parson tried to modulate her passion into a lighter and less

34

tragic key. He accompanied his caresses with apt quotations from the livelier classics. *Quantum, quale latus, quam juvenile femur!** In the intermissions of love he told improper stories from the *Dames Galantes* of Brantôme, he whispered into her ear a few of the enormities so diligently catalogued by Sanchez in his folio on matrimony. But her face never changed its expression. It was like a face in marble, a face on a tomb, closed, unresponsive, pure even of life. And when at last she reopened her eyes, it was as though she were looking at him from another world, a world where there was only suffering and a fixed despair. The look disquieted him; but to his solicitous questioning her only answer was to lift her hands, catch him by his thick black curls and pull him down to her mouth, to her proffered throat and breast.

Then one day, in the middle of his story about King Francis's drinking cups for debutantes—those flagons engraved on the inside with amorous postures, which revealed themselves a little more completely with every sip of the concealing wine—she interrupted him with the curt announcement that she was going to have a baby, and immediately burst into a paroxysm of uncontrollable sobbing.

Shifting his hand from the bosom to the bowed head and changing his tone, without any transition, from the bawdy to the clerical, the parson told her that she must learn to bear her cross with Christian resignation. Then, remembering the visit he had promised to pay to poor Mme. de Brou, who had a cancer of the womb and needed all the spiritual consolation he could give her, he took his leave.

After that he was too busy to give her any more lessons. Except as a penitent, Philippe never saw him alone. And when, in the confessional, she tried to speak to him as a person—as the man she had loved, the man who, as she still believed, had loved her—she found, confronting her, only the priest, only the transubstantiator of bread and wine, the giver of absolution and the assigner of penance. How eloquently he urged her to repent, to throw herself on the divine mercy! And when she mentioned their past love, he rebuked her with an almost prophetic indignation, for thus complacently wallowing in her filth; when she asked him despairingly what she was to do,

* How broad, how fine a flank, what a youthful thigh!

35

he told her with unction that, as a Christian, she must be, not merely resigned to the humiliation which it was God's good pleasure that she should suffer; she must embrace and actively will it. Of his own share in her misadventure he would not allow her to speak. Every soul must bear the burden of its own wrongdoing. One's own sins were not excused by the sins which others might, or might not, have committed. If she came to the confessional, it was in order to ask forgiveness for what she had done, not to inquire into the conscience of others. And with that, bewildered and in tears, she would be dismissed.

The spectacle of her unhappiness evoked in him neither pity nor remorse, but only a sense of grievance. The siege had been tedious, the capture without glory, the subsequent enjoyment only moderate. And now with this precipitate and untimely fecundity, she was threatening his honor, his very existence. A little bastard on top of all his other troubles—it would be the ruin of him! He had never really cared for the girl; now he actively disliked her. And she was no longer even pretty. Pregnancy and worry had conspired to give her the expression of a whipped dog, the complexion of a child with worms. In conjunction with all the rest, her temporary unattractiveness made him feel not only that he had no further obligations toward her, but that she had done him an injury and, by impugning his taste, insulted him into the bargain. It was with a good conscience that he now took the course which, since there was no acceptable alternative, he would have had to take even with a bad one. He decided to brazen it out, to deny everything. Not only would he act and speak, he would even think and inwardly feel, as though nothing of the kind had ever, or could have, happened, as though the very idea of an intimacy with Philippe Trincant were absurd, preposterous, utterly out of the question.

> *Le cœur le mieux donné tient toujours à demi,*
> *Chacun s'aime un peu mieux toujours que son ami.*

CHAPTER TWO

THE weeks passed. Philippe went abroad less and less frequently and at last even gave up going to church. She was ill, she said, and had to keep to her room. Her friend, Marthe le Pelletier, a girl of good family, but orphaned and very poor, came to live in the house as her nurse and companion. Still suspecting nothing, still indignant if anyone even so much as hinted at the truth or breathed a word against the parson, M. Trincant talked with parental concern about peccant humors and impending phthisis. Dr. Fanton, the attending physician, discreetly said nothing to anybody. The rest of Loudun either winked and sniggered, or else indulged in the pleasures of righteous indignation. When they met him, the parson's enemies dropped envenomed hints; his graver friends shook their heads at him, the more Rabelaisian dug him in the ribs and offered ribald congratulations. To all of them Grandier replied that he did not know what they were talking about. For those who were not already prejudiced against him, his frank yet dignified manner and the manifest sincerity of his words were proof enough of his innocence. It was morally impossible that such a man could have done the things his calumniators accused him of. In the houses of such distinguished persons as M. de Cerisay and Mme. de Brou he was still a welcome guest. And their doors remained open to him, even after that of the Public Prosecutor had been closed. For, in the end, even Trincant's eyes were opened to the true nature of his daughter's indisposition. Cross-questioned, she confessed the truth. From having been the parson's staunchest friend Trincant became, overnight, the most implacable and the most dangerous of his enemies. Grandier had forged another and an essential link in the chain that was to draw him to his doom.

The baby came at last. Through the closed shutters, through the heavy quilts and curtains, by which it had been hoped to stifle every sound, the screaming of the young mother, muffled but perfectly distinct, gave notice of the blessed event to all M. Trincant's eagerly expectant neighbors. Within an hour the news was all over town and by the following morning a scurrilous "Ode to the Public Prosecutor's Bastard Granddaughter" had been pinned to the doors of the law court. Some Protestant hand was suspected; for M. Trincant was exceedingly orthodox and had taken every opportunity to thwart and harass his heretical fellow citizens.

Meanwhile, with a self-sacrificing generosity, which stands out all the more conspicuously because of the prevailing moral squalor, Marthe le Pelletier had publicly assumed the baby's maternity. It was she who had sinned, she who had been forced to hide her shame. Philippe was merely the benefactress who had given her a place of refuge. Nobody, of course, believed a word of it; but the gesture was admired. When the infant was a week old, Marthe placed it with the young peasant woman who had agreed to serve as its foster mother. The act was done conspicuously, so that all the world could see. Still unconvinced, the Protestants went on talking. To silence their ribald skepticism, the Public Prosecutor resorted to a peculiarly odious legal stratagem. He had Marthe le Pelletier arrested in the open street and brought before a magistrate. There, under oath and in the presence of witnesses, she was required to sign an act, whereby she officially recognized the child as hers and accepted the responsibility for its future maintenance. Because she loved her friend, Marthe signed. One copy of the act was filed in the record office, the other M. Trincant triumphantly pocketed. Duly attested, the lie was now legally true. For minds trained in the law, legal truth is the same thing as truth without qualification. To everyone else, as the Public Prosecutor discovered to his chagrin, the equivalence seems very far from evident. Even after he had read the act aloud, even after they had seen the signature with their own eyes, touched the official seal with their own fingers, his friends only smiled politely and talked about something else, while his enemies laughed aloud and made offensive remarks. Such was the malignity of the Protestants, that one of their ministers publicly maintained that perjury is a graver sin than fornication, and that the liar who forswears himself in order to conceal a scandal is more deserving of hell-fire than the person by whose lewdness the scandal was originally caused.

A long and eventful century separated the middle age of Dr. Samuel Garth from the youth of William Shakespeare. In government, in social and economic organization, in physics and mathematics, in philosophy and the arts, there had been revolutionary changes. But there was at least one institution that remained, at the end of the period, exactly what it had been at the beginning—the drugstore. In the apothecary's shop described by Romeo,

> a tortoise hung,
> An alligator stuff'd, and other skins
> Of ill-shap'd fishes, and about the shelves
> A beggarly account of empty boxes,
> Green earthen pots, bladders and musty seeds.

In his *Dispensary* Garth paints an almost identical picture.

> Here mummies lay, most reverently stale,
> And there the tortoise hung her coat of mail;
> Not far from some large shark's devouring head
> The flying fish their finny pinions spread.
> Aloft in rows large poppy heads were strung
> And, near, a scaly alligator hung;
> In this place drugs in musty heaps decay'd
> In that dried bladders and drawn teeth were laid.

This temple of science, which is at the same time a magician's laboratory and a side show at a country fair, is a most expressive symbol of that strange agglomeration of incongruities, the seventeenth-century mind. For the age of Descartes and Newton was also the age of Fludd and Sir Kenelm Digby; the age of logarithms and analytical geometry was no less the age of the weapon salve, the Sympathetic Powder, the theory of Signatures. Robert Boyle, who wrote *The Sceptical Chemist* and was one of the founders of the Royal Society, left a volume of recipes for home remedies. Culled from an oak at the full moon, mistletoe berries dried, powdered and mixed with black cherry water, will cure epilepsy. For apoplectic fits, one must take mastic (the resin exuded by lentisk bushes on the island of Chios), extract the essential oil by distillation in a copper alembic and blow two or three drops, through a quill, into one of the patient's nostrils, "and after a while into the other." The scientific spirit was already vigorously alive. But no less vigorously alive was the spirit of the medicine man and the witch.

M. Adam's pharmacy in the Rue des Marchands was of the middle rank, neither beggarly nor grandiose, but solidly provincial. Too modest for mummies or a rhinoceros horn, it could yet boast of several West Indian turtles, the foetus of a whale and an eight-foot crocodile. And the stock was plentiful and varied. On the shelves were all the herbs of the Galenists' repertory, all the new-fangled chemicals of the followers of Valentine and Paracelsus. Rhubarb and aloes were there in plenty; but so was calomel or, as M. Adam preferred to call it, *Draco mitigatus*, the mitigated Dragon. There was colocynth, if you liked a vegetable liver pill; but there was also Tartar emetic and metallic antimony, if you were ready to venture on a more modern treatment. And if you had had the misfortune to be lucky in love with the wrong kind of nymph or swain, you could take your choice between *Arbor vitae* and *Hydrargyrum cum Creta*, between Sarsaparilla and an inunction of Blue Ointment. With all these, as well as with dried vipers, horses' hoofs and human bones, M. Adam could supply his customers out of stock. The more costly specifics—powdered sapphires, for example, or pearls—had to be specially ordered and paid for in advance.

From this time forth the apothecary's shop became the regular meeting place and headquarters of a cabal, whose single aim was to be revenged on Urbain Grandier. The leading spirits in this conspiracy were the Public Prosecutor, his nephew, Canon Mignon, the *Lieutenant Criminel*, and his father-in-law, Mesmin de Silly, Mannoury, the surgeon, and M. Adam himself, whose position as pill-maker, tooth-drawer and clyster-giver to the community provided him with unrivaled opportunities for the collection of information.

Thus, from Mme. Chauvin, the notary's wife, he had learned (in strictest confidence, while he made up a vermifuge for her little Théophile) that the parson had just invested eight hundred livres in a first mortgage. The rascal was growing rich.

And here was a piece of bad news. From M. d'Armagnac's second footman's sister-in-law, who had a female complaint and was a regular customer for dried mugwort, the apothecary had heard that Grandier was to dine next day at the Castle. At this the Public Prosecutor frowned, the *Lieutenant Criminel* swore and shook his head. D'Armagnac was not merely the Governor; he was one of the King's favorites. That such a man should be the parson's friend and protector was indeed deplorable.

There was a long and gloomy silence, broken at last by Canon Mignon, who declared that their only hope lay in a good scandal. Somehow or other they would have to arrange to catch him in *flagrante delicto*. What about the vintner's widow?

Sadly the apothecary had to admit that, in that quarter, he had nothing to report that was at all satisfactory. The widow herself knew how to keep her mouth shut, her maid had proved incorruptible, and when, the other night, he had tried to peep through a chink in the shutters, someone had leaned out of an upper window with a brimming chamber pot. . . .

Time passed. With a serene and majestic impudence, the parson went about his business and his pleasures as usual. And soon the strangest rumors began to reach the apothecary's ears. The parson was spending more and more of his time with the town's most distinguished prude and *dévote*, Mlle. de Brou.

Madeleine was the second of the three daughters of René de Brou, a man of substantial fortune and noble birth, related to all the best families of the province. Her two sisters were married, one to a physician, the other to a country gentleman; but at thirty Madeleine was still unwed and fancy free. Suitors had not been lacking; but she had rejected every offer, preferring to stay at home, look after her aging

41

parents and think her own thought. She was one of those quiet and enigmatic young women, who repress strong emotions under a grave aloofness of manner. Esteemed by her elders, she had few friends among her contemporaries and juniors, who regarded her as a prig and, because she did not take pleasure in their loud amusements, a spoilsport. Besides she was altogether too pious. Religion was all very well; but it should never be allowed to invade the sanctities of private life. And when it came to frequent communion, confessing every other day and kneeling for hours, as Madeleine used to do, in front of the image of Our Lady—well, that was really too much of a good thing. They left her alone. It was precisely what Madeleine wanted them to do.

Then her father died. And a little later her mother developed a cancer. During her long and painful illness, Grandier had found time, in the intervals between Philippe Trincant and the vintner's widow, to visit the poor lady and bring her the consolations of religion. On her deathbed Mme. de Brou recommended her daughter to his pastoral care. The parson promised to guard Madeleine's material and spiritual interests as though they were his own. In his peculiar fashion he was to keep that promise.

Madeleine's first thought, after her mother's death, was to sever all her worldly ties and enter religion. But when she consulted her spiritual director, she found that he was against the plan. Outside the cloister, Grandier insisted, she could do more good than within. Among the Ursulines or the Carmelites, she would be hiding her light under a bushel. Her place was here, at Loudun; her vocation, to give a shining example of wisdom to all those foolish virgins whose thought was only of perishable vanities. He spoke eloquently and there was a divine unction in his words. His eyes were bright, his whole face seemed to shine with an inner fire of zeal and inspiration. He looked, Madeleine thought, like an apostle, like an angel. Everything he said was true, axiomatically, self-evidently.

She went on living in the old house; but it seemed very dark now, very empty, and she took to spending a great part of each day with her friend (almost her only friend), Françoise Grandier, who lived with her brother at the parsonage. Sometimes—what could be more natural?—Urbain would join them as they sat there, stitching for the poor or richly embroidering for Our Lady or one of the saints; and suddenly the world would seem brighter and so full of a divine significance that she felt her soul overflowing with happiness.

This time Grandier fell into his own trap. His strategy—the old familiar strategy of the professional seducer—had called for coolness in the face of a deliberately kindled fire, for a detached sensuality pitting itself against passion and exploiting the infinities of love for its own strictly limited purposes. But as the campaign advanced, something went wrong—or rather something went right. For the first time in his life Grandier found himself in love; in love not merely with the prospect of future sensualities, not merely with an innocence which it would be fun to corrupt, a social superiority whose humiliation would be his triumph, but with a woman recognized as a person and loved for what she actually was. The rake underwent a conversion to monogamy. It was a great step forward —but a step forward which a priest of the Roman Church could not take without involving himself in endless difficulties, ethical and theological, ecclesiastical and social. It was in order to get clear of some of these difficulties that Grandier wrote the little treatise on the celibacy of the clergy, to which reference was made in an earlier chapter. Nobody likes to think of himself as immoral and heretical; but at the same time nobody likes to renounce a course of action dictated by powerful impulses, especially when these impulses are recognized as being in their nature good, as tending toward a higher and more abundant life. Hence all the curious literature of rationalization and justification—rationalization of impulse or intuition in terms of whatever philosophy happens, at the given time and place, to be fashionable, justification of unorthodox actions by reference to the current moral code, reinterpreted to fit the particular occasion. Grandier's treatise is a characteristic specimen of this touching and often exceedingly odd branch of apologetics. He loves Madeleine de Brou and knows that this love of his is something intrinsically good; but according to the bylaws of the organization to which he belongs, even this intrinsically good love is bad. He must therefore find some argument to prove that the bylaws do not mean what they say or that he himself did not mean what he said when he agreed, under oath, to abide by them. For a clever man, nothing is easier than to find arguments that will convince him that he is doing right when he is doing what he wants to do. For Grandier the arguments in his treatise seemed irrefragably convincing. What is somewhat more remarkable, they seemed irrefragably convincing to Madeleine. Religious almost to scrupulosity, virtuous not only on principle, but by habit and temperament, she regarded the rules of the Church as so many categorical imperatives and would have died rather than sin against chastity. But she was in love—for the first time and with a passion the more violent for having taken possession of a nature so inward, so long and so consistently held in check. The heart had its reasons, and when Grandier argued that the vow of celibacy was not binding and that a priest might marry, she believed him. If she became his wife, she would be allowed to love him—indeed, it would be her duty to love him. Ergo—for logic is irresistible —the ethics and theology of her lover's treatise were beyond reproach. And so it came to pass that one midnight, in the empty, echoing church, Grandier fulfilled his promise to Mme. de Brou by going through a ceremony of marriage with the orphan she had left to his care. As priest he asked himself whether he took this woman to be his wedded wife, and as bridegroom he answered in the affirmative, he slipped the ring upon her finger. As priest he invoked a blessing, and as groom he knelt to receive it. It was a fantastic ceremony; but in defiance of law and custom, of Church and state, they chose to believe in its validity. Loving one another, they knew that, in the sight of God, they were truly married.*

In the sight of God, perhaps—but most certainly not in the sight of men. So far as the good people of Loudun were concerned, Madeleine was merely the latest of their parson's concubines—a little *sainte nitouche*, who looked as though butter wouldn't melt in her mouth, but in fact was no better than she should be; a prude who

* "From the proceedings of the Huguenot synod of Poitiers in 1560, it is evident that priests not infrequently secretly married their concubines, and, when the woman was a Calvinist, her equivocal position became a matter of grave consideration with her Church." (Henry C. Lea, *History of Sacerdotal Celibacy*, from Chapter XXIX, "The Post-Tridentine Church.")

had suddenly revealed herself as a whore and was prostituting her body in the most shameless manner to this cassocked Priapus, this goat in a biretta.

Among those who met each afternoon under M. Adam's crocodile, indignation was louder, malignity more venomous than in any other quarter. Loathing the parson, but unable, so discreetly had he managed his affairs, to turn this latest outrage to his disadvantage, they indemnified themselves for their enforced inaction by resorting to bad language. There was nothing they could do; but at least they could talk. And talk they did—to so many people and in terms so insulting that Madeleine's relatives decided at last that something would have to be done about it. What they thought of Madeleine's liaison with her confessor is not recorded. All we know is that, like Trincant, they were strong believers in the power of legal truth to take the place of truth unqualified. *Magna est veritas legitima, et praevalebit.** Acting upon this maxim, they persuaded Madeleine to bring an action for slander against M. Adam. The case was heard before the Parlement of Paris and the apothecary was found guilty. A local landowner, who was no friend of the de Brous and who detested Grandier, stood surety for him and an appeal was lodged. There was a second hearing, and the decision of the lower court was confirmed. Poor M. Adam was sentenced to pay six hundred and forty livres parisis in damages, to bear the entire costs of the two trials and, in the presence of the magistrates of the city and of Madeleine de Brou and her relations, to kneel, bareheaded, and to say "in a loud and intelligible voice that he had, temerariously and maliciously, uttered atrocious and scandalous words against the said damsel, for the which he was to ask pardon of God, of the King, of Justice and of the said Mademoiselle de Brou, acknowledging her to be a maiden of virtue and honor." And so it was done. Legal truth had triumphantly prevailed. Lawyers themselves, the Public Prosecutor and the *Lieutenant Criminel* admitted defeat. In any future attack on Grandier, Madeleine, they saw, would have to be left in peace. After all, her mother had been a Chauvet; de Cerisay was her cousin; de Brous had intermarried with the Tabarts, the Dreux, the

* The legal truth is great, and shall prevail.

Genebauts. Whatever she might do, a girl with relatives of such importance could not possibly be anything but *fille de bien et d'honneur*. Meanwhile, it was too bad that the apothecary should have been completely ruined. However, such is life, such the mysterious dispensations of Providence. All of us have our little crosses, and every man, as the apostle so justly remarked, shall bear his own burden.

Two new recruits were now added to the cabal against Grandier. The first was a lawyer of some importance, Pierre Menuau, the King's Advocate. For years past he had pestered Madeleine with proposals of marriage. Her refusals had not discouraged him and he still had hopes of some day winning the girl, the dowry and the ramifying family influence. Great, therefore, was his fury on discovering that Madeleine had bilked him of what he regarded as his rights by bestowing herself upon the parson. Trincant listened sympathetically to his outcry and, by way of consolation, offered him a place on the council of war. The invitation was accepted with alacrity and from now on Menuau was one of the most active members of the cabal.

The second of Grandier's new enemies was a friend of Menuau's, called Jacques de Thibault, a country gentleman who had been a soldier and was now, as an unofficial agent for Cardinal Richelieu, dabbling in provincial politics. From the first Thibault had disliked the parson. A twopenny-halfpenny little priest, a member of the lower middle classes—and he sports the mustaches of a cavalryman, he affects the manners of a lord, he shows off his Latin as though he were a Doctor of the Sorbonne! And now he has the impudence to debauch the King's Advocate's intended bride! Obviously this sort of thing could not be allowed to go on.

Thibault's first step was to address himself to one of Grandier's most powerful friends and protectors, the Marquis du Bellay. He talked so loud and backed up his denunciations with a catalogue of so many real and imaginary offenses that the Marquis changed camps and henceforward treated his erstwhile friend as *persona non grata*. Grandier was deeply hurt and not a little disquieted. Officious friends hastened to tell him of the part which Thibault had played in the affair and, the next time the two men met, the parson (who was in full canonicals and about to enter the church of Sainte-Croix) accosted his enemy with bitter words of reproach. For all answer Thibault lifted his malacca cane and aimed a blow at Grandier's head. A new phase of the battle of Loudun had begun.

Grandier was the first to act. Vowing vengeance on Thibault, he set off the very next morning for Paris. Violence against the person of a priest was sacrilege, was blasphemy in action. He would appeal to the Parlement, to the Attorney General, to the Chancellor, to the King himself.

Within the hour M. Adam was fully informed of his departure and the purpose of his journey. Dropping his pestle, he hurried off to tell the Public Prosecutor, who immediately sent a servant to summon the other members of the cabal. They came and, after some discussion, worked out a plan of counterattack. While the parson was away in Paris complaining to the King, they would go to Poitiers and complain to the Bishop. A document was drawn up in the best legal style. In it Grandier was accused of having debauched innumerable married women and young girls, of being profane and impious, of never reading his breviary and of having committed fornication within the precincts of his church. To transform these statements into legal truths was easy. M. Adam was dispatched to the cattle market and soon came back with two seedy-looking individuals who professed themselves willing, for a small consideration, to sign anything that might be set before them. Bougreau knew how to write, but Cherbonneau could only make his mark. When it was all over, they took their money and went gleefully away to get drunk.

Next morning the Public Prosecutor and the *Lieutenant Criminel* mounted their horses and rode at their leisure to Poitiers. There they called on the Bishop's legal representative, the Promoter of the Officiality. To their great delight they found that Grandier was already on the diocesan black list. Rumors of the parson's amorous exploits had reached the ears of his superiors. And to lubricity and indiscretion had been added the graver sin of uppishness. Only recently, for example, the fellow had had the insolence to encroach on episcopal authority by granting, and being paid for, a dispensation to marry without the preliminary publication of banns. It was time to clip the cockerel's wings. These gentlemen from Loudun had arrived most opportunely.

Carrying a letter of recommendation from the Promoter of the Officiality, Trincant and Hervé trotted off to see the Bishop, who was residing in his splendid castle of Dissay some four leagues out of town.

Henry-Louis Chasteignier de la Rochepozay was that rare phenomenon, a prelate by grace of noble birth who was at the same time a man of learning and the author of portentous works of Biblical exegesis. His father, Louis de la Rochepozay, was the patron and lifelong friend of Joseph Scaliger, and the young lord and predestined bishop had had the advantage of being tutored by that incomparable scholar, "the greatest intellect," in Mark Pattison's words, "that has ever spent itself in acquiring knowledge." It is greatly to his credit that, in spite of Scaliger's Protestantism and in the teeth of the Jesuits' abominable campaign of slander against the author of *De emendatione temporum,* he remained steadfastly loyal to his old master. Toward all other heretics M. de la Rochepozay showed himself implacably hostile. He detested the Huguenots, who were so numerous in his diocese, and did everything in his power to make their lives uncomfortable. But like charity, like the rain which falls on the garden parties of the just as well as on those of the unjust, bad temper is divinely impartial. When his own Catholics annoyed him, the Bishop was ready to treat them just as badly as he treated the Protestants. Thus, in 1614, according to a letter written by the Prince de Condé to the Regent, Marie de Médicis, there were two hundred families encamped outside the town and unable to return to their houses because their pastor, *plus meschant que le diable,* had ordered his arquebusiers to shoot at them if they tried to pass through the gates. And what was their crime? Fidelity to the governor appointed by the Queen, but disliked by M. de la Rochepozay. The Prince asked Her Majesty to punish "the unheard-of insolence of this priest." Nothing, of course, was done, and the good Bishop continued to reign at

Poitiers until, in 1651, at a ripe old age, he was carried off by an apoplectic stroke.

A testy aristocrat and petty tyrant, a book-loving scholar, for whom the world beyond his study door was merely a source of maddening interruptions to the serious business of reading—such was the man who now gave audience to Grandier's enemies. In half an hour he had come to a decision. The parson was a nuisance and must be taught a lesson. A secretary was sent for and an order for Grandier's arrest and transfer to the episcopal prisons at Poitiers was drawn up, signed and sealed. The document was then handed over to Trincant and the *Lieutenant Criminel* to be made use of at their discretion.

In Paris, meanwhile, Grandier had lodged his complaint with the Parlement and been received (thanks to d'Armagnac) in private audience by the King. Deeply moved by the parson's recital of his wrongs, Louis XIII gave orders that justice should be done with all possible expedition, and within a matter of days Thibault was served a summons to appear before the Parlement of Paris. He set out immediately, taking with him the order for Grandier's arrest. The case was heard. Everything seemed to be going in favor of the parson, when Thibault dramatically produced the Bishop's warrant and handed it to the judges. They read it and immediately adjourned the case until such time as Grandier should have cleared himself with his superior. It was a triumph for the parson's enemies.

At Loudun, in the meantime, an official inquiry into Grandier's behavior was being conducted, at first under the impartial presidency of the *Lieutenant Civil*, Louis Chauvet, and later, when Chauvet had resigned in disgust, under that, pre-eminently partial, of the Public Prosecutor. Accusations now poured in from all sides. The Reverend Meschin, one of Grandier's vicars at St. Peter's, affirmed that he had seen the parson sporting with women on the floor (surely a little too stony for such amusements) of his own church. Another clergyman, the Reverend Martin Boulliau, had hidden behind a pillar and spied upon his colleague while he talked to Mme. de Dreux, the deceased mother-in-law of M. de Cerisay, the *Bailli*, in the family pew. Trincant improved this testimony by substituting the words, "committing the veneric act," for the original statement, in which there was merely a question of "speaking to the said lady while laying his hand upon her arm." The only persons who did not bear witness against the parson were those whose testimony would have been the most convincing—the easy-going servant girls, the dissatisfied wives, the all too consolable widows, and Philippe Trincant, and Madeleine de Brou.

On the advice of d'Armagnac, who promised to write on his behalf to M. de la Rochepozay and the Promoter of the Officiality, Grandier decided to present himself voluntarily before the Bishop. Returning secretly from Paris, he spent only a single night at the parsonage. Next day, at sunrise, he was in the saddle again. By breakfast time the apothecary knew everything. An hour later, Thibault, who had returned to Loudun two days before, was galloping along the road to Poitiers. Going directly to the episcopal palace, he informed the authorities that Grandier was in town, trying to avoid the humiliation of arrest by a show of voluntary submission. At all costs he must not be allowed to play such a trick. The Promoter of the Officiality agreed with him. As Grandier left his lodging to walk to the palace, he was arrested by the King's Sergeant and led off, protesting, but *sans scandale, ès prisons episco-pales dudict Poitiers.*

The episcopal prisons of the said Poitiers were situated in one of the towers of his lordship's palace. Here Grandier was consigned to the jailer, Lucas Gouiller, and locked up in a dank and almost lightless cell. The date was November 15, 1629. Less than a month had passed since the quarrel with Thibault.

It was bitterly cold, but the prisoner was not allowed to send for warm clothes and when, a few days later, his mother asked permission to visit him, it was refused. After two weeks of this horribly rigorous confinement he wrote a piteous letter to M. de la Rochepozay. "My lord," it began, "I had always believed and even taught that affliction was the true road to heaven, but I had never made trial of it until your goodness, moved by fear for my perdition and a desire for my salvation, flung me into this place, where fifteen days of misery have brought me nearer to God than forty years of previous prosperity had ever done." This is followed by an elaborately literary passage, full of conceits and Biblical allusions. God, it seems, has "happily conjoined the face of a man with that of the lion, in other words your moderation with the passion of my enemies who, wishing to destroy me like another Joseph, have brought about my advancement in the kingdom of God." So much so that his hate has been turned into love, his thirst for vengeance into a desire to serve those who have wronged him. And after a flowery paragraph about Lazarus, he concludes with the plea that, since the end of punishment is amendment of life and since, after two weeks in prison, his own life has been amended, he should forthwith be released.

It is always hard to believe that frank and unaffected emotion can find expression in the curious devices of a labored style. But literature is not the same as life. Art is governed by one set of rules, conduct by another. The early seventeenth-century absurdity of Grandier's epistolary manner is perfectly compatible with a real sincerity of feeling. There is no reason to doubt the genuineness of his belief that affliction had brought him nearer to God. Unfortunately for himself, he knew too little about his own nature to realize that a renewal of prosperity would infallibly (unless he made enormous and persistent efforts) undo the work of affliction, and undo it, not in fifteen days, but in the first fifteen minutes.

Grandier's letter did not mollify the Bishop. Still less did the letters he now received from M. d'Armagnac and M. d'Armagnac's good friend, the Archbishop of Bordeaux. That this odious little man should have such influential friends was bad enough. But that these friends should venture to dictate to him, a de la Rochepozay, a scholar compared with whom the Archbishop was no better than one of his own horses, that they should presume to advise him what to do with an insubordinate priestling—this was absolutely intolerable. He gave orders that Grandier should be treated even worse than before.

The parson's only visitors, during all this unhappy time, were the Jesuits. He had been their pupil and they did not now desert him. Along with spiritual consolations the good fathers brought him warm socks and letters from the outside world. From these last he learned that d'Armagnac had won over the Attorney General, that the Attorney General had ordered Trincant, as Public Prosecutor of Loudun, to reopen the case against Thibault, that Thibault had come to d'Armagnac with a view to an accommodation, but that *Messieurs les esclezeasticques* (the governor's orthography is consistently astounding) had advised against any compromise, since it would *faire tort à vostre ynosance*. The parson took new heart, wrote another letter to the Bishop about his own case, but got no answer; wrote yet another, when Thibault directly approached him with an offer to settle out of court, and still got no answer. Early in December the witnesses who had been paid to accuse him were heard at Poitiers. Even upon judges prejudiced in their favor, the impression they made was altogether deplorable. Next it was the turn of Grandier's vicar, Gervais Meschin, and the other clerical Peeping Tom who had seen him in the pew with Mme. de Dreux. Their testimony turned out to be almost as unconvincing as that of Bougreau and Cherbonneau. To find anyone guilty on such evidence seemed impossible. But M. de la Rochepozay was not the man to be turned aside from his course by such trifles as equity or legal procedure. On the third of January, sixteen hundred and thirty, judgment was finally pronounced. Grandier was condemned to fast on bread and water every Friday for three months and was forbidden, for five years in the diocese of Poitiers and forever in the town of Loudun, to exercise the sacerdotal function. For the parson this sentence spelled financial ruin and the blasting of all his hopes of future preferment. But meanwhile he was a free man again— free to live once more in his own well-warmed house, to eat a good dinner (except on Fridays), to talk with his relatives and friends, to be visited (with what an infinity of precautions!) by the woman who believed herself to be his wife—and free, finally, to appeal from M. de la Rochepozay to his ecclesiastical superior, the Archbishop of Bordeaux. With copious expressions of respect, but none the less firmly, Grandier wrote to Poitiers announcing his decision to take the case to the metropolitan. Incensed beyond measure, M. de la Rochepozay could yet do nothing to prevent this intolerable affront to his pride. Canon law—could anything be more subversive?—conceded that worms had rights and even permitted them, in certain circumstances, to turn.

To Trincant and the other members of the cabal, the news that Grandier intended to appeal was most unwelcome. The Archbishop was on intimate terms with d'Armagnac, and disliked M. de la Rochepozay. There was every reason to fear that the appeal, if made, would be successful. In which case Loudun would be saddled with the parson forever. To prevent that appeal from being made, Grandier's enemies themselves appealed—not to the higher ecclesiastical court, but to the Parlement of Paris. The Bishop and his officiality were ecclesiastical judges and could impose only spiritual punishments, such as fasting and, in extreme cases, excommunication. There could be no hanging, no maiming or branding, no condemnation to the galleys, except at the decree of a civil magistrate. If Grandier was guilty enough to merit interdiction *a divinis*, then most certainly he was guilty enough to be tried before the high court. The appeal was lodged and a date at the end of the following August was set for the trial.

This time it was the parson's turn to feel disturbed. The case of René Sophier, the country parson who, only six years before, had been burned alive for "spiritual incests and sacrilegious impudicities" was as fresh in his memory as in that of the Public Prosecutor. D'Armagnac, at whose country house he spent most of that spring and summer, reassured him. After all, Sophier had been caught in the act, Sophier had no friends at court. Whereas here there was no evidence and the Attorney General had already promised his assistance, or at least his benevolent neutrality. Everything would be all right. And, in effect, when the case came up for a hearing, the judges did the very thing which Grandier's enemies had hoped they would not do: they ordered a new trial before the *Lieutenant Criminel* of Poitiers. This time the judges would be impartial, the witnesses would find themselves subjected to the most searching cross-examination. The prospects were so alarming that Cherbonneau vanished into thin air and Bougreau not merely withdrew his accusation, but confessed that he had been paid to put his name

53

to it. Of the two priests the elder, Martin Boulliau had long since disavowed the statements attributed to him by the Public Prosecutor, and now, a few days before the opening of the new trial, the younger, Gervais Meschin, came to Grandier's brother and, in a fit of panic mingled perhaps with remorse, dictated a statement to the effect that everything he had said as to Grandier's impiety, his sporting with maids and matrons on the floor of the church, his midnight parties with women in the parsonage, was totally untrue and that he had made statements at the suggestion and on the solicitation of those who were conducting the inquiry. No less damning was the testimony volunteered by one of the canons of Sainte-Croix who now revealed that Trincant had come to him secretly and had tried first to wheedle and then to browbeat him into making unfounded accusations against his colleague.

When the case came to trial there was no evidence against the parson, but a great deal of evidence against his accusers. Thoroughly discredited, the Public Prosecutor found himself on the horns of a dilemma. If he told the truth about his daughter, Grandier would be condemned and his own disgraceful conduct explained and in some measure excused. But to tell the truth would be to expose Philippe to dishonor and himself to contempt or a derisive pity. He held his peace. Philippe was saved from ignominy; but Grandier, the object of all his hatred, was absolved and his own reputation, as a gentleman, as a lawyer, as a public servant, was irreparably tarnished.

There was now, for Grandier, no more danger of being burned alive for spiritual incests; but the interdiction *a divinis* remained in force and, since M. de la Rochepozay would not relent, there was nothing for it but to proceed with the appeal to the metropolitan. The archbishopric of Bordeaux was at this time a family living of the house of Escoubleau de Sourdis. Thanks to the fact that his mother, Isabeau Babou de la Bourdaisière, was the aunt of Gabrielle d'Estrées, the favorite mistress of Henri IV, François de Sourdis had risen very rapidly in his chosen career. At twenty-three he was given a cardinal's hat and the following year, 1599, became Archbishop of Bordeaux. In 1600 he made a journey to Rome, where he was nicknamed, a little unkindly, *Il Cardinale*

Sordido, arcivescovo di Bordello. Returning to his see, he divided his time between founding religious houses and quarreling, over trifles but ferociously, with the local Parlement, which at one moment he excommunicated with all the solemnities of bell, book and candle. In 1628, after a reign of almost thirty years, he died and was succeeded by his younger brother, Henri de Sourdis.

Tallemant's notes on the new Archbishop begin as follows. "Mme. de Sourdis, his mother, told him on her deathbed that he was the son of the Chancellor de Chiverny, that she had procured for him the bishopric of Maillezais and several other benefices, and that she begged him to be content with a diamond, without asking anything from the property of her late husband. He answered: 'Mother, I was never willing to believe that you were no better than you should be (*que vous ne valiez rien*); but I now perceive that it is true.' This did not prevent him from getting the fifty thousand crowns of his lawful portion like the other brothers and sisters, for he won his lawsuit."[*]

As Bishop of Maillezais (another family living, which his uncle had occupied before him), Henri de Sourdis led the life of a gay young courtier. Debarred from the responsibilities of marriage, he did not feel it necessary to deny himself the pleasures of love. Because he wasted so much of his substance upon these pleasures, Mlle. du Tillet, with characteristically Gallic thriftiness, advised his brother's wife, Jeanne de Sourdis, to *faire l'amour avec M. l'évesque de Maillezais, vostre beau-frère.* " 'Jesus, Mademoiselle! What are you saying?' cried Mme. de Sourdis. 'What am I saying?' the other retorted. 'I am saying that it is not good that money should go out of the family. Your mother-in-law did the same thing with *her* brother-in-law, who was also Bishop of Maillezais.' "[†]

In the intervals of love the young Bishop occupied himself chiefly with war, first on land as Quartermaster General and Intendent of Artillery, and later at sea, as a captain of ships and as First Lord of the Admiralty. In this last capacity he virtually created the French Navy.

At Bordeaux Henri de Sourdis followed in his brother's foot-

---

[*] Tallemant des Réaux, *Historiettes* (Paris, 1854), II, p. 337.
[†] *Ibid.*, I, p. 189.

steps by quarreling with the Governor, M. d'Epernon, over such questions as the Archbishop's right to a state entry and the Governor's claim to a first choice of the freshest fish. Matters were carried to such a pitch that one day the Governor ordered his men to stop and turn back the Archbishop's coach. To avenge this insult the Archbishop excommunicated M. d'Epernon's guards and suspended in advance any priest who should say Mass in his private chapel. At the same time he gave orders that public prayers for the Duke of Epernon's conversion should be read in all the churches of Bordeaux. The infuriated Duke counterattacked by forbidding the holding of any meeting of more than three persons within the precincts of the archiepiscopal palace. When this order was communicated to him, M. de Sourdis rushed out into the streets, calling upon the people to protect the liberty of the Church. Issuing from his own quarters to quell the tumult, the Governor came face to face with the Archbishop and, in a frenzy of exasperation, struck him with his cane. M. de Sourdis pronounced him *ipso facto* excommunicate. The dispute was referred to Richelieu, who chose to support M. de Sourdis. The Duke was banished to his estates and the Archbishop remained in triumphant possession of the field. In later life M. de Sourdis himself fell into disgrace. "During his exile," writes Tallement, "he learned a little theology."

Such a man was perfectly fitted to understand and appreciate Urbain Grandier. Himself devoted to the sex, he viewed the parson's peccadilloes with sympathetic indulgence. Himself a fighter, he admired pugnacity even in an underling. Besides, the parson talked well, refrained from cant, had a fund of useful information and amusing anecdotes, and was altogether a most agreeable companion. "*Il vous affectionne bien fort*," d'Armagnac wrote to the parson, after the latter's visit to M. de Sourdis in the spring of 1631, and the liking soon found a practical expression. The Archbishop gave orders that the case should be reviewed by the Officiality of Bordeaux.

All this time the great nationalistic revolution, initiated by Cardinal Richelieu, had been making steady progress and now, almost suddenly, it began to affect the private life of every personage involved in this petty provincial drama. To break the power of the Protestants and the feudal magnates, Richelieu had persuaded the King and Council to order the demolition of every fortress in the realm. Innumerable were the towers already razed, the moats filled in, the ramparts transformed into tree-lined alleys. And now it was the turn of the castle of Loudun. Founded by the Romans, rebuilt and enlarged again and again throughout the Middle Ages, it was the strongest fortress in all Poitou. A circuit of walls defended by eighteen towers crowned the hill upon which the city was built, and within this circuit was a second moat, a second wall and, overtopping all the rest, the huge medieval keep, restored in 1626 by the present Governor, Jean d'Armagnac. The repairs and interior remodelling had cost him a pretty penny; but he had received private assurances from the King, whom he served as first lord of the bedchamber, that, even if the rest of the castle were destroyed, the donjon would be left standing.

Richelieu, meanwhile, had his own views on the matter, and they did not coincide with the King's. For him d'Armagnac was merely an unimportant little courtier and Loudun a nest of potentially dangerous Huguenots. True, these Huguenots had remained loyal during all the recent uprisings of their coreligionists—in the South under the Duc de Roharn, at La Rochelle in alliance with the English. But today's loyalty was no guarantee against tomorrow's rebellion. And anyhow they were heretics. No, no, the castle must be razed and, along with the castle, must go all the ancient privileges of a town which, by remaining predominantly Protestant, had proved itself unworthy of them. The Cardinal's plan was to transfer these privileges to his own town, the neighboring and still hypothetical city of Richelieu, which was now building, or to be built, around the home of his ancestors.

At Loudun public sentiment was strongly against the demolition of the castle. It was a time when domestic peace was still a precarious novelty. Deprived of their fortress, the townspeople, Catholic as well as Protestant, felt that they would be (in d'Armagnac's words) "at the mercy of all kinds of soldiery and subject to frequent pillage." Moreover, rumors of the Cardinal's secret intentions were already abroad. By the time he had done with it, poor old Loudun would be no better than a village—and a half-deserted village at that. Because of his friendship with the Governor, Grandier was unequivocally on the side of the majority. His private enemies, almost without exception, were Cardinalists, who cared nothing for the future of Loudun, but were only concerned to curry favor with Richelieu by clamoring for demolition and working against the Governor. At the very moment when Grandier seemed about to score a final victory, he was threatened by a power enormously greater than any with which he had yet had to cope.

All this time the parson's social position was oddly paradoxical. He had been interdicted *a divinis*; but he was still the Curé of St. Peter's, where his brother, the first vicar, acted on his behalf. His friends were still kind; but his enemies treated him as an outcast, beyond the pale of respectable society. And yet, from behind the scenes, this outcast was exercising most of the functions of a royal governor. D'Armagnac was compelled to spend the greater part of his time at court, in attendance upon the King. During his absence he was represented at Loudun by his wife and a faithful lieutenant. Both the lieutenant and Mme. d'Armagnac had been given explicit orders to consult with Grandier on every important issue. The disgraced and suspended priest was acting as the town's vice-governor and the guardian of the family of its first citizen.

In the course of that summer of 1631 M. Trincant retired into private life. His colleagues and the public at large had been profoundly shocked by the revelations made at Grandier's second trial. A man who was prepared, for the sake of private vengeance, to commit perjury, to suborn witnesses, to falsify written testimony, was obviously unfitted to hold a responsible legal position. Under quiet but persistent pressure Trincant resigned. Instead of selling (as he was entitled to do) the reversion of his post, he gave it away to Louis Moussaut—but gave it on a condition. The young lawyer would not become Loudun's Public Prosecutor until after his marriage with Philippe Trincant. For Henri IV, Paris had been worth a Mass. For M. Moussaut a good job was worth his fiancée's lost virginity and the ribaldry of the Protestants. After a quiet wedding,

Philippe settled down to serve her sentence—forty years of loveless marriage.

In the following November Grandier was summoned to the Abbey of Saint-Jouin-de-Marnes, one of the favorite residences of the much-beneficed Archbishop of Bordeaux. Here he learned that his appeal from M. de la Rochepozay's sentence had been successful. The interdiction *a divinis* was lifted and he was free once again to exercise his functions as Curé of St. Peter's. M. de Sourdis accompanied this announcement with some friendly and eminently sensible advice. Legal rehabilitation, he pointed out, would not disarm the fury of his enemies, it would tend rather to intensify it. Seeing that these enemies were numerous and powerful, would it not be wiser, more conducive to a quiet life, to leave Loudon and start afresh in some other parish? Grandier promised to consider these suggestions, but had already made up his mind to do nothing about them. He was the parson of Loudun and at Loudun he intended to stay, in spite of his enemies—or rather because of them. They wanted him to go; very well, he would remain, just to annoy them and because he enjoyed a fight, because, like Martin Luther, he loved to be angry.

Besides these, the parson had other and less discreditable reasons for wishing to stay. Loudun was Madeleine's home, and it would be very difficult for her to leave it. And there was his friend, Jean d'Armagnac, who now had as much need of Grandier's help as Grandier had once had need of his. To leave Loudun in the midst of the battle over the castle would be like deserting an ally in the face of the enemy.

On his way home from Saint-Jouin, Grandier dismounted at the parsonage of one of the villages on his road and asked if he might cut a branch from the handsome bay tree growing in the garden. The old priest gladly gave his permission. Nothing like bay leaves, he remarked, for improving the flavor of wild duck and roast venison. And nothing like bay leaves, Grandier added, for celebrating a triumph. It was with the victor's laurel in his hand that he rode through the streets of Loudun. That evening, after nearly two years of silence, the parson's ringing voice was heard again in

St. Peter's. Beneath the apothecary's crocodile, meanwhile, the members of the cabal acknowledged their defeat and grimly debated their next move.

A new phase of the struggle was to open sooner than they or anyone else expected. A day or two after Grandier's triumphant return from Saint-Jouin, a distinguished visitor arrived in town and took lodgings at the Swan and Cross. This visitor was Jean de Martin, Baron de Laubardemont, First President of the Court of Appeal (*cour des aides*) of Guyenne, a member of the Council of State and now His Majesty's special Commissioner for the demolition of the castle of Loudun. For a man of only forty-one M. de Laubardemont had gone far. His career was a demonstration of the fact that, in certain circumstances, crawling is a more effective means of locomotion than walking upright, and that the best crawlers are also the deadliest biters. All his life Laubardemont had systematically crawled before the powerful and bitten the defenseless. And now he was reaping his reward; he had become one of His Eminence's favorite subordinates.

In appearance and manner the Baron had modeled himself, two hundred and some odd years before the event, on Dickens's Uriah Heep. The long, squirming body, the damp hands incessantly rubbed, the constant protestations of humility and good will—all were there. And so was the underlying malignancy, so was the ruthless eye to the main chance.

This was Laubardemont's second visit to Loudun. He had come there in the previous year to represent the King at the baptism of one of d'Armagnac's children. For this reason the Governor, somewhat naïvely, believed that Laubardemont was his devoted friend. But the Baron had no friends and was devoted only to the powerful. D'Armagnac wielded no effective power; he was merely the favorite of a King, who had invariably shown himself too weak to say no to his first minister. The favorite had had His Majesty's assurance that the donjon would not be razed; but His Eminence had made up his mind that it must go. This being so, it was a foregone conclusion that sooner or later (and more probably sooner) the King would withdraw his promise. Whereupon the favorite would be revealed for what he was—a mere cipher, a titled nonentity. Before leaving for Poitou, Laubardemont had called on the Governor and made the usual offers of service, the customary protestations of everlasting friendship. And while at Loudun he was assiduous in his attentions to Mme. d'Armagnac, he went out of his way to be polite to the parson. Secretly, however, he held long consultations with Trincant, Hervé, Mesmin de Silly and the other Cardinalists. Grandier, whose private intelligence service was at least as good as the apothecary's, was very soon apprised of these meetings. He wrote to the Governor, warning him to be on his guard against Laubardemont and, above all, against Laubardemont's master, the Cardinal. D'Armagnac replied triumphantly that the King had just written personally to his Commissioner with explicit orders that the keep was to be left standing. That would settle the matter, once and for all.

The royal missive was delivered about the middle of December, 1631. Laubardemont merely put it in his pocket and said nothing about it. The demolition of the outer walls and towers went steadily forward and when, in January, Laubardemont left Loudun to attend to more pressing business elsewhere, the wreckers were getting very close to the keep. Grandier questioned the engineer in charge of the work. His orders were to demolish everything. Acting on his own initiative, the parson gave orders to the soldiers under the Governor's command to form a cordon round the inner fortress.

In February Laubardemont returned and, perceiving that, for the moment, the game was up, apologized to Mme. d'Armagnac for his unaccountable oversight and finally published the King's letter. Temporarily the keep had been saved, but for how long and at what price? Michel Lucas, His Majesty's private secretary and a faithful agent of the Cardinal, received orders to undermine d'Armagnac's influence with his royal master. As for the parson—he would be dealt with in due course and as occasion offered.

Grandier and d'Armagnac scored their last and their most suicidal victory in the early summer of 1632. A courier was bribed, a budget of letters from the Cardinalists to Michel Lucas was intercepted. These letters contained, along with much malicious slander against the Governor, clear proofs that the men who had written them were working wholeheartedly for the ruin of Loudun. D'Armagnac, who was staying at his country house of Lamotte, rode unannounced into the city and, to the sound of the tocsin, summoned an assembly of the people. The incriminating letters were read aloud, and such was the popular fury that Hervé, Trincant and the rest had to go into hiding. But the Governor's triumph was short-lived. Returning a few days later to court, he found that the news of his exploit had preceded him and that the Cardinal had taken it very badly. La Vrillière, the Secretary of State, and a faithful friend, took him aside and told him that he would have to choose between his donjon and his offices under the crown. In no circumstances would His Eminence permit him to keep both. And in any case, whatever might be the present intentions of His Majesty, the donjon was going to be demolished. D'Armagnac took the hint. From that time forth he offered no further resistance. A year later the King wrote another letter to his Commissioner. "Monsieur de Laubardemont, having heard of your diligence . . . I write this letter to express my satisfaction, and because the donjon still remains to be demolished, you will not fail to cause it to be razed entirely, without reserving anything." As usual, the Cardinal had had his way.

Meanwhile Grandier had been fighting his own battles as well as the Governor's. Within a few days of his reinstatement as Curé of St. Peter's, his enemies appealed to the Bishop of Poitiers for permission to receive the sacraments from other hands than those, so notoriously impure, of their parish priest. M. de la Rochepozay was only too happy to oblige. By doing so he would be punishing the man who had dared to appeal against his sentence and at the same time would be telling the Archbishop exactly what he thought of him and his precious absolutions. This dispensation gave occasion for new scandals. In the summer of 1632 Louis Moussaut and his wife, Philippe, came to St. Peter's with their first-born. Instead of leaving the christening to one of his vicars, Grandier offered, with inconceivable bad taste, to perform the rite himself. Moussaut produced the Bishop's dispensation. Grandier insisted that it was illegal and, after a violent altercation with his ex-mistress's husband, brought a lawsuit to enforce his claims.

While the new case was pending, an old one had been revived. Forgotten were all the Christian sentiments of the letter he had written from prison—all those fine phrases about hate having turned into love, the thirst for vengeance giving place to a desire to serve those who had wronged him. Thibault had struck him, and Thibault should be made to pay. D'Armagnac repeatedly advised him to settle out of court. But the parson ignored all Thibault's offers of an accommodation and, as soon as he had been rehabilitated, pressed the old charges for all they were worth. But Thibault had friends at court, and though Grandier finally won his case, the damages assigned were humiliatingly small. For the sake of twenty-four livres parisis he had destroyed the last hope of reconciliation, or at least of an understanding, with his enemies.

CHAPTER THREE

WHILE Urbain Grandier was thus engaged in riding the wheel of fortune from triumph to defeat and back again to precarious triumph, a younger contemporary of his was fighting another kind of battle for a prize incomparably higher. As a schoolboy at the College of Bordeaux, Jean-Joseph Surin must often have seen, among the theological students or the Jesuit novices, a particularly handsome young priest, must often heard his masters speak approvingly of M. Grandier's zeal and M. Grandier's abilities. Grandier left Bordeaux in 1617, and Surin was never to set eyes on him again. When he came to Loudun in the late autumn of 1634, the parson was already dead, and his ashes had been scattered to the four winds.

Grandier and Surin—two men nearly of an age, brought up in the same school, by the same masters, in the same humanistic and religious discipline, both priests, the one secular, the other a Jesuit, and yet predestined to be the inhabitants of incommensurable universes. Grandier was the average sensual man—only a little more so. His universe, as the record of his life sufficiently proves, was "the world," in the sense in which that word is used so frequently in the Gospels and Epistles. "Woe unto the world because of offenses!" "I pray not for the world." "Love not the world, neither the things that are in the world. If any man love the world, the love of the Father is not in him. For all that is in the world, the lust of the flesh, and the lust of the eyes, and the pride of life, is not of the Father, but of the world. And the world passeth away, and the lusts thereof; but he that doeth the will of God abideth for ever."

"The world" is man's experience as it appears to, and is molded by, his ego. It is that less abundant life, which is lived according to the dictates of the insulated self. It is nature denatured by the distorting spectacles of our appetites and revulsions. It is the finite divorced from the Eternal. It is multiplicity in isolation from its non-dual Ground. It is time apprehended as one damned thing after another. It is a system of verbal categories taking the place of the fathomlessly beautiful and mysterious particulars which constitute reality. It is a notion labeled "God." It is the Universe equated with the words of our utilitarian vocabulary.

Over against "the world" stands "the other world," the Kingdom of God within. Towards this Kingdom Surin had, since the beginnings of his self-conscious life, always felt himself attracted. Rich and distinguished, his family was also pious, with a piety that was practical and self-sacrificing. Before he died, Jean-Joseph's father had deeded a considerable property to the Society of Jesus, and after her husband's death, Mme. Surin realized a long-cherished dream by entering the cloister as a Carmelite nun. The elder Surins must have brought up their son with a systematic and conscientious severity. Fifty years later, looking back over his childhood, Surin could discover only one short interlude of happiness. He was eight, and there had been a case of plague in the household. The child was quarantined in a cottage in the country. The season was summer, the place most beautiful, his governess had orders to let him enjoy himself, his relations came to visit him, bringing all kinds of wonderful presents. "My days were spent in playing and running wild, without having to be afraid of anyone." (What a painfully revealing phrase!) "After this quarantine, I was sent to learn my letters, and my bad times began, and a leading of Our Lord that lay so heavy upon me that, from that time until four or five years ago, my sufferings were very great and went on increasing until they reached the highest pitch of which, so I think, our nature is capable."

Jean-Joseph was put to school with the Jesuits. They taught him all he knew, and when the time came for him to choose a vocation, it was to the Society that he unquestioningly turned. From another source, meanwhile, he had learned something even better than good Latin, something even more important than scholastic theology. During some five years of Surin's boyhood and adolescence the Prioress of the Carmelite convent at Bordeaux was a Spanish nun, called Sister Isabel of the Angels. Sister Isabel had been a companion and disciple of St. Teresa and, in middle life, was assigned, with several other nuns, to the missionary work of bringing to France St. Teresa's new model of an order and St. Teresa's spiritual practices and mystical doctrine. To any pious soul who genuinely desired to listen, Sister Isabel was always ready to expound these high and arduous teachings. Among those who came to her most regularly and listened most earnestly, was a rather undersized schoolboy of twelve. The boy was Jean-Joseph, and this was the way he liked to spend his half-holidays. Through the bars of the parlor grating, he listened spellbound to a voice that talked, in laboring and guttural French, of the love of God and the bliss of union, of humility and self-naughting, of the purification of the heart and the emptying of the busy and distracted mind. Listening, the boy felt himself filled with the heroic ambition to do battle with world and flesh, with principalities and powers—to fight and conquer, that he might be fit, at last, to give himself to God. Wholeheartedly he threw himself into the spiritual combat. Shortly after his thirteenth birthday he was vouchsafed what seemed to be a sign of God's favor, a presage of ultimate victory. Praying one day in the Carmelite church, he became aware of a supernatural light, a light that seemed to reveal the essential nature of God and at the same time to manifest all the divine attributes.

The memory of that illumination and of the unearthly bliss by which the experience had been accompanied never left him. It preserved him, in the same sort of social and educational environment as Grandier's and as Bouchard's, from identifying himself, as these others had done, with "the lusts of the flesh, the lusts of the eye, and the pride of life." It was not that that pride and those lusts left him unmoved. On the contrary, he found them horribly attractive. Surin was one of those frail, nervous beings in whom the sexual impulse is powerful almost to frenzy. Moreover, his talents as a writer were considerable and in later years he was tempted, not unnaturally, to equate his total personality with those gifts and become a professional man of letters, primarily concerned with the problems of aesthetics. This invitation to succumb to the most respectable of "the lusts of the eye" was reinforced by vanity and worldly ambition. He would have relished the taste of fame, would have enjoyed, while seeming of course to deprecate, the praise of critics, the plaudits of an adoring public. But the last infirmity of noble mind is just as fatal, so far as the spiritual life is concerned, as the first infirmity of the ignoble. Jean-Joseph's temptations, the creditable no less than the discreditable, were very powerful; but in the light of that remembered glory he could recognize them for what they were. Surin died a virgin, burned the greater part of his literary productions and was content to be not merely not famous, but (as we shall see) positively infamous. Painfully, with heroic perseverance and against the unimaginable obstacles which will be described in a later chapter, he addressed himself to the task of achieving Christian perfection. But before we embark on the history of his strange pilgrimage, let us pause for a little to examine what it is that drives men and women to undertake such voyages into the unknown.

II

Introspection, observation and the records of human behavior in the past and at the present time, make it very clear that an urge to self-transcendence is almost as widespread and, at times, quite as powerful as the urge to self-assertion. Men desire to intensify their consciousness of being what they have come to regard as "themselves," but they also desire—and desire, very often, with irresistible violence—the consciousness of being someone else. In a word, they long to get out of themselves, to pass beyond the limits of that tiny island universe, within which every individual finds himself confined. This wish for self-transcendence is not identical with the wish to escape from physical or mental pain. In many cases, it is true, the wish to escape from pain reinforces the desire for self-transcendence. But the latter can exist without the former. If this were not so, healthy and successful individuals, who have (in the jargon of psychiatry) "made an excellent adjustment to life," would never feel the urge to go beyond themselves. But in fact they do. Even among those whom nature and fortune have most richly endowed, we find, and find not infrequently, a deep-seated horror of their own selfhood, a passionate yearning to get free of the repulsive little identity to which the very perfection of their "adjustment to life" has condemned them (unless they appeal to the Higher Court) without reprieve. Any man or woman, the most happy (by the world's standards) no less than the most wretched, may come, suddenly or gradually, to what the author of *The Cloud of Unknowing* calls "the naked knowing and feeling of thine own being." This immediate awareness of selfhood begets an agonizing desire to go beyond the insulated ego. "I am gall," writes Hopkins,

> I am gall, I am heartburn. God's most deep decree
> Bitter would have me taste: my taste was me;
> Bones built in me, flesh filled, blood brimmed the curse.
> Selfyeast of spirit a dull dough sours. I see
> The lost are like this, and their scourge to be
> As I am mine, their sweating selves; but worse.

Complete damnation is being one's sweating self, but worse. Being one's sweating self, but not worse, merely no better, is partial damnation, and this partial damnation is everyday life, is our consciousness, generally dulled, but sometimes acute and "naked," of behaving like the average sensual human beings we are. "All men have matter of sorrow," says the author of *The Cloud*, "but most specially he feeleth matter of sorrow who knoweth and feeleth that he *is*. All other sorrows in comparison to this be but as it were game to earnest. For he may make sorrow earnestly that knoweth and feeleth not only what he is, but *that* he is. And who has never felt this sorrow, let him make sorrow; for he hath never yet felt perfect sorrow. This sorrow, when it is had, cleanseth the soul not only of sin, but also of the pain it hath deserved for sin; and also it maketh a soul able to receive that joy, the which reaveth from a man all knowing and feeling of his being."

If we experience an urge to self-transcendence, it is because, in some obscure way and in spite of our conscious ignorance, we know who we really are. We know (or, to be more accurate, something within us knows) that the ground of our individual knowing is identical with the Ground of all knowing and all being; that Atman (Mind in the act of choosing to take the temporal point of view) is the same as Brahman (Mind in its eternal essence). We know all this, even though we may never have heard of the doctrines in which the primordial Fact has been described, even though, if we happen to be familiar with them, we may regard these doctrines as so much moonshine. And we also know their practical corollary, which is that the final end, purpose and point of our existence is to make room in the "thou" for the "That," is to step aside so that the Ground can come to the surface of our consciousness, is to "die" so completely that we can say, "I am crucified with Christ; nevertheless I live; yet not I, but Christ liveth in me." When the phenomenal ego transcends itself, the essential Self is free to realize, in terms of a finite consciousness, the fact of its own eternity, together with the correlative fact that every particular in the world of experience partakes of the timeless and the infinite. This is liberation, this is enlightenment, this is the beatific vision, in which all things are perceived as they are "in themselves" and not in relation to a craving and abhorring ego.

The primordial Fact that That art thou is a fact of individual consciousness. For the purposes of religion, this fact of consciousness has to be externalized and objectified by the projection of an infinite deity, standing apart from the finite. At the same time the primordial Duty of getting out of the way, so that the Ground can come to the surface of the finite consciousness, is projected outward as the duty to win salvation within the framework of the Faith. From these two original projections religions have derived their dogmas, their theories of mediation, their symbols, their rites, their rules and precepts. Those who conform to the rules, who worship the mediators, who perform the rites, who believe in the dogmas and adore a God "out there," beyond the finite, may expect, with the aid of divine grace, to achieve salvation. Whether or not they achieve the enlightenment, which accompanies the realization of the primordial Fact, depends on something other than the faithful practice of religion. Insofar as it helps the individual to forget himself and his ready-made opinions about the universe, religion will prepare the way for realization. Insofar as it arouses and justifies such passions as fear, scrupulosity, righteous indignation, institutional patriotism and crusading hate, insofar as it harps on the saving virtues of certain theological notions, certain hallowed arrangements of words, religion is an obstacle in the way of realization.

The primordial Fact and the primordial Duty can be formulated, more or less adequately, in the vocabulary of all the major religions. In the terms employed by Christian theology we may define realization as the soul's union with God as a Trinity, a three in one. It is simultaneously union with the Father, the Son and the Holy Ghost—union with the source and Ground of all being, union with the manifestation of that Ground in a human consciousness and union with the spirit which links the Unknowable to the known.

Union with any single person of the Trinity, to the exclusion of the other two, is not realization. Thus, union exclusively with the Father is a knowledge, by ecstatic participation, of the Ground in its eternal essence and not, at the same time, in its manifestation in the finite. The completely liberating and enlightening experience is that of the eternal in time, the non-dual in multiplicity. For the Bodhisattva, according to the Mahayanist tradition, the world-obliterating ecstasies of the Hinayanist Sravaka are not realization, but barriers to realization. In the West the assault on Quietism was motivated by ecclesiastical considerations and resulted in persecution. In the East the Sravaka was not punished; he was merely told that he was on the wrong track. "The Sravaka," says Ma-tsu, "is enlightened, and yet going astray. The ordinary man is off the right path, and yet in a way enlightened. The Sravaka fails to perceive that Mind as it is in itself knows no stages, no causation, no imagination. Disciplining himself in the cause, he has attained the result and abides in the Samadhi of Emptiness for ever so many aeons. However enlightened in this way, the Sravaka is not at all on the right track. From the point of view of the Bodhisattva this (the abiding in the Samadhi of Emptiness) is like suffering the tortures of hell. The Sravaka has buried himself in emptiness and does not know how to get out of his quiet contemplation, for he has no insight into the Buddha-nature."

Unitive knowledge of the Father alone excludes a knowledge of the world as it is "in itself"—a multiplicity manifesting the non-dual Infinite, a temporal order participating in the eternal. If the world is to be known as it is "in itself," there must be union not only with the Father, but with the Son and Holy Spirit as well.

Union with the Son is the assimilation of the personality to a model of loving selflessness. Union with the Holy Spirit is at once the means to, and the fruit of the individual's self-transcendence into loving selflessness. Together they make possible the awareness of what, unconsciously, we enjoy at every moment—union with the Father. In cases where union with the Son is pursued too exclusively—where attention is centered upon the humanity of the historical mediator—religion tends to become an affair, outwardly, of "works" and inwardly of imaginings, visions and self-induced emotions. But in themselves neither works, nor visions, nor emotions directed toward a remembered or imagined person, are enough. Their value, so far as liberation and enlightenment are concerned, is purely instrumental. They are means to selflessness (or to be more precise, they *may* be means to selflessness) and thus make it possible for the individual, who does the works, or sees the visions and feels the emotions, to become conscious of the divine Ground in which, without knowing it, he has always had his being. The complement of works, imaginings and emotions is faith—not faith in the sense of belief in a set of theological and historical affirmations, nor in the sense of a passionate conviction of being saved by someone else's merits, but faith as confidence in the order of things, faith as a theory about human and divine nature, as a working hypothesis resolutely acted upon in the expectation that what began as an assumption will come to be transformed, sooner or later, into an actual experience, by participation, of a reality which, for the insulated self, is unknowable.

Unknowableness, we may remark, is normally an attribute not

only of the divine Ground of our being, but also of much else that lies, so to speak, between this Ground and our everyday consciousness. To those, for example, who undergo tests for ESP, or prevision, there is no perceptible distinction between success and failure. The process of guessing *feels* exactly the same, whether the result be a score attributable to mere chance, or markedly above or below that figure. This is consistently true of test situations in the laboratory. But it is not always true of situations of a more significant kind. From the many well-authenticated cases on record it is clear that ESP and prevision sometimes take place spontaneously, and that the persons in whom they occur are aware of the event and strongly convinced of the truth of the information which is being conveyed. In the spiritual field we find analogous records of spontaneous theophanies. By a grace of sudden intuition, the normally unknowable makes itself known, and the knowledge is self-validating beyond the possibility of doubt. In men and women who have achieved a high degree of selflessness, these insights, from being rare and brief, may become habitual. Union with the Son through works and union with the Holy Spirit, through docility to inspiration, make possible a conscious and transfiguring union with the Father. In this state of union objects are no longer perceived as related to an insulated ego, but are known "as they are in themselves"—in other words, as they are in relation to, in ultimate identity with, the divine Ground of all being.

For the purposes of enlightenment and liberation, a too exclusive union with the Spirit is no less unsatisfactory than a too exclusive union with the Father in world-obliterating ecstasy, or with the Son in outward works and inward imaginings and emotions. Where union with Spirit is sought to the exclusion of the other unions, we find the thought-patterns of occultism, the behavior-patterns of psychics and sensitives. Sensitives are persons who have been born with, or have acquired, the knack of being conscious of events taking place on those subliminal levels, where the embodied mind loses its individuality and there is a merging with the psychic medium (to use a physical metaphor), out of which the personal self has been crystallized. Within this medium are many other crystallizations, each one with its blurred edges, its melting and interpenetrating boundaries. Some of these crystallizations are the minds of other embodied beings; others, the "psychic factors" which survive bodily death. Some, no doubt, are the idea-patterns, created by suffering, enjoying and reflecting individuals and persisting, as objects of possible experience, "out there" in the psychic medium. And, finally, yet others of these crystallizations may be nonhuman entities, beneficent, malicious or merely alien. Foredoomed to failure are all those who aim exclusively at union with the Spirit. If they ignore the call to union with the Son through works, if they forget that the final end of human life is the liberating and transfiguring knowledge of the Father, in whom we have our being, they will never reach their goal. For them, there will be no union with the Spirit; there will be a mere merging with spirit, with every Tom, Dick and Harry of a psychic world, most of whose inhabitants are no nearer to enlightenment than we are, while some may actually be more impenetrable to the Light than the most opaque of incarnate beings.

Obscurely, we know who we really are. Hence our grief at having to seem to be what we are not, and hence the passionate desire to overstep the limits of this imprisoning ego. The only liberating self-transcendence is through selflessness and docility to inspiration (in other words, union with the Son and the Holy Spirit) into the consciousness of that union with the Father in which, without knowing it, we have always lived. But liberating self-transcendence is easier to describe than to achieve. For those who are deterred by the difficulties of the ascending road, there are other, less arduous alternatives. Self-transcendence is by no means invariably upward. Indeed, in most cases, it is an escape either downward into a state below that of personality, or else horizontally into something wider than the ego, but not higher, not essentially other. We are forever trying to mitigate the effects of the collective Fall into insulated selfhood by another, strictly private fall into animality and mental derangement, or by some more or less creditable self-dispersion into art or science, into politics, a hobby or a job. Needless to say, these substitutes for upward self-transcendence, these escapes into subhuman or merely human surrogates for Grace, are unsatisfactory at the best and, at the worst, disastrous.

III

The *Provincial Letters* take rank among the most consummate masterpieces of literary art. What precision, what verbal elegance, what a pregnant lucidity! And what delicate sarcasm, what an urbane ferocity! The pleasure we derive from Pascal's performance is apt to blind us to the fact that, in the squabble between Jesuits and Jansenists, our incomparable virtuoso was fighting for what, in the main, was the worse cause. That the Jesuits finally triumphed over the Jansenists was certainly no unmixed blessing. But at least it was less of a curse than would have been, in all probability, the triumph of Pascal's party. Committed to the Jansenist doctrine of predestined damnation for almost everyone and to the Jansenist ethic of unbending puritanism, the Church might easily have become an instrument of almost unmitigated evil. As it actually turned out, the Jesuits prevailed. In doctrine, the extravagances of Jansenist Augustinianism were tempered by a dose of semi-Pelagian common sense. (At other periods the extravagances of Pelagianism—those of Helvétius, for example, those of J. B. Watson and Lysenko in our own day—have had to be tempered by appropriate doses of semi-Augustinian common sense.) In practice rigorism gave place to a more indulgent attitude. This more indulgent attitude was justified by a casuistry whose aim was always to prove that what looked like a mortal sin was in fact venial; and this casuistry was rationalized in terms of the theory of Probabilism, by means of which the multiplicity of authoritative opinions was used in order to give the sinner the benefit of every possible doubt. To the rigid and all too consistent Pascal, Probabilism seemed utterly immoral. For us, the theory and the kind of casuistry it justified possess one enormous merit: between them they reduce to absurdity the hideous doctrine of everlasting damnation. A hell, from which one can be saved by a quibble that would carry no weight with a police magistrate, cannot be taken very seriously. The intention of the Jesuit casuists and moral philosophers

74

was, by leniency, to keep even the worldliest and most sinful men and women within the bounds of the Church and thereby to strengthen the organization as a whole and their own Order in particular. To some extent they achieved this intended end. But at the same time they achieved a considerable schism within the fold and, implicitly, a *reductio ad absurdum* of one of orthodox Christianity's cardinal doctrines—the doctrine of infinite punishment for finite offenses. The rapid spread, from 1650 onward, of deism, "free thought" and atheism was an end-product of many co-operating causes. Among those causes were Jesuit casuistry, Jesuit Probabilism and those *Provincial Letters*, in which, with unsurpassable artistic skill, Pascal ferociously caricatured them.

The Jesuits who played a part, directly or at one remove, in our strange drama were singularly unlike the good fathers of the *Provincial Letters*. They had nothing to do with politics; they had hardly any contacts with "the world" and its denizens; the austerity of their lives was heroic almost to madness, and they preached the same austerity to their friends and disciples, who were all, as were they themselves, contemplatives dedicated to the achievement of Christian perfection. They were mystics in that school of Jesuit mysticism, whose most eminent representative had been Father Alvarez, the director of St. Teresa. Alvarez was censured by one General of the Society for practicing and teaching contemplation, as opposed to discursive meditation along the lines of the Ignatian exercises. A later General, Aquaviva, exonerated him and, in so doing, laid down what may be called the official Jesuit policy in regard to contemplative prayer. "Those persons are to be blamed who attempt prematurely and temerariously to launch out into high contemplation. However, we must not go to the lengths of flying in the face of the constant experience of the holy Fathers by despising contemplation and forbidding it to our members. For it is well established by the experience and authority of many Fathers that true and profound contemplation possesses more force and efficacity than all other methods of prayer, both for subduing and casting down human pride and for exciting lukewarm souls to execute their Superiors' commands and work with ardor for the salvation of souls."

75

During the first half of the seventeenth century those members of the Society who showed a marked vocation for the mystical life were permitted, and indeed encouraged, to devote themselves to contemplation within the framework of their essentially active Order. At a later period, after the condemnation of Molinos and during the bitter controversy over Quietism, passive contemplation came to be regarded by the majority of Jesuits with considerable suspicion.

In the last two volumes of his *Histoire Littéraire du Sentiment Religieux en France*, Bremond picturesquely dramatizes the conflict between the "asceticist" majority within the Order and a minority of frustrated contemplatives. Pottier, the learned Jesuit historian of Lallemant and his disciples, has subjected Bremond's thesis to severe and destructive criticism. Contemplation, he insists, was never officially condemned and individual contemplatives continued, even in the worst days of the anti-Quietist movement, to flourish within the Society.

In the sixteen-thirties Quietism was still half a century in the future, and the debate over contemplation had not yet been envenomed by accusations of heresy. For Vitelleschi, the General, and his hierarchy of Superiors, the problem was purely practical. Did the practice of contemplation produce better Jesuits than the practice of discursive meditation, or did it not?

From 1628 until his retirement, for reasons of health, in 1632, a great Jesuit contemplative, Father Louis Lallemant held the post of Instructor at the College of Rouen. Surin was sent to Rouen in the autumn of 1629 and remained there, with a group of twelve or fifteen other young priests, who had come for their "second novitiate," until the late spring of 1630. Throughout that memorable semester he listened to daily lectures by the Instructor and prepared himself, by prayer and penance, for a life of Christian perfection within the framework of the Ignatian rule.

The outlines of Lallemant's teaching as recorded briefly by Surin and, at greater length, by his fellow pupil, Father Rigoleuc, were worked up from the original notes by a later Jesuit, Father Cham-

76

pion, and issued, in the last years of the seventeenth century, under the title of *La Doctrine Spirituelle du Père Louis Lallemant*.

In Lallemant's doctrine there was nothing basically novel. How could there be? The end pursued was that unitive knowledge of God, which is the goal of all who aspire to upward self-transcendence. And the means to that end were strictly orthodox—frequent communion, a scrupulous fulfillment of the Jesuit vow of obedience, systematic mortification of the "natural man," self-examination and a constant "guard of the heart," daily meditations on the Passion and, for those who were ready for it, the passive prayer of "simple regard," the alert waiting on God in the hope of an infusion of the grace of contemplation. The themes were ancient; but the manner, in which Lallemant first experienced and then expressed them, was personal and original. The Doctrine, as formulated by the master and his pupils, has its own special character, its tone and peculiar flavor.

In Lallemant's teaching special emphasis was laid on purification of the heart and docility to the leadings of the Holy Ghost. In other words, he taught that conscious union with the Father can only be hoped for, where there has been union with the Son through works and devotion, and union with the Spirit in the alert passivity of contemplation.

Purification of the heart is to be achieved by intense devotion, by frequent communion and by an unsleeping self-awareness, aimed at the detection and mortification of every impulse to sensuality, pride and self-love. Of devotional feelings and imaginings, and of their relations to enlightenment, there will be occasion to speak in a later chapter. In this place our themes are the processes of mortification and the "natural man," who has to be mortified. The corollary of "Thy kingdom come" is "our kingdom go." On that matter all are agreed. But all are not agreed as to the best way of making our kingdom go. Should it be conquered by force of arms? Or should it be converted? Lallemant was a rigorist, who took a very gloomy and Augustinian view of the total depravity of fallen nature. As a good Jesuit, he advocated leniency toward sinners and the worldly. But the tone of his theological thought was deeply pessimistic, and toward himself and all those who aspired to perfection he was im-

77

placable. For them, as for him, no course was open but that of a mortification pushed to the limits of human endurance. "It is certain," writes Champion in his brief biography of Father Lallemant, "that his bodily austerities exceeded his strength and that their excess, in the judgment of his most intimate friends, greatly shortened his life."

It is interesting, in this context, to read what Lallemant's other contemporary, John Donne, the Romanist turned Anglican, the repentant poet turned preacher and theologian, has to say on this matter of self-punishment. "Foreign crosses, other men's merits are not mine; spontaneous and voluntary crosses, contracted by mine own sin, are not mine; neither are devious, and remote, and unnecessary crosses, my crosses. Since I am bound to take up my cross, there must be a cross that is mine to take up, a cross prepared by God, and laid in my way, which is temptations or tribulations in my calling; and I must not go out of my way to seek a cross; for so it is not mine, nor laid for my taking up. I am not bound to hunt after a persecution, nor to stand it and not fly, nor to affront a plague and not remove, nor to open myself to an injury and not defend. I am not bound to starve myself by inordinate fasting, nor to tear my flesh by inhuman whipping and flagellations. I am bound to take up my cross; and that is only mine, which the hand of God hath laid for me, that is, in the way of my calling, temptations and tribulations incident to that."

These views are by no means exclusively Protestant. At one time or another they have been expressed by many of the greatest Catholic saints and theologians. And yet physical penance, carried often to extreme lengths, remained a common practice in the Roman Church for long centuries. There were two reasons for this, one doctrinal and the other psycho-physiological. For many, self-punishment was a substitute for purgatory. The alternative was between torture now and much worse torture in the posthumous future. But there were also other and obscurer reasons for bodily austerities. For those whose goal is self-transcendence, fasting, insomnia and physical pain are "alteratives" (to borrow a word from the older pharmacology); they bring about a change of state, they cause the patient to be other than he was. On the physical level these alteratives, if administered to excess, may result in a downward self-transcendence, ending in disease and even, as in Lallemant's case, in premature death. But on the way to this undesirable consummation, or in cases where they are used with moderation, physical austerities may be made the instruments of horizontal and even of upward self-transcendence. When the body goes hungry, there is often a period of unusual mental lucidity. A lack of sleep tends to lower the threshold between the conscious and the subconscious. Pain, when not too extreme, is a tonic shock to organisms deeply and complacently sunk in the ruts of habit. Practiced by men of prayer, these self-punishments may actually facilitate the process of upward self-transcendence. More frequently, however, they give access, not to the divine Ground of all being, but to that queer "psychic" world which lies, so to say, between the Ground and the upper, the more personal levels of the subconscious and conscious mind. Those who gain access to this psychic world—and the practice of physical austerities would seem to be a royal road to the occult—often acquire powers of the kind which our ancestors called "supernatural" or "miraculous." Such powers and the psychic states accompanying them were often confused with spiritual enlightenment. In fact, of course, this kind of self-transcendence is merely horizontal, and not upward. But psychic experiences are so strangely fascinating that many men and women have been willing and even eager to undergo the self-tortures which make them possible. Consciously and as theologians, Lallemant and his disciples never believed that "extraordinary graces" were the same as union with God, or indeed that they had any necessary connection with it. (Many "extraordinary graces," as we shall see, are indistinguishable in their manifestations from the workings of "evil spirits.") But conscious belief is not the sole determinant of conduct and it seems possible that Lallemant and probable that Surin felt themselves strongly drawn toward the austerities which did in fact help them to obtain "extraordinary graces,"* and that they rationalized this attraction in terms of such

* "The consolations and pleasures of prayer," Surin writes in one of his letters, "go hand in hand with bodily mortification." Unpunished bodies, we read elsewhere, "are hardly capable of receiving the visits of angels. To be loved and caressed by God, one must either suffer much inwardly, or else maltreat one's body."

orthodox beliefs as that the natural man is intrinsically evil and must be got rid of at any cost and by any means, however violent.

Lallemant's hostility to nature was directed outward as well as inward. For him, the fallen world was full of snares and riddled with pitfalls. To take pleasure in creatures, to love their beauty, to inquire overmuch into the mysteries of mind and life and matter—these, to him, were dangerous distractions from the proper study of mankind, which is not man, not nature, but God and the way to a knowledge of God. For a Jesuit the problem of achieving Christian perfection was peculiarly difficult. The Society was not a contemplative order, whose members lived in seclusion and devoted their lives only to prayer. It was an active order, an order of apostles, dedicated to the saving of souls and pledged to fight the battles of the Church in the world. Lallemant's conception of the ideal Jesuit is summed up in the notes, in which Surin recorded his master's teaching. The essence, the whole point of the Society consists in this: that it "joins together things which in appearance are contrary, such as learning and humility, youth and chastity, diversity of nations and a perfect charity. . . . In our life we must mingle a deep love of heavenly things with scientific studies and other natural occupations. Now, it is very easy to rush to one extreme or the other. One may have too great a passion for the sciences and neglect prayer and spiritual things. Or, if one aspires to become a spiritual man, one may neglect to cultivate, as one should, such natural talents as doctrinal knowledge, eloquence and prudence." The excellence of the Jesuit spirit consists in this, "that it honors and imitates the manner in which the divine was united with all that was human in Jesus Christ, with the faculties of his soul, with the members of his body, with his blood, and it deified all. . . . But this alliance is difficult. That is why those among us who do not realize the perfection of our spirit, tend to cling to natural and human advantages, being destitute of the supernatural and the divine." The Jesuit who fails to live up to the spirit of the Society turns into the Jesuit of popular imagination, and not infrequently of historical fact—worldly, ambitious, intriguing. "The man who fails to apply himself wholeheartedly to the inner life falls inevitably into these defects; for the poverty-stricken and starving soul must needs cling to something in the hope of satisfying its hunger."*

For Lallemant, the life of perfection is a life simultaneously active and contemplative, a life lived at the same time in the infinite and the finite, in time and in eternity. This ideal is the highest which a rational being can conceive—the highest and at the same time the most realistic, the most conformable to the given facts of human and divine nature. But when they discussed the practical problems involved in the realization of this ideal, Lallemant and his disciples displayed a narrow and self-stultifying rigorism. The "nature" which is to be united with the divine is not nature in its totality, but a strictly limited segment of human nature—a talent for study, or for preaching, for business or for organization. Nonhuman nature finds no place in Surin's summary and is only passingly referred to in the longer account of Lallemant's teaching given by Rigoleuc. And yet Christ told his followers to consider the lilies—and to consider them, be it noted, in an almost Taoist spirit, not as emblems of something all too human, but as blessedly other, as autonomous creatures living according to the law of their own being and in union (perfect except for its unconsciousness) with the Order of Things. The author of *Proverbs* bids the sluggard consider the ways of the prudent ant. But Christ delights in the lilies precisely because they are not prudent, because they neither toil nor spin and yet are incomparably lovelier than the most gorgeous of Hebrew kings. Like Walt Whitman's "Animals,"

> They do not sweat and whine about their condition,
> They do not lie awake in the dark and weep for their sins,
> They do not make me sick discussing their duty to God,
> Not one is dissatisfied, not one is demented with the
> mania for owning things,
> Not one kneels to another, nor to his kind that lived
> thousands of years ago,
> Not one is respectable or industrious over the whole earth.

* "The Jesuits have tried to combine God and the world, and have gained only the contempt of both" (Pascal).

Christ's lilies are worlds apart from the flowers with which St. Francis de Sales opens his chapter on the purification of the soul. These flowers, he tells Philothea, are the good desires of the heart. The *Introduction* abounds in references to nature—but to nature as seen through the eyes of Pliny and the authors of the bestiaries, to nature as emblematic of man, nature as consistently the schoolmarm and the moralist. But the lilies of the field enjoy a glory which has this in common with the Order of the Garter—that "there's no damned merit about it." That, precisely, is their point; that is why, for us human beings, they are so refreshing and, on a level much deeper than that of morality, so profoundly instructive. "The Great Way," says the Third Patriarch of Zen,

> The Great Way is no harder than men themselves
> Make it by not refusing to prefer;
> For where there is no abhorrence, where there is no
> Frenzy to have, the Way lies manifest.

As always in real life, we are in the midst of paradoxes and antinomies—bound to choose the good rather than the evil, but bound at the same time, if we wish to realize our union with the divine Ground of all being, to choose without craving and aversion, without imposing upon the universe our own notions of utility or morality.

Insofar as they ignore nonhuman nature, or treat it as merely symbolic of human nature, as merely instrumental and subordinate to man, the teachings of Lallemant and Surin are characteristic of their time and country. French literature of the seventeenth century is astonishingly poor in expressions of any but a strictly utilitarian or symbolic interest in birds, flowers, animals, landscape. In the whole of *Tartufe*, for example, there is only one reference to nonhuman nature—a single line, and that most marvelously unpoetical.

La campagne à present n'est pas beaucoup fleurie. No truer word was ever spoken. So far as literature was concerned, the French countryside, during those years which led up to and included the Grand Siècle, were almost flowerless. The lilies of the field were there all right; but the poets did not consider them. The rule had its exceptions, of course; but they were few—Théophile de Viau, Tristan l'Hermite and, later, La Fontaine, who occasionally wrote of the brute creation not as men in fur and feathers, but as beings of another, though related, order, to be looked at as they are in themselves and to be loved for their own sake and for God's. In the *Discours à Madame de la Sablière* there is a beautiful passage on the then fashionable philosophy, whose exponents proclaim:

> *Que la beste est une machine;*
> *Qu'en elle tout se fait sans choix et par ressorts:*
> *Nul sentiment, point d'âme, en elle tout est corps . . .*
> > *L'animal se sent agité*
> > *De mouvements que le vulgaire appelle*
> *Tristesse, joye, amour, plaisir, douleur cruelle,*
> > *Ou quelque autre de ces estats.*
> *Mais ce n'est point cela; ne cous y trompez pas.*

This summary of the odious Cartesian doctrine—a doctrine, incidentally, not so far removed from the orthodox Catholic view that the brutes are without souls and may therefore be used by human beings as though they were mere things—is followed by a series of examples of animal intelligence, in the stag, the partridge and the beaver. The whole passage is as fine, in its own way, as anything in the whole range of reflective poetry.

It stands, however, almost alone. In the writings of La Fontaine's great contemporaries, nonhuman nature plays almost no part whatever. The world in which Corneille's enormous heroes act out their tragedies is that of a closely organized, hierarchical society. "*L'espace cornélien c'est la Cité*," writes M. Octave Nadal. The yet more strictly limited universe of Racine's heroines and the somewhat featureless males, who serve as pretexts for their anguish, is as windowless as the Cornelian City. The sublimity of these post-Senecan tragedies is stuffy and confined, the pathos without air, without elbow room, without background. We are far indeed from *King Lear* and *As You Like It*, from *A Midsummer Night's Dream* and *Macbeth*. In practically any comedy or tragedy of Shakespeare one cannot read twenty lines without being made aware that, behind the clowns, the criminals, the heroes, behind the flirts and the weeping queens, beyond all that is agonizingly or farcically human, and yet symbiotic with man, immanent in his consciousness and consubstantial with his being, there lie the everlasting data, the given facts of planetary and cosmic existence on every level, animate and inanimate, mindless and purposively conscious. A poetry that represents man in isolation from nature, represents him inadequately. And analogously a spirituality which seeks to know God only within human souls, and not at the same time in the nonhuman universe with which in fact we are indissolubly related, is a spirituality which cannot know the fullness of divine being. "My deepest conviction," writes an eminent Catholic philosopher of our time, M. Gabriel Marcel, "my deepest and most unshakable conviction—and if it is heretical, so much the worse for orthodoxy—is that, whatever all the thinkers and doctors have said, it is not God's will at all to be loved by us *against* the Creation, but rather glorified *through* the Creation, and with the Creation as our starting point. That is why I find so many devotional books intolerable." In this respect, the least intolerable book of seventeenth-century devotion would be Traherne's *Centuries of Meditations*. For this English poet and theologian, there is no question of a God set up against the creation. On the contrary, God is to be glorified through the creation, to be realized in the creation—infinity in a grain of sand and eternity in a flower. The man who, in Traherne's phrase, "attains the World" in disinterested contemplation, thereby attains God, and finds that all the rest has been added. "Is it not a sweet thing to have all covetousness and ambition satisfied, suspicion and infidelity removed, courage and joy infused? Yet is all this in the fruition of the World attained. For thereby is God seen in all his wisdom, power, goodness and glory." Lallemant speaks of the mingling of seemingly incompatible elements, the natural and the supernatural, in the life of perfection. But, as we have seen, what he calls "nature" is not nature in its fullness, but merely an excerpt. Traherne advocated the same mingling of incompatibles, but accepted nature in its totality and in its smallest details. The lilies and the ravens are to be considered, not *quoad nos*, but selflessly, *an sich*—which is the same as saying "in God." And here is sand and a flower growing from

84

among the grains: contemplate these things lovingly and you will see them transfigured by the immanence of eternity and infinity. It is worth remarking that this experience of a divinity immanent in natural objects came also to Surin. In a few brief notations he records that there were times when he actually perceived the full majesty of God in a tree, a passing animal. But, strangely enough, he never wrote at any length about this beatific vision of the Absolute in the relative. And even to the recipients of his spiritual letters he never suggested that obedience to Christ's injunction to consider the lilies might help the blindly groping soul to come to a knowledge of God. One can only suppose that the acquired belief in the total depravity of fallen nature was stronger, in his mind, than the givenness of his own experience. The dogmatic words he had learned at Sunday School were opaque enough to eclipse the immediate Fact. "If you wish to see It before your eyes," writes the Third Patriarch of Zen, "have no fixed notions either for or against It." But fixing notions is the professional occupation of theologians, and both Surin and his master were theologians before they were seekers for enlightenment.

In Lallemant's scheme of *ascesis* purification of the heart was to be accompanied and completed by constant docility to the leadings of the Holy Ghost. One of the seven Gifts of the Spirit is Intelligence, and the vice opposed to Intelligence is "coarseness in regard to spiritual things." This coarseness is the ordinary state of the unregenerate, who are more or less completely blind to the inner light and more or less completely deaf to inspiration. By mortifying his self-regarding impulses, by setting up a witness to his thoughts and "a little sentinel to keep an eye on the movements of the heart," a man can sharpen his perceptions to the point where he becomes aware of the messages coming up from the obscure depths of the mind—messages in the form of intuitive knowledge, of direct commands, of symbolic dreams and phantasies. The heart that is constantly watched and guarded becomes capable of all the graces and in the end is truly "possessed and governed by the Holy Spirit."

But on the way to this consummation there may be possessions of a very different kind. For by no means all inspirations are divine, or even moral, even relevant. How are we to distinguish between the leadings of the not-I who is the Holy Spirit and of that other not-I who is sometimes an imbecile, sometimes a lunatic and sometimes a malevolent criminal? Bayle cites the case of a pious young Anabaptist, who felt inspired one day to cut off his brother's head. The predestined victim had read his Bible, knew that this sort of thing had happened before, recognized the divine origin of the inspiration and, in the presence of a large assemblage of the faithful, permitted himself, like a second Isaac, to be decapitated. Such teleological suspensions of morality, as Kierkegaard elegantly calls them, are all very well in the Book of Genesis, but not in real life. In real life we have to guard against the gruesome pranks of the maniac within. Lallemant was very well aware that many of our inspirations are most certainly not from God, and was careful to take due precautions against illusion. To those of his colleagues who objected that his doctrine of docility to the Holy Ghost was suspiciously like the Calvinist doctrine of the inner spirit, he answered: first, that, it was an article of faith that no good work could be accomplished without a leading of the Holy Spirit in the form of an inspiration and, second, that divine inspiration presupposed the Catholic Faith, the traditions of the Church and the obedience due to ecclesiastical superiors. If an inspiration prompted a man to go against the faith or the Church, it could not possibly be divine.

This is one way—and a very effective way—of guarding against the extravagances of the indwelling maniac. The Quakers had another. Persons who felt a concern to do something unusual or momentous were advised to consult with a number of "weighty Friends" and to abide by their opinion as to the nature of the inspiration. Lallemant advocates the same procedure. Indeed, he asserts that the Holy Ghost actually "prompts us to consult with judicious persons and to conform our conduct to the opinion of others."

No good work can be accomplished without an inspiration of the Holy Spirit. This, Lallemant could point out to his critics, is an article of the Catholic faith. To those of his colleagues who "complained that they did not have this kind of leading by the Holy Spirit and that they were unable to experience it," he answered that, if they were in a state of grace, such inspirations were never wanting, even though they might be unaware of them. And he added that they would certainly become aware of divine inspiration if they behaved themselves as they ought. But instead of that, "they chose to live outside themselves, hardly ever coming home to look into their own souls, making the examination of conscience (to which they were bound by their vows) in a very superficial way and taking into consideration only such faults as are obvious to outsiders, without trying to seek out their inner roots in the passions and in dominant habits, and without examining the state and tendency of the soul and the feelings of the heart." That such persons could not experience the leading of the Holy Ghost was hardly surprising. "How could they know it? They do not even know their inward sins, which are their own acts freely performed by themselves. But as soon as they choose to create within themselves the appropriate conditions for such knowledge, they will infallibly have it."

All this explains why most would-be good works are ineffective to the point of being almost bad. If hell is paved with good intentions, it is because most people, being self-blinded to the inner light, are actually incapable of having a purely good intention. For this reason, says Lallemant, action must always be in direct proportion to contemplation. "The more inward we are, the more we may undertake outward activities; the less inward, the more we should refrain from trying to do good." Again, "one busies oneself with works of zeal and charity; but is it from a pure motive of zeal and charity? Is it not, perhaps, because one finds a personal satisfaction in this kind of thing, because one does not care for prayer or study, because one cannot bear to stay in one's room, cannot stomach seclusion and recollectedness?" A priest may have a large and devoted congregation; but his words and works will bear fruit "only in proportion to his union with God and his detachment from his own interests." The appearances of doing good are often profoundly deceptive. Souls are saved by the holy, not by the busy. "Action must never be allowed to be an obstacle to our union with God, but must serve rather to bind us more closely and lovingly to Him." For "just as there are certain humors which, when they are too abundant, cause the death of the body, so in the religious life, when action predominates to excess and is not tempered by prayer and meditation, it infallibly stifles the spirit." Hence the fruitlessness of so many lives, seemingly so meritorious, so brilliant and so productive. Without the selfless inwardness which is the condition of inspiration, talent is fruitless, zeal and hard work produce nothing of spiritual value. "A man of prayer can do more in a single year than another can accomplish in a whole lifetime." Exclusively outward work may be effective in changing outward circumstances; but the worker who wishes to change men's reactions to circumstances— and one can react destructively and suicidally to even the best environment—must begin by purifying his own soul and making it capable of inspiration. A merely outward man may work like a Trojan and talk like Demosthenes; but "an inward man will make more impression on hearts and minds by a single word animated by the spirit of God" than the other can do by all his efforts, all his cleverness and learning.

How does it actually feel to be "possessed and governed by the Holy Spirit?" This state of conscious and continuous inspiration was described, with the most delicate precision of self-analysis, by Surin's younger contemporary, Armelle Nicolas, affectionately known throughout her native Brittany as *la bonne Armelle*. This uneducated servant girl, who lived the life of a contemplative saint while cooking the dinner, scrubbing floors and looking after the children, was incapable of writing her own story. But fortunately it was written for her by a very intelligent nun, who succeeded in drawing her out and in recording her confidences almost verbatim.* "Losing sight of herself and all the workings of her mind, Armelle no longer envisaged herself as acting in anything, but as suffering and passively submitting to the workings which God accomplished in and by her; so that it seemed to her that, while she possessed a body, it was only that she might be moved and governed by the Spirit of God. It was into this state that she entered after God had so peremptorily commanded her to make room for Him. . . . When

* See Le Gouvello, *Armelle Nicolas*, 1913; H. Bremond, *Histoire Littéraire du Sentiment Religieux en France* (Paris, 1916).

she thought of her body or her mind, she no longer said "my body," or "my mind"; for the word "my" had been banished, and she used to say that everything belonged to God.

"I remember hearing her say that, from the time that God had made Himself the absolute master of her being, she had been dismissed as effectively as, in the past, she herself had given notice" (Armelle's metaphors were all drawn from the professional vocabulary of a maid of all work) "to those other things" (her bad habits, her self-regarding impulses). "Once dismissed, her mind was not permitted to see or understand what God was working in the inmost recesses of her soul, nor to interfere with its own workings. It was as though her mind remained, huddled up, outside the door of this central chamber, where God alone might freely enter, waiting there like a lackey for his master's orders. And the mind did not find itself alone in this situation; but it seemed sometimes that an infinite number of angels kept it company, standing around the dwelling-place of God, so as to prevent anything from crossing the threshold." This state of things lasted some time. Then God permitted her conscious self to enter the central chamber of the soul—to enter and actually *see* the divine perfections with which it was now filled, with which, indeed, it had always been filled; but like everyone else, she had not known it. The inner Light was intense beyond her capacity to bear it, and for a time her body suffered excruciatingly. In the end, she acquired some measure of tolerance and was able to support the consciousness of her enlightenment without too much distress.

Remarkable in itself; Armelle's self-analysis is doubly interesting as being yet another piece among the many pieces of evidence all pointing to the same conclusion: namely, that the phenomenal self is underlain by a Pure Ego or Atman, which is of the same nature as the divine Ground of all being. Outside the central chamber where (until the soul has become selfless) "none but God may enter," between the divine Ground and the conscious self, lies the subliminal mind, almost impersonal at its melting fringe, but crystallizing, as the phenomenal self is approached, into the personal subconscious with its accumulations of septic rubbish, its swarms of rats and black beetles and its occasional scorpions and vipers. This personal subconscious is the haunt of our indwelling criminal lunatic, the *locus* of Original Sin. But the fact that the ego is associated with a maniac is not incompatible with the fact that it is also associated (all unconsciously) with the divine Ground. We are born with Original Sin; but we are also born with Original Virtue—with a capacity for grace, in the language of Western theology, with a "spark," a "fine point of the soul," a fragment of unfallen consciousness, surviving from the state of primal innocence and technically known as the *synteresis*. Freudian psychologists pay far more attention to Original Sin than to Original Virtue. They pore over the rats and the black beetles, but are reluctant to see the inner Light. Jung and his followers have shown themselves to be somewhat more realistic. Overstepping the limits of the personal subconscious, they have begun to explore the realm where the mind, growing more and more impersonal, merges into the psychic medium, out of which individual selves are crystallized. Jungian psychology goes beyond the immanent maniac, but stops short of the immanent God.

And yet, I repeat, there is plenty of evidence for the existence of an Original Virtue underlying Original Sin. Armelle's experience was not unique. The knowledge that there is a central chamber of the soul, blazing with the light of divine love and wisdom, has come, in the course of history, to multitudes of human beings. It came, among others, to Father Surin—and came, as will be recorded in a later chapter, in conjunction with a knowledge, no less immediate and no less overpowering, of the horrors at large in the psychic medium and the poisonous vermin in the personal subconscious. At one and the same instant he was aware of God and of Satan, he knew beyond all doubt that he was eternally united with the divine Ground of all being, and yet was convinced that he was already and irrevocably damned. In the end, as we shall see, it was the consciousness of God that prevailed. In that tormented mind, Original Sin was finally swallowed up in the infinity of a much more Original, because timeless, Virtue.

Mystical experiences, theophanies, flashes of what has been called cosmic consciousness—these are not to be had for the asking, cannot be repeated uniformly and at will in the laboratory. But if the experience of the central chamber of the soul is not to be commanded, certain experiences of approach to that center, of being within its field, of standing at the door (in Armelle's words) among a company of angels, are repeatable, if not uniformly indeed (for only the most elementary psychological experiences can be repeated with anything like uniformity), but at least sufficiently often to indicate the nature of the transcendent Limit, toward which they all converge. For example, those who have experimented with hypnosis find that, at a certain depth of trance, it happens not too infrequently that subjects, if they are left alone and not distracted, will become aware of an immanent serenity and goodness that is often associated with a perception of light and of spaces vast but not solitary. Sometimes the entranced person feels impelled to speak about his or her experience. Deleuze, who was one of the best observers in the second generation of Animal Magnetists, records that this state of somnambulism is characterized by a complete detachment from all personal interests, by the absence of passion, by indifference to acquired opinions and prejudices and by "a novel manner of viewing objects, a quick and direct judgment, accompanied with an intimate conviction. . . . Thus the somnambulist possesses at the same time the torch which gives him his light and the compass that points out his way. This torch and this compass," Deleuze concludes, "are not the product of somnambulism; they are always in us, but the distracting cares of the world, the passions and, above all, pride, and attachment to perishable things prevent us from perceiving the one and consulting the other."* (Less dangerously and more effectively than the drugs which sometimes produce "anaesthetic revelations,"† hypnotism temporarily abolishes distractions and allays the passions, leaving the consciousness free to occupy itself with what lies beyond the haunt of the immanent maniac.) "In this new situation," Deleuze continues, "the mind is filled with religious ideas, with which, perhaps, it was never before

* See J. P. F. Deleuze, *Practical Instruction in Animal Magnetism*, trans. T. C. Hartshorn (New York, 1890).
† See William James, *Varieties of Religious Experience*.

occupied." Between the somnambulist's new way of viewing the world and his normal state there is a difference "so prodigious that he sometimes feels as though he were inspired; he regards himself as the organ of a superior intelligence, but this does not excite his vanity."

Deleuze's findings are confirmed by those of an experienced woman psychiatrist who for many years has made a study of automatic writing. In conversation this lady has informed me that, sooner or later, most automatists produce scripts in which certain metaphysical ideas are set forth. The theme of these scripts is always the same: namely, that the ground of the individual soul is identical with the divine Ground of all being. Returning to their normal state, the automatists read what they have written and often find it in complete disharmony with what they have always believed.

In this context it seems worth while to remark that (as F. W. H. Myers pointed out many years ago) the moral tone of mediumistic utterances about life in general is almost invariably above reproach. Because of their style, such utterances may be dismissed as mere twaddle. But however soggy the language, however commonplace the thoughts (and for the last thirty centuries at least, all the great truths have been commonplaces), the twaddle is always harmless and might even, if psychics could only write a little better, be uplifting. The inference to be drawn from all this is that in certain states of trance mediums go beyond the personal subconscious, beyond the verminous realm of Original Sin, into an area of subliminal mind in which, like a radiation from some distant source, the influence of Original Virtue makes itself faintly but still distinctly felt. Meanwhile, of course, if they neglect to make union with the Father their end and union with the Son, through works, a means to that end, they are in constant danger of finding themselves inspired, not by the Holy Ghost, but by all manner of inferior entities, some indigenous to their own personal subconscious, others existing "out there" in the psychic medium, some harmless or positively helpful, but others in the highest degree undesirable.

With these inferential confirmations of the reality of mystical experience, with this evidence at one remove, Lallemant and his disciples did not have to concern themselves. They had their first-hand knowledge and, to validate it, an authoritative literature ranging from the *Mystical Theology* of Dionysius the Areopagite to the almost contemporary writings of St. Teresa and St. John of the Cross. Of the reality and the divine nature of the end, to which purification of the heart and docility to the Holy Spirit were the principal means, there was never, in their minds the slightest question. In the past great servants of God had written of their experiences, and the orthodoxy of these writings had been guaranteed by the Doctors of the Church. And now, in the present, they themselves had lived through the agonizing Dark Nights of the senses and the will, and had known the peace which passeth all understanding.*

* For a further discussion of this subject, the reader is referred to the "Epilogue" on page 313.

CHAPTER FOUR

FOR those who had no vocation for it, life in a seventeenth-century convent was merely a succession of boredoms and frustrations, mitigated in some slight degree by an occasional *Schwaermerei*, by gossip with visitors in the parlor, and by absorption, during leisure hours, in some innocent but entirely footling hobby. Father Surin, in his *Letters*, speaks of the ornaments in plaited straw, upon which many good sisters of his acquaintance spent the greater part of their spare time. Their masterpiece, in this line, was a miniature straw coach, drawn by six straw horses, and destined to adorn the dressing table of an aristocratic patroness. Of the nuns of the Visitation Father de la Colombière writes that, though the rules of the order are admirably designed to lead souls to the highest perfection, and though he has met certain Visitandines of exalted holiness, it remains true, nevertheless, "that religious houses are filled with persons who keep their rules, get up, go to Mass, to prayer, to confession, to communion merely because it is the habit, because the bell tolls and because others do the same. Their heart has almost no part in what they do. They have their little notions, their little plans, which keep them busy; the things of God enter their minds only as things indifferent. Relatives and friends, whether within the convent or without, use up all their affections, so that there is left over for God only some kind of sluggish and forced emotion by no means acceptable to Him. . . . Communities which ought to be furnaces in which souls are forever on fire with the love of God, remain instead in a condition of frightful mediocrity, and God grant that things may not go from bad to worse."

To Jean Racine, Port-Royal seemed uniquely admirable because of "the solitude of the parlor, the little eagerness shown by the nuns to enter into conversation, their lack of curiosity about the things of the world and even about the affairs of their neighbors." From this catalogue of Port-Royal's merits we can infer the corresponding defects of other, less remarkable convents.

The house of Ursuline nuns, which was established at Loudun in 1626, was neither better nor worse than the average. Most of the seventeen nuns were young noblewomen, who had embraced monastic life, not out of any overmastering desire to follow the evangelical counsels and achieve Christian perfection, but because there was not enough money at home to provide them with dowries commensurate with their birth and acceptable to suitors of corresponding rank. There was nothing scandalous in their conduct and nothing particularly edifying. They observed their rule, but observed it with resignation rather than enthusiasm.

Life at Loudun was hard. The nuns of the new foundation had arrived without money in a town that was half Protestant and wholly stingy. The only house they could afford to rent was a gloomy old building, which nobody else would live in because it was notoriously haunted. They had no furniture and for some time were compelled to sleep on the floor. The pupils, on whom they relied for their living, were slow in presenting themselves, and for a time these blue-blooded de Sazillys and d'Escoubleaus, these de Barbezières and de la Mottes, these de Belciels and de Dampierres, were compelled to work with their hands and to go without meat, not only on Fridays, but on Mondays, Tuesdays, Wednesdays and Thursdays as well. After a few months, snobbery came to their rescue. When bourgeois Loudun discovered that, for a very modest fee, it could have its female offspring taught good French and courtly manners by a second cousin once removed of Cardinal de Richelieu, by an even closer relative of Cardinal de Sourdis, by the younger daughter of a marquis and a niece of the Bishop of Poitiers, boarders and day pupils came thick and fast.

With them, at last, came prosperity. Servants were hired to do the dirty work, beef and mutton reappeared on the refectory table and the mattresses were taken off the floor and placed on wooden bedsteads.

In 1627 the Prioress of the new community was transferred to another house of the order and a new superior was appointed in her place. Her name in religion was Jeanne des Anges; in the world it had been Jeanne de Belciel, daughter of Louis de Belciel, Baron de Coze, and of Charlotte Goumart d'Eschillais, who came of a family hardly less ancient and eminent than his own. Born in 1602, she was now in her middle twenties, her face rather pretty, but her body diminutive almost to dwarfishness and slightly deformed—presumably by some tubercular affection of the bones. Jeanne's education had been only slightly less rudimentary than that of most young ladies of her time; but she was possessed of considerable native intelligence, combined, however, with a temperament and a character, which had made her a trial to others and her own worst enemy. Because of her deformity the child was physically unattractive; and the consciousness of being misshapen, the painful knowledge that she was an object either of repugnance or of pity, aroused in her a chronic resentment, which made it impossible for her either to feel affection or to permit herself to be loved. Disliking and consequently disliked, she lived in a defensive shell, issuing forth only to attack her enemies—and everybody, *a priori*, was an enemy—with sudden sarcasms or strange outbursts of jeering laughter. "I noticed," Surin was to write of her, "that the Mother Superior had a certain jocosity of nature which excited her to laugh and crack jokes (*bouffonner*) and that the demon, Balaam, did his best to cherish and maintain this humor. I saw that this spirit was wholly opposed to the seriousness with which one ought to take the things of God, and that it fostered in her a certain glee which destroys the compunction of heart indispensable to a perfect conversion to God. I saw that a single hour of this kind of jocularity was enough to ruin everything I had built up in the course of many days, and I induced in her a strong desire to rid herself of this enemy." There is a laughter that is perfectly compatible with "the things of God"—a laughter of humility and self-criticism, a laughter of good-natured tolerance, a laughter in lieu of despair or indignation at the world's perverse absurdity. Very different from any of these, Jeanne's laughter was either of derision or of cynicism. Directed against others, never against herself, the first was a symptom of the unreconciled hunchback's desire to be revenged on destiny by putting other people in their place—and their place, in spite of all appearances, was below her. Motivated by the same craving for compensatory dominance, the second was a more impersonal jeering and joking at all that, by current standards, was most solemn, lofty and grand.

Persons of Jeanne's character are apt to make a good deal of trouble, both for themselves and for other people. Incapable of coping with a very unpleasant child, her parents packed her off to an elderly aunt, who was the prioress of a neighboring abbey. After two or three years she was ignominiously returned; the nuns could do nothing with her. Time passed, and life in the paternal château became so odious to her that even a cloister seemed preferable to home. She entered the Ursuline house at Poitiers, passed through the usual novitiate and took her vows. As might have been expected, Jeanne did not make a very satisfactory nun; but her family was rich and influential, and the Superior deemed it expedient to put up with her. And then, almost overnight, there was a marvelous change for the better. Ever since her coming to Loudon Sœur Jeanne had behaved with exemplary piety and diligence. The young woman who, at Poitiers, had been so insubordinate, so wanting in zeal, so slack in the performance of her duties, was now the perfect religious—obedient, hard-working and devout. Deeply impressed by this conversion, the retiring Prioress recommended Sister Jane as the person best fitted to take her place.

Fifteen years later the convert gave her own version of this episode. "I took good care," she wrote, "to make myself indispensable to those in authority, and since there were but few nuns, the Superior was obliged to assign me to all the offices of the

97

community. It was not that she could not do without me, for she had other nuns more capable and better than I; it was merely that I imposed upon her by a thousand little compliances and so made myself necessary to her. I knew so well how to adapt myself to her humor and to prevail upon her, that at last she found nothing well done except what was done by me; she even believed that I was good and virtuous. This puffed up my heart to such an extent that I had no difficulty in performing actions which seemed to be worthy of esteem. I knew how to dissimulate and I made use of hypocrisy, so that my Superior might go on thinking well of me and be favorable to my inclinations; and in effect she granted me many privileges which I abused, and since she was herself good and virtuous and believed that I too intended to go to God with Christian perfection, she often invited me to converse with worthy monks, which I did in order to humor her and to pass the time."

When the worthy monks took their leave, they would push through the grille some newly translated classic of the spiritual life. One day it was a treatise by Blosius; another, the life of the Blessed Mother Teresa of Avila, written by herself, with St. Augustine's *Confessions* and Del Rio on angels thrown in for good measure. As she read these books, as she learned to discuss their contents with the prioress and the good fathers, Sœur Jeanne found her attitude insensibly changing. These pious talks in the parlor, these studies in the literature of mysticism, ceased to be mere time-killers and became means to a specific end. If she read the mystics, if she talked with the visiting Carmelites of perfection, it was not at all "for the sake of her own advancement in the spiritual life, but solely in order to seem clever and to outshine all the other nuns in every kind of company." The unreconciled hunchback's craving for superiority had found another outlet, a new and fascinating field in which to operate. There were still occasional outbursts of sarcasm and cynical buffoonery; but in the graver intervals Sister Jane was now the expert in spirituality, the learned consultant on all matters of mystical theology. Exalted by her new-found knowledge, she could now look down on her sisters with an altogether delightful mingling of contempt and pity. True, they were pious, they were trying, poor things, to be good—but with what a piddling kind of virtue, what an ignorant and, one might say, brutish devotion! What did *they* know of extraordinary graces? What of spiritual touches, of rapts and inspirations, of aridities and the night of the senses? And the answer, the highly gratifying answer to all these questions was that they knew nothing at all. Whereas she— the little dwarf with one shoulder higher than the other—she knew practically everything.

Mme. Bovary came to a bad end because she imagined herself to be the kind of person she in fact was not. Perceiving that Flaubert's heroine embodied a very widespread human tendency, Jules de Gaultier coined from her name the word "bovarism" and wrote a book on the subject, which is well worth the reading. Bovarism i by no means invariably disastrous. On the contrary, the process of imagining that we are what we are not, and of acting upon this imagination, is one of the most effective mechanisms of education. The title of the most enduring of all books of Christian devotion— *The Imitation of Christ*—bears eloquent witness to this fact. It is by thinking and acting in any given situation, not as we would normally think and act, but rather as we imagine that we should do, if we were like some other and better person, that we finally cease to be like our old selves and come, instead, to resemble our ideal model.

Sometimes, of course, the ideal is low and the chosen model more or less undesirable. But the bovaristic mechanism of imagining ourselves to be what we are not, and of thinking and acting as though that fancy were a fact, remains the same. There is, for example, a bovarism in the realm of vice—the bovarism of the good boy who conscientiously takes to drinking and whoring in order to be like some generally admired he-man or daredevil. There is a bovarism in the field of hierarchical relationships—the bovarism of the bourgeois snob who imagines himself to be an aristocrat and tries to behave as such. There is a political bovarism—the bovarism of those who practice the imitation of Lenin or Webb or Mussolini. There is a cultural and aesthetic bovarism—the bovarism of the *précieuses ridicules*, the bovarism of the modern philistine who is converted overnight from the cover of the *Saturday Evening Post* to Picasso. And finally there is bovarism in religion—and we have at one end of the scale the saint who wholeheartedly imitates Christ and, at the other, the hypocrite who tries to look like a saint in order the more effectively to pursue his own unholy ends. In the middle ground, somewhere between the two extremes of Tartufe and St. John of the Cross, there exists a third, hybrid variety of religious bovarists. These, the absurd but often touching comedians of the spiritual life, are neither consciously wicked nor resolutely holy. Their all too human desire is to make the best of both worlds. They aspire to be saved—but without going to too much trouble; they hope to be rewarded—but only for looking like heroes, only for talking like contemplatives, not for doing or being. The faith which sustains them is the illusion, half recognized as such, half earnestly believed in, that by saying "Lord, Lord" sufficiently often they will contrive, somehow or other, to enter into the Kingdom of Heaven.

Without "Lord, Lord," or some more elaborate doctrinal or devotional equivalent, the process of religious bovarization would be difficult, in some cases all but impossible. The pen is mightier than the sword in this sense; that it is by means of verbalized thought that we direct and maintain our efforts. But it is possible to make use of words as a substitute for effort, to live in a purely verbal universe and not in the given world of immediate experience. To change a vocabulary is easy; to change external circumstances or our own ingrained habits is hard and tiresome. The religious bovarist who is not prepared to undertake a wholehearted imitation of Christ contents himself with the acquisition of a new vocabulary. But a new vocabulary is not the same thing as a new environment or a new character. The letter kills, or merely leaves inert; it is the spirit, it is the reality underlying verbal signs, which gives new life. Phrases which, at their first formulation, expressed significant experiences, tend (such is the nature of human beings and their religious organizations) to become a mere jargon, a pious slang, by means of which the hypocrite disguises his conscious wickedness and the more or less harmless comedian tries to deceive himself and impress his fellows. As we should expect, Tartufe speaks and teaches others to speak the language of the sons and servants of God.

> De toutes amitiés il détache mon âme,
> Et je verrai mourir frère, enfants, mère et femme
> Que je m'en soucierais autant que de cela.

We recognize a distorted echo of the Gospels, a parody of the Ignatian and Salesian doctrine of holy indifference. And how movingly, when at last he is unmasked, does the hypocrite confess his total depravity! All the saints have always believed themselves to be enormous sinners, and Tartufe is no exception to the rule.

> Oui, mon frère, je suis un méchant, un coupable,
> Un malheureux pécheur, tout plein d'iniquité,
> Le plus grand scélérat qui jamais ait été.

It is the language of St. Catherine of Siena—and the language, when she remembers to speak it, of Sœur Jeanne des Anges in her *Autobiography*.

Even when he is making passes at Elmire, Tartufe employs the phraseology of the devout. "*De vos regards divins l'ineffable douceur*"—applied to God or to Christ, the words are to be found in the writings of every Christian mystic. "*C'en est fait*," cries the indignant Orgon, when at last he discovers the truth,

> C'en est fait, je renonce à tous les gens de bien;
> J'en aurai désormais une horreur effroyable,
> Et m'en vais devenir pour eux pire qu'un diable.

His more sensible brother has to give him a little lecture on semantics. Because some *gens de bien* are not what they seem to be, it does not follow that all are villains or comedians. Every case must be considered on its own merits.

In the course of the seventeenth century several eminent directors of souls—Cardinal Bona was one of them, the Jesuit, Father Guilloré was another—published exhaustive treatises on the problems of distinguishing false spirituality from the genuine article, mere words from living substance, fraud and phantasy from "extraordinary graces." Subjected to tests of the kind proposed by these writers, it seems most improbable that Sœur Jeanne would for long have succeeded in "getting away with it." Unhappily, her directors were only too uncritically anxious to give her the benefit of every doubt. Sane or hysterical, but in either condition the consummate actress, Sœur Jeanne had the misfortune to be taken seriously on every occasion except, as we shall see, the one when she was doing her best to tell the plain unvarnished truth.

If her directors took her seriously, it was either because they had their own, not too creditable reasons for believing in her extraordinary graces, or else because they were committed by temperament and *Weltanschauung* to this kind of illusion. How seriously, we may now ask, did she take herself? How seriously was she taken by her fellow nuns? We can only guess at the answers to these questions.

There must be times when, however word-perfect in their impressive roles, the comedians of the spiritual life become uneasily conscious that something is not quite right, that perhaps, after all, God is not mocked and that even human beings may not (appalling thought!) be quite so dumb as one might be led to suppose.

This last truth seems to have dawned upon Sœur Jeanne at a fairly early stage in her long-drawn impersonation of St. Teresa. "God," she writes, "very often permitted that things should happen to me at the hands of creatures, which gave me much pain." Through the obscuring veils of this odd jargon we divine the ironic shrug with which Sister X received some specially eloquent discourse on the Spiritual Marriage, the hard-boiled comment made by Sister Y on Jeanne's new trick, in church, of rolling up her eyes and pressing her hands, like some saint in a baroque picture, over a bosom wildly palpitating with extraordinary graces. We all imagine ourselves to be simultaneously clear-sighted and impenetrable; but, except when blinded by some infatuation, other people can see through us just as easily as we can see through them. The discovery of this fact is apt to be exceedingly disconcerting.

Fortunately for Sœur Jeanne—or perhaps very unfortunately—the first Prioress of the Loudun house was less perspicacious than those other creatures, whose ironic skepticism had given her so much pain. Deeply impressed by her young pupil's holy conversation and exemplary behavior, the good mother had felt no hesitation in recommending Jeanne's appointment as Prioress. And now the appointment had been made, and here she was—only twenty-five and the head of a house, the queen of a tiny empire, whose seventeen subjects were bound by Holy Obedience to take her orders and listen to her advice.

Now that victory had been won, now that the fruits of a long and arduous campaign were securely in her grasp, Sœur Jeanne felt that she was entitled to a holiday. She went on with her mystical reading, she continued, on occasion, to talk very learnedly about Christian perfection; but in the intervals she permitted herself—indeed, as Superior, she actually commanded herself—to take it easy. In the parlor, where she was now free to spend as much time as she liked, the new Prioress indulged in interminable conversations with her friends and acquaintances of the uncloistered world. Years later she piously expressed the wish that she might be permitted to set forth "all the faults I committed and caused to be committed in the course of conversations which were not strictly necessary; for then it would be seen how dangerous it is to expose young nuns with such facility at the grilles of their convent parlors, even though their talk may seem to be wholly spiritual." Yes, even the most spiritual discourses, as the Prioress knew only too well, had a curious way of winding up as something very different. One started out with a series of edifying remarks about the devotion to St. Joseph, about meditation and the precise moment when it might be allowed to give place to the prayer of simple regard, about holy indifference and the practice of the presence of God—one started with these things and then, before one knew where one was or how precisely one had got there, one was discussing, yet again, the exploits of the fascinating and abominable M. Grandier.

"That shameless creature in the Rue du Lion d'Or. . . . That young hussy who was M. Hervé's housekeeper before he got married. . . . That cobbler's daughter who was now in the service of Her Majesty, the Queen Mother, and who kept him posted about all that went on at court. . . . And his penitents. . . . One shudders to think. . . . Yes, in the sacristy, Reverend Mother, in the sacristy—not fifteen paces from the Blessed Sacrament. . . . And that poor little Trincant, seduced, you might say, under her father's nose, in his own library. And now it was Mlle. de Brou. Yes, that prude, that precisian. So much attached to virginity that she would never marry. So devout that, when her mother died, she talked of turning Carmelite. Instead of which. . . ."

Instead of which. . . . In her own case, the Prioress reflected, there had been no "instead." A novice at nineteen, a nun when she was barely of age. And yet, after the death of her sisters and her two brothers, her parents had begged her to come home and get married and give them grandchildren. Why had she refused? Why, though she hated this dismal life between four walls, had she persisted in taking the final vows? Was it for the love of God, or out of dislike for her mother? Was it to spite M. de Coze or to please Jesus?

She thought with envy of Madeleine de Brou. No choleric father, no prying mother; plenty of money; and her own mistress, free to do as she pleased. And now she had Grandier.

Envy modulated into hatred and contempt.

This hypocrite, with her pale face like the face of a virgin martyr in a picture book! This soft-spoken dissembler, with her beads and her long prayers and her pocket edition of the Bishop of Geneva in red morocco! And all the time, under those black weeds, behind those downcast eyes, what a burning, what lechery! No better than that slut in the Rue du Lion d'Or, no better than the cobbler's daughter, or the little Trincant. And these at least had the excuse of being young or widowed; which was more than could be said for that old maid of thirty-five, with a figure like a Maypole and no looks at all. Whereas she, the Prioress, was still in her twenties, and Sister Claire de Sazilly used to say that her face under its coif was like an angel's, peeping through a cloud. And what eyes! Everybody had always admired her eyes—even her mother, even her detestable old aunt, the Abbess. If only she could get him as far as the parlor! Then she would look at him through the grille—look at him fixedly, searchingly, with eyes that should reveal her soul in all its nakedness. Yes, in all its nakedness; for the grille was not the adjunct of modesty; it was in lieu of modesty. Restraint had been taken out of the mind and embodied in an iron lattice. Behind bars one could be shameless.

But, alas, the opportunity for shamelessness never presented itself. The parson had no reasons, either professional or personal, for visiting the convent. He was not the nuns' director, he had no relatives among their pupils. His lawsuits and his parochial duties left him no leisure for mindless chatter, or talk about perfection, and his mistresses left him no appetite for new and hazardous "embarkations." Month succeeded month, year followed year, and the Prioress had still found no occasion for the deployment of those irresistible eyes of hers; so far as she was concerned, Grandier remained merely a name—but a name of power, a name that conjured up unavowable phantasies, spirits familiar and unclean, a demon of curiosity, an incubus of concupiscence.

A bad reputation is the mental equivalent of the purely physiological appeals issued by animals during their mating seasons—cries, odors and even, in the case of certain moths, infrared radiation. In a woman, a name for promiscuity constitutes a standing invitation to every male within gossip range. And how fascinating, even to the most respectable ladies, is the professional seducer, the hardened breaker of hearts! In the imagination of his female parishioners Grandier's amorous exploits took on heroic proportions. He became a mythical figure, part Jupiter, part Satyr—bestially lustful and yet, or therefore, divinely attractive. At the time of his trial, a married lady, belonging to one of Loudun's most honorable families, testified that, after administering communion, the parson had looked at her fixedly, whereupon she "was seized with a violent love for him, which began with a little thrill in all her members." Another met him in the street and was incontinently overcome by "an extraordinary passion." A third merely looked at him as he was entering a church and felt "exceedingly great emotions, together with impulses such that she would very much have liked to sleep with him there and then." All these ladies were notoriously virtuous and of unblemished reputation. Each of them, moreover, had a home with a man in it and a growing family. The poor Prioress had nothing to do, no husband, no children and no vocation. What wonder if she too fell in love with the delicious monster! *"La mère prieure en fut tellement troublée, qu'elle ne parlait plus que de Grandier, qu'elle disait estre l'objet de touttes ses affections."* That double *t* in *touttes* seems to raise *all* to a higher power, so that Grandier becomes the object of affections beyond the limit of experience, affections which it was impossible for anyone to feel—and yet she felt them in all their monstrous and perverse enormity. The thought of the parson haunted her continuously. Her meditations, which should have been a practice of the presence of God, were a practice, instead, of the presence of Urbain Grandier, or rather of the obscenely fascinating image which had crystallized, in her fancy, around his name. Hers was the unobjective and therefore limitless and insane desire of the moth for the star, of the schoolgirl for the crooner, of the bored and frustrated housewife for Rudolph Valentino. On such merely carnal sins as gluttony and lust, the body imposes, by its very nature and constitution, certain limits. But however weak the flesh, the spirit is always indefinitely willing. To sins of the will and the imagination kind nature sets no limits. Avarice and the lust for power are as nearly infinite as anything in this sublunary world can be. And so is the thing which D. H. Lawrence called "sex in the head." As heroic passion, it is one of the last infirmities of noble mind. As imagined sensuality, it is one of the first infirmities of the insane mind. And in either case (being free of the body and the limitations imposed by fatigue, by boredom, by the essential irrelevance of material happenings to our ideas and fancies), it partakes of the infinite. Behind her bars the Prioress found herself the victim of an insatiable monster, her own imagination. In her own person she combined the trembling and lacerated quarry with an infernal analogue of the Hound of Heaven. As might have been expected, her health broke down and by 1629 Sœur Jeanne was suffering from a psychosomatic "derangement of the stomach which," according to Dr. Rogier and the surgeon Mannoury, "rendered her so weak that it was with difficulty that she could walk."

All this time, let us remember, the Ursulines' *pensionnat* was purveying reading and writing, the catechism and deportment, to a growing enrollment of young girls. How, one wonders, did the pupils react to the ministrations of a headmistress in the clutch of a sexual obsession, of teachers already infected by the hysteria of their principal? To this question the documents provide, unfortunately, no answer. All we know is that it was not until a later stage of the proceedings that indignant parents began to remove their children from the good sisters' care. For the present, it would seem, the mental atmosphere of the convent was not so manifestly abnormal as to arouse alarm. Then, early in the fifth year of the Prioress's reign, there occurred a series of events which, though unimportant in themselves, were destined to have enormous consequences.

The first of these events was the death of the Ursulines' director, Canon Moussaut. A most worthy priest, the Canon had conscientiously done his best for the new community, but his best, since he was on the brink of second childhood, had not been very good. He understood nothing of his penitents; and his penitents, on their side, paid no attention to anything he said.

At the news of Moussaut's death, the Prioress tried her hardest to look sad; but inwardly she was filled with an effervescent elation. At last, at last!

As soon as the old gentleman was safely buried, she dispatched a letter to Grandier. It began with a paragraph about the irreparable loss sustained by the community, went on to stress her own and her sisters' need for spiritual guidance by some director no less wise and holy than the dear defunct, and ended with an invitation to Grandier to step into the Canon's shoes. Except for the spelling, which had always been Sœur Jeanne's weakest point, the letter was altogether admirable. Reading through the fair copy, the Prioress could not see how he could possibly resist an appeal at once so heartfelt, so pious, so delicately flattering.

But Grandier's answer, when it came, was a polite refusal. Not only did he feel himself unworthy of so high an honor; he was also much too busy with his duties as a parish priest.

From the pinnacle of joy, the Prioress tumbled headlong into a disappointment in which grief was mingled with hurt pride, and out of which there grew, as she ruminated the bitter cud of her defeat, a cold persistent rage, a steady malignancy of hatred.

To implement this loathing was by no means easy; for the parson inhabited a world into which it was impossible for a cloistered nun to penetrate. She could not go to him; and he would not go to her. Their nearest approach to a personal contact came when Madeleine de Brou called at the convent to visit her niece, who was one of the boarders. Entering the parlor, Madeleine found the Prioress confronting her on the other side of the grille. She uttered a polite greeting and was answered by a torrent of abuse that became more shrilly violent with every passing moment. "Whore, strumpet, debaucher of priests, committer of the ultimate sacrilege!" Through the bars the Prioress spat at her rival. Madeleine turned and fled.

The last hope of a personal, face-to-face vengeance was now gone. But one thing, at least, Sœur Jeanne could still do: she could associate herself and the whole community under her charge with Grandier's avowed enemies. Without delay she sent for the man who, of all the local clerics, had the most cogent reasons for detesting him. Ill-favored, congenitally lame, devoid of talent no less than of charm, Canon Mignon had always envied the parson's good looks, quick wit and easy successes. To this general and, so to say, antecedent antipathy had been added, over the years, a number of more specific grounds for dislike—Grandier's sarcasms, the seduction of Mignon's cousin, Philippe Trincant, and, more recently, a quarrel over a piece of property disputed between the collegial church of Ste. Croix and the parish of St. Pierre. Acting against the advice of his fellow canons, Mignon had taken the case to court and, as they had all prophesied, lost it. He was still smarting under this humiliation, when the Prioress summoned him to the convent parlor, and, after talking at large about the spiritual life and in particular of the parson's scandalous behavior, invited him to become the nuns' confessor. The offer was immediately accepted. A new ally had joined the forces leagued against Grandier. Precisely how that ally was to be made use of, Mignon did not yet know. But, like a good general, he was prepared to seize every opportunity that might present itself.

In the Prioress's mind, meanwhile, the new hatred for Grandier had not abolished, had not even mitigated, the old obsessive desires. The imagined hero of her waking or nocturnal dreams remained the same; but now he was no longer the Prince Charming, for whom one left the casement open at night, but an importunate incubus, who delighted in inflicting upon his victim the outrage of an unwelcome but irrepressible pleasure. After Moussaut's death Sœur Jeanne dreamed on several occasions that the old man had come back from purgatory to implore his former penitents for the assistance of their prayers. But even as he plaintively spoke, everything changed and "it was no longer the person of her late confessor, but the face and semblance of Urbain Grandier who, altering his words and behavior at the same time as his figure, talked to her of amours, plied her with caresses no less insolent than unchaste, and pressed her to grant him what was no longer hers to dispose of, that which, by her vows, she had consecrated to her divine Bridegroom."

In the mornings the Prioress would recount these nocturnal adventures to her fellow nuns. The tales lost nothing in the telling and, within a very little while, two other young ladies—Sœur Claire de Sazilly (Cardinal Richelieu's cousin) and another Claire, a lay sister, were also having visions of importunate clergymen and hearing a voice that whispered the most indelicate propositions in their ears.

The next, the determining event in the long series which led at last to the parson's destruction, was a rather silly practical joke. Devised by a committee of the younger nuns and their older pupils, for the purpose of frightening the babies and the pious and simple-minded elders, the joke was a simple hallowe'en affair of pretended apparitions and poltergeists. The house, in which the nuns and their boarders were lodged, had a reputation, as we have already seen, for being haunted. Its occupants were therefore well prepared to be terrified when, shortly after the old Canon's death, a white-sheeted figure was seen to glide about the dormitories. After the first visitation, all doors were carefully bolted; but the phantoms either made their way along the leads and entered through the windows, or else were admitted by their fifth column within the rooms. Clothes were plucked off the beds, faces were touched by icy fingers. Overhead, in the attics, there was a groaning and a rattling of chains. The children screamed; the Reverend Mothers crossed themselves and appealed to St. Joseph. In vain. After a few quiet nights the ghosts would be back again. The school and convent were in a panic.

Seated at his listening post in the confessional, Canon Mignon knew about everything—about the incubi in the cells, about the ghosts in the dormitories, about the practical jokers in the attics. He knew about everything—and suddenly a light dawned and the finger of Providence was manifest. All things, he now perceived, were working together for good. He would work with them. To this end, he reprimanded the jokers, but ordered them to say nothing about their pranks. He instilled a new terror into the victims of those pranks by telling them that the things they had taken for ghosts were more probably devils. And he confirmed the Mother Superior and her fellow visionaries in their hallucinations by assuring them that their nightly visitants were real and manifestly satanic. After which he repaired, with four or five of the parson's most influential enemies, to M. Trincant's country house at Puydardane, a league from town. There, before the assembled council of war, he gave an account of what was happening in the convent and showed how the situation might be exploited to Grandier's disadvantage. The matter was discussed and a plan of campaign, complete with secret weapons, psychological warfare and a supernatural intelligence service, was drawn up. The conspirators parted in the highest of spirits. This time, they all felt, they had him—on toast.

Mignon's next step was to call on the Carmelites. What he needed was a good exorcist. Could the Reverend Fathers provide one? Enthusiastically the Prior gave him, not one, but three—Fathers Eusèbe de Saint-Michel, Pierre-Thomas de Saint-Charles and Antonin de la Charité. With Mignon, they set to work at once and were so successful in their operations that, within a few days, all except two or three of the oldest nuns were having nightly visits from the parson.

After a time rumors began to leak out of the haunted nunnery, and in a little while it was a matter of common knowledge that the good sisters were all possessed by devils, and that the devils laid the blame for everything on the sprightly M. Grandier. The Protestants, as can be imagined, were delighted. That a popish priest had conspired with Satan to debauch an entire convent of Ursulines was almost enough to console them for the fall of La Rochelle.

As for the parson himself, he merely shrugged his shoulders. After all, he had never so much as set eyes on the Prioress and her frantic sisters. What these demented women said about him was merely the product of their malady—melancholy adust combined with a touch of *furor uterinus.* Debarred from men, the poor things must needs imagine an incubus. When these remarks were reported to Canon Mignon he only smiled and remarked that he laughs best who laughs last.

Meanwhile the labor of exorcising all these demoniacs was so great that, after some months of heroic wrestling with the demons, the Canon had to call for reinforcements. The first to be summoned was Pierre Rangier, the Curé of Veniers, a man who owed his very considerable influence in the diocese and his universal unpopularity to the fact that he had made himself the Bishop's spy and secret agent. With Rangier participating in the exorcisms, the Canon could feel confident that there would be no skepticism in high places. The possession would be official and orthodox.

To Rangier's was soon added the collaboration of another priest of a very different stamp. M. Barré, Curé of Saint-Jacques in the neighboring town of Chinon, was one of those negative Christians, to whom the Devil is incomparably more real and more interesting than God. He saw the print of cloven hoofs in everything; he recognized Satan's work in all the odd, all the disastrous, all the too pleasurable events of human life. Enjoying nothing so much as a good tussle with Belial or Beelzebub, he was forever fabricating and exorcising demoniacs. Thanks to his efforts, Chinon was full of raving girls, bewitched cows, husbands unable, because of some sorcerer's malignant spells, to perform their conjugal duties. In his parish nobody could complain that life was uninteresting; what with the Curé and the Devil, there was never a dull moment.

Mignon's invitation was accepted with alacrity, and a few days later Barré arrived from Chinon at the head of a procession formed by a large body of his more fanatical parishioners. To his great disgust he found that, up to this time, the exorcisms had been conducted behind closed doors. To hide one's light under a bushel—what an idea! Why not give the public a chance to be edified? The doors of the Ursulines' chapel were thrown open; the mob poured in. At his third attempt, Barré succeeded in sending the Mother Superior into convulsions. "Bereaved of sense and reason," Sœur Jeanne rolled on the floor. The spectators were delighted, especially when she showed her legs. Finally, after many "violences, vexations, howlings and grindings of teeth, two of which at the back of the mouth were broken," the Devil obeyed the order to leave his victim in peace. The Prioress lay exhausted; M. Barré wiped the sweat from his forehead. And now it was the turn of Canon Mignon and Sœur Claire de Sazilly, of Father Eusebius and the lay sister, of M. Rangier and Sister Gabrielle of the Incarnation. The performance ended only with the ending of the day. The spectators trooped out into the autumnal twilight. It was universally agreed that, not since the coming of those traveling acrobats, with the two dwarfs and the performing bears, had poor old Loudun been treated to such a good show as this. And all free of charge—for of course you didn't *have* to put anything in the bag, when it was passed round, and if you *did* give something, a farthing would make as good a jingle as a sixpence.

Two days later, on October 8th, 1632, Barré won his first major victory, by routing Asmodeus, one of the seven devils who had taken up residence in the body of the Prioress. Speaking through the lips of the demoniac, Asmodeus revealed that he was entrenched in the lower belly. For more than two hours Barré wrestled with him. Again and again the sonorous Latin phrases rumbled forth. *"Exorciso te, immundissime spiritus, omnis incursio adversarii, omne phantasma, omnis legio, in nomine Domini nostri Jesus Christi; eradicare et effugare ab hoc plasmate Dei."** And then there would be a sprin-

* "I exorcize thee, most unclean spirit, every onslaught of the Adversary, every specter, every legion, in the name of our Lord Jesus Christ; be thou uprooted and put to flight from this creature of God."

kling of holy water, a laying on of hands, a laying on of the stole, of the breviary, of relics. "*Adjuro te, serpens antique, per Judicem vivorum et mortuorum, per factorem tuum, per factorem mundi, per eum qui habet potestatem mittendi te in gehennam, ut ab hoc famulo Dei, qui ad sinum Ecclesiae recurrit, cum metu et exercitu furoris tui festinus discedas.*"* But instead of departing, Asmodeus merely laughed and uttered a few playful blasphemies. Another man would have admitted defeat. Not so M. Barré. He ordered the Prioress to be carried to her cell and sent in haste for the apothecary. M. Adam came, bringing with him the classical emblem of his profession, the huge brass syringe of Molièresque farce and seventeenth-century medical reality. A quart of holy water was ready for him. The syringe was filled, and M. Adam approached the bed on which the Mother Superior was lying. Perceiving that his last hour was at hand, Asmodeus threw a fit. In vain. The Prioress's limbs were pinioned, strong hands held down the writhing body and, with the skill born of long practice, M. Adam administered the miraculous enema. Two minutes later, Asmodeus had taken his departure.†

In the autobiography which she wrote some years later, Sœur Jeanne assures us that during the first months of her possession, her mind was so confused that she could remember nothing of what had happened to her. The statement may be true—or it may not. There are many things which we would like to forget, which we do our best to suppress, but which in fact we go on remembering only too vividly. M. Adam's syringe, for example. . . .

From insulated selfhood there are many ways of escape into a larval condition of subhumanity. This state partakes of the Nothingness, which is the theme of so many of Mallarmé's poems.

* "I conjure thee, ancient serpent, by the Judge of the living and the dead, by thy maker, by the maker of the world, by him who has the power to cast thee into gehenna, that from this servant of God, who hastens back to the bosom of the Church, thou with the fears and afflictions of thy fury speedily depart."

† Barré was not the inventor of this adjunct to exorcism. Tallemant records that a French nobleman, M. de Fervaque, had used it successfully on a possessed nun of his acquaintance. Today, in South Africa, there are Negro sects which practice baptism by colonic lavage.

> *Mais ta chevelure est une rivière tiède,*
> *Où noyer sans remords l'âme qui nous obsède,*
> *Et trouver le Néant que tu ne connais pas.*

But for many persons, absolute Nothingness is not enough. What they want is a Nothing with negative qualities, a Nonentity that stinks and is hideous.

> *Une nuit que j'étais près d'une affreuse juive,*
> *Comme au long d'un cadavre un cadavre étendu.* . . .

This also is an experience of Nothingness—but with a vengeance. And it is precisely in Nothingness-with-a-vengeance that certain minds discover what is, for them, the most satisfying kind of experienced otherness. In Jeanne des Anges, the longing for self-transcendence was powerful in proportion to the intensity of her native egotism and the frustrating circumstances of her environment. In later years she was to pretend to try, and even actually to try without pretense, to achieve an upward self-transcendence into the life of the spirit. But at this stage in her career the only avenue of escape that presented itself was a descent into sexuality. She had begun by deliberately indulging in the imagination of an intimacy with her *beau ténébreux*, the unknown but titillatingly notorious M. Grandier. But in time deliberate and occasional indulgence turned into irresistible addiction. Habit converted her sexual phantasies into an imperious necessity. The *beau ténébreux* took on an autonomous existence that was altogether independent of her will. Instead of being the mistress of her imagination, she was now its slave. Slavery is humiliating; and yet the consciousness of being no longer in control of one's own thoughts and actions is a form, inferior no doubt, but effective, of that self-transcendence to which all human beings aspire. Sœur Jeanne had tried to free herself from her servitude to the erotic images she had conjured up; but the only freedom she could achieve was freedom to be the self she abhorred. There was nothing for it but to slide down again into the dungeon of her addiction.

And now, after months of this inward struggle, she was in the hands of the egregious M. Barré. The phantasy of a downward self-transcendence had been transformed into the brute fact of his actually treating her as something less than human—as some queer kind of animal, to be exhibited to the rabble like a performing ape, as a less than personal creature fit only to be bawled at, manipulated, sent by reiterated suggestion into fits and finally subjected, against what remained of her will and in spite of the remnants of her modesty, to the outrage of a forcible colonic irrigation. Barré had treated her to an experience that was the equivalent, more or less, of a rape in a public lavatory.*

The person who was once Sœur Jeanne des Anges, Prioress of the Ursulines of Loudun, had been annihilated—annihilated, not in the Mallarméan fashion, but in the Baudelairean, with a vengeance. Parodying the Pauline phrase, she could say of herself, "I live, yet

* In the medical practice of the seventeenth and eighteenth centuries, the clyster was employed as freely and frequently as is the hypodermic syringe today. "Clysters," writes Robert Burton, "are in good request. Trincavellius esteems of them in the first place, and Hercules of Saxonia is a greater approver of them. I have found (saith he) by experience that many hypochrondriacal melancholy men have been cured by the sole use of clysters. For without question," Burton adds in another passage, "a clyster, opportunely used, cannot choose in this, as in most other maladies, but to do very much good." From earliest infancy all members of the classes that could afford to call in the physician or the apothecary were familiar with the giant syringe and the suppository —with copious rectal doses of "Castilian soap, honey boiled to a consistence or, stronger, of Scammony, Hellebore, etc." It is, therefore, not surprising to find that, when he describes his childish diversions with the *petites demoiselles*, who used to come and play with his sisters, Jean-Jacques Bouchard (the Prioress's exact contemporary) speaks, as of a thing known to everyone, of the *petits bastons*, with which small boys and girls were in the habit of pretending to give one another clysters. But the child is father of the man and mother of the woman, and for generations the apothecary's monstrous syringe continued to haunt the sexual imagination, not merely of the small fry, but also of their elders. More than a hundred and fifty years after M. Barré's exploit, the heroes and heroines of the Marquis de Sade, in their laborious efforts to extend the range of sexual enjoyment, were making frequent use of the exorcist's secret weapon. A generation earlier than the Marquis, François Boucher had produced, in *L'Attente du Clystère*, the most terrific pin-up girl of the century, perhaps of all time. From the savagely obscene and the gracefully pornographic there is an easy modulation to Rabelaisian fun and the smoking-room joke. One remembers the Old Woman in *Candide* with her little witticisms about canulas and *nous autres femmes*. One thinks of the amorous Sganarelle, in *Le Médecin malgré Lui*, tenderly begging Jacqueline for leave to give her, not a kiss, but *un petit clystère dulcifiant*. M. Barré's, with its quart of holy water, was a *petit clystère sanctifiant*. But, sanctifying or dulcifying, the thing remained what it was intrinsically and what, by convention and at that particular moment of history, it had become—an all but erotic experience, an outrage to modesty, and a symbol enriched by a whole gamut of pornographic overtones and harmonics, which had entered into the folkways and become a part of the circumambient culture.

115

not I, but dirt, but humiliation, but mere physiology liveth in me."
During the exorcisms she was no longer a subject; she was only an
object with intense sensations. It was horrible, but it was also
wonderful—an outrage but at the same time a revelation and, in the
literal sense of the word, an ecstasy, a standing outside of the
odious and all too familiar self.

At this period, it should be noted, Sœur Jeanne had no intimate
sense of being a demoniac. Mignon and Barré told her that she was
infested by devils and in the ravings induced by their exorcisms
she herself would say as much. But she had, as yet, no feeling of
being possessed by the seven demons (six after the departure of
Asmodeus) who were supposed to be encamped in her tiny body.
Here is her own analysis of the situation.

"I did not then believe that one could be possessed without having given consent to, or made a pact with, the devil; in which I was
mistaken, for the most innocent and even the most holy can be
possessed. I myself was not of the number of the innocent; for
thousands upon thousands of times I had given myself over to the
devil by committing sin and making continual resistance to grace.
. . . The demons insinuated themselves into my mind and inclinations, in such sort that, through the evil dispositions they found
in me, they made of me one and the same substance with themselves. . . . Ordinarily the demons acted in conformity with the
feelings I had in my soul; this they did so subtly that I myself did
not believe that I had any demons within me. I felt insulted when
people showed that they suspected me of being possessed, and if
anyone talked to me of my possession by the demons, I felt a violent
emotion of anger and could not control the expression of my
resentment." This means that the person who could not help
dreaming of M. Grandier, the person whom M. Barré was treating
as a kind of laboratory animal, was not conscious, outside the
exorcisms and during waking hours, of being in any way abnormal.
The ecstasies of humiliation and of hallucinatory sensuality were
being inflicted upon a mind that still felt itself to be that of an
average sensual woman who had had the bad luck to land in a
convent, when she ought to have married and reared a family.

Of the state of mind of M. Barré and the other exorcists we know nothing at firsthand. They left no autobiographies and wrote no letters. Until Father Surin made his entry upon the scene, some two years later, the history of the men involved in this prolonged psychological orgy is completely lacking in personal touches. Fortunately for us, Surin was an introvert with an urge to self-revelation, a born "sharer" whose passion for confession amply made up for the reticences of his colleagues. Writing of these early years spent at Loudun and, later, at Bordeaux, Surin complains of being subjected to almost continual temptations of the flesh. Given the circumstances of an exorcist's life in a convent of demoniac nuns, the fact is hardly surprising. At the center of a troop of hysterical women, all in a state of chronic sexual excitement, he was the chartered Male, imperious and tyrannical. The abjection in which his charges were so ecstatically wallowing served only to emphasize the triumphant masculinity of the exorcist's role. Their passivity heightened his sense of being the master. In the midst of uncontrollable frenzies, he was lucid and strong; in the midst of so much animality he was the only human being; in the midst of demons, he was the representative of God. And as the representative of God, he was privileged to do what he liked with these creatures of a lower order—to make them perform tricks, to send them into convulsions, to manhandle them as though they were recalcitrant sows or heifers, to prescribe the enema or the whip.* In their more lucid moments

* In the letter which he wrote after a visit to Loudun in 1635, Thomas Killigrew describes the treatment meted out to that ravishing Sister Agnes, whose good looks and startlingly immodest behavior had earned her, among the *habitués* of the exorcism, the affectionate nickname of *le beau petit diable*. "She was very young and handsome, of a more tender look and slender shape than any of the rest. . . . The loveliness of her face was clothed in a sad sable look which, upon my coming into the chapel, she hid, but presently unveiled again." (Killigrew was only twenty at the time, and uncommonly handsome.) "And though she stood now, bound like a slave in the friar's hand, you might see through all her misfortunes, in her black eyes, the unruined arches of many triumphs." *Like a slave in the friar's hand*—the words are painfully apt. A little later, as Killigrew records, the wretched girl was a slave under the friar's feet. For after having thrown her into convulsions and made her roll on the floor, the good father triumphantly stood on his recumbent victim. "I confess it was so sad a sight," says Killigrew, "I had no power to see the miracle wrought of her recovery, but went from thence to the inn."

the demoniacs would confide to their masters—with what an obscene delight in thus trampling underfoot the conventions which had been an essential part of their personality!—the most unavowable facts about their physiological condition, the most lurid phantasies dredged up from the oozy depths of the subconscious. The kind of relation that could exist between exorcists and supposedly demoniac nuns is well illustrated by the following extract from a contemporary account of the possession of the Ursulines of Auxonne, which began in 1658 and continued until 1661. "The nuns declare, and so do the priests, that by means of exorcism, they (the priests) relieved them of hernias, *qu'ils leur ont fait rentrer des boyaux qui leur sortaient de la matrice*, that they cured them in an instant of the lacerations of the womb caused by the sorcerers, that they caused the expulsion *des bastons couverts de prépuces de sorciers qui leur avoient esté mis dans la matrice, des bouts de chandelles, des bastons couverts de langes et d'aultres instruments d'infamie, comme des boyaux et aultres choses desquelles les magiciens et les sorciers s'étaient servis pour faire sur elles des actions impures.* They also declare that the priests cured them of colics, stomach aches and headaches, that they cured hardenings of the breast by confession; that they checked hemorrhages by exorcism, and, by means of holy water taken through the mouth, that they put an end to bloatings of the belly caused by copulation with demons and sorcerers.

"Three of the nuns announce, without beating about the bush, that they have undergone copulation with demons and been deflowered. Five others declare that they have suffered, at the hands of sorcerers, magicians and demons, actions which modesty forbids them to mention, but which in fact are none other than those described by the first three. The said exorcists bear witness to the truth of all the above statements." (See *Barbe Buvée et la pretendue possession des Ursulines d'Auxonne*, by Dr. Samuel Garnier, Paris, 1895, pp. 14-15.)

What a cozy squalor, what surgical intimacies! The dirt is moral as well as material; the physiological miseries are matched by the spiritual and the intellectual. And over everything, like a richly smelly fog, hangs an oppressive sexuality, thick enough to be cut with a knife and ubiquitous, inescapable. The physicians who, at the order of the Parlement of Burgundy, visited the nuns, found no evidence of possession, but many indications that all or most of them were suffering from a malady to which our fathers gave the name of *furor uterinus*. The symptoms of this disease were "heat accompanied by an inextinguishable appetite for venery" and an inability, on the part of the younger sisters, to "think or talk about anything but sex."

Such was the atmosphere in a convent of demoniac nuns, and such the persons with whom, in an intimacy that was a compound of the intimacies existing between gynecologist and patient, trainer and animal, adored psychiatrist and loquacious neurotic, the officiating priest passed many hours of every day and night. For the exorcists of Auxonne the temptations were too powerful and there is good reason to believe that they took advantage of their situation to seduce the nuns committed to their charge. No such accusation was brought against the priests and monks who worked on Sœur Jeanne and the other hysterics of Loudun. There was, as Surin bore witness, a constant temptation; but it was resisted. The long-drawn debauch took place in the imagination and was never physical.

The expulsion of Asmodeus was so notable a victory and the nuns were by this time so well trained to act their demoniac parts that Mignon and the other enemies of Grandier now felt themselves strong enough to take official action. Accordingly, on the eleventh of October, Pierre Rangier, the parson of Veniers, was sent to the office of the city's Chief Magistrate, M. de Cerisay. He gave an account of what had happened and invited the *Bailli* and his Lieutenant, Louis Chauvet, to come and see for themselves. The invitation was accepted and that same afternoon the two magistrates, with their clerk, called at the convent, were received by Barré and Canon Mignon and taken up "to a high-ceilinged room furnished with seven small beds, one of which was occupied by the lay sister and another by the Mother Superior. The latter was surrounded by several Carmelites, by some nuns of the convent, by Mathurin Rousseau, priest and Canon of Sainte-Croix and by the surgeon, Mannoury."

At the sight of the *Bailli* and his Lieutenant, the Prioress (in the words of the minutes drawn up by the Magistrate's clerk) "began to make very violent movements, with certain noises like the grunts of a small pig, then buried herself under the bedclothes, ground her teeth and made various other contortions such as might be made by a person out of her wits. At her right was a Carmelite and on her left hand the said Mignon, who stuck two fingers, namely the thumb and the forefinger, in the said Mother Superior's mouth and performed exorcisms and conjurations in our presence."

In the course of these exorcisms and conjurations it transpired that Sœur Jeanne had been possessed through the material agency of two diabolic "pacts"—one consisting of three hawthorn prickles, the other of a bunch of roses which she had found on the stairs and stuck in her belt, "whereupon she was attacked by a great trembling in her right arm and was seized by love for Grandier all the time of her orisons, being unable to keep her mind on anything except the representation of Grandier's person which had been inwardly impressed upon her."

Asked in Latin, "Who sent these flowers?" the Prioress, "after having delayed and hesitated, answered as though under constraint, *Urbanus*. Thereupon the said Mignon said, *Dic qualitatem*. She said, *Sacerdos*. He said, *Cujus ecclesiae?* and the said nun replied, *Santi Petri*,* which last words she pronounced rather badly."

When the exorcism was over, Mignon took the *Bailli* aside and, in the presence of Canon Rousseau and M. Chauvet, remarked that the present case seemed to bear a striking resemblance to that of Louis Gauffridi, the Provençal priest who, twenty years earlier, had been burned alive for bewitching and debauching certain Ursulines of Marseilles.

With the mention of Gauffridi, the cat was out of the bag. The strategy of the new campaign against the parson stood clearly revealed. He was to be accused of sorcery and magic, brought to trial and, if acquitted, ruined in reputation, if condemned, sent to the stake.

* ". . . Urbain. . . . Tell his rank. . . . Priest. . . . Of what church? . . . Saint Peter's. . . ."

CHAPTER FIVE

AND so Grandier was accused of sorcery and the Ursulines were possessed by devils. We read these statements and smile; but before the smile can expand into a grin or explode in a guffaw, let us try to discover what precisely was the meaning attached to these words during the first half of the seventeenth century. And since, at this period, sorcery was everywhere a crime, let us begin with the legal aspects of the problem.

Sir Edward Coke, the greatest English lawyer of the late Elizabethan and Jacobean age, defined a witch as "a person who hath conference with the Devil, to consult with him or to do some act." Under the Statute of 1563 witchcraft was punished by death only when it could be proved that the witch had made an attempt on someone's life. But in the first year of James's reign this statute was replaced by a new and harsher law. After 1603 the capital offense was no longer murder by supernatural means, but the simple fact of being proved a witch. The act performed by the accused might be harmless, as in the case of divination, or even beneficent, as in the case of healing by means of spells and charms. If there were proof that it had been performed through "conference with the Devil," or by the intrinsically diabolical methods of magic, the act was criminal and the performer of it was to be condemned to death.

This was an English and a Protestant ruling; but it was fully in accord with Canon Law and Catholic practice. Kramer and Sprenger, the learned Dominican authors of the *Malleus Maleficarum* (for almost two centuries the textbook and *vade mecum* of all witch-hunters, Lutheran and Calvinist no less than Catholic) cite many authorities to prove that the proper penalty for witchcraft, fortune-telling, the practice of any kind of magic art, is death. "For witchcraft is high treason against God's majesty. And so they (the accused) are to be put to the torture to make them confess. Any person, whatever his rank or position, upon such an accusation may be put to the torture. And he who is found guilty, even if he confess his crime, let him be racked, let him suffer all other tortures prescribed by law in order that he may be punished in proportion to his offence."*

Behind these laws stood an immemorial tradition of demonic intervention in human affairs and, more specifically, the revealed truths that the devil is the Prince of this World and the sworn enemy of God and God's children. Sometimes the devil works on his own account; sometimes he does his mischiefs through the instrumentality of human beings. "And if it be asked whether the Devil is more apt to injure men and creatures by himself than through a witch, it can be said that there is no comparison between the two cases. For he is infinitely more apt to do harm through the agency of witches. First, because he thus gives greater offence to God by usurping to himself a creature dedicated to Him. Secondly, because, when God is the more offended, He allows him the more power of injuring men. And thirdly, for his own gain, which he places in the perdition of souls."†

In medieval and early modern Christendom the situation of sorcerers and their clients was almost precisely analogous to that of Jews under Hitler, capitalists under Stalin, Communists and fellow travelers in the United States. They were regarded as the agents of a Foreign Power, unpatriotic at the best and, at the worst, traitors, heretics, enemies of the people. Death was the penalty meted out to these metaphysical Quislings of the past and, in most parts of the contemporary world, death is the penalty which awaits the political

* Kramer and Sprenger, *Malleus Maleficarum*, trans. the Rev. Montague Summers (London, 1948), pp. 5-6.
† *Ibid.*, p. 122.

and secular devil-worshipers known here as Reds, there as Reactionaries. In the briefly liberal nineteenth century men like Michelet found it difficult not merely to forgive, but even to understand the savagery with which sorcerers had once been treated. Too hard on the past, they were at the same time too complacent about their present and far too optimistic in regard to the future—to *us*! They were rationalists who fondly imagined that the decay of traditional religion would put an end to such deviltries as the persecution of heretics, the torture and burning of witches. *Tantum religio potuit suadere malorum.** But looking back and up, from our vantage point on the descending road of modern history, we now see that all the evils of religion can flourish without any belief in the supernatural, that convinced materialists are ready to worship their own jerry-built creations as though they were the Absolute, and that self-styled humanists will persecute their adversaries with all the zeal of Inquisitors exterminating the devotees of a personal and transcendent Satan. Such behavior-patterns antedate and outlive the beliefs which, at any given moment, seem to motivate them. Few people now believe in the Devil; but very many enjoy behaving as their ancestors behaved when the Fiend was a reality as unquestionable as his Opposite Number. In order to justify their behavior, they turn their theories into dogmas, their bylaws into First Principles, their political bosses into Gods and all those who disagree with them into incarnate devils. This idolatrous transformation of the relative into the Absolute and the all too human into the Divine, makes it possible for them to indulge their ugliest passions with a clear conscience and in the certainty that they are working for the Highest Good. And when the current beliefs come, in their turn, to look silly, a new set will be invented, so that the immemorial madness may continue to wear its customary mask of legality, idealism and true religion.

In principle, as we have seen, the law relating to witchcraft was exceedingly simple. Anyone who deliberately had dealings with the devil was guilty of a capital crime. To describe how this law was administered in practice would require much more space than can here be given. Suffice it to say that, while some judges were mani-

* So great the evil religion has aroused.

festly prejudiced, many did their best to give the accused a fair trial. But even a fair trial was, by our present Western standards, a monstrous caricature of justice. "The laws," we read in *Malleus Maleficarum*, "allow that any witness whatever is to be admitted in evidence against them." And not only were all and sundry, including children, and the mortal enemies of the accused, admitted as witnesses; all kinds of evidence were also admitted—gossip, hearsay, inferences, remembered dreams, statements made by demoniacs. Always in order, torture was frequently (though by no means invariably) employed to extort confessions. And along with torture went false promises in regard to the final sentence. In the *Malleus** this matter of false promises is discussed with all the authors' customary acumen and thoroughness. There are three possible alternatives. If he chooses the first, the judge may promise the witch her life (on condition, of course, that she reveal the names of other witches) and may intend to keep the promise. The only deception he practices is to let it be understood by the accused that the death penalty is to be commuted to some mild punishment, such as exile, whereas *in petto* he has decided to condemn her to perpetual solitary confinement on bread and water.

A second alternative is preferred by those who think that, "after she has been consigned to prison in this way, the promise to spare her life should be kept for a time, but that after a certain period she should be burned."

"A third opinion is that the judge may safely promise the accused her life, but in such a way that he should afterward disclaim the duty of passing sentence upon her, deputing another judge in his place."

(How richly significant is that little word, "safely"! Systematic lying is something which puts the liar's soul into considerable jeopardy. *Ergo*, if you find it expedient to lie, be sure to make such mental reservations as will cause you to seem to yourself—if not to others, or to a God who is most certainly not mocked—a worthy candidate for paradise.)

To contemporary Western eyes, the most absurd, as well as the

* Kramer and Sprenger, *op. cit.*, p. 228.

most iniquitous feature of a medieval or early-modern witch trial was the fact that almost any of the odd and untoward events of daily life might legitimately be treated as the effects of diabolic intervention brought about by the magic arts of a sorcerer. Here, for example, is a part of the evidence on which one of the two witches tried in 1664, at Bury St. Edmunds, before the future Lord Chief Justice, Sir Matthew Hale, was condemned to be hanged. In the course of a quarrel, the accused had cursed and threatened one of her neighbors. After this, the man testified, "so soon as his sows pigged, the pigs would leap and caper, and immediately fall down dead." Nor was this all. A little later he was "vexed with a number of lice of extraordinary bigness." Against such supernatural vermin, the current methods of disinfection were unavailing and the witness had no alternative but to consign two of his best suits to the flames. Sir Matthew Hale was a just judge, a lover of moderation, a man of wide learning, scientific as well as literary and legal. That he should have taken this kind of evidence seriously seems now almost incredible. But the fact remains that he did take it seriously. The reason is to be sought, presumably, in the fact that, as well as all the rest, Hale was exceedingly pious. But in a fundamentalist age piety involved belief in a personal devil and the duty to extirpate the witches who were his servants. Moreover, granted the truth of everything contained in the Judeo-Christian tradition, there was an antecedent probability that, if preceded by an old woman's curse, the death of piglets and the multiplication of lice were supernatural events, due to the intervention of Satan on behalf of one of his votaries.

Into the Biblical lore of devils and witches had been incorporated a number of popular superstitions which came at last to be treated with the same veneration as was accorded to revealed truths of Scripture. For example, until late in the seventeenth century, all inquisitors and most civil magistrates accepted without question the validity of what may be called the physical tests of witchcraft. Did the body of the accused exhibit unusual marks? Could you find in it any spots insensitive to the prick of a needle? Were there, above all, any of those "little teats," or supernumerary nipples, at which some familiar—toad or cat—might suck and fatten? If so, your suspect was undoubtedly a witch; for tradition affirmed that these were the brands and seals with which the devil marked his own. (Since nine per cent of all males and a little under five per cent of all females are born with supernumerary nipples, there was never any shortage of predestined victims. Nature punctually did her part; the judges, with their unexamined postulates and first principles, did the rest.)

Of the other popular superstitions which had crystallized into axioms there are three which, because of the enormous miseries entailed by their general acceptance, deserve at least a brief mention. These are the beliefs that, by invoking the devil's aid, witches can cause tempests, diseases and sexual impotence. In the *Malleus* Kramer and Sprenger treat these notions as self-evident truths, established not merely by common sense but also by the authority of the greatest Doctors. "St. Thomas, in his commentary on Job, says as follows: It must be confessed that, with God's permission, the devils can disturb the air, raise up winds and make the fire fall from heaven. For, although in the matter of taking various shapes, corporeal nature is not at the command of any Angel, either good or bad, but only at that of God the Creator, yet, in the matter of local motion, corporeal nature has to obey the spiritual nature. . . . But winds and rain and other similar disturbances of the air can be caused by the mere movement of vapours released from the earth or the water; therefore the natural power of devils is sufficient to cause such things. So says St. Thomas."*

As for diseases, "there is no infirmity, not even leprosy or epilepsy, which cannot be caused by witches, with God's permission. And this is proved by the fact that no sort of infirmity is excluded by the Doctors."†

The authority of the Doctors is confirmed by our authors' personal observations. "For we have often found that certain people have been visited with epilepsy or the falling sickness by means of eggs which have been buried with dead bodies, especially the dead

* *Ibid.*, p. 147.
† *Ibid*, p. 134.

bodies of witches . . . particularly when these eggs have been given to a person either in food or drink."*

In regard to impotence, our authors draw a sharp distinction between the natural variety and the supernatural. Natural impotence is the incapacity to have sexual relations with any member of the opposite sex. Supernatural impotence, caused by magic spells and devils, is incapacity in relation to one person only (especially a wife or husband), potency being unimpaired in regard to all other members of the opposite sex. It should be noted, say the authors, that God permits more bewitchments to be performed in relation to the generative powers than in any other department of human life, the reason being that, since the Fall, there exists in everything that pertains to sex "a greater corruption than in the case of other human actions."

Devastating storms are not uncommon, selective impotence affects most men at some time or another, and disease is never absent. In a world where law, theology and popular superstition were all agreed in holding witches responsible for these everyday occurrences, the occasions for spying and the opportunities for delation and persecution were innumerable. At the height of the sixteenth-century witch hunts, social life in certain parts of Germany must have been very like social life under the Nazis, or in a country newly subjected to Communist domination.

Under torture, or moved by a sense of duty or some hysterical compulsion, a man would denounce his wife, a woman her best friends, a child its parents, a servant his master. And these were not the only evils to be met with in a devil-haunted society. On many individuals the incessant suggestions of bewitchment, the daily warnings against the devil had a disastrous effect. Some of the more timorous were driven out of their minds, some actually killed by the ever-present fear. On the ambitious and the resentful this harping on supernatural dangers had quite another effect. In order to win the prizes they so frantically coveted, men like Bothwell, women like Mme. de Montespan were ready to exploit the resources of black magic to their criminal limit. And if one felt one-

* *Ibid.*, p. 137.

self oppressed and frustrated, if one bore a grudge against society at large and one's neighbors in particular, what more natural than that one should appeal to those who, according to St. Thomas and the rest, were capable of doing such enormous mischiefs? By paying so much attention to the devil and by treating witchcraft as the most heinous of crimes, the theologians and the inquisitors actually spread the beliefs and fostered the practices which they were trying so hard to repress. By the beginning of the eighteenth century witchcraft had ceased to be a serious social problem. It died out, among other reasons, because almost nobody now bothered to repress it. For the less it was persecuted, the less it was propagandized. Attention had shifted from the supernatural to the natural. From about 1700 to the present day all persecutions in the West have been secular and, one might say, humanistic. For us, Radical Evil has ceased to be something metaphysical and has become political or economic. And that Radical Evil now incarnates itself, not in sorcerers and magicians (for we like to think of ourselves as positivists), but in the representatives of some hated class or nation. The springs of action and the rationalizations have undergone a certain change; but the hatreds motivated and the ferocities justified are all too familiar.

The Church, as we have seen, taught that witchcraft was a terrible and ubiquitous reality, and with appropriate ruthlessness the Law acted upon that teaching. To what extent was Public Opinion in accord with the official view of the matter? The sentiments of the unlettered and inarticulate majority can only be inferred from their recorded actions and from the comments of the educated.

In its chapter devoted to the bewitchment of animals, the *Malleus* throws a curious sidelight on that medieval village life, for which the sentimentalists, whose dislike of the present blinds them to the no less enormous horrors of the past, still nostalgically yearn. "There is not," we read, "even the smallest farm where women do not injure each other's cows by drying up their milk (through the use of spells), and very often killing them." Four generations later we find, in the writings of two English divines, George Gifford and Samuel Harsnett, essentially similar accounts of rustic life in a devil-haunted society. "Some woman," writes Gifford, "doth fall out bitterly with her neighbour; there followeth some great hurt. . . . There is a suspicion conceived. Within few years after she is in some jar with another. He is also plagued. This is noted of all. Great fame is spread of the matter. Mother W. is a witch. . . . Well, Mother W. doth begin to be very odious and terrible unto many, her neighbours dare say nothing but yet in their hearts they wish she were hanged. Shortly after another falls sick and doth pine. The neighbours come to visit him. 'Well, neighbour,' saith one, 'do you not suspect some naughty dealing? Did you never anger Mother W.?' 'Truly, neighbour,' saith he, 'I have not liked the woman a long time. I cannot tell how I should displease her, except it were this other day, my wife prayed her, and so did I, that she would keep her hens out of my garden. . . . I think verily she hath bewitched me.' Everybody saith now that Mother W. is a witch indeed. . . . It is out of all doubt, for there were which saw a weasel run from her houseward into his yard even a little before he fell sick. The sick man dieth and taketh it upon his death that he is bewitched. Then is Mother W. apprehended and sent to prison; she is arraigned and condemned and, being at the gallows, taketh it upon her death that she is not guilty."* And here is what Harsnett writes in his *Declaration of Egregious Popish Impostures*. "Why then, ho, beware, look about you, my neighbours! If any of you have a sheep sick of the giddies, or an hog of the mumps, or an horse of the staggers, or a knavish boy of the school, or an idle girl of the wheel, or a young drab of the sullens, and hath not fat enough for her porridge, nor her father and mother butter enough for their bread . . . and then withal old Mother Nobs hath called her by chance 'idle young hussy,' or bid the devil scratch her, then no doubt but Mother Nobs is the witch."† These pictures of rustic communities solidly based on superstition, fear and mutual malice are curiously depressing—all the more so because they are so modern, so topical and up-to-date. They remind us all too forcibly of certain pages in

* George Gifford, *A Discourse of the Subtill Practices of Devils by Witches*, as quoted in W. Notestein, *A History of Witchcraft in England*, p. 71.
† Notestein, *op. cit.*, p. 91.

La Vingt-Cinquième Heure and *1984*—pages in which the Rumanian describes the nightmare events of the present and the immediate past, the Englishman foretells the yet more diabolic future.

The foregoing accounts by educated men of inarticulate Public Opinion are sufficiently illuminating. But deeds speak even louder than words, and a society that periodically lynches its witches proclaims, most emphatically, its faith in magic and its fear of the devil. Here is an example drawn from French history and almost contemporary with the events related in this book. In the summer of 1644, after a very violent and destructive hailstorm, the inhabitants of several villages near Beaune banded together in order to take vengeance on the incarnate fiends who had thus wantonly ruined their crops. Under the leadership of a seventeen-year-old boy, who claimed to have an infallible nose for witches, they ducked a number of women and then beat them to death. Other suspects were burned with red-hot shovels, pushed into brick kilns or thrown headlong from high places. To put an end to this panic reign of terror, the Parlement of Dijon had to send two special commissioners at the head of a strong force of police.

We see then that inarticulate Public Opinion was in full agreement with the theologians and the lawyers. Among the educated, however, there was no such unanimity of approval. Kramer and Sprenger write with indignation of those—and at the end of the fifteenth century they were already numerous—who doubted the reality of witchcraft. They point out that all the theologians and canonists are at one in condemning the error of "those who say that there is no witchcraft in the world, but only in the imagination of men who, through their ignorance of hidden causes, which no man yet understands, ascribe certain natural effects to witchcraft, as though they were effected not by hidden causes, but by devils working either by themselves or in conjunction with witches. And though all the other Doctors condemn this error as a pure falsehood, St. Thomas impugns it more vigorously and stigmatizes it as actual heresy, saying that this error proceeds from the root of infidelity."*

This theoretical conclusion raises a practical problem. The question arises whether people who maintain that witches do not exist

* Kramer and Sprenger, *op. cit.*, p. 56.

are to be regarded as notorious heretics, or whether they are to be regarded as gravely suspect of holding heretical opinions. It seems that the first opinion is the correct one. But though all persons "convicted of such evil doctrine" have deserved excommunication, with all the penalties thereto attached, "we must take into consideration the very great number of persons who, owing to their ignorance, will surely be found guilty of this error. And since the error is very common, the rigor of strict justice may be tempered with mercy." On the other hand, "let no man think he may escape by pleading ignorance. For those who have gone astray through ignorance of this kind may be found to have sinned very gravely."

In a word, the official attitude of the Church was such that, though disbelief in witchcraft was undoubtedly a heresy, the disbeliever was in no immediate danger of punishment. Nevertheless, he remained gravely suspect and, if he persisted in his false doctrine after being apprised of the Catholic truth, might get into serious trouble. Hence the caution displayed by Montaigne in the eleventh chapter of his Third Book. "The witches of my neighborhood are in danger of their lives when anyone brings to bear fresh witness to the reality of their visions. To reconcile the examples which Holy Writ gives us of such things—examples most certain and irrefutable—and to bring them into comparison with those that happen in modern times, since we can see neither the causes of them nor the means by which they took place, needs a greater ingenuity than ours." It may be that God alone can tell what is a miracle and what is not. God must be believed; but do we have to believe a mere man, "one of ourselves, who is amazed at his own telling—and he must necessarily be amazed, if he is not out of his wits." And Montaigne concludes with one of those golden sentences which deserve to be inscribed over the altar of every church, above the bench of every magistrate, on the walls of every lecture hall, every senate and parliament, every government office and council chamber. "After all," (write the words in neon, write in letters as tall as a man!) "after all, it is rating one's conjectures at a very high price to roast a man alive on the strength of them."

Half a century later Selden showed himself less cautious, but also less humane. "The law against witches does not prove that there be any; but it punishes the malice of those people that use such means to take away men's lives. If one should profess that by turning his hat thrice, and crying 'Buzz,' he could take away a man's life, though in truth he could do no such thing, yet this were a just law made by the State that whosoever should turn his hat thrice and cry 'Buzz,' with an intention to take away a man's life, shall be put to death." Selden was enough of a skeptic to disapprove the elevation of conjectures to the rank of dogmas; but at the same time he was lawyer enough to think that roasting a man alive for thinking he was a witch might be right and proper. Montaigne had also been bred to the law; but his mind had obstinately refused to take the legalistic stain. When he thought of witches, he found himself considering, not their punishable malice, but their perhaps not incurable malady. "In all conscience," he writes, "I should rather have prescribed them hellebore [a drug supposed to be effective in purging melancholy and therefore in curing madness] than hemlock."

The first systematic assaults against the practice of witch-hunting and the theory of diabolic intervention came from the German physician, Johann Weier, in 1563, and from Reginald Scot, the Kentish squire, who published his *Discovery of Witchcraft* in 1584. The nonconformist Gifford and the Anglican Harsnett shared Scot's skepticism in regard to contemporary instances of witchcraft, but could not go so far as he did in questioning the Biblical references to possession, magic and pacts with the devil.

Over against the skeptics we find a notable array of believers. First in eminence as in time stands the great Jean Bodin who tells us that he wrote his *Démonomanie des Sorciers*, among other reasons, "to serve as an answer to those who endeavor, by their books, as far as possible to excuse sorcerers; insomuch as it seems as if they were influenced by the Devil himself to publish these fine books." Such skeptics, Bodin thinks, deserve to be sent to the stake along with the witches whom their doubts serve to protect and justify.

In his *Demonologie* James I took up the same position. The rationalistic Weier, he says, is an apologist for sorcerers, and by his book he "bewrays himself to have been one of that profession."

Of James I's eminent contemporaries, Sir Walter Raleigh and Sir Francis Bacon seem to have been on the side of the believers. Later in the century we find the case for witchcraft being argued in England by philosophers like Henry More and Cudworth, by learned physicians and scholars such as Sir Thomas Browne and Glanvil, and by lawyers of the caliber of Sir Matthew Hale and Sir George Mackenzie.

In seventeenth-century France all the theologians accepted the reality of witchcraft; but not all of the clergy were practicing witch-hunters. To many the whole business seemed extremely indecorous and a menace to good order and public tranquility. They deplored the zeal of their more fanatical colleagues and did their best to restrain it. A similar situation existed among the lawyers. Some of them were only too happy to burn a woman *"pour avoir, en pissant dans un trou, composé une nuée de grêle qui ravagea le territoire de son village"* (this particular burning took place at Dôle, in 1610); but there were others, the moderates, who believed, no doubt, in the theory of witches, but were unwilling, in practice, to proceed against them.

But under an absolute monarchy the decisive opinion is that of the King. Louis XIII was much concerned with the devil, but his son was not. In 1672 Louis XIV gave orders that all the persons recently condemned for witchcraft by the Parlement of Rouen should have their sentences commuted to banishment. The Parlement protested; but their arguments, the theological no less than the legal, left the Monarch unmoved. It was his good pleasure that these witches should not be burned, and that was sufficient, that was that.

When considering the events which took place at Loudun we must clearly distinguish between the alleged possession of the nuns and the alleged cause of that possession—the magic arts employed by Grandier. In what follows I shall deal in the main with the question of Grandier's guilt, leaving the problem of possession to be considered in a later chapter.

Father Tranquille, a member of one of the earlier teams of exorcists, published in 1634 a *True Relation of the Just Proceedings*

Observed in the Matter of the Possession of the Ursulines of Loudun and in the Trial of Urbain Grandier. The title is deceptive; for the pamphlet is not a true relation of anything, but merely a polemic, a rhetorical defense of the exorcists and the judges against what was quite evidently a general skepticism and an almost universal disapprobation. In 1634, it is clear, most educated people were doubtful of the reality of the nuns' possession, were convinced of Grandier's innocence and were shocked and disgusted by the iniquitous conduct of his trial. Father Tranquille rushed into print in the hope that a little pulpit eloquence would bring his readers to a more proper frame of mind. His efforts were not successful. True, the King and Queen were firm believers; but their courtiers, almost to a man, were not. Of the persons of quality who came to see the exorcisms, very few believed in the genuineness of the possession—and, of course, if the possession were not real, then Grandier could not be guilty. Most of the visiting physicians came away with the conviction that the phenomena they had seen were all too natural. Ménage, Théophraste Renaudot, Ismaël Boulliau—all the men of letters, who wrote about Grandier after his death, stoutly maintained his innocence.

On the side of the believers were the great masses of illiterate Catholics. (The illiterate Protestants, it goes without saying, were in this case unanimously skeptical.) That all the exorcists believed in Grandier's guilt and the genuineness of the possession seems certain. They believed even when, like Mignon, they had helped to fake the evidence which sent Grandier to the stake. (The history of spiritualism makes it very clear that fraud, especially pious fraud, is perfectly compatible with faith.) Of the opinions of the mass of the clergy we know next to nothing. As professional exorcists, the members of the religious orders were presumably on the side of Mignon, Barré and the rest. But what of the secular priests? Did they care to believe, and to preach, that one of their number had sold his soul to the devil and put a spell on seventeen Ursulines?

We know at least that among the higher clergy opinion was sharply divided. The Archbishop of Bordeaux was convinced that Grandier was innocent and that the nuns were suffering from a combination of Canon Mignon and *furor uterinus*. The Bishop of

Poitiers, on the other hand, was convinced that the nuns were really possessed and that Grandier was a sorcerer. And what of the supreme ecclesiastical authority, what of the Cardinal-Duke? In one context, as we shall see, Richelieu was completely skeptical; in another he exhibited the faith of a charcoal burner. The thing was obviously a hoax; and yet, in a Pickwickian sense, and sometimes even in a non-Pickwickian sense, it was all perfectly true.

Magic, whether white or black, was the art and science of compassing natural ends by supernatural (though not divine) means. All witches made use of magic and the powers of more or less evil spirits; but some of them were also adherents of what in Italy was called *la vecchia religione*.

"In order to clear the ground," writes Miss Margaret Murray in the introduction of her valuable study, *The Witch-Cult in Western Europe*, "I make a sharp distinction between Operative Witchcraft and Ritual Witchcraft. Under Operative Witchcraft I class all charms and spells, whether used by a professed witch or a professed Christian, whether intended for good or for evil, for killing or for curing. Such charms and spells are common to every nation and country, and are practised by the priests and people of every religion. They are part of the common heritage of the human race. . . . Ritual Witchcraft—or, as I propose to call it, the Dianic cult—embraces the religious beliefs and ritual of the people known in late medieval times as 'Witches.' The evidence proves that, underlying the Christian religion was a cult practised by many classes of the community, chiefly, however, by the more ignorant or those in the less thickly inhabited parts of the country. It can be traced back to pre-Christian times and appears to be the ancient religion of Western Europe."

In that year of grace, sixteen hundred and thirty-two, more than a thousand years had gone by since Western Europe was "converted to Christianity"; and yet the ancient fertility religion, considerably corrupted by the fact of being chronically "agin the government," was still alive, still boasted its confessors and heroic martyrs, still had an ecclesiastical organization—identical, according to Cotton Mather, to that of his own Congregational Church. The fact of the old faith's survival seems somewhat less astonishing, when we remember that, after four centuries of missionary effort, the Indians of Guatemala are not perceptibly more Catholic today than they were in the first generation after the coming of Alvarado.* In another seven or eight hundred years the religious situation in Central America may have come, perhaps, to resemble that which prevailed in seventeenth-century Europe, where a majority of Christians bitterly persecuted a minority attached to the older faith.

(In some districts the members of the Dianic cult and their fellow travelers may actually have constituted a majority of the population. Remy, Boguet and de Lancre have left accounts respectively of Lorraine, the Jura and the Basque country, as they found them at the turn of the seventeenth century. From their books it is clear that in these outlying regions, most people were, to some extent at least, of the old religion. Hedging their bets, they worshiped God by day and the devil at night. Among the Basques many priests used to celebrate both kinds of Mass, the black as well as the white. Lancre burned three of these eccentric clergymen, lost five who escaped from the condemned cell, and vehemently suspected a host of others.)

The central ceremony of Ritual Witchcraft was the so-called "Sabbath"—a word of unknown origin, having no relation to its Hebrew homonym. Sabbaths were celebrated four times a year—on Candlemass Day, February 2nd, on Rood Mass Day, May 1st, on Lammas Day, August 1st, and on the eve of All Hallows, October 31st. These were great festivals, often attended by hundreds of devotees, who came from considerable distances. Between Sabbaths there were weekly "Esbats" for small congregations in the villages where the ancient religion was still practiced. At all high Sabbaths the devil himself was invariably present, in the person of some man who had inherited, or otherwise acquired, the honor of being the incarnation of the two-faced god of the Dianic cult. The worshipers paid homage to the god by kissing his reverse face—a mask worn, beneath an animal's tail, on the devil's backside. There was then, for some at least of the female devotees, a ritual copulation with the god, who was equipped for this purpose with an artificial phallus of

* See Maud Oakes, *The Two Crosses of Todos Santos* (New York, 1951).

horn or metal. This ceremony was followed by a picnic (for the Sabbaths were celebrated out of doors, near sacred trees or stones), by dancing and finally by a promiscuous sexual orgy that had, no doubt, originally been a magical operation for increasing the fertility of the animals on which primitive hunters and herdsmen depend for their livelihood. The prevailing atmosphere at the Sabbaths was one of good fellowship and mindless, animal joy. When captured and brought to trial, many of those who had taken part in the Sabbath resolutely refused, even under torture, even at the stake, to abjure the religion which had brought them so much happiness.

In the eyes of the Church and of the civil magistrates membership in the devil's party was an aggravation of the crime of witchcraft. A witch who had attended the Sabbath was worse than a witch who had strictly confined herself to private practice. To attend the Sabbath was to profess openly that one preferred the Dianic cult to Christianity. Moreover, the witches' organization was a secret society which might be used by ambitious leaders for political purposes. That Bothwell had thus made use of the Scottish covens seems almost certain. Still more certain is the fact that Elizabeth and her Privy Council were convinced, rightly or wrongly, that foreign and native Catholics were employing witches and magicians to take the Queen's life. In France, according to Bodin, the sorcerers constituted a kind of Mafia, with members in every class of society and branches in every town and village.

That his crime might seem more abominable, Grandier was accused at his trial not merely of operative witchcraft, but also of participation in the rites of the Sabbath, of membership in the diabolic church.

The spectacle thus evoked of a pupil of the Jesuits solemnly renouncing his baptism, of a priest hurrying from the altar to do homage to the devil, of a grave and learned ecclesiastic dancing jigs with conjurors and tumbling in the hay with an assortment of witches, goats and incubi, was one well calculated to appall the pious, to tickle the groundlings and to bring joy to the Protestants.

CHAPTER SIX

D E CERISAY'S preliminary investigations had left him convinced that there was no genuine possession—only a sickness, improved by some little fraud on the part of the nuns, by a great deal of malice on the part of Canon Mignon and by the superstition, fanaticism and professional self-interest of the other ecclesiastics involved in the affair. There could be no cure, it was obvious, until the exorcisms had been stopped. But when he tried to put an end to these suggestions, which were systematically driving the nuns out of their wits, Mignon and Barré triumphantly produced a written order from the Bishop, charging them to go on exorcising the Ursulines until further notice. Unwilling to risk a scandal, de Cerisay gave his permission for the exorcisms to continue, but insisted on being present during the performance. On one of these occasions, it is recorded, there was a terrifying noise in the chimney and a cat suddenly appeared in the fireplace. The animal was pursued, caught, sprinkled with holy water, signed with the cross and adjured in Latin to depart. After which it was discovered that this devil in disguise was the nuns' pet Tom, who had been out on the tiles and was taking a short cut home. The laughter was loud and Rabelaisian.

Next day Mignon and Barré had the impudence to shut the convent door in de Cerisay's face. With his fellow magistrates he was kept waiting outside in the autumnal weather, while, contrary to his orders, the two priests exorcised their victims without official witnesses. Returning to his chambers, the indignant judge dictated a letter to the exorcists. Their actions, he declared, were such as to create "a vehement suspicion of trickery and suggestion." Moreover, "the Superior of the convent having publicly accused and defamed Grandier, by saying that he had a compact with the devils, nothing thereafter should have been done in secret; on the contrary, everything must now be done in the face of justice and in our presence." Alarmed by so much firmness, the exorcists apologized and reported that the nuns had calmed down and that consequently further exorcisms would, for the time being, be unnecessary.

Meanwhile Grandier had ridden to Poitiers to appeal to the Bishop. But when he called, M. de la Rochepozay was indisposed and could only send a message by his chaplain to the effect that "M. Grandier should sue before the royal judges and that he, the Bishop, would be most happy if he could obtain justice in this affair."

The parson returned to Loudun and at once applied to the *Bailli* for a restraining order against Mignon and his accomplices. De Cerisay promptly issued an injunction forbidding anyone, of whatever rank or quality, to harm or traduce the said Curé of Saint-Pierre. At the same time he expressly ordered Mignon to do no more exorcising. The Canon retorted that he was answerable only to his ecclesiastical superiors and that he did not recognize the *Bailli's* authority in a matter which, since it involved the devil, was wholly spiritual.

In the interval Barré had returned to his parishioners at Chinon. There were no more public exorcisms. But every day Canon Mignon spent long hours with his penitents, reading them chapters from Father Michaelis's best-selling report of the Gauffridy case, assuring them that Grandier was as great a magician as his Provençal colleague and that they too had been bewitched. By this time the behavior of the good sisters had become so eccentric that the parents of their pupils took fright; soon the boarders were all withdrawn and such few day pupils as still ventured into the convent brought back the most disquieting reports. Halfway through their arithmetic lesson, Sister Claire of St. John had started to laugh uncontrollably, as though someone were tickling her. In the refectory Sister Martha had had a fight with Sister Louise of Jesus. What screaming! And the bad language!

Late in November, Barré was called back from Chinon and, under his influence, everybody's symptoms at once became much worse. The convent was now a madhouse. Mannoury, the surgeon, and Adam, the apothecary, took alarm and summoned the leading physicians of the town in consultation. They came and, after examining the nuns, made a written report to the *Bailli*. Their conclusions were as follows: "the nuns are certainly transported, but we do not consider that this has happened through the workings of demons and spirits. . . . Their alleged possession seems to us more illusory than real." To all but the exorcists and Grandier's enemies, this report seemed conclusive. Grandier made another appeal to de Cerisay and de Cerisay renewed his efforts to put a stop to the exorcisms. Once again Mignon and Barré defied him, and once again he shrank from the scandal that would follow the use of physical force against priests. Instead, he wrote a letter to the Bishop, appealing to his lordship to put a stop to an affair which was "the sorriest piece of knavery invented for many ages past." Grandier, he went on, had never seen the nuns or had anything to do with them; "and if he had devils at his beck and call, he would have used them to avenge the violences and insults to which he has been subjected."

To this letter M. de la Rochepozay vouchsafed no reply. Grandier had offended him by appealing from his decision. Therefore anything that might be done to harm the parson was entirely right, proper and just.

De Cerisay now wrote a second letter, this time to the head of the Officiality. More fully than to the Bishop he entered into the details of the grotesque and horrible farce which was being played at Loudun. "M. Mignon is already saying that M. Barré is a saint, and they are reciprocally canonizing one another without waiting for the judgment of their superiors." Barré corrects the devil when he goes astray in the labyrinth of grammar, and challenges unbelievers "to do as he does and put a finger in the demoniac's mouth.

Father Rouseau, a Cordelier, was caught and bitten so hard that he was constrained to pull the nun's nose with his other hand, to make her let go, crying, '*Au diable, au diable!*' much louder than our kitchen maids cry, '*Au chat, au chat!*' when puss has run off with something. After which the question was propounded why the fiend had bitten a consecrated finger, and it was concluded that the Bishop must have been stingy with the holy oils, and that the unction did not get as far as the finger." Several fledgling priests tried their hands at exorcism, among them a brother of Philippe Trincant. But this young man made so many mistakes in Latin—*hoste* as the vocative of *hostis*, and *da gloria Deo*—that the educated public could not keep a straight face and he had to be withdrawn. Moreover, adds de Cerisay, "even at the height of her convulsions, the nun on whom he was working would not permit M. Trincant to put his fingers in her mouth (for he is somewhat dirty) and insistently asked for another priest." In spite of all which "the good father Guardian of the Capuchins is astonished at the hardness of heart of the people of Loudun and amazed by their reluctance to believe. At Tours, he assures us, he would have got them to swallow such a miracle as easily as butter. He and certain others have declared that those who do not believe are atheists and already damned."

This letter also remained unanswered, and the horrible farce was allowed to go on, day after day, until the middle of December, when M. de Sourdis came most opportunely to stay at his abbey, Saint-Jouin-des-Marnes. Unofficially by Grandier and officially by de Cerisay the Archbishop was informed of what was happening and asked to intervene. M. de Sourdis immediately sent his personal physician to look into the matter. Knowing that the doctor was a man who would tolerate no nonsense and that his master, the Metropolitan, was frankly skeptical, the nuns took fright and during the whole time of the investigation behaved themselves like so many lambs. There was no sign of possession. The doctor made his report to this effect and in the last days of December, 1632, the Archbishop published an ordinance. Henceforward Mignon was not to exorcise at all, and Barré might do so only in conjunction with two exorcists appointed by the Metropolitan, a Jesuit from Poitiers and an Oratorian from Tours. No one else might take part in the exorcisms.

The prohibition was almost unnecessary; for during the months that followed there were no devils to exorcise. No longer stimulated by priestly suggestions, the frenzies of the nuns gave place to a dismal, morning-after condition, in which mental confusion was mingled with shame, remorse and the conviction of enormous sin. For what if the Archbishop were right? What if there never had been any devils? Then all these monstrous things they had done and said could be imputed to them as crimes. Possessed, they were guiltless. Unpossessed, they would have to answer, at the Last Judgment, for blasphemy and unchastity, for lies and malice. At their feet hell yawned appallingly. And meanwhile, to make matters worse, there was no money and everybody had turned against them. Everybody—the parents of their pupils, the pious ladies of the town, the crowds of sightseers, and even their own relatives. Yes, even their own relatives; for now that they had ceased to be possessed, now that, in the judgment of the Archbishop, they were either impostors or the victims of melancholy and enforced continence, they had become disgraces to their families, and as such were repudiated, disavowed, their allowances cut off. Meat and butter disappeared from the refectory table, servants from the kitchen. The nuns were forced to do their own housework; and when the housework was done, they had to earn their bread by taking in plain sewing, by spinning wool for rapacious cloth merchants who took advantage of their needs and their misfortunes by paying them even less than the current rate for sweated labor. Hungry, oppressed by incessant toil, haunted by metaphysical terrors and a sense of guilt, the poor women looked back nostalgically to the happy days of their possession. Winter gave place to spring, and spring to a no less wretched summer. Then, in the autumn of 1633, hope revived. The King had changed his mind about the castle keep, and M. de Laubardemont was once again a guest at the Swan and Cross. Mesmin de Silly and the other cardinalists were exultant. D'Armagnac had lost the game; the castle was doomed. Nothing now remained but to get rid of the insufferable parson. At his very first interview with the King's Commissioner, Mesmin broached the subject of the possession. Laubardemont listened attentively. As a man who, in his time, had judged and burned several dozens of witches, he could legitimately claim to be an expert in matters supernatural.

Next day he called at the convent in the Rue Paquin. Canon Mignon confirmed Mesmin's story; so did the Mother Superior; so did the Cardinal's kinswoman, Sister Claire de Sazilly, and so did Laubardemont's two sisters-in-law, the demoiselles de Dampierre. The bodies of all the good sisters had been infested by evil spirits; the spirits had been introduced by magic, and the magician was Urbain Grandier. These truths had been vouched for by the devils themselves, and were therefore beyond doubt. And yet His Grace, the Archbishop, had said there was no real possession, and thereby disgraced them in the eyes of the world. It was a monstrous injustice, and they begged M. de Laubardemont to use his influence with His Eminence and His Majesty to have something done about it. Laubardemont was sympathetic, but made no promises. Personally, he liked nothing better than a good witch trial. But how did the Cardinal feel about such matters? It was hard indeed to say. Sometimes he seemed to take them very seriously indeed. But the next time you saw him, the chances were that he would be talking about the supernatural in the derisive tones of a disciple of Charron or Montaigne. By those who serve him, a great man must be treated as a mixture between a god, a naughty child and a wild beast. The god must be worshiped, the child amused and bamboozled and the wild beast placated and, when aroused, avoided. The courtier who, by an unwelcome suggestion, annoys this insane trinity of superhuman pretension, subhuman ferocity and infantile silliness, is merely asking for trouble. The nuns might weep and implore; but until he had discovered which way the wind was blowing, Laubardemont had no intention of doing anything to help them.

A few days later Loudun was honored by the visit of a very distinguished personage, Henri de Condé. This prince of the blood royal was a notorious sodomite, who combined the most sordid avarice with an exemplary piety. In politics he had once been an anti-Cardinalist, but now that Richelieu's position seemed impregnable, he had become the most fawning of His Eminence's sycophants. Informed of the possession, the prince at once expressed a desire to see for himself. Canon Mignon and the nuns were only too happy to oblige. Accompanied by Laubardemont and a numerous suite, Condé drove in state to the convent, was received by Mignon and ushered into the chapel, where a solemn Mass was celebrated. At first the nuns observed the most perfect decorum; but at the moment of communion, the Prioress, Sœur Claire and Sœur Agnès went into convulsions and rolled on the floor, howling obscenities and blasphemies. The rest of the community followed suit and for an hour or two the church looked like a mixture between a bear-garden and a brothel. Greatly edified, the prince declared that doubt was no longer possible and urged Laubardemont to write at once to the Cardinal, informing His Eminence of what was going on. "But the Commissioner," as we learn from a contemporary narrative, "gave no inkling as to what he thought about this strange spectacle. However, after returning to the inn, he felt himself deeply moved by compassion for the deplorable condition of the nuns. To cloak his real feelings, he invited Grandier's friends to dinner and, along with them, Grandier himself." It must have been a delightful party.

To spur the overcautious Laubardemont into action, the parson's enemies now came forward with a new and graver accusation. Grandier was not merely a sorcerer, who had denied his faith, rebelled against God and bewitched a whole convent of nuns; he was also the author of a violent and obscene attack on the Cardinal, published six years earlier, in 1627, under the title, *Lettre de la Cordonnière de Loudun.* Almost certainly Grandier did not write this pamphlet; but since he was the friend and correspondent of the lady-cobbler after whom the lampoon was named, since he had once very likely been her lover, it was not altogether unreasonable to suppose that he might have written it.

Catherine Hammon was a bright and pretty little proletarian who, in 1616, while Marie de Médicis was staying at Loudun, attracted the Queen's attention, was taken into her service and soon became, officially, the royal shoemaker and, unofficially, a royal confidante and factotum. Grandier had known her (all too intimately, it was said) during the period of the Queen's exile at Blois, when the girl came home for a time to Loudun. Later on, when she returned to her post, Catherine, who knew how to write, kept the parson informed of what was going on at court. Her letters were so amusing that Grandier used to read their spicier passages aloud to his friends. Among those friends was M. Trincant, the Public Prosecutor and father of the delicious Philippe. It was this same M. Trincant, no longer his friend, but the most implacable of his enemies, who now accused Catherine Hammon's correspondent of being the author of the *Cordonnière*. This time Laubardemont made no effort to conceal his feelings. What the Cardinal really thought about witches and devils might be uncertain; but what he thought about critics of his administration, his family and himself had never been in any doubt. To disagree with Richelieu's political opinion was to invite dismissal from the public service, financial ruin and exile; to insult him was to run the risk of death on the gallows or even (since an edict of 1626 had declared that libelous pamphleteering was a crime of *lèse-majesté*) at the stake or on the wheel. For only printing the *Cordonnière*, a wretched tradesman had been sent to the galleys. If he were ever caught, what would be done to the author? Confident, this time, that his zeal would find favor in the sight of His Eminence, Laubardemont took copious notes of all that M. Trincant said. And meanwhile Mesmin had not been idle. Grandier, as we have seen, was an avowed enemy of the monks and friars, and with very few exceptions the monks and friars of Loudun were the avowed enemies of Grandier. The Carmelites had the most substantial reasons for hating Grandier; but the Carmelites were in no position to give effect to their hatred. The Capuchins had suffered less at Grandier's hands, but their power to hurt him was incomparably greater. For the Capuchins were colleagues of Father Joseph, and were in regular correspondence with that *Eminence Grise* who was the confidant, chief advisor and right-hand man of the Cardinal. It was to the Gray Friars, therefore, and not to the White that Mesmin confided the new accusations against Grandier. The response was all that he could have desired. A letter to Father Joseph was immediately drafted, and Laubardemont, who was on the point of returning to Paris, was asked to deliver it in person. Laubardemont accepted the commission and, the same day, invited Grandier and his friends to a farewell dinner, at which he drank the parson's health, assured him of undying friendship and promised to do everything in his power to assist him in his struggle against a cabal of unscrupulous enemies. So much kindness, and offered so generously, so spontaneously! Grandier was moved almost to tears.

Next day Laubardemont rode to Chinon, where he spent the evening with the most sincerely fanatical believer in the parson's guilt. M. Barré received the royal Commissioner with all due deference and, at his request, handed over the minutes of all the exorcisms, in the course of which the nuns had accused Grandier of bewitching them. After breakfast, on the following morning, Laubardemont was entertained by the antics of some local demoniacs; then bidding farewell to the exorcist, he took the road to Paris.

Immediately after his arrival, he had an interview with Father Joseph, then, a few days later, a more decisive interview with the two Eminences, the scarlet and the gray, in consultation. Laubardemont read M. Barré's minutes of the exorcisms, and Father Joseph read the letter in which his Capuchin colleagues had accused the parson of being the long-sought author of the *Cordonnière*. Richelieu decided that the matter was grave enough to be considered at the next meeting of the Council of State. On the day appointed (November 30, 1633), the King, the Cardinal, Father Joseph, the Secretary of State, the Chancellor and Laubardemont assembled at Ruel. The possession of the Ursulines of Loudun was the first item on the agenda. Briefly but luridly Laubardemont told his story, and Louis XIII, who was a firm and terrified believer in devils, unhesitatingly decided that something would have to be done about it. A document was then and there drawn up, signed by the King, countersigned by the Secretary of State, and sealed, in yellow wax, with the Great Seal. By the terms of this document Laubardemont was commissioned to go to Loudun, investigate the facts of the possession, examine the accusations leveled by the devils against Grandier and, if they appeared to be well-founded, bring the magician to trial.

In the sixteen twenties and thirties, witch trials were still of common occurrence; but of all the dozens of persons accused, during these years, of trafficking with the devil, Grandier was the only one in whose case Richelieu took a keen and sustained interest. Father Tranquille, the Capuchin exorcist who, in 1634, wrote a pamphlet on behalf of Laubardemont and the devils, declares that "it is to the zeal of the Eminentissimous Cardinal that we owe the first undertaking of this affair"—a fact to which "the letters he wrote to M. de Laubardemont sufficiently bear witness." As for the Commissioner, "he never instituted any procedure for proving the possession without first fully informing His Majesty and my lord Cardinal." Tranquille's testimony is confirmed by that of other contemporaries, who write of the almost daily exchange of letters between Richelieu and his agent at Loudun.

What were the reasons for this extraordinary concern over a case, apparently, of such small importance? Like His Eminence's contemporaries, we must be content with guesses. That the desire for personal vengeance was an important motive seems certain. In 1618, when Richelieu was only Bishop of Luçon and Abbot of Coussay, this whippersnapper of a parson had been rude to him. And now there was good reason to believe that the same Grandier was responsible for the outrageous libels and insults contained in the *Cordonnière*. True, the accusation was one which it would be all but impossible to substantiate in a court of law. But for merely having been suspected of such a crime, the man deserved to be got rid of. And this was not all. The guilty parson was the incumbent of a guilty parish. Loudun was still a stronghold of Protestantism. Too prudent to compromise themselves at the time of the uprising which ended in 1628 with the capture of La Rochelle, the Huguenots of Poitou had done nothing to deserve open and systematic persecution. The Edict of Nantes still stood and, intolerable as they were, the Calvinists had to be tolerated. But now suppose that it could be proved, out of the mouths of the good sisters, that these gentlemen of the so-called Reformed Religion had been in secret league with an enemy even worse than the English—with the devil himself? In that case there would be ample justification for doing what he had long been planning to do: namely, to deprive Loudun of all its rights and privileges, and to transfer them to his own brand-new city of Richelieu. And even this was not all. The devils might be useful in yet other ways. If people could be made to believe that Loudun was but the beachhead of a regular invasion from hell, then it might be possible to revive the Inquisition in France. And how convenient that would be! How greatly it would facilitate the Cardinal's self-appointed task of centralizing all power in the absolute monarchy! As we know from our own experience of such secular devils as the Jews, the Communists, the Bourgeois Imperialists, the best way to establish and justify a police state is to keep harping on the dangers of a Fifth Column. Richelieu made only one mistake: he overestimated his compatriots' belief in the supernatural. Seeing that he was in the middle of the Thirty Years' War, he would probably have done better with a Fifth Column of Spaniards and Austrians than with mere spirits, however infernal.

Laubardemont lost no time. By December 6th he was back again at Loudun. From a house in the suburbs he sent secretly for the Public Prosecutor and the Chief of Police, Guillaume Aubin. They came. Laubardemont showed them his commission and a royal warrant for Grandier's arrest.

Aubin had always liked the parson. That night he sent Grandier a message, informing him of Laubardemont's return and urging immediate flight. Grandier thanked him; but, fondly imagining that innocence had nothing to fear, ignored his friend's advice. Next morning, on his way to church, he was arrested. Mesmin and Trincant, Mignon and Menuau, the apothecary and the surgeon—in spite of the earliness of the hour, they were all on hand to see the fun. It was to the sound of jeering laughter that Grandier was led away to the coach, which was to carry him to his appointed prison in the castle of Angers.

The parsonage was now searched, and all Grandier's books and papers were impounded. Disappointingly enough, his library contained not a single work on the Black Art; but it did contain (and this was very nearly as damning) a copy of the *Lettre de la Cordonnière*, together with the manuscript of that *Treatise on Sacerdotal Celibacy*, which Grandier had written in order to salve the conscience of Mlle. de Brou.

In convivial moments Laubardemont had been heard to remark that if he could get hold of only three lines of a man's handwriting, he could find a reason for hanging him. In the *Treatise* and the pamphlet against the Cardinal, he already had the amplest justification not merely for a hanging, but for the rack, the wheel, the stake. And the search had revealed other treasures. For example, there were all the letters written to the parson by Jean d'Armagnac—letters which, if he ever made a nuisance of himself, could certainly be used to send the royal favorite into exile or to the scaffold. And here were the absolutions granted by the Archbishop of Bordeaux. At the moment M. de Sourdis was doing very well at the Admiralty; but if at any time he should do less well, these proofs that he had once absolved a notorious magician might come in very handy. Meanwhile, of course, they must be kept out of Grandier's hands; for if he could show no proof that he had been absolved by the Metropolitan, then his condemnation by the Bishop of Poitiers still held good. And if it still held good, Grandier was the priest who had performed the veneric act in church. And if he were capable of *that*, then, obviously, he was capable of bewitching seventeen nuns.

The weeks that followed were a long orgy of licensed spite, of perjury consecrated by the Church, of hatred and envy, not merely unrepressed, but officially rewarded. The Bishop of Poitiers issued a monitory, denouncing Grandier and inviting the faithful to inform against him. The injunction was eagerly obeyed. Whole volumes of malicious gossip were transcribed by Laubardemont and his clerks. The case of 1630 was reopened, and all the witnesses who had confessed to perjury now swore that all the lies they had recanted were gospel truth. At these preliminary hearings Grandier was neither present in person, nor represented by counsel. Laubardemont did not permit the case for the defense to be stated, and when Grandier's mother protested against the iniquitous and even illegal methods which were being employed, he merely tore up her petitions. In

January, 1634, the old lady gave notice that she was appealing, in her son's name, to the Parlement of Paris. Laubardemont, meanwhile, was at Angers, cross-questioning the prisoner. His efforts were fruitless. Grandier, who had been informed of the appeal and who felt confident that his case would soon be tried before another and less manifestly prejudiced judge, refused to answer the Commissioner's questions. After a week of alternate browbeating and cajolery, Laubardemont gave up in disgust and hurried back to Paris and the Cardinal. Set in motion by old Mme. Grandier, the ponderous machinery of the law was slowly but surely grinding its way toward an appeal. But an appeal was the last thing that either Laubardemont or his master desired. The judges of the high court were passionately concerned with legality, and jealous, on principle, of the executive branch of the government. If they were permitted to review the case, Laubardemont's reputation as a lawyer would be ruined and His Eminence would have to give up a scheme to which, for reasons best known to himself, he was greatly attached. In March, Richelieu took the matter to the Council of State. The devils, he explained to the King, were counterattacking, and only by the most energetic action could they be checked and turned back. As usual, Louis XIII permitted himself to be convinced. The Secretary of State drew up the necessary documents. Under the royal hand and seal it was now decreed that "without regard to the appeal at present lodged with the Parlement, which His Majesty hereby annuls, my lord Laubardemont shall continue the action initiated against Grandier . . . : to which end the King renews his commission for as long as may be necessary, debars the Parlement of Paris and all other judges from taking cognizance of the case, and forbids the parties from suing before them, under penalty of a fine of five hundred livres."

Thus placed above the law and armed with unlimited powers, the Cardinal's agent returned to Loudun early in April and began at once to set the stage for the next act of his gruesome comedy. The city, he found, had no prison strong enough, or uncomfortable enough, to house a magician. The attic of a house belonging to Canon Mignon was placed at the Commissioner's disposal. To make it devil-proof, Laubardemont had the windows bricked up, the door fitted with a new lock and heavy bolts and the chimney (that witches' postern) closed with a stout iron grating. Under military escort, Grandier was brought back to Loudun and locked up in this dark and airless cell. No bed was allowed him and he had to sleep, like an animal, on a truss of straw. His jailers were a certain Bontemps (who had borne false witness against him in 1630) and Bontemps's shrewish wife. Throughout the long trial, they treated him with unwavering malignity.

Having secured his prisoner, Laubardemont now turned all his attention to the principal, indeed the only, witnesses for the prosecution—Sœur Jeanne and the sixteen other demoniacs. Disobeying the orders of their Archbishop, Canon Mignon and his colleagues had been working hard to undo the salutary effects of six months of enforced quiet. After a few public exorcisms the good sisters were all as frantic as they had ever been. Laubardemont gave them no respite. Day after day, morning and evening, the wretched women were taken in batches to the various churches of the city and put through their tricks. These tricks were always the same. Like modern mediums, who go on doing exactly what the Fox Sisters did a hundred years ago, these earlier demoniacs and their exorcists were incapable of inventing anything new. Time after time there were the all too familiar convulsions, the same old obscenities, the conventional blasphemies, the boastful claims, constantly repeated, but never substantiated, to supernormal powers. But the show was good enough, and dirty enough, to attract the public. By word of mouth, in pamphlets and broadsheets, from hundreds of pulpits, news of the possession spread far and wide. From every province of France and even from abroad, sightseers came flocking to the exorcisms. With the eclipse of the Carmelites' miracle-working Notre-Dame de Recouvrance, Loudun had lost almost the whole of its tourist trade. Now, thanks to the devils, all and more than all was restored. The inns and the lodging houses were filled to capacity, and the good Carmelites, who had a monopoly of the lay demoniacs (for the hysterical infection had spread beyond the convent walls) were now as prosperous as in the best of the good old days of the pilgrimages. Meanwhile the Ursulines were growing positively rich. From the royal treasury they now received a regular subsidy, which was augmented by the alms of the faithful and the handsome gratuities left by those tourists of high rank, for whom some specially miraculous performance had been staged.

During the spring and summer of 1634 the main purpose of the exorcisms was not the deliverance of the nuns, but the indictment of Grandier. The aim was to prove, out of the mouth of Satan himself, that the parson was a magician and had bewitched the nuns. But Satan is, by definition, the Father of Lies, and his evidence is therefore worthless. To this argument Laubardemont, his exorcists and the Bishop of Poitiers replied by affirming that, when duly constrained by a priest of the Roman Church, devils are bound to tell the truth. In other words, anything to which a hysterical nun was ready, at the instigation of her exorcist, to affirm on oath, was for all practical purposes a divine revelation. For inquisitors, this doctrine was a real convenience. But it had one grave defect: it was manifestly unorthodox. In the year 1610 a committee of learned theologians had discussed the admissibility of diabolic evidence and issued the following authoritative decision. "We, the undersigned Doctors of the Faculty of Paris, touching certain questions which have been proposed to us, are of the opinion that one must never admit the accusation of demons, still less must one exploit exorcisms for the purpose of discovering a man's faults or for determining if he is a magician; and we are further of the opinion that, even if the said exorcisms should have been applied in the presence of the Holy Sacrament, with the devil forced to swear an oath (which is a ceremony of which we do not at all approve), one must not for all that give any credit to his words, the devil being always a liar and the Father of Lies." Furthermore, the devil is man's sworn enemy, and is therefore ready to endure all the torments of exorcism for the sake of doing harm to a single soul. If the devil's evidence were admitted, the most virtuous people would be in the greatest danger; for it is precisely against these that Satan rages most violently "Wherefore St. Thomas (Book 22, Question 9, Article 22) maintains with the authority of St. Chrysostom, *Daemoni, Etiam Vera Dicenti, Non*

Est Credendum. [The devil must not be believed, even when he tells the truth]." We must follow the example of Christ, who imposed silence on the demons even when they spoke truth, by calling him the Son of God. "Whence it appears that, in the absence of other proofs, one must never proceed against those who are accused by devils. And we note that this is well observed in France, where judges do not recognize these depositions." Twenty-four years later, Laubardemont and his colleagues recognized nothing else. For the humanity and good sense of the orthodox view, the exorcists had substituted, and the Cardinal's agents had eagerly accepted, a heresy that was both monstrously silly and dangerous in the extreme. Ismaël Boulliau, the astronomer-priest who had served under Grandier as one of the vicars of Saint-Pierre du Marché, qualified the new doctrine as "impious, erroneous, execrable and abominable—a doctrine which turns Christians into idolaters, undermines the very foundations of the Christian religion, opens the door to calumny and will make it possible for the devil to immolate human victims in the name, not of Moloch, but of a fiendish and infernal dogma." That the fiendish and infernal dogma was fully approved by Richelieu is certain. The fact is recorded by Laubardemont himself and by the author of the *Démonomanie de Loudun,* Pillet de la Mesnardière, the Cardinal's personal physician.

Licensed, sometimes even suggested, and always respectfully listened to, the diabolic depositions came pouring in just as fast as Laubardemont needed them. Thus he found it desirable that Grandier should be not merely a magician, but also a high priest in the Old Religion. The word went round, and immediately one of the lay demoniacs obliged by confessing (through the mouth of a devil who had been duly constrained by one of the Carmelite exorcists) that she had prostituted herself to the parson, and that the parson had expressed his appreciation by offering to take her to the Sabbath and make her a princess at the devil's court. Grandier affirmed that he had never so much as laid eyes on the girl. But Satan had spoken and to doubt his word would be sacrilege.

Some witches, as is well known, have supernumerary nipples; others acquire, at the touch of the devil's finger, one or more small areas of insensibility, where the prick of a needle causes no pain and draws no blood. Grandier had no extra teats; *ergo* he must carry, somewhere on his person, those pain-free spots, by which the Evil One marks his own. Where precisely were those spots? As early as April 26th the Prioress had given the answer. There were five marks in all—one on the shoulder, at the place where criminals are branded, two more on the buttocks, very near the fundament, and one on either testicle. (*A Quoi Rèvent les Jeunes Filles?*) To confirm the truth of this statement, Mannoury, the surgeon, was ordered to do a little vivisection. In the presence of two apothecaries and several doctors, Grandier was stripped, shaved all over, blindfolded and then systematically pricked to the bone with a long, sharp probe. Ten years before, in Trincant's drawing room, the parson had made fun of this ignorant and pompous ass. Now the ass was getting his own back, and with a vengeance. The pain was excruciating and, through the bricked-up windows, the prisoner's screams could be heard by an ever-growing crowd of the curious in the street below. In the official summary of the counts on which Grandier was condemned, we learn that, owing to the great difficulty of locating such small areas of insensibility, only two out of the five marks described by the Prioress were actually discovered. But, for Laubardemont's purposes, two were amply sufficient. Mannoury's methods, it may be added, were admirably simple and effective. After a score of agonizing jabs, he would reverse the probe and press the blunt end against the parson's flesh. Miraculously, there was no pain. The devil had marked the spot. Had he been permitted to go on long enough, there is no doubt that Mannoury would have discovered all the marks. Unfortunately, one of the apothecaries (an untrustworthy stranger from Tours) was less complaisant than the village doctors whom Laubardemont had assembled to control the experiment. Catching Mannoury in the act of cheating, the man protested. In vain. His minority report was merely ignored. Meanwhile, Mannoury and the others had proved themselves to be most gratifyingly co-operative. Laubardemont was able to announce that Science had now corroborated the revelations of hell.

For the most part, of course, Science did not have to corroborate; *ex hypothesi*, the revelations of hell were true. When Grandier was confronted by his accusers, they rushed at him like a pack of Maenads, screaming through the mouths of all their devils that it was he who had bewitched them, he who, every night for four whole months, had prowled through the convent making passes at them and whispering obscene cajoleries in their ears. Conscientiously Laubardemont and his clerks made notes of everything that was said. The minutes were duly signed, countersigned and filed in duplicate at the record office. Factually, theologically and now legally, it was all true.

To make the parson's guilt still truer the exorcists produced a number of "pacts," which had appeared mysteriously in the cells, or (better still) had been vomited up, undigested, in the midst of a paroxysm. It was by means of these pacts that the good sisters had been, and were still being, bewitched. Here, for example, was a piece of paper, stained with three drops of blood and containing eight orange pips; here, a bundle of five straws; here, a little package of cinders, worms, hairs and nail parings. But it was Jeanne des Anges who, as usual, outdid all the rest. On June 17th, while possessed by Leviathan, she threw up a pact containing (according to her devils) a piece of the heart of a child, sacrificed in 1631 at a witches' Sabbath near Orléans, the ashes of a consecrated wafer and some of Grandier's blood and semen.

There were moments when the new doctrine was a source of embarrassment. One morning, for example, a devil (duly constrained and in the presence of the Blessed Sacrament) remarked that M. de Laubardemont was a cuckold. The clerk conscientiously recorded the statement and Laubardemont, who had not been present at the exorcism, signed the minute without reading it, and appended the usual postscript to the effect that, to the best of his knowledge, everything contained in the *procès-verbal* was true. When the matter came to light, there was much Rabelaisian laughter. It was annoying, of course, but of no serious consequence. Compromising documents could always be destroyed, stupid clerks dismissed and impertinent devils recalled to their duty by a good scolding or even a smacking. All in all, the advantages of the new doctrine far outweighed its drawbacks.

One of these advantages, as Laubardemont was quick to realize, consisted in this: that it was now possible (through the mouth of a devil who had been duly constrained in the presence of the Sacrament) to flatter the Cardinal in an entirely new and supernatural manner. In the minutes of an exorcism of May 20, 1634, written entirely in Laubardemont's hand, we read the following: "*Question*: 'What do you say about the great Cardinal, the protector of France?' The devil answered, swearing by the name of God, 'He is the scourge of all my good friends.' *Question*: 'Who are your good friends?' *Answer*: 'The heretics.' *Question*: 'What are the other heroic aspects of his person?' *Answer*: 'His work for the relief of the people, the gift of government, which he has received from God, his desire to preserve peace in Christendom, the single-minded love he bears to the King's person.' " It was a handsome tribute and, coming as it did, direct from hell, it could be accepted as the simple truth. The nuns were far gone in hysteria, but never so far gone as to forget which side their bread was buttered. Throughout the possession, as Dr. Legué has pointed out,* God, Christ and the Virgin were constantly blasphemed, but never Louis XIII and never, above all, His Eminence. The good sisters knew well enough that, against Heaven, they could let off steam with impunity. But if they were rude to the Cardinal. . . . Well, see what was happening to M. Grandier.

* Gabriel Legué, *Documents pour servir à l'Histoire Médicale des Possédées de Loudun* (Paris, 1874).

CHAPTER SEVEN

AT ANY given time and place certain thoughts are completely unthinkable. But this radical unthinkableness of certain thoughts is not paralleled by any radical unfeelableness of certain emotions, or any radical undoableness of the actions inspired by such emotions. Anything can at all times be felt and acted upon, albeit sometimes with great difficulty and in the teeth of general disapproval. But though individuals can always feel and do whatever their temperament and constitution permit them to feel and do, they cannot think about their experiences except within the frame of reference which, at that particular time and place, has come to seem self-evident. Interpretation is in terms of the prevailing thought-pattern, and this thought-pattern conditions to some extent the expression of urges and emotions, but can never completely inhibit them. For example, a firm belief in eternal damnation can coexist in the believer's mind with the knowledge that he or she is committing mortal sin. In this context let me quote the eminently judicious remarks which Bayle has hidden away in a note on Thomas Sanchez, that learned Jesuit who, in 1592, published a folio on Marriage, which his contemporaries and immediate successors regarded as by far the filthiest book ever written. "We do not know the domestic privacy of the ancient Pagans, as we know those of the countries where auricular confession is practiced; and therefore we cannot tell whether marriage was so brutishly dishonored among the Pagans as it is among the Christians; but at least it is probable that the Infidels did not surpass, in this respect, many persons who believe all the doctrines of the Gospel. They therefore believe what the Scripture teaches us of Heaven and Hell, they believe in purgatory and the other doctrines of the Romish communion; and yet in the midst of this persuasion, you see them plunged into abominable impurities, which are not fit to be named, and which draw down severe reproaches upon the head of such authors as dare to mention them. I observe this against those who persuade themselves that the corruption of manners proceeds from men's doubting or being ignorant that there is another life after this." In 1592 sexual behavior was evidently very similar to what it is today. The change has been only in the thoughts about that behavior. In early modern times the thoughts of a Havelock Ellis or a Krafft-Ebing would have been unthinkable. But the emotions and actions described by these modern sexologists were just as feelable and doable in an intellectual context of hell-fire as they are in the secularist societies of our own time.

In the paragraphs which follow I shall describe very briefly the frame of reference within which the men of the early seventeenth century did their thinking about human nature. This frame of reference was so ancient and so intimately associated with traditional Christian doctrine that it was universally regarded as a structure of self-evident truths. Today, though still most lamentably ignorant, we know enough to feel quite certain that, in many respects, the older thought-pattern was inadequate to the given facts of experience.

How, we may ask, did this manifest inadequacy of theory affect the behavior of men and women in the ordinary affairs of daily life? The answer would seem to be that, in some instances, the effect was imperceptible, in other cases, great and momentous.

A man can be an excellent practical psychologist and yet be completely ignorant of the current psychological theories. What is even more remarkable is that a man can be well versed in psychological theories which are demonstrably inadequate, and yet remain, thanks to his native insight, an excellent practical psychologist.

On the other hand, a wrong theory of human nature (such as the theory which explains hysteria in terms of diabolic possession) may evoke the worst passions and justify the most fiendish of cruelties. Theory is simultaneously not very important and very important indeed.

What was the theory of human nature, in terms of which Grandier's contemporaries interpreted ordinary behavior and such strange happenings as those which took place at Loudun? The answers to this question will be given, for the most part, in the words of Robert Burton, whose chapters on the anatomy of the Soul contain a brief and remarkably lucid summary of the philosophy which everyone, before the time of Descartes, took for granted and regarded as practically axiomatic.

"The soul is immortal, created of nothing, and so infused into the child or embryo in his mother's womb, six months after conception; not as the brutes, which are *ex traduce* (handed on by parent to offspring) and, dying with them, vanish into nothing." The soul is simple in the sense that it cannot be split or disintegrated. In the etymological sense of the word, it is a psychological atom—something which cannot be cut up. But this simple and indivisible soul of man has a three-fold manifestation. It is in some sort a trinity in unity, comprising a vegetal, a sensitive and a rational soul. The vegetal soul is defined as " 'a substantial act of an organical body, by which it is nourished, augmented and begets another like unto itself.' In which definition, three several operations are specified—*altrix, auctrix, procreatrix*. The first is nutrition, whose object is nourishment, meat, drink and the like; his organ, the liver in sensible creatures, in plants, the root or sap. His object is to turn the nutriment into the substance of the body nourished, which he performs by natural heat. . . . As this nutritive faculty serves to nourish the body, so doth the augmenting faculty (the second operation or power of the vegetal faculty) to the increasing of it in quantity . . . and to make it grow till it comes to his due proportion and perfect shape." The third faculty of the vegetal soul is the procreative—the faculty of reproducing its kind.

Next in order is the sensitive soul, "which is as far beyond the other in dignity as a beast is preferred to a plant, having those vegetal powers included in it. 'Tis defined as an 'Act of an organical body, by which it lives, hath sense, appetite, judgment, breath and motion.' . . . The general organ is the brain, from which principally the sensible operations are derived. The sensible soul is divided into two parts, apprehending or moving. . . . The apprehensive faculty is subdivided into two parts, inward or outward. Outward, as the five senses, of touching, hearing, seeing, smelling, tasting. . . . Inward are three—common sense, phantasy, memory." Common sense judges, compares and organizes the messages brought to it by the special organs of sense, such as the eye and the ear. Phantasy examines more fully the data of common sense, "and keeps them longer, recalling them to mind again, or making new of his own." Memory takes all that comes to it from phantasy and the common sense and "stores it away in a good register."

In man imagination "is subject and governed by reason, or at least should be; but in brutes it hath no superior, but is *ratio brutorum*, all the reason they have." The second power of the sensitive soul is the moving faculty, which in turn is "divided into two faculties, the power of appetite, and of moving from place to place.

And finally there is the rational soul, "which is defined by philosophers to be 'the first substantial act of a natural, human, organical body, by which a man lives, perceives and understands, freely doing all things, and with election.' Out of which definition we may gather that this rational soul includes the powers and performs the duties of the two other, which are contained in it, and all three faculties make one soul, which is inorganical of itself, although it be in all parts (of the body), and incorporeal, using their organs and working by them. It is divided into two parts, differing in office only, not in essence: the understanding, which is the rational power apprehending; the will, which is the rational power moving; to which two, all the other rational powers are subject and reduced."

Such was the theory in terms of which our ancestors thought about themselves and tried to explain the facts of human experience and behavior. Because it was very old, and because many of its elements were theological dogmas, or corollaries of dogmas, the theory seemed axiomatically true. But if the theory were true, then certain notions, which today seem obvious to the point of self-evidence, could not be entertained and were for all practical purposes unthinkable. Let us consider a couple of concrete examples.

Here is Miss Beauchamp, a blameless but rather sickly young woman, full of high principles, inhibitions and anxiety. From time to time she plays truant from herself and behaves like a very naughty and exuberantly healthy child of ten. Questioned under hypnosis, this *enfant terrible* insists that she is not Miss Beauchamp, but someone else called Sally. After some hours or days, Sally disappears and Miss Beauchamp returns to consciousness—but returns only to her own consciousness, not to Sally's; for she remembers nothing of what was done, in her name and through the agency of her body, while the latter was in control. Sally, on the contrary, knows all that goes on in Miss Beauchamp's mind and makes use of that knowledge to embarrass and torment the other tenant of their shared body. Because he could think of these odd facts in terms of a well-substantiated theory of subconscious mental activity, and because he was acquainted with the techniques of hypnosis, Dr. Morton Prince, the psychiatrist in charge of this famous case, was able to solve Miss Beauchamp's problems and to bring her, for the first time in many years, to a state of physical and mental health.

In certain respects the case of Sœur Jeanne was essentially similar to that of Miss Beauchamp. Periodically she took a holiday from her habitual self, and from being a respectable nun of good family became, for a few hours or days, a savage, blaspheming, utterly shameless virago, who called herself now Asmodeus, now Balaam, now Leviathan. When the Prioress returned to self-consciousness, she had no recollection of what these others had said and done in her absence. Such were the facts. How were they to be explained? Some observers attributed the whole deplorable business to deliberate fraud; others to "melancholy"—a derangement of the humoral equilibrium of the body, resulting in a derangement of the mind. For those who could not, or would not, accept these hypotheses, only one alternative explanation remained—diabolic possession. Given the theory in terms of which they had to think, it was impossible for them to come to any other conclusion. By a definition which was the corollary of a Christian dogma, the "soul"—in other words, the conscious and personal part of the mind—was an atom, simple and indivisible. The modern notion of a split personality was therefore unthinkable. If two or more selves appeared, concurrently or alternately, to occupy the same body, it could not be because of a disintegration of that not too securely tied bundle of psycho-physical elements which we call a person; no, it must be because of a temporary expulsion from the body of the indivisible soul and its temporary replacement by one or more of the innumerable super-human spirits who (it was a matter of revealed truth) inhabited the universe.

Our second example is that of a hypnotized person—any hypno-tized person—in whom the operator has produced a state of cata-lepsy. The nature of hypnosis and the way in which suggestion acts upon the autonomic nervous system are still imperfectly under-stood; but at least we know that it is very easy to put certain per-sons into a trance and that, when they are in this state, some part of their subconscious mind will cause their body to obey the sug-gestions given by the operator, or sometimes by their own supra-liminal selves. At Loudun this cataleptic rigidity, which any competent operator can induce in any good subject, was regarded by the faithful as a work of Satan. Necessarily so; for the nature of current psychological theories was such that the phenomenon must be due *either* to deliberate cheating, *or* to a supernatural agency. You might search the writings of Aristotle and Augustine, of Galen and the Arabians; in none of them could you find any hint of what we now call the subconscious mind. For our ancestors there was only the soul or conscious self, on the one hand, and on the other God, the saints and a host of good and evil spirits. Our conception of a vast intermediate world of subconscious mental activity, much more extensive and, in certain respects, more effective than the activity of the conscious self, was unthinkable. The current theory of human nature had left no place for it; consequently, so far as our ancestors were concerned, it did not exist. The phenomena which we now explain in terms of this subconscious activity had either to be denied altogether, or else attributed to the action of nonhuman spirits. Thus, catalepsy was either a humbug or a symptom of diabolic infestation. When he attended an exorcism in the autumn of 1635, young Thomas Killigrew was invited by the friar in charge of the proceedings to feel the nun's stony limbs—to feel, to confess the power of the Evil One and the yet greater power of the Church Militant, and then, God willing, to be converted from heresy, as his good friend Walter Montague had been in the preceding year. "I must tell you the truth," wrote Killigrew in a letter describing the event, "I only felt firm flesh, strong arms and legs held out stiff." (Note how completely the nuns have ceased to be regarded as human beings with a right to privacy or respect. The good father who performs the exorcisms behaves exactly like the proprietor of a side show at a fair. "Step up, ladies and gentlemen, step up! Seeing is believing, but pinching our fat girl's legs is the naked truth." These spouses of Christ have been turned into cabaret performers and circus freaks.) "But others," Killigrew continues, "affirm that she was all stiff, and heavy as iron; but they had more faith than I, and it seemed that the miracle appeared more visible to them than to me." How significant is that word "miracle"! If the nuns are not shamming, then the corpselike rigidity of their limbs *must* be due to supernatural causes. No other explanation is possible.

The coming of Descartes and the general acceptance of what at that time seemed a more "scientific" theory of human nature did not improve matters; indeed, in some respects it caused men's thinking about themselves to become less realistic than it had been under the older dispensation. Devils passed out of the picture; but along with the devils went any kind of serious consideration of the phenomena once attributed to diabolic agency. The exorcists had at least recognized such facts as trance, catalepsy, split personality and extrasensory perception. The psychologists who came after Descartes were inclined either to dismiss the facts as nonexistent, or to account for them, if they did not permit themselves to be dismissed, as the product of a something called "imagination." For men of science, "imagination" was almost synonymous with "illusion." The phenomena attributed to it (such as the cures which Mesmer effected during the magnetic sleep) might safely and properly be ignored. Descartes's mighty effort to think geometrically about human nature had led, no doubt, to the formulation of some admirably "clear ideas." But unhappily these clear ideas could be entertained only by those who chose to ignore a whole class of highly significant facts. Pre-Cartesian philosophers took account of these facts and were compelled by their own psychological theories to attribute them to supernatural causes. Today we are able to accept the facts and to explain them without having recourse to devils. We can think of the mind (as opposed to the "spirit," or "pure ego," or "Atman") as something radically different from the Cartesian and pre-Cartesian soul. The soul of the earlier philosophers was dogmatically defined as simple, indivisible and immortal. For us, it is manifestly a compound, whose identity, in Ribot's words, "is a question of number." This bundle of elements can be disintegrated and, though it probably survives bodily death, it survives in time, as something subject to change and to ultimate dissolution. Immortality belongs not to the psyche but to the spirit, with which, if it so chooses, the psyche may identify itself. According to Descartes, minds have consciousness as their essence; they can interact with the matter in their own body, but not directly with other matter or with other minds. Pre-Cartesian thinkers would probably have agreed with all these propositions except the first. Consciousness, for them, was the essence of the rational soul; but many of the operations of sensitive and vegetal souls were unconscious. Descartes regarded the body as a self-regulating automaton, and therefore had no need to postulate the existence of these subsidiary souls. Between the conscious "I" and what one may call the Physiological Unconscious, we now infer the existence of wide ranges of subconscious mental activity. Moreover, we have to admit, if we accept the evidence for extrasensory perception and psychokinesis, that on the subconscious level minds can and do act directly upon other minds and upon matter outside their respective bodies. The queer happenings which Descartes and his followers chose to ignore, and which his predecessors accepted as facts, but could only explain in terms of diabolic infestation, are now recognized as being due to the natural operations of a mind, whose range, whose powers and whose weaknesses are all far greater than a study of its conscious aspect would lead us to believe.

We see, then, that if the idea of fraud were excluded, the only purely psychological explanation of what was happening at Loudun was an explanation in terms of sorcery and possession. But there were many who never thought of the matter in purely psychological terms. To them it seemed obvious that such phenomena as were manifested by Sœur Jeanne could be explained in terms of physiology and ought to be treated accordingly. The more Draconian among them prescribed the application to the bare skin of a good birch rod. Tallemant records that the Marquis de Couldray-Montpensier withdrew his two possessed daughters from the hands of the exorcists and "had them well fed and soundly whipped; the devil took his leave immediately." At Loudun itself, during the later stages of the possession, the whip was prescribed with increasing frequency, and Surin records that devils who merely laughed at the rites of the Church were often routed by the discipline.

In many cases old-fashioned whipping was probably just as effective as modern shock treatment, and for the same reasons: namely, that the subconscious mind developed such a fear of the tortures prepared for its body that, rather than undergo them again, it decided to stop behaving as though it were crazy.* Up to the opening years of the nineteenth century, shock treatment by whipping was regularly employed in all cases of unequivocal insanity.

* Full and accurate accounts of psychiatric treatment and its results exist from the latter part of the eighteenth century onward. A well-known psychologist, who has studied these documents, tells me that they all seem to point to one significant conclusion: namely, that in mental disorders the proportion of cures has remained, for nearly two hundred years, remarkably constant, whatever the nature of the psychiatric methods employed. The percentage of cures claimed by modern psychoanalysts is no higher than the percentage of cures claimed by the alienists of 1800. Did the alienists of 1600 do as well as their successors of two and three centuries later? No certain answer can be given; but I would guess that they did not. In the seventeenth century the mentally sick were treated with a consistent inhumanity, which must often have aggravated the disease. We shall have occasion, in a later chapter, to return to this topic.

> In the bonny halls of Bedlam,
>   Ere I was one-and-twenty,
> I had bracelets strong, sweet whips ding-dong,
>   And prayer and fasting plenty.
> Now I do sing, "Any food, any feeding,
>   Feeding, drink or clothing?
> Come dame, or maid, be not afraid,
>   Poor Tom will injure nothing."

Poor Tom was a subject of Queen Elizabeth. But even in the days of George III, two hundred years later, the two houses of Parliament passed a bill authorizing the court physicians to scourge the lunatic king.

For simple neurosis or hysteria, birching was not the invariable treatment. These maladies were caused, according to the medical theories current at the time, by too much black bile, in the wrong place. "Galen," says Robert Burton, "imputeth all to the cold that is black, and thinks that, the spirits being darkened and the substance of the brain cloudy and dark, all the objects thereof appear terrible, and the mind itself, by these dark, obscure, gross fumes, ascending from black humours, is in continual darkness, fear and sorrow." Averroës scoffs at Galen for his reasons; so does Hercules de Saxonia. But they are "copiously censured and confuted by Aelianus Montaltus, Lodovicus Mercatus, Altomarus, Guiancrius, Bright, Laurentius Valesius. *Distemperature,* they conclude, *makes black juice, blackness obscures the spirits, the spirits obscured cause fear and sorrow.* Laurentius supposeth these black fumes offend especially the Diaphragma, or midriff, and so, consequently, the mind, which is obscured as the Sun by a cloud. To this opinion of Galen almost all the Greeks and Arabians subscribe, the Latins new and old; as children are affrighted in the dark, so are melancholy men at all times, as having the inward cause with them, and still carrying it about. Which black vapours, whether they proceed from the black blood about the heart, (as Thomas Wright, Jesuit, thinks in his treatise of the passions of the mind) or stomach, spleen, midriff, or all the misaffected parts together, it boots not; they keep the mind in a perpetual dungeon, and oppress it with continual fears, anxieties, sorrows, etc."

The physiological picture is of a kind of smoke or fog arising from unwholesome blood or diseased viscera, and either directly darkening the brain and mind, or else in some way clogging the tubes (for the nerves were regarded as hollow pipes) along which the natural, vital and animal spirits are supposed to flow.

In reading the scientific literature of early modern times one is struck by its strange mingling of the wildest supernaturalism with the crudest, the most naïve kind of materialism. This primitive materialism differs from modern materialism in two important respects. In the first place the "matter" with which the older theory deals is something which does not lend itself (owing to the nature of the descriptive terms employed) to exact measurement. We hear only of heat and cold, dryness and moisture, lightness and heaviness. No attempt is ever made to elucidate the meaning of these qualitative expressions in terms of quantity. In its fine structure the "matter" of our ancestors was nonmeasurable, and consequently nothing much could ever be done about it. And where nothing can be done, very little can be understood.

The second point of difference is no less important than the first. To us, "matter" reveals itself as a something in perpetual activity— a something, indeed, whose essence is nothing other than activity. All matter is forever *doing something*, and of all forms of matter the colloids composing living bodies are the most frantically busy— but with a frenzy marvelously integrated, so that the activity of one part of the organism regulates and in turn is regulated by the activities of other parts, in a harmonious dance of energies. For the ancients, and for medieval and early modern thinkers, matter was mere stuff, intrinsically inert, even in the living body where its activities were due exclusively to the workings of the vegetal soul in plants, of the vegetal and sensitive soul in the brutes, and, in man, of that trinity in unity, the vegetal, sensitive and rational soul. Physiological processes were explained not in terms of chemistry, for chemistry as a science was nonexistent; nor in terms of electrical impulses, for nothing was yet known of electricity; nor in terms of cellular activity, for there was no microscope and nobody had ever seen a cell; they were explained (with no trouble at all) in terms of action on inert matter by special faculties of the soul. There was a faculty of growth, for example, a faculty of nutrition, a faculty of secretion—a faculty for any and every process that might be observed. For philosophers it was wonderfully convenient; but when men tried to pass from words to the given facts of nature, they found that the theory of special faculties was of no practical use whatever.

The crudity of the older materialism is clearly expressed in the language of its exponents. Physiological problems are discussed in metaphors drawn from what goes on in the kitchen, the smelter and the privy. There are boilings and simmerings and strainings; there are refinings and extractions; there are putrefactions, miasmic exhalations from the cesspool and their pestilential condensations upstairs, on the *piano nobile*. In terms such as these, fruitful thinking about the human organism is very difficult. The good doctors were men with a natural gift, who did not permit their learning to interfere too much with their diagnostic intuitions and their talent for helping nature to perform her miracles of healing. Along with much useless or dangerous nonsense, there is in Burton's huge compilation not a little excellent sense. Most of the nonsense derives from the current scientific theories; most of the sense from the openminded empiricism of shrewd and kindly men who loved their fellows, had a special knack with the sick and trusted in the *vis medicatrix Naturae*.

For details of the strictly medical treatment of melancholy, whether due to natural or supernatural causes, the reader is referred to Burton's absurd and charming book. For our present purposes it is enough to remark that, during the whole time of the possession, Sœur Jeanne and her fellow nuns were under constant medical supervision. In their case, unfortunately, none of the more sensible methods of treatment described by Burton were ever applied. For them there was no question of a change of air, of diet, of occupation. They were merely bled and purged and made to swallow innumerable pills and draughts. So drastic was this medication that some of the independent physicians who examined them were of the opinion that their disease was aggravated (as so many diseases are still aggravated) by overzealous attempts to bring about a cure. The nuns, they discovered, were being given large and frequent doses of antimony. Perhaps that was all that was wrong with them.

(To appreciate the full historical import of this diagnosis, we must bear in mind that, at the time of the possession, what may be called the Battle of Antimony had been raging for three generations and was still going strong. By the heretical anti-Galenists the metal and its compounds were regarded as miracle drugs, specific for practically everything. Under pressure from the orthodox right wing of the medical profession, the Parlement of Paris had issued an edict prohibiting their use in France. But the law had proved to be unenforceable. Half a century after its passage, Grandier's good friend and Loudun's most famous medical son, Théophraste Renaudot, was zealously proclaiming the virtue of antimony. His younger contemporary, Gui Patin, the author of the famous *Letters*, was no less violent on the other side. In the light of modern research we can see that Patin was more nearly in the right than Renaudot and the other anti-Galenists. Certain compounds of antimony are specific in the treatment of the tropical disease known as kala-azar. In most other conditions, the use of the metal or its compounds is hardly worth the risks involved. Medically speaking, there was no justification for such indiscriminate use as was made of the drug during the sixteenth and seventeenth centuries. From the economic point of view, however, the justification was ample. M. Adam and his fellow apothecaries sold Perpetual Pills of metallic antimony. These were swallowed, irritated the mucous membrane as they passed through the intestine, thus acting as a purgative, and could be recovered from the chamber pot, washed and used again, indefinitely. After the first capital outlay, there was no further need for spending money on cathartics. Dr. Patin might fulminate and the Parlement forbid; but for the costive French bourgeois, the appeal of antimony was irresistible. Perpetual Pills were treated as heirlooms and after passing through one generation were passed on to the next.)

It is worth remarking parenthetically that Paracelsus, the greatest of the early anti-Galenists, owed his enthusiasm for antimony to a false analogy. "Just as antimony purifies gold and leaves no slag in it, in the same form and shape it purifies the human body."* The same kind of false analogy between the arts of the metalworker and the alchemist on the one hand and the arts of the doctor and dietician on the other led to the belief that the value of foods increased with their increasing refinement—that white bread was better than brown, that a much-stewed bouillon was superior to the unconcentrated meats and vegetables of which it was composed. It was assumed that "coarse" foods coarsened the people who ate them. "Cheese, milk and oatcakes," Paracelsus says, "cannot give one a subtle disposition." It was only with the isolation of the vitamins, a generation ago, that the old false analogies with alchemy ceased to play havoc with our theories of diet.

The existence of a well developed medical treatment of "melancholy" was in no way incompatible with the existence of a widespread belief, even among the doctors, in the reality of possession and diabolic infestation. Some people, writes Burton "laugh at all such stories." But on the opposite side are "most lawyers, divines, physicians, philosophers." Ben Jonson, in *The Devil is an Ass*, has left us a vivid description of the seventeenth-century mind, divided between credulity and skepticism, between a reliance on the supernatural (above all in its less creditable aspects) and a bumptious confidence in the new-found powers of applied science. In the play, Fitzdottrel is introduced as a dabbler in the magic arts, who longs to meet with a devil, because devils know the site of hidden treasures. But to this belief in magic and the power of Satan is conjoined a no less powerful belief in the quasi-rational and pseudo-scientific schemes of those fraudulent inventors and company promoters whom our fathers called "projectors." When Fitzdottrel tells his wife that his projector has worked out a plan, which will infallibly make him eighteen million pounds and secure him a dukedom, she shakes her head and tells him not to put too much trust "in these false spirits." "Spirits!" cries Fitzdottrel,

* Paracelsus, *Selected Writings* (New York, 1951), p. 318.

Spirits! O no such thing, wife; wit, mere wit.
This man defies the Devil and all his works.
He does't by engine and devices, he!
He has his winged ploughs that go with sails,
Will plough you forty acres at once! and mills
Will spout you water ten miles off.

However farcically the figure of fun, Fitzdottrel is nonetheless a truly Representative Man. He stands for a whole epoch, whose intellectual life was straddled insecurely between two worlds. That he tried to make the worst of both worlds, instead of the best, is also sadly typical. For the unregenerate, occultism and "projects" are considerably more attractive than pure science and the worship of God in spirit.

In Burton's book, as in the history of the nuns of Loudun, these two worlds coexist and are taken for granted. There is melancholy and there is an approved medical treatment for melancholy. At the same time it is well known that magic and possession are common causes of disease, both of mind and of body. And no wonder! For "not so much as an hair-breadth empty in heaven, earth, or waters, above or under the earth. The air is not so full of flies in summer as it is at all times of invisible devils; this Paracelsus stiffly maintains, and that they have every one their several Chaos." The number of these spirits must be infinite; "for if that be true that some of our Mathematicians say: if a stone could fall from the starry heaven or eighth sphere, and should pass every hour an hundred miles, it would be 65 years, or more, before it would come to ground, by reason of the great distance of heaven from earth, which contains, as some say, 170 million 803 miles . . . how many such spirits may it contain?" In the circumstances, the truly surprising thing was not the fact of an occasional possession, but the fact that most people could go through life without becoming demoniacs.

II

We have seen that the plausibility of the hypothesis of possession was exactly proportionate to the inadequacy of a physiology without cell structure or chemistry, and of a psychology which took practically no account of mental activity on subconscious levels. Once universal, belief in possession is entertained at the present time only by Roman Catholics and Spiritists. The latter explain certain phenomena of the séance room in terms of the temporary possession of the medium's organism by the surviving psyche of some dead human being. The former deny possession by departed souls, but explain certain cases of mental and physical derangement in terms of possession by devils, certain psychophysical accompaniments of mystical or premystical states in terms of possession by some divine agency.

There is nothing, so far as I can see, self-contradictory in the idea of possession. The notion is not one to be ruled out *a priori*, on the ground that it is a "a relic of ancient superstition." It should be treated rather as a working hypothesis, which may be cautiously entertained in any case where other forms of explanation are found to be inadequate to the facts. In practice modern exorcists seem to be agreed that most cases of suspected possession are in fact due to hysteria and can best be treated by the standard methods of psychiatry. In a few instances, however, they find evidence of something more than hysteria and assert that only exorcism and the casting out of the possessing spirit can effect a cure.

Possession of a medium's organism by the discarnate spirit, or "psychic factor," of defunct human beings has been invoked to explain certain phenomena, such as evidential scripts and utterances, for which it would otherwise be difficult to account. The earlier evidence for such possession may be conveniently studied in F. W. H. Myers's *Human Personality and Its Survival of Bodily Death*, the more recent in Mr. G. N. M. Tyrell's *The Personality of Man*.

Professor Oesterreich, in his richly documented study of the subject* has pointed out that, while belief in diabolic possession sharply declined during the nineteenth century, belief in possession by departed spirits became, during the same period, much more common. Thus, neurotics who, at an earlier epoch, would have attributed their malady to devils, were inclined, after the rise of the Fox

* T. K. Oesterreich. *Les Possédés*, trans. René Sudre (Paris, 1927).

Sisters, to lay the blame on the discarnate souls of evil men or women. With the recent advances in technology, the notion of possession has taken a new form. Neurotic patients often complain that they are being influenced, against their will, by some kind of radio messages transmitted by their enemies. The Malicious Animal Magnetism which haunted poor Mrs. Eddy's imagination for so many years has now been transformed into Malicious Electronics.

In the sixteen hundreds there was no radio and very little belief in possession by discarnate spirits. Burton cites the opinion that devils are merely the souls of the malevolent dead, but cites it only to remark that it is an "absurd tenet." For him, possession was a fact, and was exclusively by devils. (For Myers, two and a half centuries later, possession was also a fact, but exclusively by the spirits of the dead.)

Do devils exist? And, if so, were they present in the bodies of Sœur Jeanne and her fellow nuns? As with the notion of possession, I can see nothing intrinsically absurd or self-contradictory in the notion that there may be nonhuman spirits, good, bad and indifferent. Nothing compels us to believe that the only intelligences in the universe are those connected with the bodies of human beings and the lower animals. If the evidence for clairvoyance, telepathy and prevision is accepted (and it is becoming increasingly difficult to reject it), then we must allow that there are mental processes which are largely independent of space, time and matter. And if this is so, there seems to be no reason for denying *a priori* that there may be nonhuman intelligences, either completely discarnate, or else associated with cosmic energy in some way of which we are still ignorant. (We are still ignorant, incidentally, of the way in which human minds are associated with that highly organized vortex of cosmic energy known as a body. That some association exists is evident; but how energy gets transformed into mental processes, and how mental processes affect energy, we still have no idea.*)

In the Christian religion devils have, until very recent times, played an exceedingly important part—and this from the very

* Consult in this context Sir Charles Sherrington's Gifford Lectures, published in 1941 under the title of *Man on His Nature.*

beginning. For, as Fr. A. Lefèvre S. J. has remarked, "the devil has but a small place in the Old Testament; his empire is not yet revealed. The New Testament discloses him as chief of the leagued forces of evil."* In the current translations of the Lord's Prayer we ask to be delivered from evil. But is it certain that *apo tou ponerou* is neuter rather than masculine? Does not the very structure of the prayer imply that the word refers to a person? "Lead us not into temptation, but (on the contrary) deliver us from the Evil One, the Tempter."

In theory and by theological definition Christianity is not Manichaeism. For Christians, evil is not a substance, not a real and elementary principle. It is merely a privation of good, a diminution of being in creatures who derive their essential being from God. Satan is not Ahriman under another name, is not an eternal principle of Darkness over against the divine principle of Light. Satan is merely the most considerable among a vast number of individual angels who, at a given moment of time, chose to separate themselves from God. It is only by courtesy that we call him *the* Evil One. There are many evil ones, of whom Satan is the Chief Executive. Devils are persons, and each one has his character, his temperament, his humors, crotchets and idiosyncrasies. There are power-loving devils, lustful devils, covetous devils, proud and conceited devils. Moreover, some devils are much more important than others; for they retain, even in hell, the positions they occupied in the heavenly hierarchy, before their fall. Those who in heaven were merely angels or archangels are lower-class devils of small account. Those who were once Dominions or Principalities or Powers, now constitute the *haute bourgeoisie* of hell. The quondam Cherubim and Seraphim are an aristocracy, whose power is very great and whose physical presence (according to the information supplied to Father Surin by Asmodeus) can make itself felt within a circle thirty leagues in diameter. At least one seventeenth-century theologian, Father Ludovico Sinistrari, maintained that human beings could be possessed, or at least obsessed, not merely by devils, but also, and more frequently, by nonmalignant spiritual entities—the fauns,

* In *Satan*, a volume of the *Etudes Carmélitaines*, (Paris, 1948).

nymphs and satyrs of the ancients, the hobgoblins of the European peasantry, the poltergeists of modern psychical researchers.* According to Sinistrari, most incubi and succubi were merely natural phenomena, no worse and no better than buttercups, say, or grasshoppers. At Loudun, unfortunately, this kindly theory was never broached. The insanely libidinous imaginings of the nuns were all attributed to Satan and his messengers.

Theologians, I repeat, have carefully guarded against Manichaean dualism; but, at all times, all too many Christians have behaved as though the devil were a First Principle, on the same footing as God. They have paid more attention to evil and the problem of its eradications than to good and the methods by which individual goodness may be deepened, and the sum of goodness increased. The effects which follow too constant and intense a concentration upon evil are always disastrous. Those who crusade, not *for* God in themselves, but *against* the devil in others, never succeed in making the world better, but leave it either as it was, or sometimes even perceptibly worse than it was, before the crusade began. By thinking primarily of evil we tend, however excellent our intentions, to create occasions for evil to manifest itself.

Though frequently Manichaean in practice, Christianity was never Manichaean in its dogmas. In this respect it differs from our modern idolatries of communism and nationalism, which are Manichaean not only in action, but also in creed and theory. Today it is everywhere self-evident that *we* are on the side of Light, *they* on the side of Darkness. And being on the side of Darkness, *they* deserve to be punished and must be liquidated (since *our* divinity justifies everything) by the most fiendish means at our disposal. By idolatrously worshiping ourselves as Ormuzd, and by regarding the other fellow as Ahriman, the Principle of Evil, we of the twentieth century are doing our best to guarantee the triumph of diabolism in our time. And on a very small stage, this precisely was what the exorcists were doing at Loudun. By idolatrously identifying God with the political interests of their sect, by concentrating their thoughts and their efforts on the powers of evil, they were doing

* See L. Sinistrari, *Demoniality* (Paris, 1879).

their best to guarantee the triumph (local, fortunately, and temporary) of that Satan, against whom they were supposed to be fighting.

For our present purposes it is unnecessary either to affirm or deny the existence of nonhuman intelligences capable of possessing the bodies of men and women. The only question we have to ask ourselves is this: granted the existence of such intelligences, is there any reason to believe that they were responsible for what happened to the Ursulines of Loudun? Modern Catholic historians are unanimously agreed that Grandier was innocent of the crime for which he was tried and condemned; but some of them—they are cited by the Abbé Bremond in his *Histoire Littéraire du Sentiment Religieux en France*—are still convinced that the nuns were the victims of a genuine possession. How such an opinion can be held by anyone who has read the relevant documents, and who has even the slightest knowledge of abnormal psychology, I confess myself unable to understand. There is nothing in the behavior of the nuns which cannot be paralleled in the many cases of hysteria recorded, and successfully treated, by modern psychiatrists. And there is no evidence that any of the nuns ever manifested any of the paranormal powers which, according to the doctrines of the Roman Church, are the hallmarks of a genuine diabolic invasion.

How is true possession to be distinguished from fraud or the symptoms of disease? The Church prescribes four tests—the language test, the test of preternatural physical strength, the test of levitation and the test of clairvoyance and prevision. If a person can on occasion understand, or better still, speak a language, of which, in his normal state, he is completely ignorant; if he can manifest the physical miracle of levitation or perform unaccountable feats of strength, and if he can correctly predict the future or describe events taking place at a distance—then that person may be presumed to be possessed by devils. (Alternatively, he may be presumed to be the recipient of extraordinary graces; for in many instances divine and infernal miracles are, most unhappily, identical. The levitation of saintly ecstatics is distinguishable from the levitation of ecstatic demoniacs only in virtue of the moral antecedents and consequences of the event. These moral antecedents and consequences are often hard to assess, and it has sometimes happened that even the holiest persons have been suspected of producing their ESP phenomena and their PK effects by diabolic means.)

Such are the official and time-hallowed criteria of diabolic possession. For us, these ESP and PK phenomena prove only that the old notion of a completely watertight soul is untenable. Below and beyond the conscious self lie vast ranges of subconscious activity, some worse than the ego and some better. Some stupider and some, in certain respects, far more intelligent. At its fringes this subconscious self overlaps and merges with not-self, with the psychic medium in which all selves bathe and through which they can directly communicate with one another and with cosmic Mind. And somewhere on these subconscious levels individual minds make contact with energy, and make contact with it not merely in their own body, but also (if the anecdotic and statistical evidence may be trusted) outside their own body. The older psychology, as we have seen, was compelled by its own dogmatic definitions to ignore subconscious mental activity; in order to account for the observed facts, it had to postulate the devil.

For the moment, let us place ourselves in the intellectual position of the exorcists and their contemporaries. Accepting as valid the Church's criteria of possession, let us examine the evidence on which the nuns were pronounced to be demoniacs and the parson, a sorcerer. We will begin with the test which, because it was the easiest of application, was in practice the most frequently applied—the test of language.

For all the Christians of an earlier day, "speaking with tongues" was an extraordinary grace, a gratuitous gift of the Holy Spirit. But it was also (such is the strangely equivocal nature of the universe) a sure symptom of possession by devils. In the great majority of cases, glossolalia is not a clear and unmistakable speaking of some hitherto unknown tongue. It is a more or less articulate, more or less systematic gibberish, exhibiting certain resemblances to some form of traditional speech and consequently interpretable, by listeners of good will, as a rather obscure utterance in some language with which they happen to be familiar. In the cases where persons in a state of trance have shown an unequivocal knowledge of some language of which they were consciously ignorant, investigation has generally revealed the fact that they had spoken the language during childhood and subsequently forgotten it, or that they had heard it spoken and, without understanding the meaning of the words had unconsciously familiarized themselves with their sound. For the rest there is, in the words of F. W. H. Myers, "little evidence of the acquisition—telepathy apart—of any actual mass of fresh knowledge, such as a new language, or a stage of mathematical knowledge unreached before." In the light of what we know, through systematic psychical research, of trance mediumship and automatic writing, it seems questionable whether any alleged demoniac ever passed the test of language in a completely unambiguous and decided manner. What is certain is that the recorded cases of complete failure are very numerous, while the recorded successes are mostly partial and rather unconvincing. Some of the ecclesiastical investigators of possession applied the language test in very ingenious and effective ways. In 1598, for example, Marthe Brossier made a great name for herself by exhibiting the symptoms of possession. One of these symptoms—a thoroughly traditional and orthodox symptom—consisted in going into convulsions every time a prayer or an exorcism was read over her. (Devils hate God and the Church; consequently they tend to fly into a rage every time they hear the hallowed words of the Bible or the prayer book.) To test Marthe's paranormal knowledge of Latin, the Bishop of Orléans opened his Petronius and solemnly intoned the somewhat unedifying story of the Matron of Ephesus. The effect was magical. Before the first sonorous sentence had been completed, Marthe was rolling on the floor, cursing the Bishop for what he was making her suffer by his reading of the Sacred Word. It is worth remarking that, far from putting an end to Marthe's career as a demoniac, this incident actually helped her to go forward to fresh triumphs. Fleeing from the Bishop, she put herself under the protection of the Capuchins, who proclaimed that she had been unjustly persecuted and made use of her to draw enormous crowds to their exorcisms.

The Petronius test was never, so far as I know, applied to the Ursulines of Loudun. The nearest approach to such a test was made by a visiting nobleman who handed the exorcist a box in which, so he whispered, there were some exceedingly holy relics. The box was applied to the head of one of the nuns, who immediately exhibited all the symptoms of intense pain and threw a fit. Much delighted, the good friar returned the box to its owner, who thereupon opened it and revealed that, except for a few cinders, it was completely empty. "Ah, my lord," cried the exorcist, "what sort of a trick have you played upon us." "Reverend Father," answered the nobleman, "what sort of a trick have you been playing upon *us*?"

At Loudun, simple language tests were frequently tried, but always without success. Here is the account of an incident which de Nion, who was a firm believer in the reality of the nuns' possession, regarded as convincingly miraculous. Speaking in Greek, the Bishop of Nîmes orders Sister Claire to bring him her beads and say an *Ave Maria*. Sister Claire responds by bringing first a pin and then some aniseed. Being urged to obey, she says, "I see you want something else," and finally brings the beads and offers to say an *Ave*.

In most cases the miracle was even less astounding. All the nuns who knew no Latin were possessed by devils who also knew no Latin. To account for this strange fact, one of the Franciscan exorcists explained in a sermon that there are uneducated devils as well as educated ones. The only educated devils at Loudun were those who had invaded the Prioress. But even Jeanne's devils were not conspicuously learned. Here is part of the *procès-verbal* of the exorcism performed before M. de Cerisay on November 24, 1632. "M. Barré holds up the Host and asks the devil, '*Quem adoras?*' Answer: '*Jesus Christus.*'* Whereupon M. Daniel Drouyn, Assessor of the Provost's Office, said in a rather loud voice, 'This devil is not congruous.' The exorcist then changed his question to, '*Quis est iste quem adoras?*' She answered, '*Jesu Christe.*'† Upon which several persons remarked, 'What bad Latin!' But the exorcist re-

---

* 'Whom do you worship?' Answer: 'Jesus Christ.'

† 'Who is it whom you worship?' She answered, '*Jesu Christe*' [instead of *Jesus Christus*].

179

torted that she had said, '*Adoro te, Jesu Christe.*'* Afterward a little nun came in, roaring with laughter and repeating, 'Grandier, Grandier!' Then the lay sister, Claire, entered the room neighing like a horse."

Poor Jeanne! She had never learnt enough Latin to understand all this nonsense about nominatives and accusatives and vocatives. *Jesus Christus, Jesu Christe*—she had given them everything she could remember; and still they said it was bad Latin!

M. de Cerisay, meanwhile, had declared that he would willingly believe in the possibility of possession, "if the said Superior would answer categorically two or three of his interrogations." But when the questions were asked, there was no reply. Completely floored, Sœur Jeanne had to take refuge in a convulsion and a little howling.

On the day following this very unconvincing demonstration, Barré went to de Cerisay and protested that his actions were pure, and without passion or evil intentions. "Placing the ciborium on his head, he prayed that it might confound him, if he had made use of any malpractices, suggestions or persuasions in regard to the nuns in all this affair. When he had finished the Prior of the Carmelites stepped forward and made similar protestations and imprecations; he also held the holy ciborium on his head and prayed that the maledictions of Dathan and Abiram might fall upon him, if he had sinned or been at fault in this affair." Barré and the Prior were probably fanatical enough to be sincerely blind to the nature of their actions, and it was, no doubt, with a clear conscience that they swore these enormous oaths. Canon Mignon, we note, thought it wiser to put nothing on his head and to call down no thunderbolts.

Among the distinguished British tourists, who visited Loudun during the years of the possession, was young John Maitland, afterward Duke of Lauderdale. Maitland's father had told him of a Scottish peasant woman, through whose mouth a demon had corrected the bad Latin of a Presbyterian minister, and the young man had consequently grown up with an *a priori* belief in possession. In the hope of confirming this belief by direct observation of demoniacs, Maitland undertook two continental journeys, one to Ant-

* 'I worship thee, Jesus Christ.'

werp, the other to Loudun. In both cases, alas, he was disappointed. At Antwerp, "I saw only some great Holland wenches hear exorcism patiently and belch most abominably." At Loudun, matters were a little livelier, but no more evidential. "When I had seen exorcising enough of three or four of them in the chapel, and could hear nothing but wanton wenches singing bawdy songs in French, I began to suspect a *fourbe*." He complained to a Jesuit, who commended his "holy curiosity" in coming to Loudun, and told him to go that evening to the parish church, where he would be amply satisfied. "In the parish church I saw a great many people gazing and a wench pretty well taught to play tricks, yet nothing so much as I have seen twenty tumblers or rope dancers do. Back I came to the nuns' chapel, where I saw the Jesuits still hard at work, at several altars, and one poor Capuchin, who was an object of pity, for he was possessed by a melancholy fancy that devils were running about his head, and was constantly applying relics. I saw the Mother Superior exorcised, and saw the hand, on which they would have made me believe the names Jesus, Maria, Joseph, were written by miracle, (but it was apparent to me that it was done with aquafortis); then my patience was quite spent, and I went to a Jesuit and told him my mind fully. He still maintained a real possession, and I desired, for a trial, to speak a strange language. He asked, 'What language?' I told him, 'I would not tell; but neither he nor all these devils should understand me.' [Presumably it was the Gaelic of his native Scotland that Maitland had in mind.] He asked me if I would be converted upon the trial (for he had discovered I was no papist). I told him, 'That was not the question, nor could all the devils in hell pervert me; but the question was, if that was a real possession, and if any could understand me, I would confess it under my hand.' His answer was, 'These devils have not traveled,' and this I replied to with loud laughter."

According to the Franciscan, these devils were uneducated; according to the Jesuit, they had never traveled. Such explanations of their inability to understand foreign languages seemed a little lame, and for the benefit of those who were unwilling to accept them, the nuns and their exorcists added a couple of new and, so they hoped, more cogent explanations. If the devils could not speak Greek or Hebrew, it was because the pact they had made with Grandier included a special clause to the effect that in no circumstances would they speak Greek or Hebrew. And if that was not enough, then there was the final, the clinching explanation, that it was not God's will that these particular devils should speak with tongues. *Deus non vult*—or as Sister Jane was apt to say, in her pidgin Latin, *Deus non volo*. On the conscious level, the blunder was doubtless attributable to mere ignorance. But in an obscure way our ignorances are often voluntary. On the subliminal level, that *Deus non volo*, that "I, God, do not wish," may very well have expressed the sentiments of Jeanne's profounder ego.

The tests for clairvoyance seem to have been as uniformly unsuccessful as the language tests. De Cerisay, for example, arranged with Grandier that the latter should spend the day at the house of one of his colleagues; then went to the convent and, in the course of the exorcism, asked the Superior to say where, at that moment, the parson was. Without hesitation, Sœur Jeanne answered that he was in the great hall of the castle with M. d'Armagnac.

On another occasion one of Jeanne's devils affirmed that he had had to take a brief trip to Paris in order to escort the soul of a newly departed *procureur du Parlement*, called M. Proust, to the infernal regions. Inquiry revealed that there had never been a *procureur* called Proust and that no *procureur* had died on the day specified.

During Grandier's trial another of the Prioress's devils swore on the sacraments that Grandier's books of magic were stored in the house of Madeleine de Brou. The house was searched. There were no books of magic—but at least Madeleine had been well frightened, humiliated and insulted, which was all that really interested the Mother Superior.

In his accounts of the possession Surin admits that the nuns often failed to pass the ESP tests devised by examining magistrates, or arranged for the edification and amusement of distinguished tourists. In consequence of these failures many members of his own order refused to believe that the nuns were suffering from anything more supernatural than melancholy and *furor uterinus*. Surin points out that these skeptics among his colleagues had never visited Loudun for more than a few days at a time. But like the spirit of God, the spirit of evil bloweth where and when it listeth. To be certain of seeing it blow, one had to be on the spot, day and night, for months at a stretch. Speaking as one of the resident exorcists, Surin affirms that Sœur Jeanne repeatedly read his thoughts before he uttered them. That a highly sensitive hysteric, such as Sœur Jeanne, could have lived nearly three years in the closest intimacy with a highly sensitive spiritual director, such as Father Surin, and not have developed some degree of telepathic rapport with him would be indeed surprising. Dr. Ehrenwald* and others have pointed out that this kind of rapport between doctor and patient is sometimes established in the course of psychoanalytic treatment. The relationship between demoniac and exorcist is probably even more intimate than that between psychiatrist and neurotic. And in this particular case, let us remember, the exorcist was obsessed by the same devils as had invaded his penitent.

Surin, then, was fully convinced that the Prioress could, on occasion, successfully read the thoughts of those around her. But by dogmatic definition anyone who could read another's thoughts was possessed by a devil—or alternatively was the recipient of an extraordinary grace. The notion that ESP might be a natural faculty, latent in all minds and manifest in a few, never seems, for a single instant, to have entered his head, or, for that matter, the head of any of his contemporaries or predecessors. Either the phenomena of telepathy and clairvoyance did not exist, or they were the work of spirits, whom one might presume, unless the thought-reader were manifestly a saint, to be devils. Surin deviated from strict orthodoxy in only one point: he believed that devils could read minds directly, whereas the most authoritative theologians were of the opinion that they could do so only indirectly, by inference from the bodily changes accompanying thought.

In the *Malleus Maleficarum*, it is asserted, on the best possible authority, that devils cannot possess the will and the understanding, but only the body and such mental faculties as are most closely allied to the body. In many cases devils do not even possess the

* See Jan Ehrenwald, M.D., *Telepathy and Medical Psychology* (New York, 1948).

183

whole of the demoniac's body, but only a small part of it—a single organ, one or two muscle groups, or bones. Pillet de la Mesnardière, one of Richelieu's personal physicians, has left us a list of the names and local habitations of all the devils who took part in the possessions of Loudun. Leviathan, he tells us, occupied the center of the Prioress's forehead; Beherit was lodged in her stomach; Balaam under the second rib on the right side; Isacaaron under the last rib on the left. Eazaz and Caron lived respectively under the heart and in the center of the forehead of Sister Louise of Jesus. Sister Agnes de la Motte-Baracé had Asmodeus under the heart and Beherit in the orifice of the stomach. Sister Claire de Sazilly harbored seven devils in her body—Zabulon in the forehead, Nephthali in the right arm; Sans Fin, alias Grandier of the Dominations, under the second rib on the right; Elymi, to one side of the stomach; the Enemy of the Virgin, in the neck; Verrine in the left temple and Concupiscence, of the Order of Cherubim, in the left rib. Sister Seraphica had a bewitchment of the stomach, consisting of a drop of water guarded by Baruch or, in his absence, by Carreau. Sister Anne d'Escoubleau had a magic barberry leaf in her stomach under the care of Elymi, who simultaneously watched over the purple damson in the stomach of her sister. Among the lay demoniacs Elizabeth Blanchard had a devil under each armpit, with another called Coal of Impurity in her left buttock. Yet others were lodged under the navel, below the heart and under the left pap. Four demons occupied the body of Françoise Filatreau—Ginnillion in the forebrain; Jabel, a wanderer through every part of the organism; Buffetison below the navel; and Dog's Tail, of the Order of Archangels, in the stomach.

From their many mansions within the victim's body the devils sallied forth, one at a time, to work upon the humors, the spirits, the senses and the phantasy. In this way they could influence the mind, even though they were unable to possess it. The will is free, and only God can look into the understanding. From this it followed that a possessed person could not directly read another's mind. If devils sometimes seemed to have ESP, it was because they were observant and clever, and could therefore infer a man's secret thoughts from his overt behavior.

At Loudun, ESP phenomena may have occurred (Surin at least was convinced of the fact). But if they did occur, they occurred spontaneously, and never in the test situations devised by the investigating lawyers and physicians. But the Church taught that devils could be compelled by the exorcist to do his bidding. If, when duly constrained, the demoniacs failed to demonstrate ESP under test conditions, then it followed, according to the rules of the theological and legal games, that they were not possessed. Unfortunately for Grandier and, indeed, for everyone else concerned, the games in this case were not played according to the rules.

From the mental criteria of possession we now pass to the physical. In regard to levitation, Sister Jane's devils had indicated at an early stage of the proceedings that, in their pact with Grandier, there was an article which specifically barred all supernatural floatings. And anyhow those who longed to see such marvels were displaying too much curiosity, *nimia curiositas*, a thing which *Deus* very definitely *non volo*. And yet though she herself had never professed to be levitated, some of her supporters confidently asserted, with M. de Nion, that on several occasions "the Mother Superior was carried off her feet and suspended in the air at a height of twenty-four inches." De Nion was an honest man, who probably believed what he said. Which only shows how extremely cautious one must always be in the matter of believing believers.

Some of the other nuns were less prudent than their Superior. Early in May, 1634, the devil Eazaz promised that he would raise Sister Louise of Jesus three feet into the air. Not to be outdone, Cerberus offered to do the same for Sister Catherine of the Presentation. Alas, neither of the young ladies succeeded in getting off the ground. A little later, Beherit, who was lodged in the pit of Sister Agnes de la Motte-Baracé's stomach, swore that he would cause Laubardemont's skull cap to leave his head and fly up to the roof of the chapel. A crowd assembled to see the miracle. It did not take place. After that, all requests for levitation were met with a polite refusal.

Tests for preternatural strength were carried out by Dr. Mark Duncan, the Scottish physician who was the Principal of the

Protestant College at Saumur. Grasping the wrists of one of the demoniacs, he found it easy to prevent her from striking him or from breaking out of his control. After this humiliating display of diabolical weakness, the exorcists confined themselves to inviting unbelievers to stick their fingers in the good sisters' mouths, and see if the devil would bite them. When Duncan and the others declined the invitation, it was held by all right-thinking people to be an acknowledgment of the reality of the possession.

From all this it must be evident that if, as the Roman Church maintained, ESP phenomena and PK effects are the hallmark of diabolic possession (or, alternatively, are extraordinary graces), then the Ursulines of Loudun were merely hysterics who had fallen into the hands, not of the fiend, not of the living God, but of a crew of exorcists, all superstitious, all hungry for publicity, and some deliberately dishonest and consciously malevolent.

In the absence of any evidence for ESP or PK, the exorcists and their supporters were compelled to fall back on even less convincing arguments. The nuns, they asserted, must be possessed by devils; for how, otherwise, could one account for the shamelessness of their actions, the smut and irreligion of their conversation? "In what school of rakes and atheists," asks Father Tranquille, "have they learned to spew forth such blasphemies and obscenities?" And with a touch almost of boastfulness, de Nion assures us that the good sisters "made use of expressions so filthy as to shame the most debauched of men, while their acts, both in exposing themselves and in inviting lewd behavior from those present, would have astounded the inhabitants of the lowest brothel in the country."* As for their

* When Sister Claire was ordered by the exorcist (as a test for ESP) to obey an order, secretly whispered by one of the spectators to another, she went into convulsions and rolled on the floor *"relevant jupes et chemises, montrant ses parties les plus secrètes, sans honte, et se servant de mots lascifs. Ses gestes devinrent si grossiers que les témoins se cachaient la figure. Elle répétait, en s' . . . des mains, Venez donc, foutez-moi."* On another occasion this same Claire de Sazilly, *se trouva si fort tentée de coucher avec son grand ami, qu'elle disait être Grandier, qu'un jous s'étant approchée pour recevoir la Sainte Communion, elle se leva soudain et monta dans sa chambre, où ayant été suivie par quelque'une des Sœurs, elle fut vue avec un Crucifix dans la main, dont elle se preparait. . . . L'honnêteté,* (adds Aubin) *ne permet pas d'écrire les ordures de cet endroit.*

oaths and blasphemies—these were "so unheard of that they could not have suggested themselves to a merely human mind."

How touchingly ingenuous this is! Alas, there is no horror which cannot suggest itself to human minds. "We know what we are," says Ophelia, "but we know not what we may be." Practically all of us are capable of practically anything. And this is true even of persons who have been brought up in the practice of the most austere morality. What is called "induction" is not confined to the lower levels of the brain and nervous system. It also takes place in the cortex, and is the physical basis of that ambivalence of sentiment which is so striking a feature of man's psychological life.* Every positive begets its corresponding negative. The sight of something red is followed by a green afterimage. The opposing muscle groups involved in any action automatically bring one another into play. And on a higher level we find such things as a hatred that accompanies love, a derision begotten by respect and awe. In a word, the inductive process is ubiquitously active. Sister Jane and her fellow nuns had had religion and chastity drummed into them from childhood. By induction, these lessons had called into existence, within the brain and its associated mind, a psychophysical center, from which there emanated contradictory lessons in irreligion and obscenity. (Every collection of spiritual letters abounds in references to those frightful temptations against the faith and against chastity, to which the seekers after perfection are peculiarly subject. Good directors point out that such temptations are normal and almost inevitable features of the spiritual life and must not be permitted to cause undue distress.†) At ordinary times these negative thoughts and feelings were repressed or, if they rose into consciousness, were

* See above p. 157 ff., and Ischlondsky, *Brain and Behaviour* (London, 1949).
† In a letter dated January 26, 1923, Dom John Chapman writes as follows: "In the 17th-18th centuries most pious souls seem to have gone through a period in which they felt sure that God had reprobated them. . . . This doesn't seem to happen nowadays. But the *corresponding trial* of our contemporaries seems to be the *feeling of not having any faith*; not temptation against any particular article (usually), but a mere feeling that religion is not true. . . . The only remedy is to *despise* the whole thing and pay no attention to it except (of course) to assure our Lord that one is ready to suffer from it as long as He wishes, which seems an absurd paradox to say to a Person one doesn't believe in."

by an effort of will denied any outlet in speech or action. Weakened by psychosomatic disease, made frantic by her indulgence in forbidden and unrealizable phantasies, the Prioress lost all power to control these undesirable results of the inductive process. Hysterical behavior is infectious, and her example was followed by the other nuns. Soon the whole convent was throwing fits, blaspheming and talking smut. For the sake of a publicity which was thought to be good for their respective Orders and the Church at large, or with the deliberate intention of using the nuns as instruments for the destruction of Grandier, the exorcists did everything in their power to foster and increase the scandal. The nuns were forced to perform their antics in public, were encouraged to blaspheme for distinguished visitors and to tickle the groundlings with displays of extravagant immodesty. We have already seen that, at the beginning of her malady, the Prioress did not believe herself to be possessed. It was only after her confessor and the other exorcists had repeatedly assured her that she was full of devils that Sister Jane came at last to be convinced that she was a demoniac and that her business, henceforth, was to behave as such. And the same was true of some at least of the other nuns. From a pamphlet published in 1634 we learn that Sister Agnes had frequently remarked, during exorcism, that she was not possessed, but that the friars had said she was and had constrained her to undergo exorcism. And "on the preceding twenty-sixth of June, the exorcist having by mistake let fall some burning sulphur on Sister Claire's lip, the poor girl burst into tears, saying that, 'Since she had been told she was possessed, she was ready to believe it, but that she did not on that account deserve to be treated in this way.' " The work begun spontaneously by hysteria was completed by the suggestions of Mignon, Barré, Tranquille and the rest. All this was clearly understood at the time. "Granted that there is no cheat in the matter," wrote the author of the anonymous pamphlet cited above, "does it follow that the nuns are possessed? May it not be that, in their folly and mistaken imagination, they believe themselves to be possessed, when in fact they are not?" This, continues our author, can happen to nuns in three ways. First, as a result of fasts, watchings and meditations on hell and Satan. Second, in consequence of some remark made by their confessor—something which makes them think they are being tempted by devils. "And thirdly, the confessor, seeing them act strangely, may imagine in his ignorance that they are possessed or bewitched, and may afterward persuade them of the fact by the influence he exercises over their minds." In the present case the mistaken belief in possession was due to the third of these causes. Like the mercurial and antimonial poisonings of earlier days, like the sulfa poisoning and serum-fevers of the present, the Loudun epidemic was an "iatrogenic disease," produced and fostered by the very physicians who were supposed to be restoring the patients to health. The guilt of the exorcists seems the more enormous when we remember that their proceedings were in direct violation of the rules laid down by the Church. According to these rules, exorcisms were to be performed in private, the demons were not to be allowed to express their opinions, they were never to be believed, they were consistently to be treated with contempt. At Loudun, the nuns were exhibited to enormous crowds, their demons were encouraged to hold forth on every subject from sex to transubstantiation, their statements were accepted as gospel truth and they were treated as distinguished visitors from the next world, whose utterances had the authority almost of the Bible. If they blasphemed and talked bawdy—well, that was just their pretty way. And anyhow bawdry and blasphemy were box office. The faithful fairly lapped them up and came back, in their thousands, for more.

Supernatural blasphemy, more than human bawdry—and if these were not sufficient proofs of diabolic possession, what about the nuns' contortions? what about their exploits in the acrobatic field? Levitation had quickly been ruled out; but if the good sisters never rose into the air, they at least performed the most amazing feats on the floor. Sometimes, says de Nion, "they passed the left foot over the shoulder to the cheek. They also passed their feet over the head, until the big toes touched the nose. Others again were able to stretch their legs so far to the left and right that they sat on the ground, without any space being visible between their bodies and the floor. One, the Mother Superior, stretched her legs to such an extraordinary extent that, from toe to toe, the distance was seven feet, though she herself was but four feet high." Reading such accounts of the nuns' performances, one is forced to the conclusion that, as well as *naturaliter Christiana*, the feminine soul is *naturaliter Drum-Majoretta*. So far as the Eternal Feminine is concerned, a taste for acrobacy and exhibitionism would seem to be built in, only awaiting a favorable opportunity to manifest itself in handsprings and back somersaults. In the case of cloistered contemplatives, such opportunities are not of frequent occurrence. It took seven devils and Canon Mignon to create the circumstances in which, at long last, it became possible for Sister Jane to do the splits.

That the nuns found a deep satisfaction in their gymnastics is proved by de Nion's statement that, though for months at a stretch they were "tortured by the devils twice a day," their health in no way suffered. On the contrary, "those who were somewhat delicate seemed healthier than before the possession." The latent drum majorettes, the cabaret dancers *in posse* had been permitted to come to the surface and, for the first time, these poor girls without a vocation for prayer were truly happy.

Alas, their happiness was not unmitigated. They had their lucid intervals. They were aware, from time to time, of what was being done to them, of what they themselves were doing to the wretched man, with whom they had all frantically imagined themselves to be in love. We have seen that, as early as June 26th, Sister Claire had been complaining of the manner in which the exorcists were treating her. On July 3rd, in the chapel of the castle, she suddenly burst into tears and, between her sobs, declared that everything she had said about Grandier, during the preceding weeks, was a tissue of lies and calumnies, and that she had acted throughout under orders from Father Lactance, Canon Mignon and the Carmelites. Four days later, in a yet wilder passion of remorse and rebellion, she tried to run away, but was caught as she left the church and brought back, struggling and weeping, to the good fathers. Emboldened by her example, Sister Agnes (that *beau petit diable*, whom Killigrew was to see, more than a year later, still groveling at the feet of her Capuchin) appealed to the spectators, who had come to see her show those now familiar legs of hers, begging with tears in her eyes to be delivered from her horrible captivity among the exorcists. But the exorcists always had the last word. Sister Agnes's entreaties, Sister Claire's attempt at flight, her retractations and qualms of conscience —these, it was only too obvious, were the work of Grandier's lord and protector, the devil. If a nun withdrew what she had said against the parson, that was proof positive that Satan was speaking through her mouth and that what she had originally affirmed was the indubitable truth.

It was in the case of the Prioress that this argument was used with the greatest effect. One of the judges wrote a brief summary of the counts on which Grandier was condemned. In the sixth paragraph of this document we read what follows. "Of all the accidents by which the good sisters were tormented, none seems stranger than that which befell the Mother Superior. The day after she gave her evidence, while M. de Laubardemont was taking the deposition of another nun, the Prioress appeared in the convent yard, dressed only in her chemise, and stood there for the space of two hours, in the pouring rain, bareheaded, a rope round her neck, a candle in her hand. When the parlor door was opened, she rushed forward, fell on her knees before M. de Laubardemont and declared that she had come to make amends for the offense she had committed in accusing the innocent Grandier. After which, having retired, she fastened the rope to a tree in the garden and would have hanged herself if the other sisters had not come running to the rescue."

Another man might have supposed that the Prioress had told a pack of lies and was suffering the well-deserved agonies of remorse. Not so M. de Laubardemont. To him it was manifest that this show of contrition had been put on by Balaam or Leviathan, constrained thereto by the spells of the magician. So far from exculpating the parson, Sœur Jeanne's confession and attempted suicide made it more certain than ever that he was guilty.

It was no good. From the prison they had built for themselves— the prison of obscene phantasies now objectified as facts, of deliberate lies now treated as revealed truths—the nuns would never be able to escape. The Cardinal had now gone so far that he could not afford to let them repent. And could they themselves have afforded to persist in that repentance? By retracting what they had said about Grandier they would condemn themselves, not merely in this world but also in the next. On second thought, they all decided to believe their exorcists. The good fathers assured them that what felt so horribly like remorse was only a diabolic illusion; that what looked in retrospect like the most monstrous of lies was actually a truth, and a truth so wholesome, so Catholic, that the Church was ready to guarantee both its orthodoxy and its correspondence with the facts. They listened, they suffered themselves to be persuaded. And when it became impossible to go on pretending to believe this abominable nonsense, they took refuge in delirium. Horizontally, on the level of everyday reality, there was no escape from their prison. And as for upward self-transcendence—there was no question, in the midst of all this fiendish preoccupation with fiends, of lifting up the soul to God. But downward the road was still wide open. And downward they went, again and again—sometimes voluntarily, in a desperate effort to escape from the knowledge of their guilt and humiliation; sometimes, when their madness and the suggestions of the exorcists were too much for them, against their will and in spite of themselves. Down into convulsions; down into swinish squalor or maniacal rage. Down, far down, below the level of personality, into that subhuman world, in which it seemed natural for an aristocrat to play tricks for the amusement of the mob, for a nun to blaspheme and strike indecent postures and shout unmentionable words. And then down, still further, down into stupor, down into catalepsy, down into the ultimate bliss of total unconsciousness, of absolute and complete oblivion.

CHAPTER EIGHT

"DULY constrained, the devil is bound to tell the truth." Granted this major premise, there was literally nothing which could not be made to follow. Thus, M. de Laubardemont disliked the Huguenots. Seventeen devil-infested Ursulines stood ready to swear on the Blessed Sacrament that the Huguenots were Satan's friends and faithful servants. This being the case, the Commissioner felt himself fully justified in disregarding the Edict of Nantes. The Calvinists of Loudun were first deprived of their cemetery. Let them bury the carcasses of their dead somewhere else. Then came the turn of the Protestant College. The school's commodious buildings were confiscated and handed over to the Ursulines. In their rented convent there had been no room for the crowds of pious sightseers who thronged the city. Now at last the good sisters could be exorcised with all the publicity they deserved and without having to traipse out in all weathers to Sainte-Croix or the Eglise du Château.

Hardly less detestable than the Huguenots were those bad Catholics who obstinately refused to believe in Grandier's guilt, in the reality of the possession and in the absolute orthodoxy of the Capuchins' new doctrine. Lactance and Tranquille fulminated against them from the pulpit. These people, they bawled, were no better than heretics; their doubt was a mortal sin and they were already as good as damned. Mesmin and Trincant, meanwhile, went about accusing the skeptics of disloyalty to the King and (yet worse) conspiracy against His Eminence. And through the mouths of Mignon's nuns and the Carmelites' lay hysterics, a score of devils announced that they were all magicians who had trafficked with Satan. From some of M. Barré's demoniacs at Chinon came word that even the irreproachable *Bailli*, M. de Cerisay, was a dabbler in the Black Art. Another demoniac denounced two priests, Fathers Buron and Frogier, for attempted rape. On the accusation of the Prioress, Madeleine de Brou was charged with witchcraft, arrested and imprisoned. Thanks to their wealth and high connections, her relatives managed to get her released on bail. But after Grandier's trial was over, Madeleine was rearrested. An appeal to *Messieurs des Grands-Jours* (the judges of the peripatetic Court of Appeal, which traveled through the kingdom, looking into scandals and miscarriages of justice) brought an injunction against Laubardemont. The Commissioner retorted with an injunction against the appellant. Fortunately for Madeleine, the Cardinal did not think her important enough to justify a quarrel with the judiciary. Laubardemont was instructed to drop the case, and the Prioress had to forego the pleasures of revenge. As for poor Madeleine, she did what her lover had dissuaded her from doing after her mother's death—took the veil and disappeared forever into a convent.

Other accusations, meanwhile, were flying as thick as dust on the wind. Now it was the local debutantes who were singled out for attack. In her playful way, Sister Agnes would declare that nowhere in the world was there so much unchastity as at Loudun. Sister Claire would name names and specify sins. Sister Louise and Sister Jane would add that all the girls were budding witches, and the proceedings would end with the usual indecent postures, filthy language and shrieks of maniacal laughter.

On other occasions respectable gentlemen were accused of having attended the Sabbath and kissed the devil's rump. And their wives had fornicated with incubi, their sisters had bewitched the neighbor's chickens, their maiden aunts had caused a virtuous young man to be impotent on his wedding night. And all the time, through the tiny airholes in his bricked-up windows, Grandier was magically distributing his sperm—to the witches as a reward, to the wives and daughters of the Cardinalists in the spiteful hope of bringing them to undeserved shame.

All these malignant ravings were recorded, verbatim, by Laubardemont and his clerks. Those who were accused by the devils—those, in other words, who were obnoxious to the Commissioner and the exorcists—were summoned to Laubardemont's office, were questioned, browbeaten, menaced with legal proceedings that might cost them their lives.

One day in July, on a tip from Beherit, Laubardemont had the doors of Sainte-Croix closed on a considerable assemblage of young ladies. The girls were then frisked by Capuchins. But the pacts with Satan which they were all supposed to be carrying about their persons were not revealed by even the most thorough search. Although Beherit had been duly constrained, for some odd reason he had failed to tell the truth.

Week in, week out, Capuchins, Recollets and Carmelites yelled and gesticulated from every pulpit; but the skeptics were not convinced, the protests against the iniquitous handling of the case against Grandier grew louder and more frequent. Anonymous rhymers made epigrams on the Commissioner. Setting old tunes to new words, men sang about him derisively in the streets and over their wine in the taverns. Under cover of darkness, pasquinades against the good fathers were nailed to the church doors. Interrogated, Dog's Tail and Leviathan named a Protestant and some schoolboys as the culprits. They were arrested; but nothing could be proved against them, and they had to be set free again. Sentries were now posted outside the churches. The only result was that the libels were pinned to other doors. On the second of July the exasperated Commissioner issued a proclamation. Henceforth it was expressly forbidden to do or even say anything "against the nuns or other persons of the said Loudun, afflicted by evil spirits, or against their exorcists, or against those who assist the exorcists." Anyone who disobeyed was liable to a fine of ten thousand livres or, if it should seem necessary, to yet graver pains, both financial and bodily. After this the critics became more cautious; the devils and the exorcists could give vent to their calumnies without risk of contradiction. In the words of the anonymous author of some contemporary *Remarques et Considérations pour la Justification du Curé de Loudun*, "God, who can only speak truth, is now dethroned and the Evil One put in His place, who utters nought but cheats and vanity; and this vanity must be believed as truth. Is not this to resuscitate paganism? People say, moreover, that it is most convenient that the devil should name so many magicians and sorcerers; for by this means they will be tried, their goods will be confiscated and a share will be given, if he likes, to Pierre Menuau, who, however, may be content, as may also his cousin, Canon Mignon, with the death of the parson and the ruin of the town's most respectable families."

At the beginning of August Father Tranquille published a short treatise, setting forth and justifying the new doctrine: "Duly constrained, the devil is bound to tell the truth." The book had the approval of the Bishop of Poitiers and was hailed by Laubardemont as the last word in orthodox theology. Doubt was no longer permissible. Grandier was a magician and so, in a smaller way, was that insolently upright M. de Cerisay. Excepting those whose parents were good Cardinalists, all the girls of Loudun were whores and witches. And half the town's population was already damned for lack of faith in the devils.

Two days after the publication of Tranquille's book, the *Bailli* summoned a meeting of notables. Loudun's predicament was discussed and it was decided that de Cerisay and his Lieutenant, Louis Chauvet, should go to Paris and petition the King for protection against the high-handed actions of his Commissioner. The only dissentient voices were those of Moussaut, the Public Prosecutor, Menuau, and Hervé, the *Lieutenant Criminel*. Asked by de Cerisay whether he accepted the new doctrine and approved of what was being done to his fellow citizens in the names of Balaam, Dog's Tail and company, Hervé replied that "the King, the Cardinal and the Bishop of Poitiers believed in the possession, and that, so far as he was concerned, was enough." For our twentieth-century ears, this appeal to the infallibility of political bosses has a remarkably modern ring.

Next day de Cerisay and Chauvet set out for Paris. They were the bearers of a petition in which the just complaints and apprehensions of the people of Loudun were clearly set forth. Laubardemont's proceedings were severely blamed and the Capuchins' new doctrine was shown to be "against the express prohibition of God's law" and contrary to the authority of the Fathers of the Church, of St. Thomas and of the whole faculty of the Sorbonne, which had formally condemned a similar doctrine in 1625. In view of all this the petitioners begged His Majesty to order the Sorbonne to examine Tranquille's book and further requested that all those defamed by the demons and their exorcists might be permitted to appeal to the Parlement of Paris, "which is the natural judge of such matters."

At court the two magistrates sought out Jean d'Armagnac, who immediately went to the King and asked him to receive them. The answer was a blunt refusal. De Cerisay and Chauvet left their petition with the King's private secretary (who was the Cardinal's creature and an avowed enemy of Loudun), then took the homeward road.

In their absence Laubardemont had issued another proclamation. It was now forbidden, under pain of a fine of twenty thousand livres, to hold any public meeting whatsoever. After this the devil's enemies gave no further trouble.

The preliminary investigations were now completed; it was time at last for the trial. Laubardemont had hoped to recruit some at least of the judges from among the principal magistrates of Loudun. He was disappointed. De Cerisay, de Bourgneuf, Charles Chauvet and Louis Chauvet—all refused to be parties to a judicial murder. The Commissioner tried cajolery; then, when that failed, hinted darkly at the consequences of His Eminence's displeasure. In vain. The four lawyers stood firm. Laubardemont was forced to look further afield—to Chinon and Châtellerault, to Poitiers and Tours and Orléans, to La Flèche and Saint-Maixent and Beaufort. In the end he had a panel of thirteen complaisant magistrates and, after some trouble with an overscrupulous lawyer called Pierre Fournier, who refused to play the game according to the Cardinal's rules, a thoroughly reliable Public Prosecutor.

By the middle of the second week of August everything was ready. After hearing Mass and taking Communion, the judges assembled in the Carmelite convent and began listening to the evidence accumulated by Laubardemont during the preceding months. The Bishop of Poitiers had formally guaranteed the genuineness of the possession. This meant that real devils had spoken through the mouths the Ursulines, and these real devils had sworn again and again that Grandier was a sorcerer. But, "duly constrained, the devil is bound to tell the truth." Therefore . . . Q.E.D.

Grandier's condemnation was so certain, and the certainty was so notorious, that tourists were already pouring into Loudun for the execution. During those hot August days thirty thousand persons— more than twice the normal population of the city—were competing for beds and meals and stake-side seats.

Most of us find it very hard to believe that we could ever have enjoyed the spectacle of a public execution. But before we start to congratulate ourselves on our finer feelings, let us remember, first, that we have never been permitted to see an execution and, second, that when executions were public, a hanging seemed as attractive as a Punch and Judy show, while a burning was the equivalent of a Bayreuth Festival or an Oberammergau Passion Play—a great event for which it was worth while to make a long and expensive pilgrimage. When public executions were abolished, it was not because the majority desired their abolition; it was because a small minority of exceptionally sensitive reformers possessed sufficient influence to have them banned. In one of its aspects, civilization may be defined as a systematic withholding from individuals of certain occasions for barbarous behavior. In recent years we have discovered that when, after a period of withholding, those occasions are once more offered, men and women, seemingly no worse than we are, have shown themselves ready and even eager to take them.

The King and the Cardinal, Laubardemont and the judges, the townspeople and the tourists—all of them knew what was going to happen. The only person for whom the condemnation was not a foregone conclusion was the prisoner. Even as late as the end of the first week in August, Grandier still believed that he was just an ordinary defendant in a trial, whose irregularities were accidental and would be set straight as soon as attention had been called to them. His *Factum* (the written statement of his case) and the letter which he smuggled out of prison for delivery to the King, were evidently written by a man who was still convinced that his judges could be moved by statements of fact and logical arguments, that they took an interest in Catholic doctrine and might be expected to bow to the authority of accredited theologians. Pathetic illusion! Laubardemont and his tame magistrates were the agents of a man who was not concerned with fact, or logic, or law, or theology, but only with personal vengeance and a political experiment, carefully designed to show how far, in this third decade of the seventeenth century, the methods of totalitarian dictatorship could safely be pushed.

When the devils' depositions had all been heard, the prisoner was called to the bar. In the *Factum*, which was read aloud by defending counsel, Grandier answered his infernal accusers, stressed the illegality of the proceedings and Laubardemont's bias, denounced the exorcists for their systematic prompting of the demoniacs, and proved that the Capuchins' new doctrine was a dangerous heresy. The Judges sat there, shifting in their chairs with unconcealed impatience, whispering among themselves, laughing, picking their noses, doodling with squeaky quills on the paper before them. Grandier looked at them, and suddenly it was manifest to him that there was no hope.

He was taken back to his cell. In the windowless attic the heat was horribly oppressive. Lying sleepless on his pile of straw, he could hear the drunken singing of some Breton sight-seers, who had come for the big show and were trying to while away the dreary time of waiting. Only a few more days now. . . . And all this horror was undeserved. He had done nothing, he was absolutely innocent. Yes, absolutely innocent. But their malice had pursued him, patiently, persistently; and now this huge machine of organized injustice was closing in on him. He could fight, but they were invincibly strong; he could use his wits and his eloquence, but they did not even listen. Now there was nothing but to beg for mercy, and they would only laugh. He was trapped—snared like one of those rabbits he had caught as a boy in the fields at home. Screaming in the noose, and the noose grew tighter as the animal struggled, but never quite tight enough to stop the screaming. To stop the screaming you had to knock it over the head with a stick. And suddenly he found himself overcome by a horrible mingling of anger and frustration and self-pity and an agonizing fear. To the screaming rabbit he had brought the release of a single, merciful blow. But *they*—what did *they* have in store for him? The words he had written at the end of his letter to the King came back to him, "I remember that, while I was a student at Bordeaux, fifteen or sixteen years ago, a monk was burned for sorcery; but the clergy and his fellow monks did their best to save him, even though he had made confession of his crime. But in my own case I may say, not without resentment, that monks and nuns and my own colleagues, canons like myself, have conspired to destroy me, though I have not been convicted of anything remotely resembling sorcery." He closed his eyes and, in imagination, saw the monk's distorted face through the roaring curtain of flame. "Jesus, Jesus, Jesus. . . ." And then the screaming became inarticulate, became the screaming of the snared rabbit, and there was nobody to take mercy, nobody to put an end to the agony.

The terror became so unbearable that, involuntarily, he cried aloud. The sound of his own voice startled him. He sat up and looked around him. The darkness was impenetrable. And suddenly he was overcome with shame. Crying in the night, like a woman, like a frightened child! He frowned to himself, he clenched his fists. Nobody should ever call him a coward. Let them do their worst! He was ready for it. They should find his courage greater than their malice, stronger than any torment their cruelty could devise.

The parson lay down again—but not to sleep. He had the will to heroism; but his body was in a panic. The heart throbbed uncontrollably. Shuddering with the mindless fears of the nervous system, his muscles were made yet tenser by his conscious effort to overcome that purely physical terror. He tried to pray; but "God" was a word without meaning, "Christ" and "Mary" were empty names. He could think only of the approaching ignominy, of death in unspeakable pain, of the monstrous injustice of which he was the victim. It was all completely unthinkable; and yet it was a fact, it was actually happening. If only he had taken the Archbishop's advice and left the parish eighteen months ago! And why had he refused to listen to Guillaume Aubin? What madness had made him stay and let himself be arrested? The fancy of what might have been made the present reality seemed even more unbearable. Even more unbearable. . . . And yet he resolved to bear it. Manfully. They hoped to see him cringe and cower. But never would he give them that satisfaction, never. Gritting his teeth, he pitted his will against their spite. But the blood was still banging in his ears, and as he turned uneasily on the straw, he realized that his body was bathed in a profuse sweat.

The horror of the night was immeasurably long; and yet here, in an instant, was the dawn, and he was nearer by a day to that other, that infinitely worse and final horror.

At five o'clock the cell door was opened and the jailer announced a visitor. It was Father Ambrose, of the Order of Augustinian Canons, who had come in pure charity to ask if he could be of any help or comfort to the prisoner. Grandier hastily dressed, then knelt and began the general confession of a whole lifetime of faults and shortcomings. They were all old sins, for which he had done penance and received absolution—old sins, and yet brand new; for now, for the first time, he recognized them for what they were: barriers against grace, doors deliberately slammed in the face of God. In words and forms he had been a Christian, he had been a priest; in thoughts and acts and feelings he had never worshiped anything but himself. "*My* kingdom come, *My* will be done"—the kingdom of lust and greed and vanity, the will to cut a figure, the will to trample underfoot, to triumph and exult. For the first time in his life he knew the meaning of contrition—not doctrinally, not by scholastic definition, but from within, as an anguish of regret and self-condemnation. When the confession was over, he was bitterly weeping, not for what he was to suffer, but for what he had done.

Father Ambrose pronounced the formula of absolution, then gave him communion, and spoke a little about the will of God. Nothing was to be asked for, he said, and nothing refused. Except for sin, all that might happen to one was not merely to be accepted with resignation; it was to be willed, moment by moment, as God's will for that particular moment. Suffering was to be willed, affliction was to be willed, the humiliations resulting from personal weakness and ineptitude were to be willed. And in the act of being willed they would be understood. And in the act of being understood they would be transfigured, would be seen, not with the eyes of the natural man, but as God saw them.

The parson listened. It was all in the Bishop of Geneva, it was all in St. Ignatius. Not only had he heard it all before; he had even said it—a thousand times and much more eloquently, much more forcefully than poor dear Father Ambrose could ever hope to say it. But the old man was in earnest, the old man obviously knew what he was talking about. Mumbled in a toothless mouth, without elegance, even without grammar—the words were like lamps, suddenly illuminating a mind that had been darkened by too much brooding over past hurts, too much relishing of future pleasures or imaginary triumphs.

"God is here," mumbled the tired old voice, "and Christ is now. Here in your prison, now in the midst of your humiliations and your sufferings."

The door was opened again, and it was Bontemps, the jailer. He had reported Father Ambrose's visit to the Commissioner, and M. de Laubardemont had sent peremptory orders that His Reverence was to leave immediately and not return. If the prisoner wanted to see a priest, he could ask for Father Tranquille or Father Lactance.

The old friar was hustled out of the room; but his words remained, and the meaning of them was becoming clearer and clearer. "God is here and Christ is now"—and, so far as the soul was concerned, could be nowhere else and at no other instant. All this pitting of the will against his enemies, all this defiance of unjust fate, these resolves to be heroic and indomitable—how futile, considering that God was always present, how utterly pointless!

At seven the parson was taken to the Carmelite convent, for another sight of the judges assembled to condemn him. But God was among them; even when Laubardemont tried to trip him up in his answers, Christ was there. On some of the magistrates the calm dignity of Grandier's manner made a profound impression. But Father Tranquille explained it very simply: it was all the devil's doing. What looked like calm was merely the brazen insolence of hell; and this dignity was nothing but the outward expression of unrepentant pride.

The judges saw the defendant only three times in all. Then, very early on the morning of the eighteenth, after the usual pious preliminaries, they rendered their decision. It was unanimous. Grandier was to be subjected to "the question" both ordinary and extraordinary; he was then to kneel at the doors of St. Peter's and St. Ursula's and there, with a rope round his neck and a two-pound taper in his hand, ask pardon of God, the King and Justice; next, he was to be taken to the Place Sainte-Croix, tied to a stake and burned alive; after which his ashes were to be scattered to the four winds. The sentence, writes Father Tranquille, was truly celestial; for Laubardemont and his thirteen judges were "as much in heaven by reason of their piety and their fervent devotions as on earth through the exercise of their functions."

No sooner had sentence been pronounced than Laubardemont sent orders to the surgeons Mannoury and Fourneau to proceed immediately to the prison. Mannoury was the first to arrive; but was so much disconcerted by what Grandier said to him about his earlier exploits with the needle that he retired in a panic, leaving to his colleague the task of preparing the victim for execution. The judges' orders were that Grandier should be shaved all over—head, face and body. Fourneau, who was convinced of the parson's innocence, respectfully apologized for what he had to do, then set to work.

The parson was stripped. The razor passed over his skin. In a few minutes his body was as hairless as a eunuch's. Next, the rich black curls were sheared to a bristly stubble; the scalp was lathered and shaved clean. Then it was the turn of the Mephistophelean mustaches and the little beard.

"And now the eyebrows," said a voice from the doorway.

Startled, they turned their heads. It was Laubardemont. Reluctantly, Fourneau did as he was told. That face, which so many women had found so irresistibly handsome, was now the mask, grotesquely bald, of the clown in a harlequinade.

"Good," said the Commissioner, "good! And now the fingernails."

Fourneau was puzzled.

"The fingernails," Laubardemont repeated. "You will now pull out the fingernails."

This time the surgeon refused to obey. Laubardemont began by being genuinely astonished. What was wrong? After all, the man was a convicted sorcerer. But the convicted sorcerer, the other retorted, was still a man. The Commissioner grew angry; but in spite of all his threats, the surgeon stood firm. There was no time to send for another operator, and Laubardemont had to be content with the partial disfigurement of his victim by shaving.

Dressed only in a long nightshirt and a pair of worn out slippers, Grandier was taken downstairs, bundled into a closed carriage and driven to the courthouse. Townspeople and tourists thronged the approaches; but only a favored few—high officials, men of rank with their wives and daughters, half a dozen faithful Cardinalists from among the bourgeoisie—were permitted to enter. Silks rustled; there was a rich glow of velvet, a glittering of jewels, a smell of civet and ambergris. In full canonicals Father Lactance and Father Tranquille entered the judgment hall. With consecrated whisks they scattered holy water over everything within range, intoning as they did so the formulas of exorcism. Then a door was opened and, in his nightgown and slippers, but with a skull cap and biretta on his shaven head, Grandier appeared on the threshold. After he too had been thoroughly sprinkled, the guards led him up the whole length of the hall and made him kneel before the judges' bench. His hands were tied behind his back, and it was therefore impossible for him to bare his head. The clerk of the court stepped forward, snatched off his hat and cap and flung them down contemptuously on the floor. At the sight of that pale, hairless clown, several of the ladies giggled hysterically. An usher called for silence. The clerk put on his spectacles, cleared his throat and started to read the sentence— first, half a page of legal jargon; then a long description of the *amende honorable* which the prisoner was to make; then the condemnation to death at the stake; then a digression about the commemorative plaque to be set up in the Ursulines' chapel at a cost of one hundred and fifty livres, chargeable to the prisoner's confiscated estate; and finally, as a kind of afterthought, a casual mention of the tortures, ordinary and extraordinary, which were to precede the burning. "Pronounced at the said Loudun, August 18, 1634, and executed," the clerk concluded emphatically, "the same day."

There was a long silence. Then Grandier addressed his judges.

"My lords," he said slowly and distinctly, "I call God the Father, God the Son and God the Holy Ghost to witness, together with the Virgin, my sole advocate, that I have never been a sorcerer, have never committed sacrilege and have never known any other magic than that of Holy Scripture, the which I have always preached. I adore my Savior and pray that I may partake in the merit of the blood of His Passion."

He raised his eyes to heaven; then, after a moment, lowered them again to look at the Commissioner and his thirteen stipendiaries. In a tone almost of intimacy, as though they were his friends, he told them that he was afraid for his salvation—afraid lest the hideous torments prepared for his body might drive his poor soul to despair and, through that gravest of sins, to eternal damnation. Surely their lordships did not intend to kill a soul? And, that being so, surely they would be pleased, in their mercy, to mitigate, if only a little, the rigor of his punishment?

He paused for a few seconds and looked questioningly from face to stony face. From the women's benches came the sound of another of those half-suppressed giggles. Once again the parson knew that there was no hope—no hope except in this God who was here and would not desert him, this Christ who was now, who would go on being now at every moment of his martyrdom.

Opening his mouth again, he began to talk about the martyrs. These holy witnesses had died for the love of God and the honor of Jesus Christ—had died on the wheel, in the flames, under the sword, riddled with arrows, torn and devoured by wild beasts. Never would he venture to compare himself with such as these; but at least he might hope that an infinitely merciful God would permit him to atone by his sufferings for all the sins of a vain and disordered life.

The parson's words were so touching, and the fate which awaited him so monstrously cruel, that all but his most inveterate enemies were moved to pity. Some of the women who had giggled at the antics of the clown now found themselves in tears. The ushers called for silence. In vain. The sobbing was uncontrollable. Laubardemont was greatly disturbed. Nothing was going according to plan. Better than anyone else he must have known that Grandier was not guilty of the crimes for which he was to be tortured and burned alive. And yet, in some sublimely Pickwickian sense, the parson *was* a sorcerer. On the basis of a thousand pages of worthless evidence, thirteen hireling judges had said so. Therefore, though certainly false, it must somehow be true. Now, by all the rules of the game, Grandier should be spending his last hours in despair and rebellion, cursing the devil who had ensnared him and the God who was sending him to hell. Instead of which, the scoundrel was talking like a good Catholic and giving the most touching, the most heart-rending example of Christian resignation. The thing was insufferable. And what would His Eminence say, when he heard that the only result of this carefully stage-managed ceremony had been to convince the spectators that the parson was innocent? There was only one thing to do, and Laubardemont, who was a man of decision, promptly did it.

"Clear the court," he ordered.

The ushers and the archers of the guard hastened to obey. Angrily protesting, the gentry and their ladies were herded out into the corridors and the waiting rooms. The doors were closed behind them. Save for Grandier, his guards and judges, the two friars and a handful of city officials, the great hall was empty.

Laubardemont now addressed the prisoner. Let him confess his guilt and reveal the names of his accomplices. Then and only then the judges might consider his appeal for mitigation of their sentence.

The parson answered that he could not name accomplices he had never had, nor confess to crimes of which he was completely innocent. . . .

But Laubardemont wanted a confession; indeed, he urgently needed one—needed it in order to confound the skeptics and silence the critics of his proceedings. From severe, his manner became, all of a sudden, positively genial. He gave orders that Grandier's hands should be untied, then pulled a paper out of his pocket, dipped a pen in the inkpot and offered it to the prisoner. If he signed, it would be unnecessary to resort to torture.

According to all the rules, a convicted criminal should have jumped at this chance to buy himself a little mercy. Gauffridi, for example, the priestly magician of Marseilles, had ended by putting his name to anything and everything. But once again Grandier refused to play the game.

"I must beg your lordship to excuse me," he said.

"Just a little signature," Laubardemont wheedled. And when the other protested that his conscience would not permit him to affirm a lie, the Commissioner implored him to reconsider his decision—for his own sake, to spare his poor body unnecessary pain, to save his imperiled soul, to cheat the devil and reconcile himself to the God he had so grievously offended.

According to Father Tranquille, Laubardemont actually wept while he was making this final appeal for a confession. We need not doubt the friar's word. Richelieu's hangman possessed a genuine gift of tears. The eye-witness account of the last hours of Cinq-Mars and de Thou paints a picture of Laubardemont blubbering like a crocodile over the young men he had just condemned to death. In the present case tears were as unavailing as threats had been. Grandier persisted in his refusal to sign a false confession. To Lactance and Tranquille, the fact was further, final proof of guilt. It was Lucifer who had closed the prisoner's mouth and hardened his heart against repentance.

Laubardemont turned off his tears. In a tone of cold fury he told the parson that this was the last proffer of mercy. Would he sign? Grandier shook his head. Laubardemont beckoned to the captain of the guards and ordered him to take the prisoner upstairs to the torture chamber. Grandier made no outcry. All he asked was that Father Ambrose might be sent for, to be with him during his ordeal. But Father Ambrose was not available. After his unauthorized visit to the prison, he had been ordered to leave the city. Grandier then asked for the assistance of Father Grillau, the Warden of the Cordeliers. But the Cordeliers were in bad odor for their refusal to accept the Capuchins' new doctrine, or to have anything to do with the possession. And anyhow Grillau was known to have been on friendly terms with the parson and his family. Laubardemont refused to let him be sent for. If the prisoner wished for spiritual consolation, he might address himself to Lactance and Tranquille—the most relentless of his enemies.

"I see what it is," said Grandier bitterly. "Not content with torturing my body, you wish to destroy my soul by plunging it into despair. One day you will have to answer for this to my Redeemer."

Since Laubardemont's time, evil has made some progress. Under Communist dictators, those who come to trial before a People's Court invariably confess the crimes of which they have been accused—confess them even when they are imaginary. In the past, confession was by no means invariable. Even under torture, even at the stake, Grandier protested his innocence. And Grandier's case was by no means unique. Many persons, women no less than men, went through similar experiences with the same indomitable constancy. Our ancestors invented the rack and the iron maiden, the boot and the water torture; but in the subtler arts of breaking the will and reducing the human being to subhumanity, they still had much to learn. In a sense, it may be, they did not even wish to learn these things. They had been brought up in a religion which taught that the will is free, the soul immortal; and they acted upon these beliefs even in relation to their enemies. Yes, even the traitor, even the convicted devil-worshiper had a soul which might yet be saved; and the most ferocious judges never refused him the consolations of a religion which went on offering salvation to the very end. Before and during execution, a priest was always at hand, doing his best to reconcile the departing criminal with his Creator. By a kind of blessed inconsistency, our fathers respected the personality even of those whom they were tormenting with red-hot pincers or breaking on the wheel.

For the totalitarians of our more enlightened century, there is no soul and no Creator; there is merely a lump of physiological raw material molded by conditioned reflexes and social pressures into what, by courtesy, is still called a human being. This product of the man-made environment is without intrinsic significance and possesses no rights to self-determination. It exists for Society and must conform to the Collective Will. In practice, of course, Society is nothing but the national State, and as a matter of brute fact, the Collective Will is merely the dictator's will-to-power, sometimes mitigated, sometimes distorted to the verge of lunacy, by some pseudoscientific theory of what, in the gorgeous future, will be good for an actuarial abstraction labeled "Humanity." Individuals are defined as the products and the instruments of Society. From this it follows that the political bosses, who claim to represent Society, are justified in committing any conceivable atrocity against such persons as they may choose to call Society's enemies. Physical extermination by shooting (or, more profitably, by overwork in a slave labor camp) is not enough. It is a matter of observable fact that men and women are not the mere creatures of Society. But official theory proclaims that they are. Therefore it becomes necessary to depersonalize the "enemies of Society" in order to transform the official lie into truth. For those who know the trick, this reduction of the human to the subhuman, of the free individual to the obedient automaton, is a relatively simple matter. The personality of man is far less monolithic than the theologians were compelled by their dogmas to assume. The soul is not the same as the Spirit, but is merely associated with it. In itself, and until it consciously chooses to make way for the Spirit, it is no more than a rather loosely tied bundle of not very stable psychological elements. This composite entity can quite easily be disintegrated by anyone ruthless enough to wish to try and skillful enough to do the job in the right way.

In the seventeenth century this particular kind of ruthlessness was hardly thinkable, and the relevant skills were therefore never developed. Laubardemont was unable to extract the confession he so urgently needed; and though he would not allow the parson to choose his confessor, he conceded in principle that even a convicted sorcerer had a right to spiritual consolation.

The services of Tranquille and Lactance were offered and, very naturally, refused. Grandier was then given a quarter of an hour in which to reconcile his soul with God and prepare for his martyrdom.

The parson knelt and began to pray out loud.

"Great God and Sovereign Judge, help of the helpless and oppressed, succor me, give me the strength to bear the pains to which I have been condemned. Receive my soul into the beatitude of your saints, remit my sins, forgive this vilest and most despicable of your servants.

"Searcher of hearts, you know I am in no wise guilty of the crimes imputed to me, and that the fire which I must undergo is but the punishment of my concupiscence. Redeemer of mankind, forgive my enemies and my accusers; but cause them to see their sins, that they may repent. Holy Virgin, protector of the penitent, graciously receive my unhappy mother into your heavenly company; console her for the loss of a son who fears no other pains but those which she must endure on that earth, from which he is so soon to depart."

He was silent. Not my will, but Thine. God here, among the instruments of torture; Christ now, in the hour of extremest anguish.

La Grange, the captain of the guards, was recording in his notebook what he remembered of the parson's prayer. Laubardemont approached and asked the young officer what he was writing. Informed, he grew angry and wanted to confiscate the notebook. But La Grange defended his property, and the Commissioner had to be content with ordering him on no account to show what he had written to anyone else. Grandier was an unrepentant magician, and unrepentant magicians are not supposed to pray.

In Father Tranquille's account of the trial and execution, and in the other narratives written from the official standpoint, the parson is made to behave in the most naïvely diabolistic manner. Instead of praying, he sings an improper song. Presented with the Crucifix, he turns away in abhorrence. The name of the Blessed Virgin never passes his lips; and though he sometimes pronouces the word "God," it is obvious to every right-thinking person that what he really means is "Lucifer."

Unfortunately for their thesis, these pious propagandists were not the only ones to leave a record of the proceedings. Laubardemont might enjoin secrecy; but he had no way of compelling La Grange to obey his orders. And there were other unbiased observers of the events—some of them, such as Ismaël Boulliau, the astronomer, known to us by name, others whose surviving manuscripts remain anonymous.

The clock struck, and the prisoner's brief respite was at an end. He was bound, stretched out on the floor, with his legs, from the knees to the feet, enclosed between four oaken boards, of which the outer pair were fixed, while the two inner ones were movable. By driving wedges into the space separating the two movable boards, it was possible to crush the victim's legs against the fixed framework of the machine. The difference between ordinary and extraordinary torture was measured by the number of progressively thicker wedges hammered home. Because it was invariably (though not immediately) fatal, the question extraordinary was administered only to condemned criminals, who were to be executed without delay.

While the prisoner was being prepared for the question, Fathers Lactance and Tranquille exorcised the ropes, the boards, the wedges and the mallets. This was very necessary; for if they were not driven out of these objects, the devils might, by their infernal arts, prevent the torture from being as excruciating as it ought to be. When the friars had finished their sprinkling and their muttering, the executioner stepped forward, raised his ponderous mallet and, like a man splitting a knotty piece of timber, brought it down with all his force. There was an uncontrollable shriek of pain. Father Lactance bent over the victim and asked in Latin if he would confess. But Grandier only shook his head.

The first wedge was driven home between the knees. Then another was inserted at the level of the feet and when that had been hammered to the head, the thin end of a third and heavier wedge was tapped into position immediately below the first. There was the thud of the mallet, the shriek of pain—then silence. The victim's lips were moving. Was it a confession? The friar cupped his ear; but all he could hear was the word "God," repeated several times, and then, "Do not abandon me, do not allow this pain to cause me to forget you." He turned to the executioner and told him to get on with his work.

At the second stroke on the fourth wedge there was a loud cracking sound. Several bones of the feet and ankles had broken. For a moment, the parson fainted away.

"*Cogne, cogne!*" Father Lactance yelled to the executioner. "Hit, hit!"

The prisoner opened his eyes again.

"Father," he whispered, "where is the charity of St. Francis?"

The disciple of St. Francis vouchsafed no answer.

"*Cogne!*" he said again. And when the blow had fallen, he turned back to the prisoner. "*Dicas, dicas!*"

But there was nothing to tell. A fifth wedge was inserted.

"*Dicas!*" The mallet hung suspended. "*Dicas!*"

The victim looked at the executioner, looked at the friar, then closed his eyes.

"Torture me as you like," he said in Latin. "In a little while it will be all one, forever."

"*Cogne!*"

The blow fell, and there was a noise of splintering bone.

Breathless and sweating in the summer heat, the executioner handed the mallet to his assistant. And now it was Tranquille's turn to talk to the prisoner. In a tone of sweet reasonableness, he set forth the manifest advantages of a confession—advantages not merely in the next world, but here and now.

The parson listened and, when he had finished, asked him a question.

"Father," he said, "do you believe on your conscience that a man ought, merely to be delivered from pain, to confess a crime he has not committed?"

Brushing aside these obviously Satanic sophisms, Tranquille continued his urgings.

The parson whispered that he was very ready to own up to all his real offenses.

"I have been a man, I have loved women. . . ."

But that was not what Laubardemont and the Franciscans wished to hear.

"You have been a magician, you have had commerce with devils."

And when the parson protested yet once more that he was innocent, a sixth wedge was hammered home, then a seventh, then an eighth. From ordinary, the question had reached the traditional limits of the extraordinary. The bones of the knees, the shins, the ankles, the feet—all were shattered. Their splinters projected through the mangled flesh and, along with the blood, there was an ooze of marrow. But still the friars could extort no admission of guilt—only that screaming and, in the intervals, the whispered name of God.

The eighth wedge was the last of the regular set. Laubardemont called for more—for a cruelty beyond the merely extraordinary. The executioner went out to the storeroom and came back with two new wedges. When he learned that they were no thicker than the last of the original set, Laubardemont flew into a rage and threatened the man with a whipping. But meanwhile, as the friars pointed out, wedge number seven at the knee could be replaced by a duplicate of wedge number eight at the ankle. One of the new wedges was inserted between the boards and this time it was Father Lactance who swung the mallet.

"*Dicas!*" he shouted after every blow. "*Dicas, dicas!*"

Not to be outdone, Father Tranquille took the mallet from his colleague, adjusted the tenth wedge and, in three mighty strokes, banged it home.

Grandier had fainted again, and it almost looked as if he might be dead before they could get him to the stake. Besides, there were no more wedges. Reluctantly—for this stubborn frustrater of all his best-laid plans deserved to be tortured forever—Laubardemont called a halt. This first phase of Grandier's martyrdom had lasted three quarters of an hour. The machine was taken apart, and the executioners lifted their victim onto a stool. He looked down at his horribly mangled legs, then at the Commissioner and his thirteen accomplices.

"Gentlemen," he said, "*attendite et videte si est dolor sicut dolor meus*. Behold, and see if there is any sorrow like unto my sorrow."

On Laubardemont's orders he was carried to another room and laid on a bench. It was a stifling day in August; but the parson was shivering with the cold of extreme surgical shock. La Grange covered him with a rug and filled a glass of wine for him to drink.

Meanwhile Lactance and Tranquille were trying to make the best of what had been a deplorably bad job. To all who questioned them they answered that indeed it was true—the magician had refused to confess, even under torture. And the reason was only too obvious. Grandier had called upon God to give him strength, and his God, who was Lucifer, had made him insensible to pain. They might have gone on all day, wedge after wedge; it would have availed them nothing.

To prove to himself that this was true, another of the exorcists, Father Archangel, resolved to make a little experiment. This experiment was described, a few days later, in a public discourse, which was recorded as follows by one of the auditors. "The said Father Archangel remarked that the devil had granted him (Grandier) insensibility inasmuch as, being stretched out on a bench, with his knees, which had been crushed by the Gehenna, covered with a green rug, this rug being raised by the said Father somewhat roughly, and the said Father even poking his legs and knees, he did not complain of the pain which the said Father might be causing him." From this it followed, first, that Grandier had felt no pain, second, that Satan had made him insensible, third, that (to quote the Capuchin's very words) "when he spoke favorably of God, he meant the devil, and when he said that he detested the devil, he meant that he detested God," and, fourthly and finally, that every precaution must be taken to make sure that, at the stake, he should feel the full effect of the flames.

When Father Archangel had gone, it was the turn, yet once more, of the Commissioner. For more than two hours Laubardemont sat beside his victim, employing all the arts of persuasion to extort the signature which would excuse his own illegal proceedings, would whitewash the Cardinal, would justify the future use of inquisitorial methods in every case where hysterical nuns could be induced by their confessors to accuse the enemies of the regime. That signature was indispensable; but try as he might—and M. de Gastynes, who was present at the interview, declared that he had "never heard anything so abominable" as those specious arguments, those cajoleries, those hypocritical sighs and sobs—the Commissioner was unable to get what he wanted. To everything he could say, Grandier replied that it was morally impossible for him to put his name to a statement which he knew, and God knew (and doubtless the Commissioner knew) to be absolutely false. In the end Laubardemont had to admit defeat. He called La Grange and told him to send for the executioners.

They came. Grandier was dressed in a shirt impregnated with sulphur; then a rope was tied round his neck and he was carried down to the courtyard, where a cart, drawn by six mules, was standing ready. He was hoisted up and set on a bench. The driver shouted to his beasts; and preceded by a company of archers and followed by Laubardemont and the thirteen tame magistrates, the cart rumbled slowly into the street. A halt was made, and the sentence was once more read aloud. Then the mules moved on. At the door of St. Peter's—the door through which, for so many years the parson had come and gone with his air of confident and majestic dignity—the procession came to a standstill. The two-pound taper was placed in Grandier's hand and he was lifted down from the cart to beg pardon, as the sentence had prescribed, for his crimes. But there were no knees to kneel on, and when they lowered him to the ground, he fell forward on his face. The executioners had to lift him up again. At this moment, Father Grillau, the Warden of the Cordeliers, issued from the church and, pushing past the archers of the guard, bent over the prisoner and embraced him.

Deeply moved, Grandier asked for his prayers and the prayers of all his community—the only one in Loudun which had steadily refused to co-operate with the parson's enemies.

Grillau promised to pray for the condemned man, urged him to put his trust in God and the Redeemer, then gave him a message from his mother. She was praying for him at the feet of Our Lady, and she sent her blessing.

Both men were weeping. A murmur of sympathy ran through the crowd. Laubardemont heard it and was furious. Would nothing ever go as he had planned it? By all the rules, the rabble should be trying to lynch this trafficker with the devil. Instead of which, they were lamenting his cruel fate. He hurried forward and peremptorily ordered the guards to send the Cordelier away. In the scuffle which followed, one of the attendant Capuchins took the opportunity to hit Grandier over his shaven head with a cudgel.

When order had been restored, the parson said what he had to say—but added, after asking pardon of God, the King and Justice, that, though a great sinner, he was completely innocent of the crime for which he was now to suffer.

While the executioners were carrying him back to the cart, a friar harangued the tourists and townspeople, assuring them that they would be committing a very grave sin if they ventured to pray for this unrepentant magician.

The procession moved on. At the door of the Ursuline convent the ceremony of asking pardon of God, King and Justice was repeated. But when the Clerk ordered him to ask pardon of the Prioress and all the good sisters, the prisoner answered that he had never done them any harm, and could only pray to God that He would forgive them. Then seeing Moussaut, the husband of Philippe Trincant and one of the most implacable of his enemies, he asked him to forget the past and added with a curious little touch of that courtly politeness for which he had been famous, *"je meurs votre serviteur*—I die your most obedient servant." Moussaut turned away his face and refused to answer.

Not all of Grandier's enemies were so un-Christian. René Bernier, one of the priests who had testified against him when he was accused of improper behavior, pushed his way through the crowd in order to ask the parson's forgiveness and to offer to say a Mass on his behalf. The parson took his hand and gratefully kissed it.

In the Place Sainte-Croix more than six thousand persons were jammed into a space which would have been uncomfortably narrow for half their number. Every window had been rented, and there were spectators even on the roofs and among the gargoyles of the church. A grandstand had been set up for the judges and Laubardemont's particular friends; but the rabble had occupied every seat and had to be dislodged by the guards at the point of the pike and halberd. It was only after a pitched battle that these very important personages could be seated.

Even the most important personage of all had the greatest difficulty in reaching the place appointed for him. It took the prisoner half an hour to cover the last hundred yards to the stake, and his guards were compelled to fight for every inch of the way.

Not far from the north wall of the church a stout post, fifteen feet high, had been driven into the ground. About its base were piled layers of faggots, logs and straw, and since the victim was no longer capable of standing on those shattered feet of his, a small iron seat had been fastened to the post a couple of feet above the firewood. For all the importance of the event, all its enormous notoriety, the expenses of the execution were remarkably modest. A certain Deliard was paid nineteen livres sixteen sols for "the wood used for the bonfire of Master Urbain Grandier, together with the post to which he was tied." For "an iron seat weighing twelve pounds, at the rate of three sols four deniers per pound, together with six nails wherewith to attach the said seat to Master Urbain Grandier's stake," Jacquet, the locksmith, received forty-two sols. For one day's hire of five horses, used by the archers kindly lent for the occasion by the Provost of Chinon, and for one day's hire of six mules, a cart and two men, the widow Morin was paid one hundred and eight sols. Four livres were spent on the prisoner's two shirts— the plain one in which he was tortured and the sulphured article in which he was burned. The two-pound candle used in the ceremony of the *amende honorable* cost forty sols, and wine for the executioners, thirteen. Add to these expenses the payment for work done by the doorkeeper of Sainte-Croix and a couple of assistants, and you had a grand total of twenty-nine livres, two sols and six deniers.

Grandier was taken down from the cart, lifted onto the iron seat and securely lashed to the post. His back was turned to the church, his face to the grandstand and the façade of a house in which he had once felt himself as much at home as in his own parsonage. It was the house where he had made all those jokes at the expense of Adam and Mannoury, where he had entertained the company with readings from Catherine Hammon's letters, where he had taught a young girl Latin and seduced her, where he had transformed his best friend into the most relentless of his enemies. Louis Trincant was sitting now at the window of his drawing room, and with him were Canon Mignon and Thibault. At the sight of the hairless clown who had once been Urbain Grandier, they laughed triumphantly. The parson looked up and met their eyes. Thibault waved his hand as though to an old friend, and M. Trincant, who was sipping white wine and water, raised his glass and drank to the father of his bastard grandchild.

Partly in shame—for he remembered those Latin lessons and his abandonment of the desperately weeping girl—and partly out of a fear lest the spectacle of their triumph might move him to bitterness and make him forget that God was even here, even now, Grandier dropped his eyes.

A hand touched him on the shoulder. It was La Grange, the captain of the guard, who had come to ask the parson's forgiveness for what he had been obliged to do. Then he made two promises: the prisoner would be allowed to make a speech and, before the fire was lighted, he would be strangled. Grandier thanked him, and La Grange turned away to give his orders to the executioner, who immediately prepared a noose.

Meanwhile the friars were busy with their exorcisms.

"*Ecce crucem Domini, fugite partes adversae, vicit leo de tribu Juda, radix David. Exorciso te, creatura ligni, in nomine Dei patris omnipotentis, et in nomine Jesus Christi filii ejus Domini nostri, et in virtute Spiritus sancti. . . ."**

They sprinkled the wood, the straw, the glowing coals of the brazier that stood ready beside the pyre; they sprinkled the earth, the air, the victim, the executioners, the spectators. This time, they swore, no devil should prevent the wretch from suffering to the extreme limit of his capacity for pain. Several times the parson tried to address the crowd; but no sooner had he begun than they threw holy water in his face or hit him on the mouth with an iron crucifix. When he flinched from the blow, the friars would shout triumphantly that the renegade was denying his Redeemer. And all the time Father Lactance kept calling on the prisoner to confess.

"*Dicas!*" he shouted.

The word caught the fancy of the onlookers and for the brief and horrible remainder of his life the Recollet was always known in Loudun as Father Dicas.

"*Dicas! Dicas!*"

For the thousandth time Grandier answered that he had nothing to confess.

"And now," he added, "give me the kiss of peace and let me die."

At first Lactance refused; but when the crowd protested against such an un-Christian malignity, he climbed onto the pile of faggots and kissed the parson's cheek.

"Judas!" cried a voice, and a score of others took up the refrain.

"Judas, Judas. . . ."

Lactance heard them and, in a passion of uncontrollable rage, jumped down from the pyre, seized a twist of straw and, lighting it in the brazier, waved the flame in the victim's face. Let him confess who he was—the devil's servant! Let him confess, let him renounce his master!

* Behold the cross of the Lord, let its enemies take flight; the lion of the tribe of Juda has conquered, the root of David. I exorcise thee, creature of wood, in the name of God the Father Almighty, and in the name of Jesus Christ his Son our Lord, and in the power of the Holy Ghost. . . ."

"Father," said Grandier with a calm and gentle dignity that contrasted strangely with the almost hysterical malice of his accusers, "I am about to meet the God who is my witness that I have spoken the truth."

"Confess," the friar fairly screamed. "Confess! . . . You have only a moment to live."

"Only a moment," the parson repeated slowly. "Only a moment —and then I go to that just and fearful judgment to which, Reverend Father, you too must soon be called."

Without waiting to hear anything more, Father Lactance threw his torch onto the straw of the pyre. Hardly visible in the bright afternoon sunshine, a little flame appeared and began to creep, growing larger as it advanced, toward the bundles of dry kindling. Following the Recollet's example, Father Archangel set fire to the straw on the opposite side of the pyre. A thin blue haze of smoke rose into the windless air. Then, with a cheerful crackling, like the noise that accompanies the drinking of mulled wine on a winter evening, by the hearth, one of the faggots caught fire.

The prisoner heard the sound and, turning his head, saw the gay dancing of flames.

"Is this what you promised me?" he called to La Grange in a tone of agonized protest.

And suddenly the divine presence was eclipsed. There was no God, no Christ, nothing but fear.

La Grange shouted indignantly at the friars and tried to extinguish the nearest flames. But there were too many of them to be stamped out; and here was Father Tranquille setting fire to the straw behind the parson's back, here was Father Lactance lighting another torch at the brazier.

"Strangle him," he ordered. And the crowd took up the cry. "Strangle, strangle!"

The executioner ran for his noose, only to discover that one of the Capuchins had surreptitiously knotted the rope so that it could not be used. By the time the knots were undone, it was too late. Between the executioner and the victim he had intended to save from this last agony there was a wall of flame, a billowing curtain of smoke. Meanwhile, with whisk and holy water pot, the friars were ridding the bonfire of its remaining devils.

"*Exorciso te, creatura ignis. . . .*"

The water hissed among the burning logs and was turned in an instant to steam. From the further side of the wall of flames came a sound of screaming. The exorcism, it was evident, had begun to take effect. The friars paused for a moment to give thanks; then, with faith renewed and energy redoubled, they set to work again.

"*Draco nequissime, serpens antique, immundissime spiritus. . . .*"

At this moment a large black fly appeared from nowhere, bumped into Father Lactance's face and dropped on the opened pages of his book of exorcisms. A fly—and as large as a walnut! And Beelzebub was the Lord of Flies!

"*Imperat tibi Martyrum sanguis,*" he shouted above the roaring of the fire, "*Imperat tibi continentia Confessorum. . . .*"

With a preternaturally loud buzz the insect took wing and disappeared into the smoke.

"*In nomine Agni, qui ambulavit super aspidem et basiliscum. . . .*"

All at once the screams were strangled by a paroxysm of coughing. The wretch was trying to cheat them by dying of suffocation! To frustrate this latest of Satan's wiles, Lactance hurled a whiskful of holy water into the smoke.

"*Exorciso te, creatura fumi. Effugiat atque discedat a te nequitia omnis ac versutia diabolicae fraudis. . . .*"

It worked! The coughing stopped. There was another cry, then silence. And suddenly, to the consternation of the Recollet and his Capuchin colleagues, the blackened thing at the center of the bonfire began to speak.

"*Deus meus,*" it said, "*miserere mei Deus.*" And then, in French, "Forgive them, forgive my enemies."

The coughing began again. A moment later the cords which bound him to the post gave way and the victim tumbled sideways among the blazing logs.

The fire burned on, the good Fathers continued to sprinkle and intone. Suddenly a flock of pigeons came swooping down from the church and started to wheel around the roaring column of flame and smoke. The crowd shouted, the archers waved their halberds at the birds, Lactance and Tranquille splashed them on the wing with holy water. In vain. The pigeons were not to be driven away. Round and round they flew, diving through the smoke, singeing their feathers in the flames. Both parties claimed a miracle. For the parson's enemies the birds, quite obviously, were a troop of devils, come to fetch away his soul. For his friends, they were emblems of the Holy Ghost and living proof of his innocence. It never seems to have occurred to anyone that they were just pigeons, obeying the laws of their own, their blessedly other-than-human nature.

When the fire had burned itself out, the executioner scattered four shovelfuls of ashes, one toward each of the cardinal points of the compass. Then the crowd surged forward. Burning their fingers, men and women rummaged in the hot flaky dust, hunting for teeth, for fragments of the skull and pelvis, for any cinder showing the black smear of burned flesh. A few, no doubt, were merely souvenir hunters; but most of them were in search of relics, for a charm to bring luck or compel reluctant love, for a talisman against headaches or constipation or the malice of enemies. And these charred odds and ends would be no less effective if the parson were guilty of the crimes imputed to him than if he were innocent. The power to work miracles lies, not in the source of a relic, but in its reputation, however acquired. Constant throughout history, a certain percentage of human beings can be restored to health or happiness by practically anything that has been well advertised—from Lourdes to witchcraft, from the Ganges to patent medicines and Mrs. Eddy, from the thaumaturgical arm of St. Francis Xavier to those "pigges bones," which Chaucer's Pardoner carried in a glass for all to see and worship. If Grandier were what the Capuchins had said he was, that was excellent: even in ashes, a sorcerer is richly charged with power. And his relics would be charged with no less power if the parson were guiltless; for in that case he would be a martyr, equal to the best of them. In a little while most of the ashes had disappeared. Horribly tired and thirsty, but happy in the thought that their pockets were bulging with relics, tourists and townsfolk drifted away in search of a drink and the chance to take off their shoes.

That evening, after only the briefest of rests and the lightest of refreshments, the good Fathers reassembled at the Ursuline convent. The Prioress was exorcised, duly went into convulsions and in response to Lactance's questioning, announced that the black fly was none other than Baruch, the parson's familiar. And why had Baruch hurled himself so rudely on the book of exorcisms? Sœur Jeanne bent herself backward until her head touched her heels, then did the splits and finally answered that he had been trying to throw the book into the fire. It was all so edifying that the friars decided to break off for the night and begin again next morning, in public.

On the following day the sisters were taken to Sainte-Croix. Many of the tourists were still in town, and the church was crowded to the doors. The Prioress was exorcised and, after the usual preliminaries, identified herself as Isacaaron, the only devil presently at home; for all the other tenants of her body had gone back to hell for the wild party which had been organized for the reception of Grandier's soul.

Judiciously questioned, Sœur Jeanne confirmed what the exorcists had been saying all along—namely, that when Grandier had said "God" he always meant "Satan," and that when he had renounced the devil, he had actually been renouncing Christ.

Lactance then wanted to know what kind of torments the parson was suffering down there, and was evidently rather disappointed when the Prioress told him that the worst of them was the privation of God.

No doubt, no doubt. But what were the *physical* tortures?

After a good deal of pressing Sœur Jeanne replied that Grandier "had a special torture for each of the sins he had committed, especially those of the flesh."

And what about the execution? Had the devil been able to prevent the wretch from suffering?

Alas, replied Isacaaron, Satan had been frustrated by the exorcisms. If the fire had not been blessed, the parson would have felt

223

nothing. But thanks to the labors of Lactance, Tranquille and Archangel he had suffered excruciatingly.

But not so excruciatingly, cried the exorcist, as he was suffering now! And with a kind of gloating horror, Father Lactance brought the conversation back to hell. In which of hell's many mansions was the magician lodged? How had Lucifer received him? What precisely was being done to him at this moment? Sister Jane's Isacaaron did his best to answer. Then, when his imagination began to flag, Sister Agnes was thrown into fits, and Beherit was invited to say his piece.

That evening, at the convent, the friars noticed that Father Lactance looked pale and seemed strangely preoccupied. Was he feeling ill?

Father Lactance shook his head. No, he was not ill. But the prisoner had asked to see Father Grillau, and they had denied him. Could it be that they had committed a sin by making it impossible for him to confess?

His colleagues did their best to reassure him, but without success. Next morning, after a sleepless night, Lactance was in a fever.

"God is punishing me," he kept repeating, "God is punishing me."

He was bled by Mannoury, was purged by M. Adam. The fever subsided for a little, then returned. And now he began to see things, to hear things. Grandier under torture, screaming. Grandier at the stake, asking God to forgive his enemies. And then devils, swarms of devils. They entered his body, they set him raving, they made him kick his legs and bite the pillows, they filled his mouth with the most horrible blasphemies.

On September 18th, exactly one month after Grandier's execution, Father Lactance knocked the crucifix out of the hand of the priest who had administered Extreme Unction, and died. Laubardemont paid for a handsome funeral, and Father Tranquille preached a sermon, in which he extolled the Recollet as a model of holiness and proclaimed that he had been murdered by Satan, who had thus revenged himself for all the affronts and humiliations inflicted on him by this most heroic of God's servants.

The next to go was Mannoury, the surgeon. One night, shortly after the death of Father Lactance, he was sent for to bleed a sick man, who lived near the Porte du Martrai. On the way home, his servant with a lantern walking ahead of him, he saw Urbain Grandier. Naked, as when he had been pricked for the devil's marks, the parson was standing in the Rue du Grand-Pavé, between the counterscarps of the castle and the Cordeliers' garden. Mannoury halted, and his servant saw him staring into the vacant blackness, heard him asking someone, who wasn't there, what he wanted. There was no answer. Then the surgeon began to tremble all over. A moment later, he fell to the ground, screaming for pardon. Within the week he, too, was dead.

After that it was the turn of Louis Chauvet, one of the upright judges who had refused to take part in the hellish tomfoolery of the trial. The Prioress and most of her nuns had accused him of being a magician, and M. Barré was able to confirm their testimony through the mouths of several demoniacs in his own parish, at Chinon. Fear of what might happen to him, if the Cardinal should choose to take these ravings seriously, preyed on Chauvet's mind. He sank into a melancholy, then into madness, then into a decline, which killed him before the winter was out.

Tranquille was of tougher fiber than the others. It was not until 1638 that he finally succumbed to the consequences of a too exclusive preoccupation with evil. By his hatred of Grandier he had helped to raise the devils; by his scandalous insistence on public exorcisms, he had done his best to keep them alive. Now the devils turned against him. God is not mocked; he was reaping what he had deliberately sown.

At first the obsessions were rare and of no great force. But little by little Dog's Tail and Leviathan gained the upper hand. During the last year of his life, Father Tranquille was behaving like the nuns whose hysteria he had so carefully fostered—rolling on the floor, cursing, yelling, sticking out his tongue, hissing, barking, neighing. Nor was this all. The "stinking Owl of Hell," as his Capuchin biographer picturesquely nicknames the devil, plagued him with hardly resistible temptations against chastity, against humility, against patience, faith and devotion. He called on the Virgin, on

St. Joseph, on St. Francis and St. Bonaventure. In vain. The possession went from bad to worse.

On Whitsunday, 1638, Tranquille preached his last sermon; for two or three days more he managed to say Mass; then he took to his bed with a sickness nonetheless mortal for being obviously psychosomatic. "He threw up ordures, which were judged to be diabolic Pacts. . . . Every time he took a little nourishment, the devils made him retch with a violence that would have killed the healthiest person." And meanwhile he suffered from headaches and pains in the heart, "of a kind of which there is no mention in Galen or Hippocrates." By the end of the week "he was vomiting filths and stinks so insupportable, that his attendants had to throw them out without delay, so fearfully was the room infected by them." On the Monday after Whitsun, Extreme Unction was administered. The devils left the dying man and forthwith entered the body of another friar, who was kneeling by the bed. The new demoniac became so frantic, that he had to be held by half a dozen of his colleagues, who had the greatest difficulty in preventing him from kicking the hardly lifeless corpse.

On the day of the funeral, Father Tranquille lay in state. "No sooner was the service over than the people flung themselves upon him. Some applied their rosaries to his body, others cut from his habit little pieces which they preserved as relics. So great was the press that the coffin was smashed, and the body disturbed in countless ways, each man tugging it toward himself so as to get his snippet. And assuredly the good Father would have been left stark naked, had it not been for several persons of honor, who formed a guard to protect him from the indiscreet devotion of the people, who, after cutting up the habit, would probably have mangled the corpse itself."

The shreds of Father Tranquille's habit, the ashes of the man he had tortured and burned alive. . . . Everything was equivocal. The magician had died a martyr; his fiendish executioner was now a saint—but a saint who was possessed by Beelzebub. Only one thing was certain: a fetish is a fetish. So lend me your knife; after you with the shears!

CHAPTER NINE

GRANDIER was gone, but Eazaz remained, Coal of Impurity remained, Zabulon went marching along. To many, the fact seemed unaccountable. But where the cause persists, the effects will always follow. It was Canon Mignon and the exorcists who had originally crystallized the nuns' hysteria into the forms of devils, and it was Canon Mignon and the exorcists who now kept the possession alive. Twice every day, Sundays excepted, the demoniacs were put through their tricks. As might have been expected, they were no better—they were even a little worse—than they had been while the magician was alive.

Toward the end of September Laubardemont informed the Cardinal that he had appealed to the Society of Jesus. The Jesuits had a reputation for learning and ability. From these masters of all the sciences the public would surely "accept, with less contradiction, the evidence for the truth of this possession."

Many Jesuits, including Vitelleschi, the General of the Order, were for politely refusing to have anything to do with the possession. But it was too late to raise objections. Laubardemont's invitation was speedily followed by a royal command. Through the King, His Eminence had spoken.

On the fifteenth of December, 1634, four Jesuit Fathers rode into Loudun. Among them was Jean-Joseph Surin. Father Bohyre, the Provincial of Aquitaine, had selected him for the task of exorcism, and had then, on the advice of his council, countermanded the order. Too late. Surin had already left Marennes. The original appointment was permitted to stand.

Surin was now thirty-four, *nel mezzo del cammin*, his character formed, the pattern of his thinking already fixed. His fellow Jesuits thought highly of his abilities, recognized his zeal and respected the austerity of his life, the fervor of his pursuit of Christian perfection. But their admiration was tempered by certain misgivings. Father Surin had all the makings of a man of heroic virtue; but there was something about him which caused the more prudent of his colleagues and superiors to shake their heads. They detected in him a certain extravagance, a too-muchness in act and word. He liked to say that "the man who does not have excessive ideas in regard to God will never come near Him." And of course it was true—provided always that the excessive ideas were of the right kind. Some of the young Father's excessive ideas, though orthodox enough, seemed to deviate from the highroad of discretion. For example, he maintained that we ought to be ready to die for the people with whom we live, "while at the same time preserving ourselves from them as though they were our enemies"—a proposition hardly calculated to improve the quality of communal living in the Society's houses and colleges. As well as antisocial, his excessive ideas made him overrighteous to the point of scrupulosity. "We ought," he said, "to bewail our vanities as sacrileges, to punish with the utmost severity our ignorances and inadvertences." And to this inhuman rigorism in the name of perfection he added what seemed to many of his elders and contemporaries an indiscreet and even dangerous interest in those "extraordinary graces," which are sometimes vouchsafed to the holy, but which are entirely unnecessary to salvation or to sanctification. "From his earliest childhood," his friend, Father Anginot was to write many years later, "he has felt powerfully drawn toward such things, and has esteemed them too highly. It has been necessary to humor him in this and to allow him to travel by a road which was not the common and ordinary way."

At the fishing port of Marennes, where he had spent most of the four years following the close of his "second novitiate" at Rouen, Surin acted as director to two remarkable women—Mme.

du Verger, the wife of a prosperous and pious merchant, and Madeleine Boinet, the converted daughter of a Protestant tinker. Both were active contemplatives and both (Mme. du Verger especially) had been favored by "extraordinary graces." Surin's interest in their visions and ecstasies was so great that he copied out long extracts from Mme. du Verger's diary and wrote circumstantial accounts of both women for circulation, in manuscript, among his friends. There was, of course, nothing wrong in all this. But why pay so much attention to a subject so essentially ambiguous, so full of snares and perils? Ordinary graces were the only ones that would bring a soul to heaven; so why bother with the extraordinary—all the more so as one never knew whether such things were from God, from imagination, from deliberate fraud or from the devil? If Father Surin wanted to go to perfection, let him go by that royal road which was good enough for the rank and file of the Society—the road of obedience and active zeal, the road of vocal prayer and discursive meditation.

What made matters worse, so far as his critics were concerned, was the fact that Surin was a sick man, a victim of neurosis or, as it was then called, "melancholy." For at least two years before his coming to Loudun, he had suffered from incapacitating psychosomatic disturbances. The slightest physical effort brought on intense muscular pains. When he tried to read, he was soon forced by excruciating headaches to give up. His mind was darkened and confused, and he lived in the midst of "agonies and pressures so extreme that he did not know what would become of him." Could it be that the singularities of his conduct and his teaching were all the products of a sick mind in an unhealthy body?

Surin records that many of his fellow Jesuits were not convinced, to the very end, that the nuns were genuinely possessed. Even before coming to Loudun, he himself was troubled by no such doubts. He was persuaded that the world is at all times visibly and miraculously interpenetrated by the supernatural. And this conviction was the source, in its turn, of a wholesale credulity. People had merely to say that they had had dealings with saints, or angels, or devils; Surin believed them without question or criticism. Most con-

spicuously he lacked "the discernment of spirits." Indeed, he was
wanting even in judgment and plain common sense. Surin was
that not uncommon paradox—a man of great abilities who is, at
the same time, a bit of a fool. He could never have echoed the
opening words of Monsieur Teste: *La bêtise n'est pas mon fort.*
Along with intelligence and sanctity, silliness *was* his strong point.

Surin's first sight of the demoniacs was at one of the public
exorcisms, at which Tranquille, Mignon and the Carmelites were
officiating. He had come to Loudun, convinced of the reality of
the possession; this spectacle raised his conviction to a higher
power of certainty. The devils, he knew, were absolutely genuine,
"and God gave him so much compassion for the state of the
possessed that he could not restrain his tears." He was wasting his
sympathy—or at least misplacing it. "The devil," writes Sœur
Jeanne, "often beguiled me by a certain pleasure, which I took
in my agitations and the other extraordinary things he did to my
body. I took an extreme delight in hearing these things spoken
about, and was happy that I gave the impression of being more
gravely tormented than the others." Unduly prolonged, every
pleasure turns into its opposite; it was only when the exorcists
went too far that the good sisters ceased to enjoy their possession.
Taken in moderation, the public exorcisms, like any other kind
of orgy, were intrinsically agreeable. This was a fact, which persons
accustomed to self-examination in the light of a strict morality,
could hardly fail to find disturbing. Despite the fact that souls
were held to be guiltless of the sinful acts performed while in the
paroxysm of possession, Sœur Jeanne suffered from a chronic
remorse of conscience. "And no wonder; for I perceived very
clearly that in most instances I was the prime cause of my disorders, and that the devil only acted upon the cues I myself had
given him." She knew that when she behaved outrageously, it was
not because she had freely willed the outrage. Nevertheless, "I
feel certain, to my great confusion, that I made it possible for the
devil to do such things, and that he would not have had the power
to do them if I had not allied myself with him. . . . When I made
a strong resistance, all these furies would disappear as suddenly as

they had come; but, alas, it happened only too frequently that I did not make a great effort to resist them." Perceiving that they were guilty, not of what they did when they were out of their wits, but of what they had failed to do before their hysteria got the better of them, the nuns suffered excruciatingly from a sense of guilt. From this conviction of sin the debauches of possession and exorcism came as so many happy holidays. Tears were in order, not for these frenzies and indecencies, but for the lucid intervals between them.

To Surin, long before his arrival in Loudun, had been assigned the honor of exorcising the Mother Superior. When Laubardemont told her that he had called in the Jesuits and that she was to have as her director the ablest and holiest young Father in the Province of Aquitaine, Sœur Jeanne had been greatly alarmed. Jesuits were not like these slow-witted Capuchins and Carmelites, whom it had always been so easy to deceive. They were clever, they were well educated; and this Father Surin was holy into the bargain, a man of prayer, a great contemplative. He would see through her at once, would know when she was really possessed and when she was only acting, or at least collaborating with her devils. She pleaded with Laubardemont to be left to her old exorcists—to dear Canon Mignon, to the good Father Tranquille and the worthy Carmelites. But Laubardemont and his master had made up their minds. They needed acceptable evidence for the possession, and only the Jesuits could provide it. With a bad grace, Sœur Jeanne submitted. During the weeks which preceded Surin's arrival, she did her best to find out everything that could be discovered about her new exorcist. She wrote letters to friends in other convents, asking for information; she pumped the local Jesuits. Her purpose in all this was to "study the humor of the man to whom I had been assigned," and, having found out all she could, "to behave toward him with as little openness as possible, without giving him any information about the state of my soul. To this resolve I was only too faithful." When the new exorcist arrived, she knew enough about his life at Marennes to be able to make sarcastic references to *ta Boinette* (her devils' derisive name for Madeleine Boinet). Surin held up his hands in amazement. It was a miracle—infernal no doubt, but manifestly genuine.

Sœur Jeanne had made up her mind to keep her secrets to herself, and she acted upon this resolution by feeling and expressing an intense aversion for her new exorcist and by going into fits (in her own words, "being troubled inwardly and outwardly by the demons") whenever Surin tried to question her about the condition of her soul. When he approached, she ran away and, if compelled to listen to him, she howled and stuck out her tongue. In all this, Sœur Jeanne remarks, "she greatly exercised his virtue. But he had the charity to attribute her disposition to the devil."

All the nuns suffered from remorse and a conviction, in spite of their devils, of having gravely sinned; but the Prioress had a more pressing and a more conspicuous reason than any of her sisters for feeling guilty. Shortly after the execution of Grandier, Isacaaron, who was a devil of concupiscence "took advantage of my slackness to give me most horrible temptations against chastity. He performed an operation upon my body, the strangest and most furious that could be imagined; thereafter he persuaded me that I was great with child, in such sort that I firmly believed the fact and exhibited all the signs." She confided in her sisters, and soon a score of devils had announced the pregnancy. The exorcists reported the matter to the Commissioner and the Commissioner reported to His Eminence. Menstruation, he wrote, had ceased for the past three months; there were constant vomitings, with a derangement of the stomach, secretion of milk and a marked enlargement of the belly. As the weeks passed, the Prioress became more and more painfully agitated. If she bore a child, she herself and, with her, the community of which she was the head and her whole Order, would be disgraced. She was filled with a despair, from which the only relief was a visit from Isacaaron. These visits were of almost nightly occurrence. In the darkness of her cell she would hear noises and feel the bed trembling. Hands drew back the sheet; voices whispered flatteries and indecencies in her ear. Sometimes there was a strange light in the room, and she would see the form of a goat, a lion, a snake, a man. Sometimes she fell into a catalepsy and while she lay there, unable to move, it was as though small animals were crawling under the bedclothes, tickling her body with their paws and probing snouts. Then the wheedling voice would ask her, yet once more, for just a little love, for just the tiniest favor. And when she answered that "her honor was in the hands of God and that He would dispose of it according to his will," she was tumbled out of bed and beaten so violently that her face was quite disfigured and her body covered with bruises. "It happened very often that he treated me in this way, but God gave me more courage than I would have dared to hope for. And yet I was so wicked that I took pride in these trifling combats, thinking that I must be very pleasing to God and that therefore had no reason for dreading, as I had done, the reproaches of my conscience. Nevertheless, I found it impossible to stifle my remorse, or to prevent myself from believing that I was not what God wished me to be."

Isacaaron was the chief culprit, and it was against Isacaaron that Surin directed all his energies, all the thunders of the ritual. *Audi ergo et time, Satana, malorum radix, fomes vitiorum.* . . . Nothing availed. "Since I would not reveal my temptations, they increased more and more." And as Isacaaron became stronger, so did Sœur Jeanne's despair, so did her anxieties on account of the steadily advancing pregnancy. Shortly before Christmas she found means to procure certain drugs—mugwort, no doubt, and aristolochium and colocynth, the three simples to which Galenic science and the desperate optimism of girls in trouble attributed abortifacient powers. But what if the child should die, unbaptized? Its soul would be lost eternally. She threw the drugs away.

Another plan now suggested itself. She would go to the kitchen, borrow the cook's largest knife, cut herself open, extract the baby, baptize it and then either recover, or die herself. On New Year's Day, 1635, she made a general confession, "without, however, revealing my plans to the confessor." The following day, armed with her knife and carrying a basin of water for the baptism, she shut herself up in a little room on the top floor of the convent. There was a crucifix in the room. Sœur Jeanne knelt before it, and prayed God to "forgive her death and that of the little creature, in case I should murder myself and it, for I was resolved to smother it as soon as it was baptized." While she was undressing, she was overtaken by *de petittes appréhensions d'estre damnée*; but these little apprehensions were not strong enough to divert her from her evil design. After taking off her habit, she cut a large hole in her chemise with a pair of scissors, picked up the knife and began to thrust it between the two ribs nearest to the stomach, "with a strong resolution to proceed to the bitter end." But though they often attempt suicide, hysterics very rarely succeed. "Behold the merciful stroke of Providence which prevented me from doing what I had intended! I was suddenly thrown down with inexpressible violence. The knife was snatched out of my hand and placed before me at the foot of the crucifix." A voice cried, "Desist!" Sœur Jeanne raised her eyes to the crucifix. The Christ detached one of his arms from the cross and held out his hand to her. Divine words were spoken, after which there was a muttering and howling of devils. The Prioress resolved, there and then, to change her way of life and be wholly converted. Meanwhile, however, the pregnancy continued and Isacaaron had by no means given up hope. One night he offered, for a consideration, to bring her a magic plaster which would, if applied to the stomach, put an end to her pregnancy. The Prioress was sorely tempted to accept his terms, but, on second thoughts decided to say no. The exasperated devil gave her a sound beating. Another time Isacaaron wept and complained so mournfully that Sœur Jeanne was touched to the heart and "felt a desire for the same thing to present itself again." It did. There seemed to be no reason why this sort of thing should not go on indefinitely.

Greatly perplexed, Laubardemont sent to Le Mans for the celebrated Dr. du Chêne. He came, made a thorough examination of the Prioress and pronounced her pregnancy to be genuine. Laubardemont's perplexity gave place to alarm. How would the Protestants take the news? Fortunately for everyone concerned, Isacaaron made his appearance at a public exorcism and flatly contradicted the doctor. All the telltale symptoms, from morning sickness to the flow of milk, had been contrived by demons. "He was then constrained to make me throw up all the accumulations of blood, which he had amassed in my body. This happened in the presence of a bishop, several doctors and many other persons." All the signs of pregnancy disappeared forthwith and never returned.

The spectators gave thanks to God; and so, with her lips, did the Prioress. But in the privacy of her mind she had her doubts. "The demons," she records, "did their best to persuade me that what had happened when Our Lord prevented me from cutting myself open, in order to be freed from my so-called pregnancy, was not from God; and therefore that I ought to treat the whole thing as mere illusion, keep quiet about it and not trouble to mention it in confession." Later on these doubts were laid to rest and she was able to convince herself that there had been a miracle.

For Surin the miracle was never in question. So far as he was concerned, everything that happened at Loudun was supernatural. His faith was gluttonous and indiscriminate. He believed in the possession. He believed in Grandier's guilt. He believed that other magicians were at work upon the nuns. He believed that the devil, duly constrained, is bound to tell the truth. He believed that public exorcisms were for the good of the Catholic religion and that innumerable libertines and Huguenots would be converted by hearing the devils testify to the reality of transubstantiation. He believed, finally, in Sister Jane and the products of her imagination. Credulity is a grave intellectual sin, which only the most invincible ignorance can justify. In Surin's case the ignorance was vincible and even voluntary. We have seen that, in spite of the prevailing intellectual climate, many of his Jesuit colleagues displayed none of his indecent eagerness to believe. Doubting the possession, they were free to refuse their assent to all the absurd and hideous nonsense which the new exorcist, with his morbid interest in extraordinary graces and disgraces, had accepted without so much as an attempt at criticism. Silliness, as we have seen, was one of Surin's strong points. But so was holiness, so was heroic zeal. His goal was Christian perfection—that dying to self, which makes it possible for a soul to receive the grace of union with God. And this goal he proposed not only for himself, but for all who could be persuaded to travel with him along the path of purification and docility to the Holy Spirit. Others had listened to him—so why not the Prioress? The idea came to him—and he felt it to be an inspiration—while he was still at Marennes. He would supplement exorcism with the kind of training in the life of the spirit, which he himself had received from Mother Isabel and Father Lallemant. He would deliver the demoniac's soul by raising it into the Light.

A day or two after his arrival at Loudun he broached the subject to Sœur Jeanne, and was answered by a peal of laughter from Isacaaron, a snarl, from Leviathan, of angry contempt. This woman, they reminded him, was their property, a common lodging house for devils; and he talked to her of spiritual exercises, he urged her to prepare her soul for union with God! Why, it was more than two years since she had even attempted to practice mental prayer. Contemplation, indeed! Christian perfection! The laughter became uproarious.

But Surin was not to be deterred. Day after day, in spite of the blasphemies and the convulsions, he returned to the charge. He had set the Hound of Heaven on her tracks, and he meant to follow his quarry to the death—the death which is eternal Life. The Prioress tried to escape; but he dogged her footsteps, he haunted her with his prayers and homilies. He spoke to her of the spiritual life, he begged God to give her the strength to undertake its arduous preliminaries, he described the beatitude of union. Sœur Jeanne interrupted him with peals of laughter, jokes about his precious Boinette, enormous belches, snatches of song, imitations of pigs at feeding time. But the voice murmured on, indefatigably.

One day, after a peculiarly horrible display of diabolic beastliness, Surin prayed that he might be permitted to suffer on behalf of the Prioress and in her stead. He wanted to feel all that the devils had caused Sœur Jeanne to feel; he was ready himself to be possessed, "provided that it should please the divine Goodness to cure her and lead her into the practice of virtue." He further asked that he might be allowed to undergo the ultimate humiliation of being regarded as a lunatic. Such prayers, the moralists and theologians assure us, ought never to be offered.* Unhappily, prudence was not one of Surin's virtues. The unwise, the utterly illegitimate petition was uttered. But prayers, if earnest, have a way of getting themselves answered—sometimes, no doubt, by a direct divine intervention; but more often, we may suspect, because the nature of ideas is such that they tend to become objectified, to take a form, material or psychological, in fact or in symbol, in the waking world or in dream. Surin had prayed that he might suffer as Sœur Jeanne had suffered. On January 19th he began to be obsessed.

Perhaps it would have happened even if he had never prayed. The devils had already killed Father Lactance, and Father Tranquille was soon to go the same way. Indeed, according to Surin, there was not one of the exorcists who was not in some degree beset by the demons they had helped to evoke and were doing their best to keep alive. No man can concentrate his attention upon evil, or even upon the idea of evil, and remain unaffected. To be more *against* the devil than *for* God is exceedingly dangerous. Every crusader is apt to go mad. He is haunted by the wickedness which he attributes to his enemies; it becomes in some sort a part of him.

Possession is more often secular than supernatural. Men are possessed by their thoughts of a hated person, a hated class, race or nation. At the present time the destinies of the world are in the hands of self-made demoniacs—of men who are possessed by, and who manifest, the evil they have chosen to see in others. They do not believe in devils; but they have tried their hardest to be possessed—have tried and been triumphantly successful. And since they believe even less in God than in the devil, it seems very

* "These extraordinary sufferings, such as possession and obsession, are, like revelations, subject to ILLUSION; it is clear that we must never desire them; we must merely accept them, in spite of ourselves, as it were. If we desire to suffer, we have means of doing so by mortifying our pride and sensuality. In this way we avoid plunging into hazards, which we are powerless to control, and of which we do not know the issue. But our imagination delights in the marvelous; it requires those romantic virtues that take the public eye. . . .

"And further; trials such as possession and obsession are a serious embarrassment, not only to the person involved, but to directors and the whole community where he or she resides. Charity forbids us to desire this kind of suffering." —A. Poulain, S.J., *The Graces of Interior Prayer*. English edition, page 436.

unlikely that they will ever be able to cure themselves of their possession. Concentrating his attention upon the idea of a supernatural and metaphysical evil, Surin drove himself to a pitch of madness uncommon among secular demoniacs. But his idea of good was also supernatural and metaphysical, and in the end it saved him.

Early in May, Surin wrote to his friend and fellow Jesuit, Father d'Attichy, giving him a full account of what had happened to him. "Since last writing, I have fallen into a state far removed from anything I could have foreseen, but thoroughly consonant with the leadings of God's Providence in regard to my soul. . . . I am engaged upon a struggle with four of hell's most malignant devils. . . . The least important battlefield is that of exorcism; for my enemies have made themselves known in secret, night and day, in a thousand different ways. . . . For the last three and a half months I have never been without a devil on duty. Things have come to such a pass that (for my sins, as I think) God has permitted . . . the devils to pass out of the possessed person's body and, entering into mine, to assault me, to throw me down, to torment me so that all can see, possessing me for several hours at a stretch like a demoniac.*

"I find it almost impossible to explain what happens to me during this time, how this alien spirit is united to mine, without depriving me of consciousness or of inner freedom, and yet constituting a second 'me,' as though I had two souls, of which one is dispossessed of my body and the use of its organs, and keeps its quarters, watching the other, the intruder, doing whatever it likes. These two spirits do battle within the limits of a field, which is the body. The very soul is as though divided, and in one of its parts is the subject of diabolical impressions and, in the other, of such feelings as are proper to it or are inspired by God. At one and the same time I feel a great peace, as being under God's good pleasure, and on the other hand (without knowing how) an overpowering rage and loathing of God, expressing itself in frantic struggles (astonishing to

* These outward manifestations of diabolic infestation did not appear until Good Friday, April 6th. From January 19th until that date, the symptoms of obsession had been purely psychological.

those who watch them) to separate myself from Him. At one and the same time I experience a great joy and delight and, on the other hand, a misery that finds vent in wailings and lamentations, like those of the damned. I feel the state of damnation and apprehend it. I feel as if I had been pierced by the pricks of despair in that alien soul which seems to be mine; and meanwhile the other soul lives in complete confidence, makes light of all such feelings, and curses the being who is their cause. I even feel that the cries uttered by my mouth come from both souls at once; and I find it hard to determine whether they are the product of joy or frenzy. The shudderings which come upon me, when the Blessed Sacrament is applied to any part of my body, are caused simultaneously (so it seems to me) by the horror of its proximity, which I find unbearable, and by a heartfelt reverence. . . .

"When, under the impulsion of one of these two souls, I try to make the sign of the cross on my mouth, the other soul turns my hand aside, or takes the finger between the teeth and savagely bites it. I find that mental prayer is never easier or more tranquil than in the midst of these agitations, while the body is rolling on the ground and the ministers of the Church are speaking to me as though to a devil, loading me with maledictions. I cannot describe to you the joy I feel in thus finding myself turned into a devil, not by rebellion against God, but by a calamity which plainly symbolizes the state to which sin has reduced me. . . .

"When the other demoniacs see me in this state, it is a joy to see how they exult, to hear how the devils make sport of! 'Physician, heal thyself! Now's the time to get up in the pulpit! A pretty sight to see *that* thing preaching!' . . . What a favor this is—to know by experience the state from which Jesus Christ has drawn me, to realize the greatness of his redemption, not by hearsay, but by the actual feeling of the state from which we have been redeemed! . . .

"This is where I now stand, this is how I am almost every day. I have become a subject of dispute. Is there true possession? Is it possible for ministers of the Church to fall into such troubles? Some say that all this is God's chastisement upon me, a punishment for some illusion; others say something else. As for me, I hold my peace and have no wish to change my fate, being firmly convinced that nothing is better than to be reduced to the utmost extremity. . . ."

(In his later writings Surin developed this theme more fully. There are, he insisted, many cases in which God makes use of possession as a part of the purgative process which must precede illumination. "It is one of God's more ordinary leadings in the ways of grace to permit the devil to possess or obsess souls which He wishes to raise to a high degree of holiness." Devils cannot possess the will, and cannot force their victims into sin. Diabolic inspirations of blasphemy, impurity and hatred of God leave the soul unstained. Indeed, they actually do good, inasmuch as they cause the soul to feel as much humiliation as it would do, if such horrors were committed voluntarily. These humiliations and the agonies and apprehensions, with which the demons fill the mind, are "the crucible which burns away, down to the quick of the heart, down to the very marrow of the bones, all self-love." And meanwhile, God Himself is at work on the suffering soul, and His operations are "so strong, so insinuating and ravishing, that one can say of this soul that it is one of the loveliest works of His mercy.")

Surin concluded his letter to Father d'Attichy with a plea for secrecy and discretion. "Except for my confessor and my superiors, you are the only person to whom I have confided these things." The confidence was sadly misplaced. Father d'Attichy showed the letter to all and sundry. Numerous copies of it were made and circulated, and within a few months it had got into print, as a broadsheet. Along with the condemned murderers and the six-legged calves, Surin took his place as a news item for the amusement of the groundlings.

From now on, Leviathan and Isacaaron were never far away. But between their assaults on his body, and actually during their obsession of his soul, Surin was able to proceed with his mission—the sanctification of Sœur Jeanne. When she ran away he followed. Cornered, she turned and raged at him. He paid no attention. Kneeling at her feet, he prayed for her; sitting beside her, he whispered the spiritual doctrine of Father Lallemant into her unwilling ears. "Interior perfection, docility to the Holy Spirit, purification of the heart, conversion of the will to God. . . ." Her devils writhed and gibbered; but he went on—went on even though, within his own mind, he could hear the sneering of Leviathan, the obscene promptings of Isacaaron, the demon of impurity.

Surin had more than the devils to contend with. Even in her hours of sanity—above all, perhaps, in her hours of sanity—the Prioress still disliked him. She disliked him because she feared him, because she was afraid of being exposed by his perspicacity as what, in her lucid intervals, she knew herself to be—half actress, half unrepentant sinner, wholly hysterical. He begged her to be frank with him. The answer was either a howling of fiends, or a declaration by the nun that there was nothing to confide.

The relations between the energumen and her exorcist were complicated by the fact that, during Easter week, Sœur Jeanne was suddenly overcome by "very evil desires and a sentiment of most lawless affection" for the man she so much feared and detested. She could not bring herself to confess her secret, and it was Surin himself who, after three hours of prayer before the Blessed Sacrament, first referred to these "infamous temptations." "If anyone," writes Sœur Jeanne, "was ever dumbfounded, it was I on this occasion." The hour was late, and he left her to ruminate her astonishment. In the end, she decided, yet once more, to change not merely her behavior toward Surin, but her whole way of life. It was a resolution of the surface will. Down below, in the subconscious, the demons had other views. She tried to read; her mind became a blank. She tried to think of God, to hold her soul in His presence; at once she developed a splitting headache, together with "strange obfuscations and weaknesses." For all these symptoms Surin had one sovereign remedy: mental prayer. She agreed to try it. The devils redoubled their fury. At the first mention of interior perfection, they threw her body into convulsions. Surin made her lie on a table and bound her securely with ropes, so that she could not move. Then he kneeled beside her and, whispering in her ear, put into words a model meditation. "I took as my subject the conversion of the heart to God and its desire to consecrate itself completely to Him. I made three separate points, which I explained in an affective manner, making all the acts on behalf of the Mother." Day after day this ceremony was repeated. Tied down, as though she were to undergo a surgical operation, the Prioress was at God's mercy. She struggled, she shouted; but through all the noise she could still hear the voice of her implacable well-wisher. Sometimes Leviathan would turn his attention to the exorcist, and suddenly Father Surin would find himself unable to speak. From the Prioress came whoops of fiendish laughter. Then the current was turned on again; the prayers, the whispered teaching continued from the point where they had been interrupted.

When the devils became too violent, Surin would reach for a silver box containing a consecrated wafer and apply it to the Prioress's heart or forehead. After the first agonized convulsion, "she was moved to great devotion, all the more so as I whispered in her ear all that it pleased God to inspire me with. She became very attentive to what I said, and was plunged in a profound recollectedness. The effect upon her heart was so great . . . that the tears streamed from her eyes."

It was a conversion—but a conversion in the context of hysteria, a conversion on the stage of an imaginary theater. Eight years before, as a young nun trying to curry favor with her Superior, Sœur Jeanne had briefly flaunted the ambition to become a second St. Teresa. Except for the old lady, nobody had been impressed. Then she was appointed Prioress, she had the run of the parlor; mysticism began to seem less interesting. After that, almost suddenly, had come her obsession with the erotic dream to which she gave the name of Grandier. Her neurosis deepened, Canon Mignon talked of devils, practiced exorcisms, lent her his own copy of Michaelis's book on the Gauffridi case. She read it and forthwith saw herself as the queen of the demoniacs. Her ambition at this time was to outdo them all in everything—in blasphemy, in grunting, in filthy language, in acrobatics. She knew, of course, that "all the disorders of her soul were founded on her own character" and that "she ought to blame herself for these disorders, without invoking extraneous causes." Under the influence of Michaelis and Mignon, these native defects had been crystallized into seven devils.

And now the devils had their own autonomous life and were her masters. To get rid of them, she would have to get rid of her bad habits and her ugly tendencies. And to do that, as her new director kept telling her, she would have to pray, to expose herself to the divine Light. Surin's ardor was infectious; she was touched by the man's sincerity, was aware, behind the symptoms of his obsession, that he knew, by profound experience, what he was talking about. After listening to him, she longed to go to God; but she longed to go in the most spectacular way possible, before a large and admiring audience. She had been the queen of the demoniacs; now she desired to be a saint—or, rather, she desired to be known as a saint, to be canonized here and now, to work miracles, to be invoked in prayer. . . .

She threw herself into the new role with all her usual energy. From thirty minutes a day, the quota of mental prayer was raised to three or four hours, and to make herself fit for illumination she undertook a course of the harshest physical austerities. She exchanged her feather bed for uncushioned boards; she made decoctions of wormwood to be poured, in lieu of sauce, over her food; she wore a hair shirt and a belt spiked with nails; she beat herself with a whip at least three times a day, and sometimes, so she assures us, for as much as seven hours in a single twenty-four hour period. Surin, who was a great believer in the discipline, encouraged her to persevere. He had noticed that devils who merely laughed at the rites of the Church were often put to flight in a few minutes by a good whipping. And the whip was as good for natural melancholy as for supernatural possession. St. Teresa had made the same discovery. "I say it again (for I have seen and have had much to do with many persons troubled with this disease of melancholy) that there is no other remedy, but to conquer them by every means in our power. . . . If words be not enough, have recourse to penances, and let them be heavy, if light penances will not do. It seems unjust," the saint adds, "to punish the sick sister, who cannot help herself, as though she were well." But, first of all, let it be remembered that these neurotics do enormous harm to the souls of others. Moreover, "I really believe that the mischief comes very often from a spirit undisciplined, wanting in humility and badly trained. . . . Under the pretense of this temper (of melancholy) Satan seeks to gain many souls. It is more common in our day than it used to be; the reason is that all self-will and license are now called melancholy." Among persons who took for granted the absolute freedom of the will and the total depravity of nature, this short way with neurotics was apparently very effective. Would it work today? In some cases, perhaps. For the rest, "talking it out" is likely, in the present intellectual climate, to have better results than self-inflicted shock treatment.

What with the exorcisms and the coming and going of the tourists, the convent chapel was becoming too noisy for the whispered colloquies between Sœur Jeanne and her director. In the early summer of 1635 they began to meet more privately in an attic under the tiles. A makeshift grille was set up. Through the bars Surin gave his instructions or expounded mystical theology. And through the bars, the Prioress told him of her temptations, her combats with the demons, her experiences (already marvelous) in the course of mental prayer. Then in silence they would meditate together, and the attic became, in Surin's words, "a house of angels and a paradise of delights," in which both were favored with extraordinary graces. One day, while meditating on the contempt to which Jesus had been exposed during his Passion, Sœur Jeanne went into an ecstasy. When it was over, she reported, through the grating, "that she had come so near to God that she had received, as it were, a kiss from his mouth."

And meanwhile what did the other exorcists think about all this? What were the opinions of the good folk of Loudun? Surin tells us that he "heard people murmuring: What can this Jesuit be doing every day with a possessed nun? I answered inwardly: You do not know the importance of the affair I am engaged on. I seemed to see heaven and hell all on fire for this soul, the one in love, the other in fury, each of them straining to carry her off." But what he saw was not seen by anyone else. All that the others knew was that, instead of subjecting his penitent to the full rigor of the exorcisms, Surin was spending hours in private conversation, trying to teach her (in spite of her devils) to lead the life of Christian perfection. To his colleagues, the attempt seemed merely foolish, all the more so as Surin was himself obsessed and in frequent need of exorcism on his own account. (In May, when Gaston d'Orléans, the King's brother, came to see the devils, he had been publicly possessed by Isacaaron, who passed out of Sœur Jeanne's body into Surin's. While the demoniac sat calm, sane and ironically smiling, her exorcist rolled on the floor. The Prince, of course, was delighted; but for Jean-Joseph it had been another in the long series of humiliations to which an inscrutable Providence was subjecting him.) Nobody questioned the purity of Surin's intentions or actions; but all regarded his conduct as indiscreet, and all deplored the gossip to which, inevitably, it gave rise. By the end of the summer the Provincial was being advised to recall him to Bordeaux.

Meanwhile the Prioress had had her full share of trials. In her new part, as the great contemplative saint, she was giving a performance which ought to have brought the house down. Instead of that, "Our Lord permitted that I should have much to suffer in my conversations with my sisters, through the workings of the devils, who tormented them; for most of them conceived a great aversion for me, on account of the change in my behavior and way of life, which they recognized in me. The demons persuaded them that it was the devil who had wrought this change, so that I might be in a position to pass judgment on their character and behavior. Whenever I was with them, the demons induced some of them to jeer at me and make fun of all I said and did, a thing which was most painful to me." During their exorcisms, the nuns used to refer to their Superior as *le diable dévot*, the devout devil. Their opinion was shared by the exorcists. Except for Surin, all the attendant Fathers were skeptical. It was in vain that Sœur Jeanne assured them that the great St. Joseph had obtained for her the gift of mental prayer, in vain that she modestly claimed to have been "raised by the Divine Majesty to the degree of contemplation, by means of which I received great illuminations, and Our Lord communicated himself to my soul in a special and private manner." Instead of prostrating themselves before this walking fount of divine wisdom, the exorcists merely told her that this was the kind of illusion to which the possessed were peculiarly subject. Confronted by so much hardness of heart, the Prioress could only retreat, either into madness, or into the attic, with her dear, good, credulous Father Surin.

But even Father Surin was a trial to her. He was ready enough to believe all that she said about her extraordinary graces; but his ideals of sanctity were uncomfortably high, and his estimation of Sœur Jeanne's character uncomfortably low. To confess that one is proud and sensual is one thing; to be told these home truths by someone else is another and very different matter. And Surin was not content with telling Sœur Jeanne what her faults were; he was forever trying to correct them. He was convinced that the Prioress was possessed by devils; but he was also convinced that the devils derived their power from the victim's own defects. By getting rid of the defects one would get rid of the demons. It was therefore necessary, in Surin's words, "to attack the horse in order to overthrow the rider." But the horse found it most unpleasant to be attacked. For, though Sœur Jeanne had resolved to "go to God with perfection," though she already saw herself as a saint and was pained when other people saw only the unconscious (or perhaps the all too conscious) comedian, she found the process of sanctification extremely painful and distressing. Surin took her very seriously as an ecstatic—and that was flattering; that was all as it should be. But, unfortunately for the Prioress, he took her still more seriously as a penitent and an ascetic. When she became too uppish, he snubbed her. When she asked for showy penances—public confession of her sin, degradation to the rank of a lay sister—he insisted, instead, on the practice of small, inconspicuous, but unremitting mortifications. When, as sometimes happened, she played the great lady, he treated her as though she were a scullery maid. Exasperated, she took refuge in Leviathan's proud anger, in Behemoth's ravings against God, in Balaam's buffoonery. Instead of resorting to exorcisms, which, by this time, all the devils thoroughly enjoyed, Surin ordered the infesting entities to whip themselves. And, since the Prioress always retained enough liberty and enough genuine desire for self-improvement to give her consent, the demons had to obey. "We can stand up to the Church," they said, "we can defy the priests. But we cannot resist the will of this bitch." Whining or cursing, according to their various temperaments, they swung the discipline. Leviathan was the hardest hitter; Behemoth, a close second. But Balaam and, above all, Isacaaron had a horror of pain, and could hardly be induced to hurt themselves. "It was an admirable spectacle," says Surin, "when the demon of sensuality inflicted the punishment." The blows were light, but the screams were piercing, the tears profuse. The devils could take less punishment than Sœur Jeanne in her normal state. Once it took a whole hour of flagellation to dispel certain psychosomatic symptoms brought on by Leviathan; but on most occasions a few minutes of self-punishment were enough. The possessor took flight, and Sœur Jeanne was free to resume the march toward perfection.

It was a tedious march and, for Sœur Jeanne at least, perfection had one grave defect: it was as inconspicuous as those nagging little mortifications prescribed by Father Surin. You were raised to the degree of contemplation, you were honored by private communications from on high. But what was there to show for it? Nothing at all. You had to tell them about the graces you had received, and all they did was to shake their heads or shrug their shoulders. And when you behaved as the blessed Mother Teresa must have behaved, they either roared with laughter or flew into a rage and called you a hypocrite. Something more convincing was needed, something spectacular, something obviously supernatural.

Diabolical miracles were no longer in order; for Sœur Jeanne had ceased to be the queen of the demoniacs and was now aspiring to immediate canonization. The first of her divine miracles took place in February, 1635. One day Isacaaron confessed that three anonymous magicians, two from Loudun, one a Parisian, had come into possession of three consecrated wafers, which they intended to burn. Surin immediately ordered Isacaaron to go and fetch the wafers, which were hidden under a mattress in Paris. Isacaaron disappeared and did not return. Balaam was then commanded to go to his assistance, stubbornly refused, but was finally forced, by the help of Surin's good angel, to obey. The orders were that the wafers should be produced at the after-dinner exorcism on the following day. At the appointed time, Balaam and Isacaaron made their appearance and, after much resistance and many contortions of the Prioress's body, announced that the wafers were in a niche above the tabernacle. "The demons then caused the Mother Superior's body, which was very small, to stretch." At the end of its elongated arm the hand was thrust into the niche and came out with a neatly folded sheet of paper containing three wafers.

To this painfully fishy marvel Surin attached enormous importance. In Sœur Jeanne's autobiography it is not so much as mentioned. Was she ashamed of the trick she had so successfully played on her trusting director? Or was it that she found the miracle essentially unsatisfactory? True, she had played the principal part in the affair; but the affair was not primarily *hers*. What she needed was a miracle all her own, and in the autumn of that same year she finally got what she wanted.

Toward the end of October, yielding to the pressure of public opinion within the Order, the Provincial of Aquitaine gave orders that Surin should return to Bordeaux and that his place at Loudun should be taken by another, less eccentric exorcist. The news got out. Leviathan exulted; but Sœur Jeanne, when she came to her senses, was greatly distressed. Something, she felt, would have to be done. She prayed to St. Joseph, and had a strong conviction "that God would help us and that this proud demon would be humiliated." After this, for three or four days, she was ill in bed; then suddenly felt well enough to ask to be exorcised. "It happened that day (it was the fifth of November) that many persons of quality were present in the church to watch the exorcisms; this was not without a special providence of God." (Special providences were the rule, where very important personages were concerned. It was always in the presence of the nobility that the devils performed their greatest feats.)

The exorcism began and "Leviathan appeared in an altogether extraordinary manner, boasting that he had triumphed over the minister of the Church." Surin counterattacked by ordering the demon to adore the Blessed Sacrament. There were the customary howls and convulsions. Then "God in his mercy granted us more than we could have dared to hope." Leviathan prostrated himself—or, to be more accurate, he prostrated Sœur Jeanne at the feet of the exorcist. He acknowledged that he had plotted against Surin's honor and begged to be forgiven; then, after one last paroxysm, he left the Prioress's body—forever. It was a triumph for Surin and a vindication of his method. Impressed, the other exorcists changed their tune, the Provincial gave him another chance. Sœur Jeanne had got what she wanted and, in doing so, had demonstrated that, while she was possessed by devils, the devils were, to some extent at least, possessed by her. They had power to make her behave like a lunatic; but when she chose to use it, she had power to make them behave as though they didn't exist.

After the departure of Leviathan, a bloody cross appeared on the Prioress's forehead and remained there, plainly visible, for three full weeks. This was good; but something much better was to follow. Balaam now announced that he was ready to go and promised that, when he took his leave, he would write his name on the Prioress's left hand, where it should remain until her death. The prospect of being thus branded indelibly with the signature of the spirit of buffoonery did not appeal to Sœur Jeanne. How much better if the demon could be constrained to write the name, say, of St. Joseph! On Surin's advice, she embarked on a course of nine consecutive communions in honor of the saint. Balaam did all he could to interrupt the novena. But illness and mental obfuscation were without avail; the Prioress struggled on. One morning, just before the hour of mass, Balaam and Behemoth—buffoonery and blasphemy—got into her head and set up such a turmoil and confusion that, though she knew quite well that she was doing wrong, she could not resist a mad impulse to rush headlong to the refectory. There "I breakfasted with such intemperateness that I ate, at this one meal, more than three famished persons could have eaten in a whole day." Communion was now out of the question. Overcome with grief, Sœur Jeanne appealed to Surin for help. He put on his stole and gave the necessary orders. "The demon re-entered my head and forthwith caused me to vomit with such abundance that it was quite inconceivable." Balaam now swore that the stomach was completely empty, and Father Surin judged that she might safely take communion. "And thus I went on with my novena to the end."

On November 29th the spirit of buffoonery finally took his leave. Among the spectators on this occasion were two Englishmen —Walter Montague, son of the first Earl of Manchester and a new-made Catholic with all the convert's will-to-believe-everything, and his young friend and protégé, Thomas Killigrew, the future playwright. A few days after the event Killigrew wrote a long letter to a friend in England, describing all that he had seen at Loudun.* The experience, he says, had been "beyond his expectation." Going from chapel to chapel in the convent church, he had seen, on the first day of his visit, four or five of the energumens, quietly kneeling in prayer, each with her exorcist kneeling behind her and holding one end of a string, the other end of which was tied round the nun's neck. Small crosses were fastened to this string, which served as a leash to control, in some small measure, the frenzies of the devils. For the moment, however, all was peace and quiet, and "I saw nothing but kneeling." In the course of the next half hour, two of the nuns became unruly. One of them flew at a friar's throat; the other stuck out her tongue, threw her arms about the neck of her exorcist and tried to kiss him. All the while, through the gratings separating the church from the convent, came a sound of howling. After that the young man was called by Walter Montague to witness a display of diabolic thought-reading. The devils succeeded with the convert, but were not so successful with Killigrew. In the intervals of this performance they offered prayers for Calvin and heaped curses on the Church of Rome. When one of the fiends departed, the tourists asked where he had gone. The nun's reply was so unequivocal that the Editor of the *European Magazine* could not bring himself to print it.

Next came the exorcism of pretty little Sister Agnes. Killigrew's account of this has already been given in an earlier chapter. The spectacle of this delicious creature being held down by a pair of

* Printed for the first (and apparently the last) time in the *European Magazine*, February, 1803.

sturdy peasants, while her friar triumphantly set his foot first on her breast, then on the white throat, filled our young cavalier with horror and disgust.

Next day it all began again; but this time the performance ended in a more interesting, a less revolting manner. "Prayers being ended," writes Killigrew, "she (the Prioress) turned herself to the friar [Surin], who cast a string of crosses about her neck, and there tied it with three knots. She kneeled still, and ceased not to pray till the strings were fastened; but then she stood up and quitted her beads; and after a reverence made to the altar, she went to a seat like a couch with one end, made purposely for the exorcism, whereof there are diverse in the chapel." [It would be interesting to know if any of these ancestors of the psychoanalyst's sofa are still extant.] "The head of this seat stood to the altar; she went to it with so much humility that you would have thought that this patience would merit enough, without the prayers of the priests, to chase out the devil. When she came to it, she lay down and helped the priest to bind her to it with two ropes, one about her waist, another about her thighs and legs. When she was bound, and saw the priest with the box wherein the sacrament was included, she sighed and trembled with a sense of the tortures she was to suffer. Nor is this a particular humility and patience that she showed; for they are all so, and in the same instances. When this exorcism was performed, another of the possessed called another of the Fathers unto her, and set her seat herself, and then lay down upon it, and tied herself upon it as the other did. 'Tis strange to see how modestly they go to the altar, when they are themselves, and how they walk in the nunneries. Their modest looks and faces express what they are (maids vowed to religion). This nun, upon the beginning of the exorcism, lay as if she had slept. . . ." Surin now set to work on the Prioress. In a few minutes Balaam made his appearance. There were writhings and convulsions, abominable blasphemies, frightful grimaces. Sœur Jeanne's belly suddenly swelled, until it looked like that of a woman far gone in pregnancy; then the breasts puffed themselves up to the size of the belly. The exorcist applied relics to each part as it was affected, and the swellings subsided. Killigrew now stepped forward and touched her hand—it was cool; felt her pulse—it was calm and slow. The Prioress pushed him aside and began to claw at her coif. A moment later the bald, close-shaven head was bare. She rolled up her eyes, she stuck out her tongue. It was prodigiously swollen, black in color and had the pimply texture of morocco leather. Surin now untied her, ordering Balaam to adore the Sacrament. Sœur Jeanne slid backward off the seat and landed on the floor. For a long time Balaam stubbornly resisted; but at last he was bullied into performing the act of worship demanded of him. "Then," writes Killigrew, "as she lay on her back, she bent her waist like a tumbler and went so, shoving herself with her heels, on her bare shaven head, all about the chapel after the friar. And many other strange, unnatural postures, beyond anything that ever I saw, or could believe possible for any man or woman to do. Nor was this a sudden motion, and away; but a continuous thing, which she did for above an hour together; and yet not out of breath nor hot with all the motions she used." All this time the tongue hung out, "swollen to an incredible bigness, and never within her mouth from the first falling into her fit; I never saw her for a moment contract it. Then I heard her, after she had given a start and a shriek that you would have thought had torn her to pieces, speak one word and that was, 'Joseph.' At which all the priests started up and cried, 'That is the sign, look for the mark!' On which one, seeing her hold out her arm, looked for it. Mr. Montague and myself did the same very earnestly; and on her hand I saw a color rise, a little ruddy, and run for the length of an inch along her vein, and in that a great many red specks, which made a distinct word; and it was the same she spake, 'Joseph.' This mark the Jesuit said the devil promised, when he went out, he would make." Minutes of the proceedings were drawn up and signed by the officiating exorcists. Montague then added a postscript in English, to which he and Killigrew put their names. And so, the letter gaily concludes, "I hope you will believe it, or at leastways say there are more liars than myself, and greater, though there be none more

　　　your humble servant than

　　　　　Thomas Killigrew."

To the name of St. Joseph were added, in due course, those of Jesus, of Mary and of François de Sales. Bright red at their first appearance, these names tended to fade after a week or two, but were then renewed by Sister Jane's good angel. The process was repeated at irregular intervals from the winter of 1635 to St. John's Day, 1662. After that date the names disappeared completely, "for no known reason," writes Surin, "except that, to be rid of the continual importunity of those whose desire to see them distracted her from Our Lord, the Mother Superior had insistently prayed to be released from this affliction."

Surin, together with some of his colleagues and a majority of the general public, believed that this novel form of stigmatization was an extraordinary grace from God. Among his educated contemporaries there was a general skepticism. These people had not believed in the reality of the possession, and they did not now believe in the divine origin of the names. Some, like John Maitland, were of the opinion that they had been etched into the skin with an acid; others that they might have been traced on the surface with colored starch. Many remarked on the fact that, instead of being distributed on both hands, all the names were crowded onto the left—where it would be easier for a right-handed person to write them.

In their edition of Sœur Jeanne's autobiography Drs. Gabriel Legué and Gilles de la Tourette, both of them pupils of Charcot, incline to the belief that the writing on the hand was produced by autosuggestion, and support this view by citing several modern examples of hysterical stigmatization. It should be added that in most cases of hysteria the skin becomes peculiarly sensitive. A fingernail lightly drawn over its surface raises a red welt that may last for several hours.

Autosuggestion, deliberate fraud or a mixture of both—we are at liberty to take our choice of explanations. For myself, I incline to the third hypothesis. The stigmata were probably spontaneous enough to seem to Jeanne herself genuinely miraculous. And if they were genuinely miraculous, there could be no harm in improving on the phenomenon so as to make it more edifying to the public and more creditable to herself. Her sacred names were like Sir Walter Scott's novels—founded on fact, but considerably beholden to imagination and art.

Sœur Jeanne had now had her own, her private miracle. And it was not merely private, it was chronic. Renewed by her good angel, the sacred names were ever present, and could be shown at any time to distinguished visitors or the crowds of common sightseers. She was now a walking relic.

Isacaaron took flight on January 7, 1636. Only Behemoth remained; but this demon of blasphemy was tougher than all the rest put together. Exorcisms, penances, mental prayer—nothing availed. Religion had been forced upon an unwilling and undisciplined mind, and the inductive reaction of that mind had been an irreligion so violent and so shocking that the normal personality had felt obliged to dissociate itself from this negation of everything it reverenced. The negation became a Someone-Else, an evil spirit leading an autonomous existence in the mind, causing confusion within and scandal without. Surin wrestled with Behemoth for ten more months; then, in October, broke down completely. The Provincial recalled him to Bordeaux, and another Jesuit took over the direction of the Prioress.

Father Ressès was a great believer in what may be called "straight" exorcism. He was persuaded, says Sœur Jeanne, that those who watched the exorcisms were greatly benefited by the sight of demons adoring the Sacrament. Surin had tried to "overthrow the rider by attacking the horse." Ressès attacked the rider directly and in public—and attacked him regardless of the horse's feelings and without any attempt to modify its behavior.

"One day," writes the Prioress, "a celebrated company being assembled, the good Father planned to perform some exorcisms for their spiritual good." The Prioress told her director that she was feeling ill and that the exorcisms would do her harm. "But the good Father, who was most anxious to perform the exorcisms, told me to take courage and trust in God; after which he began the exorcism." Sœur Jeanne was put through all her tricks, with the result that she took to her bed with a high fever and a pain in her side. Dr. Fanton, a Huguenot, but the best physician in the town, was called in. She was bled three times and given medicine. It was so effective that there was "an evacuation and flux of blood lasting seven or eight days." She felt better; then, after a few more days, fell ill again. "Father Ressès thought fit to recommence the exorcisms; after which I was troubled by violent nausea and vomiting." This was followed by fever, pain in the side and spitting of blood. Fanton was recalled, pronounced that she had pleurisy, bled her seven times in as many days and administered four clysters. After which he informed her that her malady was mortal. That night Sœur Jeanne heard an inward voice. It told her that she would not die, but that God would bring her into the last extremity of danger in order, the more gloriously, to manifest His power by healing her when she was at the very doors of death. For two days she seemed to grow steadily worse and weaker, so much so that, on the seventh of February, Extreme Unction was administered. The doctor was then sent for, and while she was awaiting his arrival Sœur Jeanne uttered the following prayer: "Lord, I have always thought that You wished to display some extraordinary mark of your power in healing me of this sickness; if this be the case, reduce me to such a state that, when he sees me, the doctor will judge that I am past help." Dr. Fanton came and pronounced that she had only one or two hours to live. Hurrying home he penned a report to Laubardemont, who was then in Paris. The pulse, he wrote, was convulsive, the stomach distended; the state of weakness was such that no remedies, not even a clyster, could have any effect. However, she was being given a small suppository in the hope that it might relieve an "oppression, so great that it cannot be described." Not that this palliative would make any real difference; for the patient was *in extremis*. At half past six Sœur Jeanne fell into a lethargy and had a vision of her good angel in the form of a wonderfully beautiful youth of eighteen, with long fair curls. The angel, we are told by Surin, was the living image of the Duc de Beaufort, son of César de Vendôme, and grandson of Henri IV and Gabrielle d'Estrées. This prince had recently been in Loudun to see the devils, and his shoulder-length bob of golden hair had made a profound impression on the Prioress. After the angel came St. Joseph, who laid his hand on Sœur Jeanne's right side, at the spot where she felt the greatest pain, and anointed her with some kind of oil. "After which I came to my senses and found myself completely cured."

It was another miracle. Yet again Sœur Jeanne had demonstrated that, to some extent at least, she possessed her possessors. She had willed and suggested the expulsion of Leviathan, and now she had willed and suggested the disappearance of all the symptoms of an acute and apparently fatal psychosomatic illness.

She got out of bed, dressed, went down to the chapel and joined her sisters in singing a *Te Deum*. Dr. Fanton was sent for again and, after being told of what had happened, remarked that the power of God is greater than that of our remedies. "Nevertheless," writes the Prioress, "he would not be converted and declined in future to take care of us."

Poor Dr. Fanton! After Laubardemont's return to Loudun, he was called before a commission of magistrates and asked to sign a certificate to the effect that his patient's restoration to health had been miraculous. He refused. Pressed to explain the reasons for this refusal he answered that the sudden passage from mortal sickness to perfect health might easily have happened in the course of nature, "By reason of the sensible issue of the humor, or by its insensible excretion through the pores of the skin, or else by the conveyance of the humor from the part where it caused these accidents to another, less important part. Furthermore the distressing symptoms produced by the humor being in a certain place can be relieved without the necessity of a change of part; this is brought about by mitigation of the humor as it is subdued by nature, or by the onset of another humor which, being less savage, will blunt the acrimony of the first humor." Dr. Fanton added "that manifest excretion is by urines and fluxes of the intestines, or by vomits, sweats and losses of blood; and that insensible excretion takes place when the parts discharge themselves insensibly; these last kinds of excretion are most frequent among patients who work up hot humors, notably bile, without seeing the signs of coction which precede such excretions, even though it may be in the moment of crisis and of the discharge of nature. It is obvious that, in the cure of diseases, smaller quantities of humors must leave the body when these have previously been evacuated by remedies, which carry away not merely the antecedent cause of diseases, but also their conjoint causes. To which must be added that, in their movements, the humors observe certain regular hours." Molière, we perceive, invented nothing: he merely recorded.

Two days passed. Then the Prioress suddenly remembered that she had not wiped away the unction which had cured her, so that some of it must still be on her chemise. In the presence of the sub-Prioress she removed her habit. "Both of us smelled an admirable odor; I took off my chemise, which we then cut at the waist. On it were five drops of this divine balm, which gave forth an excellent perfume."

"Where are your young mistresses?" Gorgibus asks at the beginning of *Les Précieuses Ridicules.* "In their room," says Marotte. "What are they up to?" "Making pomade for the lips." It was an age when every woman of fashion had to be her own Elizabeth Arden. Recipes for face creams and hand lotions, for rouge and perfume, were treasured as secret weapons or generously exchanged between particular friends. In her youth at home, and even since her profession, Sœur Jeanne had been a famous cosmetician and amateur pharmacist. St. Joseph's unction came, we may suspect, from a source some way this side of heaven. But, meanwhile, there the Five Drops were, for all to see. "It is not to be believed," writes the Prioress, "how great was the devotion of the people toward this blessed unction and how many miracles God worked by means of it."

Sœur Jeanne now had two first-class prodigies to her credit, with a stigmatized hand and a perfumed chemise as perpetual witnesses to the extraordinary graces she had received. But this was not yet enough. At Loudun, she felt, her light had been put under a bushel. True, there were the tourists, the visiting princes, lords and prelates. But think of all the millions who would never make the pilgrimage! Think of the King and Queen! Think of His Eminence! Think of all the Dukes and Marquises, all the Marshals of France, all the Papal Legates, the Envoys Plenipotentiary and Extraordinary, the Doctors of the Sorbonne, the Deans, the Abbots, the Bishops and Archbishops! Shouldn't *these* be given a chance to admire the marvels, to see and hear the humble recipient of such astounding favors?

Coming from her own lips, the suggestion might have seemed presumptuous, and so it was Behemoth who first broached the subject. When, after the most strenuous of exorcisms, Father Ressès asked him why he so stubbornly resisted, the fiend replied that he would never leave the Prioress's body until that body had made a pilgrimage to the tomb of St. François de Sales at Annecy, in Savoy. Exorcism followed exorcism. Under the torrent of anathemas Behemoth merely smiled. To his earlier ultimatum he now added another condition: Father Surin must be recalled—otherwise even the trip to Annecy would be of no avail.

By the middle of June Surin was back at Loudun. But the pilgrimage proved harder to arrange. Vitelleschi, the General of the Order, did not like the idea of one of his Jesuits promenading through France with a nun; and on his side the Bishop of Poitiers did not like the idea of one of his nuns promenading with a Jesuit. Besides, there was the question of money. The royal treasury was, as usual, empty. What with the subsidies to the nuns and the salaries of the exorcists, the possession had already cost a pretty penny. There was nothing to spare for jaunts to Savoy. Behemoth stuck to his guns. As a great concession, he agreed to take his leave at Loudun —but only if Sœur Jeanne and Surin were permitted to make a vow to go to Annecy afterward. In the end he had his way. Surin and Sœur Jeanne were permitted to meet at the tomb of St. Francis, but would have to go and come by different roads. The vows were made and, a little later, on October 15th, Behemoth departed. Sœur Jeanne was free. Two weeks later Surin returned to Bordeaux. The following spring Father Tranquille died in a paroxysm of demoniac frenzy. The treasury ceased to pay the salary of the surviving exorcists, who were all recalled to their various houses. Left to themselves such devils as remained soon took their leave. After six years of incessant struggle, the Church Militant gave up the fight. Its enemies promptly disappeared. The long orgy was at an end. If there had been no exorcists, it would never have begun.

CHAPTER TEN

WITH Sœur Jeanne's pilgrimage we emerge for a few brief weeks from the shades of a provincial cloister into the great world. It is the world of the history books, the world of royal personages and intriguing courtiers, the world of duchesses with a taste for love and prelates with a taste for power, the world of high policy and high fashion, of Rubens and Descartes, of science, literature, learning. From Loudun and the company of a mystic, seven devils and sixteen hysterics, the Prioress now stepped out into the full glare of the seventeenth century.

The charm of history and its enigmatic lesson consist in the fact that, from age to age, nothing changes and yet everything is completely different. In the personages of other times and alien cultures we recognize our all too human selves and yet are aware, as we do so, that the frame of reference within which we do our living has changed, since their day, out of all recognition, that propositions which seemed axiomatic then are now untenable and that what we regard as the most self-evident postulates could not, at an earlier period, find entrance into even the most boldly speculative mind. But however great, however important for thought and technology, for social organization and behavior, the differences between then and now are always peripheral. At the center remains a fundamental identity. Insofar as they are incarnated minds, subject to physical decay and death, capable of pain and pleasure, driven by craving and abhorrence and oscillating between the desire for self-assertion and the desire for self-transcendence, human beings are faced, at every time and place, with the same problems, are confronted by the same temptations and are permitted by the Order of Things to make the same choice between unregeneracy and enlightenment. The context changes, but the gist and the meaning are invariable.

Sœur Jeanne was in no position to understand the prodigious developments in scientific thought and practice, which had begun to take place in the world around her. Of those aspects of seventeenth-century culture represented by Galileo and Descartes, by Harvey and van Helmont, the Prioress was totally unaware. What she had known as a child and what she now rediscovered in the course of her pilgrimage was the social hierarchy and the conventions of thought and feeling and behavior, to which the existence of that hierarchy gave rise.

In one of its aspects the culture of the seventeenth century, especially in France, was simply a prolonged effort, on the part of the ruling minority, to overstep the limitations of organic existence. More than at almost any other period of recent history, men and women aspired to identify themselves with their social persona. They were not content merely to bear a great name; they longed to *be* it. Their ambition was actually to *become* the offices they held, the dignities they had acquired or inherited. Hence the elaboration of baroque ceremonial, hence those rigid and complex codes of precedence, of honor, of good manners. Relations were not between human beings, but between titles, genealogies and positions. Who had the right to sit in the royal presence? For Saint-Simon, at the end of the century, the question was one of capital importance. Three generations earlier, similar questions had preyed upon the mind of the infant Louis XIII. By the time he was four he had come to feel very strongly that his bastard half-brother, the Duke of Vendôme, should not be permitted to eat his meals with him or remain covered in his presence. When Henri IV decreed that "Féfé Vendôme" was to sit at the Dauphin's table and keep his hat on while dining, the little Prince was forced to obey—but with the worst possible grace. Nothing more vividly illuminates the theory and practice of the

260

Divine Right of Kings than this matter of the royal hat. At nine years of age Louis XIII passed from the care of a governess to that of a governor. In the presence of a being who was, by definition, divine, the King's tutor remained permanently hatless. And this rule held good even when (as the late King and the Queen Mother had charged him to do) he was inflicting corporal punishment on his pupil. On these occasions the monarch, with his hat on, but his pants off, was birched till the blood ran by a subject, reverently bareheaded, as though before the Sacrament on the altar. The spectacle, as we try to visualize it, is unforgettably instructive. "There's a divinity doth hedge a king, rough-hew him how we may."

The longing to be something more than mere flesh and blood reveals itself very clearly in the arts of our period. Kings and queens, lords and ladies, liked to think of themselves as Rubens represented their persons and their allegorized characteristics—as superhumanly energetic, divinely healthy, heroically commanding. They were ready to pay through the nose in order to see themselves as Van Dyck portraits—elegant, refined, infinitely aristocratic. In the theater they loved the heroes and heroines of Corneille, loved them for their mere size, loved them for their monolithic and superhuman consistency, their cult of the will, their worship of themselves. And ever more strictly, as the years went by, they insisted on the unities of time, place and action; for what they wished to see in their tragic theater was not life as it is, but life corrected, life reduced to order, life as it might be if only men and women were something other than what in fact they are.

In the field of domestic architecture the desire for a more than human grandiosity was no less conspicuously displayed. The fact was remarked by a poet who was a boy when the Palais Cardinal was building and who died before Versailles was completed—Andrew Marvell.

> Why should, of all things, man unrul'd
> Such unproportioned dwellings build?
> The beasts are by their dens express'd
> And birds contrive an equal nest;

The low-roofed tortoises do dwell
In cases fit of tortoise-shell:
No creature loves an empty space;
Their bodies measure out their place.
But he, superfluously spread,
Demands more room alive than dead,
And in his hollow palace goes
Where winds, as he, themselves may lose.
What need of all this marble crust
T'impark the wanton mote of dust?

And as the marble crusts expanded, the periwigs of the wanton
motes imparked within them became more luxuriant, the heels of
their shoes yet higher. Tottering on stilts and crowned with tower-
ing piles of horsehair, the Grand Monarch and his courtiers proclaimed themselves larger than life and hairier than Samson at the
height of his virility.

Needless to say, these attempts to overstep the limits set by nature
were always unsuccessful. Doubly so; for not only did our seventeenth-century ancestors fail to *be*, they failed even to *seem*, superhuman. The absurd and bumptious spirit was willing enough; but
the flesh was incurably weak. The *Grand Siècle* did not possess the
material and organizational resources, without which the game of
pretending to be superhuman cannot be played. That sublimity,
those prodigies of grandeur, which Richelieu and Louis XIV so
ardently desired, can be achieved only by the greatest of stage
managers, by a Ziegfeld, a Cochran, a Max Reinhardt. But great
showmanship depends on an armory of gadgets, a well-stocked
property room and the highly trained and disciplined collaboration
of all concerned. In the *Grand Siècle* such training and discipline
were lacking, and even the material basis of theatrical sublimity—
the *machina* which introduces and, indeed, creates the *deus*—was
deficient. Even Richelieu, even the Sun King were "Old Men of
Thermopylae, who never did anything properly." Versailles itself
was curiously unimpressive—gigantic but trivial, grandiose but of
no effect. Seventeenth-century pageantry was sloppy to a degree.
Nothing was adequately rehearsed, and the most grotesque of avoid-
able mishaps would mar the most solemn of occasions. Consider,

for example, the case of *La Grande Mademoiselle*, that pathetic figure of fun who was Louis XIV's first cousin. After death, according to the curious custom of the time, her body was dissected and buried piecemeal—here the head and there a limb or two, here the heart and there the entrails. These last were so badly embalmed that, even after treatment, they went on fermenting. The gases of putrefaction accumulated and the porphyry urn containing the viscera became a kind of anatomic bomb, which suddenly exploded, in the middle of the funeral service, to the horror and dismay of all present.

Such physiological accidents were by no means exclusively posthumous. The authors of memoirs and the collectors of anecdotes abound in stories about belching in high places, about the breaking of wind in a royal presence, about the gamy aroma of kings, the bromidrosis of dukes and marshals. Henri IV's feet and armpits enjoyed an international reputation. Bellegarde had a perpetually running nose, Bassompierre a set of toes which rivaled those of his royal master. The copiousness of these anecdotes and the delighted amusement, which the telling of them evidently evoked, were in direct proportion to the enormity of kingly and aristocratic pretensions. It was precisely because great men tried to seem more than human that the rest of the world welcomed any reminder that, in part at least, they were still merely animal.

Identifying himself with a persona which was simultaneously princely, sacerdotal, political and literary, Cardinal Richelieu comported himself as though he were a demigod. But the wretched man had to play his part in a body which disease had rendered so repulsive that there were times when people could hardly bear to sit in the same room with him. He suffered from tubercular osteitis of his right arm and a fissure of the fundament, and was thus forced to live in the fetid atmosphere of his own suppuration. Musk and civet disguised but could not abolish this carrion odor of decay. Richelieu could never escape from the humiliating knowledge that he was an object, to all around him, of physical abhorrence. This brutally violent contrast between the quasi-divine persona and the body of death, with which it was associated, strongly impressed the popular imagination. When the relics of St. Fiacre (the miraculous specific for hemorrhoids) were brought from Meaux to the Cardinal's palace, an anonymous poet celebrated the occasion with a copy of verses which would have delighted Dean Swift.

> *Cependant sans sortir un pas hors de sa chambre*
> *Qu'il faisait parfumer toute de musc et d'ambre,*
> *Pour n'estonner le Sainct de cette infection*
> *Qui du parfait ministre est l'imperfection,*
> *Et modérer un peu l'odeur puantissime*
> *Qui sort du cul pourry de l'Eminentissime. . . .*

And here is another fragment from a ballad describing the great man's last illness.

> *Il vit grouiller les vers dans ses salles ulcères,*
> *Il vit mourir son bras —*
> *Son bras qui l'Europe alluma tant de guerres,*
> *Qui brusla tant d'autels. . . .*

Between the rotting body of the actual man and the glory of the persona, the gulf was unbridgeable. In Jules de Gaultier's phrase, "the Bovaric angle" separating fact from phantasy approximated to one hundred and eighty degrees. To a generation, which had been brought up to regard the divine right of kings and priests and nobles as axiomatic, and which *therefore* welcomed every opportunity of pricking the bubble of its rulers' pretensions, the case of Cardinal Richelieu was the most acceptable of parables. *Hubris* invites its corresponding *Nemesis*. That dreadful stench, those worms battening on the living corpse, seemed poetically just and appropriate. During the Cardinal's last hours, when the relics had failed to work and the doctors had given him up, an old peasant woman, who had a reputation as a healer, was called to the great man's bedside. Muttering spells, she administered her panacea—four ounces of horse dung macerated in a pint of white wine. It was with the taste of excrement in his mouth that the arbiter of Europe's destinies gave up the ghost.

When Sœur Jeanne was taken to see him, Richelieu was at the highest pinnacle of his glory, but already a sick man, suffering much pain and in constant need of medical attention. "My lord Cardinal had been bled that day, and all the doors of his château of Ruel were closed, even to bishops and marshals of France; nonetheless we were introduced into his antechamber, though he himself was in bed." After dinner ("it was magnificent, and we were served by his pages") the Mother Superior and an Ursuline companion were ushered into the bedroom, knelt to receive His Eminence's benediction and could only with difficulty be persuaded to rise and take chairs. ("The contestation of politeness on his part and of humility on ours lasted quite a long time; but at last I was obliged to obey.")

Richelieu began the conversation by remarking that the Prioress was under great obligations to God, inasmuch as He had chosen her, in this age of unbelief, to suffer for the honor of the Church, the conversion of souls and the confounding of the wicked.

Sœur Jeanne replied with a paean of gratitude. She and her sisters would never forget that, while the rest of the world had treated them as crazy impostors, His Eminence had been to them not merely a father, but a mother, a nurse and a protector as well.

But the Cardinal would not permit himself to be thanked. On the contrary, he felt himself extremely obliged to Providence for having given him the opportunity and the means to assist the afflicted. (All these things, the Prioress remarks, were spoken "with a ravishing grace and much sweetness.")

Next, the great man asked if he might look at the sacred names inscribed on Sister Jane's left hand. And after the sacred names it was the turn of the unction of St. Joseph. The chemise was unfolded. Before taking it into his hands, the Cardinal piously took off his nightcap; then he sniffed at the blessed object and exclaiming, "That smells perfectly good!" kissed it twice. After which, holding the chemise "with respect and admiration," he pressed it against a reliquary which was standing on the table beside the bed—presumably in order to recharge its contents with the mana inhering in the unction. At his request the Prioress described (for the how many hundredth time?) the miracle of her healing, then knelt for another blessing. The interview was over. Next day His Eminence sent her five hundred crowns to defray the expenses of her pilgrimage.

One reads Sœur Jeanne's account of this interview, then turns to the letters in which the Cardinal had ironically twitted Gaston d'Orléans with his credulity in regard to the possession. "I am delighted to hear that the devils of Loudun have converted Your Highness and that you have now quite forgotten the oaths with which your mouth was habitually filled." And again, "the assistance you will receive from the master of the devils of Loudun will be powerful enough to enable you, in a very short time, to make a long journey on the road to virtue." On another occasion he learns by a courier who is "one of the devils of Loudun" that the Prince has contracted a disease, whose nature is sufficiently indicated by the fact that "you have deserved it." Richelieu commiserates with His Highness and offers him "the exorcisms of the good Father Joseph" as a remedy. Addressed to the King's brother by the man who had had Grandier burned for trafficking with devils, these letters are as astounding for their insolence as for their ironic skepticism. The insolence may be attributed to that urge to "score off" his social superiors which remained, throughout life, an incongruously childish element in the Cardinal's complex character. And what of the skepticism, the cynical irony? What was His Eminence's real opinion of witchcraft and possession, of the calligraphic stigmata and the blessed chemise? The best answer, I would guess, is that, when he felt well and was in the company of laymen, the Cardinal regarded the whole affair as either a fraud, or an illusion, or a mixture of both. If he affected to believe in the devils, it was solely for political reasons. Like Canning, he had called in the New World to redress the balance of the Old—the only difference being that, in *his* case, the New World was not America, but hell. True, the public's reaction to the devils had been unsatisfactory. In the face of so general a skepticism, his plans for an inquisitorial Gestapo to fight sorcery and incidentally to strengthen the royal authority had had to be abandoned. But it is always good to know what *not* to do, and the experiment, though negative in its results, had been well worth making. True, an innocent man had been tortured and burned alive. But after all one can't make omelettes without breaking eggs. And anyhow the parson had been a nuisance and was better out of the way.

But then the trouble in his shoulder would flare up again, and his fistula would keep him awake at nights with its intolerable pain. The doctors were called in; but how little they could do! The efficacy of medicine depended upon the *vis medicatrix Naturae*. But in this wretched body of his nature seemed to have lost her healing power. Could it be that his sickness had a supernatural origin? He sent for relics and holy images, he asked for prayers to be said on his behalf. And meanwhile, in secret, he consulted his horoscope, he fingered his tried and trusted talismans, he repeated under his breath the spells he had learned in childhood from his old nurse. When sickness came, when the doors of his palace were closed "even to bishops and marshals of France," he was ready to believe in anything—even in Urbain Grandier's guilt, even in the unction of St. Joseph.

For Sœur Jeanne, the interview with His Eminence was but one in a long series of triumphs and excitements. From Loudun to Paris, and from Paris to Annecy, she moved in a blaze of glory, traveling from popular ovation to popular ovation, and from one aristocratic reception to others yet more flattering to her vanity.

At Tours she was received, with marks of "extraordinary kindness" by the Archbishop, Bertrand de Chaux, an old gentleman of eighty, much addicted to gambling, who had recently made himself notoriously ridiculous by falling head over ears in love with a lady fifty years his junior, the charming Mme. de Chevreuse. "He'll do anything I like," she used to say. "All I have to do is, when we are at table, to let him pinch my thigh." After listening to Sœur Jeanne's story, the Archbishop gave orders that the sacred names should be examined by a committee of physicians. The examination was made, and the Prioress came through with flying colors. From four thousand a day the crowds of sightseers besieging the convent, in which she was lodged, rose to seven thousand.

There was another interview with the Archbishop, this time to meet Gaston d'Orléans, detained at Tours by his liaison with a sixteen-year-old girl called Louise de la Marbelière, who later bore him a son, was duly abandoned by her royal lover and finally became a nun. "The Duke of Orléans came to meet me as far as the door of the drawing room; he welcomed me warmly, congratulated me on my deliverance and said, 'I once came to Loudun; the devils who were in you gave me a great fright; they served to cure me of my habit of swearing, and there and then I resolved to be a better man than I had been up till that time.'" After which he hurried back to Louise.

From Tours the Prioress and her companions proceeded to Amboise. So many people wanted to look at the sacred names that it was necessary to keep the convent parlor open until eleven at night.

At Blois, next day, the doors of the inn at which Sœur Jeanne was dining, were forcibly broken open by the crowd.

At Orléans, she was visited at the Ursuline convent by the bishop, who examined her hand and then exclaimed, "We must not hide God's work, we must give satisfaction to the people!" The doors of the convent were then thrown open, so that the crowds could gaze their fill at the sacred names through the grating.

In Paris the Prioress lodged at the house of M. de Laubardemont. Here she was visited frequently by M. de Chevreuse and the Prince de Guémenée, as well as by a daily multitude of twenty thousand members of the lower orders. "What was most embarrassing," writes Sœur Jeanne, "was that people were not content merely to look at my hand, but asked me a thousand questions about the possession and the expulsion of the devils; which obliged us to issue a printed booklet, in which the public was informed of the most considerable events which had occurred during the entrance of the demons into my body and their departure therefrom, with additional matter regarding the impression of the sacred names upon my hand."

There followed a visit to M. de Gondi, Archbishop of Paris. His politeness in accompanying the Prioress as far as her coach made such an impression that all Paris now thronged to see her and it became necessary to seat this supernatural equivalent of a movie star at a window on the ground floor of the Hotel de Laubardemont, where the mob could look at her. From four in the morning until ten at night she sat there, her elbow on a cushion, her miraculous hand dangling out of the window. "I was given no leisure to hear Mass or to eat my meals. The weather was very hot and the crowd so increased the heat that my head began to swim and I finally fell in a faint on the floor."

The visit to Cardinal Richelieu took place on the twenty-fifth of May and a few days later, at the command of the Queen, the Prioress was taken in Laubardemont's coach to Saint-Germain-en-Laye. Here she had a long conversation with Anne of Austria, who for more than an hour held the miraculous hand between her own royal fingers, "gazing in admiration at a thing which, until then, had never been seen, since the first beginnings of the Church. She exclaimed, 'How can anyone disapprove of a thing so marvelous, a thing that inspires so much devotion? Those who decry and condemn this marvel are the enemies of the Church.'"

A report of the marvel was brought to the King, who decided to come and see for himself. He looked attentively at the sacred names, then said, "I never doubted the truth of this miracle; but seeing it as I now see it, I find my faith strengthened." Then he sent for those of his courtiers who had shown themselves most skeptical as to the reality of the possession.

"What do you say to that?" the King asked, showing them Sœur Jeanne's hand.

"But these people," writes the Prioress, "would not give in. Moved by a principle of charity, I have never mentioned the names of these gentlemen."

The only embarrassing moment in what was otherwise a perfect day came when the Queen asked to be given a little piece of the sacred chemise, "in order that she might obtain from God, through the prayers of St. Joseph, a happy delivery." (At this time Anne of Austria was six months pregnant with the future Louis XIV.) The Prioress had to answer that she did not think it was the will of God that a thing so precious should be cut in pieces. If Her Majesty absolutely commanded it, she was ready to leave her the whole chemise. However, she ventured to point out that, if the chemise were left in her possession, an infinite number of souls devoted to St. Joseph would derive great consolation from seeing with their own eyes a true relic of their patron saint. The Queen allowed herself to be persuaded, and the Prioress returned to Paris with her chemise intact.

After that visit to Saint-Germain everything seemed a little flat—even a two-hour interview with the Archbishop of Sens, even crowds of thirty thousand, even a chat with the papal Nuncio, who said that "it was one of the finest things ever seen in the Church of God," and that he simply couldn't understand how "the Huguenots contrived to persist in their blindness after so sensible a proof of the verities they had opposed."

Sœur Jeanne and her companions left Paris on the twentieth of June and found the usual crowds, prelates and very important persons awaiting them at every halt. At Lyon, which they reached fourteen days after their departure from Paris, they were visited by the Archbishop, Cardinal Alphonse de Richelieu, the Prime Minister's elder brother. It had been intended by his parents that Alphonse should become a Knight of Malta. But all Knights of Malta had to be able to swim, and since Alphonse could never learn to swim, he had to be content with the family bishopric of Luçon, which he soon resigned in order to become a Carthusian monk. After his brother's accession to power, he was taken out of the Grande Chartreuse, made Archbishop first of Aix, then of Lyon, and given a Cardinal's hat. He had the reputation of an excellent prelate, but was subject to occasional fits of mental derangement. During these fits he would put on a crimson robe embroidered with gold thread and affirm that he was God the Father. (This kind of thing seems to have run in the family; for there is a tradition, which may or may not be true, that his younger brother sometimes imagined himself to be a horse.)

Cardinal Alphonse's interest in the sacred names was intense to the point of being surgical. Could they be erased by natural means? He took a pair of scissors and began the experiment. "I took the liberty," writes Sœur Jeanne, "of saying, 'My lord, you are hurting me.'" The Cardinal then sent for his doctor and ordered him to shave the names off. "I objected and said, 'My lord, I have no orders from my superiors to undergo these trials.' My lord Cardinal asked me who these superiors might be." The Prioress's answer was a master stroke. Her superior of superiors was the Cardinal-Duke, Cardinal Alphonse's brother. The experiment was promptly called off.

Next morning, who should turn up but Father Surin. He had already been to Annecy and was on his way home. Afflicted by hysterical dumbness, which he attributed to the operations of the devil, Surin prayed for deliverance at the tomb of St. François de Sales—in vain. The Visitandines of Annecy possessed a large supply of dried blood, which the saint's valet had collected, over a long period of years, adding to his stock every time his master was bled by the barber-surgeon. The Abbess, Jeanne de Chantal, was so much distressed by Surin's affliction that she gave him a clot of this dried blood to eat. For a moment he was able to speak. "Jesu Maria," he cried; but that was all, and he could say no more.

After some discussion and a consultation with the Jesuit fathers of Lyon, it was decided that Surin and his companion, Father Thomas, should turn back and accompany the Prioress to the goal of her pilgrimage. On the road to Grenoble something which Sœur Jeanne qualifies merely as "somewhat extraordinary" took place. Father Thomas intoned the *Veni Creator*, and immediately Father Surin responded. From that moment he was able (at least for some time) to speak without impediment.

At Grenoble Surin made use of his new-found voice to preach a number of eloquent sermons on the unction of St. Joseph and the sacred names. There is something at once lamentable and sublime in the spectacle of this great lover of God passionately maintaining that evil had been good and falsehood, truth. Shouting from the pulpit, he spends the last resources of a sick body, a mind tottering on the brink of disintegration, in an effort to persuade his hearers of the rightness of a judicial murder, the otherworldliness of hysteria and the miraculousness of fraud. It was all done, of course, for the greater glory of God. But the subjective morality of intentions requires to be supplemented by the objective and utilitarian morality of results. One may mean well; but if one acts in an unrealistic and inappropriate manner, the consequences can only be disastrous. By their credulity and their reluctance to think of human psychology in any but the old, dogmatic terms, men like Surin made it certain that the breach between traditional religion and developing science should come to seem unbridgeable. Surin was a man of great ability, and therefore had no right to be as silly as, in this instance, he proved himself to be. That he made himself a martyr to his zeal cannot excuse the fact that this zeal was misdirected.*

At Annecy, which they reached a day or two after leaving Grenoble, they found that the fame of St. Joseph's unction had preceded them. People came from as much as eight leagues away to see and smell. From morning till night Surin and Thomas were kept busy at the task of bringing the sacred chemise into contact with the objects brought for that purpose by the faithful—rosaries, crosses, medals, even bits of cotton and paper.

The Prioress, meanwhile, was lodged in the Visitandine convent, whose Abbess was Mme. de Chantal. We turn to her autobiography, expecting to find that she has devoted at least as many pages to this saintly friend and disciple of St. François as she had given to Anne of Austria or the unspeakable Gaston d'Orléans. But we are disappointed. The only reference to St. Jeanne Chantal occurs in the following paragraph.

"The places, where the unction was, became dirty. Madame de Chantal and her nuns laundered the linen on which the unction was, and the unctions retained their ordinary color."

What were the reasons for this strange silence in regard to a person so remarkable as the founder of the Visitation? One can only speculate. Can it be that Mme. de Chantal was too perspicacious and that, when Sœur Jeanne embarked upon her celebrated impersonation of St. Teresa, she was not impressed? Saints tend to acquire a most embarrassing gift for looking through the persona at the real self behind the mask, and it may be that poor Sister Jane suddenly found herself spiritually naked before this formidably

* "Superstition—Concupiscence," says Pascal. And again: "A natural vice, like incredulity, and no less pernicious—superstition."

gentle old woman—naked and, all of a sudden, overpoweringly ashamed.

At Briare, on the homeward road, the two Jesuits took leave of their companions. Sœur Jeanne was never again to see the man who had sacrificed himself in order to bring her back to sanity. Surin and Thomas turned westward to Bordeaux; the others took the road to Paris, where Sœur Jeanne had a rendezvous with the Queen. She reached Saint-Germain just in time. During the night of September 4, 1638, the labor pains began. The Blessed Virgin's girdle, which had been brought from Notre-Dame du Puy, was fastened about the Queen's waist and the Prioress's chemise was spread over the royal abdomen. At eleven o'clock on the following morning Anne of Austria was safely delivered of the male child who, five years later, was to become Louis XIV. "Thus it was," wrote Surin, "that St. Joseph demonstrated his mighty power, not only in securing for the Queen a happy delivery, but also in presenting France with a King incomparable in power and in greatness of mind, a King of rare discretion, of admirable prudence and of a godliness without previous example."

As soon as the Queen was out of all danger, Sœur Jeanne packed up her chemise and took the homeward road to Loudun. The doors of the convent opened, then closed behind her, forever. Her crowded hour of glorious life was over; but she could not immediately reconcile herself to the humdrum routine, which was henceforth to be her lot. A little before Christmas she fell ill with congestion of the lungs. Her life, according to her own account, was despaired of. "Our Lord," she told her confessor, "has given me a great desire to go to heaven; but he has also conveyed to me the knowledge that, if I were to remain on earth a while longer, I could do Him some service. And so, Reverend Father, if you will but apply the holy unction, I shall most assuredly be healed." The miracle seemed so certain to occur, that Sœur Jeanne's confessor as good as sent out invitations for the blessed occasion. On Christmas night "there assembled in our church an incredible multitude of people desirous of witnessing my recovery." Persons of quality were accommodated with seats in a chamber adjoining the Prioress's bedroom, into which they could look through a grating. "After nightfall, I being at the height of my sickness, Father Alange, a Jesuit, in full canonicals, including the chasuble, entered our room, bearing the holy unction. Drawing near to my bed, he placed the relic on my head and began to repeat the litanies of St. Joseph which he intended to say in their entirety. No sooner had he placed that holy deposit (*dépôt*) on my head than I felt myself entirely cured. However, I decided to say nothing until the good father had finished the litanies. Then I announced the fact and asked for my clothes."

Perhaps this second and all too punctual miracle failed to make any very great impression on the public. In any case it was the last of its kind.

Time passed. The Thirty Years' War went on and on. Richelieu grew richer and richer, and the people more and more miserable. There were peasant revolts against high taxes, and bourgeois revolts (in which Pascal's father participated) against the lowering of interest rates on government bonds. Among the Ursulines of Loudun life went on as usual. Every few weeks the Good Angel (who was still M. de Beaufort, but in miniature, being now only three and a half feet high and not more than sixteen years old) renewed the fading names on the Prioress's left hand. Enclosed now in a handsome reliquary, her chemise, with the unction of St. Joseph, had taken its place among the convent's most precious and most efficacious relics.

At the end of 1642 Richelieu died and was followed to the grave, a few months later, by Louis XIII. On behalf of the five-year-old King, Anne of Austria and her lover, Cardinal Mazarin, ineptly ruled the country.

In 1644 Sœur Jeanne began to write her memoirs and acquired a new Jesuit director, Father Saint-Jure, to whom she sent her own and Surin's still unfinished, work on the devils. Saint-Jure lent the manuscripts to the Bishop of Evreux, and the Bishop, who was in charge of the demoniacs of Louviers, proceeded to direct this new and, if possible, even more revolting orgy of madness and malice along the lines laid down at Loudun. "I think," Laubardemont wrote to the Prioress, "I think that your correspondence with Father Saint-Jure has been of great service in this present affair."

Less successful than the Louviers affair was the possession organized by M. Barré at Chinon. At first all seemed to be going well. A host of young women, including some belonging to the best families of the town, succumbed to the psychological infection. Blasphemy, convulsions, denunciations, obscenity—everything was in order. Unfortunately, one of the demoniac girls, called Beloquin, had a grudge against M. Giloire, a local priest. Going to church early one morning, she poured a bottleful of chicken's blood on the high altar, then announced, during M. Barré's exorcism, that it was her own, shed at midnight, while M. Giloire was violating her. Barré, of course, believed every word of it and began to question the other girls' devils, with a view to collecting more incriminating evidence against his colleague. But the woman, from whom Beloquin had bought the chicken, confided her suspicions to a magistrate. The *Lieutenant Criminel* started an investigation. Barré was indignant and Beloquin counterattacked with excruciating pains in the hypochondries, magically induced, so her devils declared, by M. Giloire. Unimpressed, the *Lieutenant Criminel* called more witnesses. To escape from him, Beloquin fled to Tours, whose Archbishop was notoriously in favor of possessions. But the Archbishop was out of town and his place had been taken by an unsympathetic Coadjutor. He listened to Beloquin's stories, then called in two midwives, who discovered that the pains, though real enough, were due to the presence in the uterus of a small pewter cannon ball. Cross-examined, the girl admitted that she had put it there herself. After which poor M. Barré was deprived of all his benefices and banished from the archidiocese of Touraine. He ended his days obscurely, as a pensioner in a monastery at Le Mans.

At Loudun, in the meantime, the devils had been tolerably quiet. On one memorable occasion, it is true, "I saw before me the forms of two exceedingly horrible men, and smelt a great stink. Each of these men carried rods; they seized me, took off my clothes, tied me to the bed post and birched me for the space of half an hour or more." Fortunately, as her chemise had been pulled up over her head, the Prioress did not see herself naked. And when the two stinking personages pulled it down again and untied her, she "did not notice that anything occurred which was contrary to modesty." There were some subsequent assaults from the same quarter; but in the main the miracles recorded by Sœur Jeanne during the next twenty years were celestial in origin. For example, her heart was split in two and marked, inwardly and invisibly, with the instruments of the Passion. On several occasions the souls of departed sisters appeared and spoke of purgatory. And all the time, of course, the sacred names were being exhibited through the parlor grating to visitors of quality, some devout, others merely curious or downright skeptical. At every renewal of the names, and frequently betweenwhiles, the Angel appeared and gave a prodigious amount of good advice, which was passed on, in interminable letters, to her director. He also gave advice to third parties—to gentlemen involved in lawsuits, to anxious mothers who wanted to know whether it would be better to marry off their daughters, rather disadvantageously, now, or to hang on in the hope of a better match presenting itself before it was too late for anything but the convent.

In 1648 the Thirty Years' War came to an end. The power of the Habsburgs was broken and a third of the inhabitants of Germany had been liquidated. Europe was now ready for the antics of the Grand Monarque and French hegemony. It was a triumph. But meanwhile there was an interlude of anarchy, Fronde succeeded Fronde. Mazarin exiled himself and returned to power; retired once more and reappeared; then vanished forever from the scene.

At about the same time, obscure and out of favor, Laubardemont died. His only son had turned highwayman and been killed. His last surviving daughter had been obliged to take the veil and was now an Ursuline at Loudun, under her father's old protégée.

In January, 1656, the first of the *Provincial Letters* was published, and four months later occurred the great Jansenist miracle—the healing of Pascal's niece's eye by the Holy Thorn preserved at Port-Royal.

A year later Saint-Jure died, and the Prioress had nobody to write to except other nuns and poor Father Surin, who was still too ill to reply. What was her joy when, at the beginning of 1658, she received a letter in Surin's hand—the first in more than twenty years. "How admirable," she wrote to her friend Mme. du Houx, now a nun of the Visitation at Rennes, "how admirable is the leading of God, who having deprived me of Father Saint-Jure, now brings the dear Father of my soul into the condition of being able to write to me! Only a few days before receiving his letter, I had written to him at length about the state of my soul."

She went on writing about the state of her soul—to Surin, to Mme. du Houx, to anyone who was ready to read and reply. If they were ever published, the Prioress's surviving letters would fill several volumes. And how many more must have been lost! Sœur Jeanne, it is evident, was still under the impression that the "inner life" is a life of constant self-analysis in public. But in fact, of course, the inner life begins where the analyzable self leaves off. The soul that goes on talking about its states thereby prevents itself from knowing its divine ground. "It was not from want of will that I have refrained from writing to you, for truly I wish you all good; but because it seemed to me that enough has been said to effect all that is needed, and that what is wanting (if anything be wanting) is not writing or speaking—whereof ordinarily there is more than enough—but silence and work." These words were addressed by St. John of the Cross to a group of nuns, who had complained that he did not answer the letters in which they had so minutely catalogued their mental states. But "speaking distracts; silence and work collect the thoughts and strengthen the spirit." Nothing, alas, could silence the Prioress. She was as copious as Mme. de Sévigné; but the gossip was exclusively about herself.

In 1660, with the Restoration, the two British tourists, who had seen Sœur Jeanne in all her diabolic glory, at last came into their own. Tom Killigrew was made a Groom of the Bedchamber and licensed to build a theater, where he might put on plays without submitting them to censorship. As for John Maitland, who had been taken prisoner at Worcester and had spent nine years in confinement—he now became Secretary of State and the new King's prime favorite.

The prioress, meanwhile, was feeling her age. She was ailing, and her double role of walking relic and verger, of sacred object and loquacious guide, fatigued her now beyond endurance. In 1662 the sacred names were renewed for the last time; thenceforward there was nothing for the devout or the curious to see. But though the miracles had ceased, the spiritual pretension remained as great as ever. "I propose," Surin wrote to her in one of his letters, "to speak to you of the prime necessity, of the very basis of grace—I mean humility. Let me beg you, then, to act in such a way that this holy humility may become the true and solid foundation of your soul. These things of which we speak in our letters—things, very often, of a sublime and lofty nature—must in no wise be permitted to compromise that virtue." In spite of his credulity, in spite of his overestimation of the merely miraculous, Surin understood his correspondent only too well. Sœur Jeanne belonged to what, at that particular moment of history, was evidently a very common subspecies of bovarists. Just how common, we may infer from a note in Pascal's *Pensées*. In St. Teresa, he writes, "what pleases God is her profound humility in revelations; what pleases men is the knowledge revealed to her. And so we work ourselves to death trying to imitate her words, imagining that thereby we are imitating her state of being. We neither love the virtue which God loves, nor do we try to bring ourselves into the state of being which God loves."

With part of her mind Sœur Jeanne was probably convinced that she actually *was* the heroine of her own comedy. With another she must have been even more certain of the contrary. Mme. du Houx who, on more than one occasion, spent long months at Loudun was of opinion that her poor friend was living almost all the time in illusion.

Did that illusion persist to the very end? Or did Sœur Jeanne at least succeed in dying, not as the heroine before the footlights, but as herself behind the scenes? It was absurd, this backstage self of hers, it was pathetic; but if she would but acknowledge the fact, if she would only cease to impersonate the authoress of the *Interior Castle*, all might still be well. So long as she insisted on pretending to be someone else, there was no chance; but if she humbly confessed to being herself, then perhaps she might discover that, in reality, she had always been Someone Else.

After her death, which came in January, 1665, the Prioress's comedy was transformed by the surviving members of the Community into the broadest of farces. The corpse was decapitated and Sœur Jeanne's head took its place, in a silver-gilt box with crystal windows, beside the sacred chemise. A provincial artist was commisioned to paint an enormous picture of the expulsion of Behemoth. At the center of the composition the Prioress was shown kneeling in ecstasy before Father Surin, who was assisted by Father Tranquille and a Carmelite. In the middle distance sat Gaston d'Orléans and his Duchess, majestically looking on. Behind them, at a window, could be seen the faces of spectators of less exalted rank. Surrounded by a gloria and accompanied by cherubim, St. Joseph hovered overhead. In his right hand he held three thunderbolts, to be hurled at the black host of imps and demons that issued from between the demoniac's parted lips.

For more than eighty years this picture hung in the Ursulines' chapel and was an object of popular devotion. But in 1750 a visiting bishop of Poitiers ordered its removal. Torn between institutional patriotism and the duty to obey, the good sisters compromised by hanging a second, yet larger painting over the first. The Prioress might be in eclipse, but she was still there. Not, however, for very long. The convent fell on evil days and in 1772 was suppressed. The picture was entrusted to a canon of Sainte-Croix, the chemise and the mummified head were sent, in all probability, to some other, more fortunate nunnery of the Order. All three have now disappeared.

CHAPTER ELEVEN

WE PARTICIPATE in a tragedy; at a comedy we only look. The tragic author feels himself into his personages; and so, from the other side, does the reader or listener. But in pure comedy there is no identification between creator and literary creature, between spectator and spectacle. The author looks, judges and records, from the outside; and from the outside his audience observes what he has recorded, judges as he has judged and, if the comedy is good enough, laughs. Pure comedy cannot be kept up for very long. That is why so many of the greatest comic writers have adopted the impure form, in which there is a constant transition from outwardness to inwardness, and back again. At one moment we merely see and judge and laugh; the next, we are made to sympathize and even to identify ourselves with one who, a few seconds before, was merely an object. Every figure of fun is potentially an Amiel or a Bashkirtseff; and every tormented author of confessions or an intimate journal can be seen, if we so desire, as a figure of fun.

Jeanne des Anges was one of those unfortunate human beings who consistently invite the outward approach, the purely comic treatment. And this in spite of the fact that she wrote confessions, which were intended to evoke the reader's heartfelt sympathy with her very considerable sufferings. That we can read these confessions and still think of the poor Prioress as a comic figure is due to the fact that she was supremely an actress; and that, as an actress, she was almost always external even to herself. The "I" who does her confessing is sometimes a pastiche of St. Augustine, sometimes the queen of the demoniacs, sometimes the second St. Teresa—and sometimes, giving the whole show away, a shrewd and momentarily sincere young woman, who knows precisely who she is and how she is related to these other, more romantic personages. Without, of course, desiring to turn herself into a figure of fun, Sœur Jeanne employs all the devices of the comic writer—the sudden shift from mask to absurd face; the emphasis, the excessive protestations; the pious verbiage that so naïvely rationalizes some all too human wish below the surface.

Moreover, Sœur Jeanne wrote her confessions without reflecting that her readers might have other sources of information about the facts therein recorded. Thus, from the official record of the counts upon which Grandier was condemned, we know that the Prioress and several other nuns were overpowered by remorse at what they had done and tried to withdraw a testimony which they knew, even in the paroxysms of hysteria, to be completely false. Sœur Jeanne's autobiography abounds in the conventional avowals of vanity, of pride, of lukewarmness. But of her greatest offense—the systematic lying which had brought an innocent man to the question and the flames—she makes no mention. Nor does she ever refer to the only creditable episode in the whole hideous story—her repentance and the public confession of her guilt. On second thoughts she preferred to accept the cynical assurances of Laubardemont and the Capuchins: her contrition was a trick of the devils, her lies were gospel truth. Any account of this episode, even the most favorable, would inevitably have spoiled her portrait of the authoress as a victim of the devil, miraculously rescued by God. Suppressing the strange and tragic facts, she chose to identify herself with an essentially bookish fiction. This sort of thing is the very stuff of comedy.

In the course of his life Jean-Joseph Surin thought, wrote and did many foolish, ill-judged and even grotesque things. But for anyone who has read his letters and his memoirs he must always remain an essentially tragic figure, in whose sufferings (however odd and however, in a certain sense, well-deserved) we always participate. We know him as he knew himself—from inside and without disguise. The "I" who does his confessing is always Jean-Joseph, never someone else, more romantic, never, as with the poor Prioress, that other, spectacular personage, who invariably ends by letting the cat out of the bag and so transforming the would-be sublime into the comic, the downright farcical.

The beginnings of Surin's long tragedy have already been described. An iron will, directed by the highest ideal of spiritual perfection and by erroneous notions as to the relations between Absolute and relative, between God and nature, had overdriven a weak constitution, a temperament in unstable equilibrium. He was a sick man even before he came to Loudun. There, though he tried to mitigate the Manichaean excesses of the other exorcists, he became the victim of a too close and intense preoccupation with the idea and the apparent fact of radical Evil. The devils derived their strength from the very violence of the campaign, which was waged against them. Strength in the nuns, and strength in their exorcists. Under the influence of an organized obsession with evil, the normally latent tendencies (tendencies to license and blasphemy, to which, by induction, a strict religious discipline always gives rise) came rushing to the surface. Lactance and Tranquille died in convulsions, "hand and foot in Belial's gripe." Surin underwent the same self-inflicted ordeal, but survived.

While working at Loudun, Surin found time, between the exorcisms and his own seizures, to write many letters. But except to his indiscreet friend, Father d'Attichy, he made no confidences. Meditation, mortification, purity of heart—these are the ordinary themes of his letters. The devils and his own trials are scarcely mentioned.

"In regard to your mental prayer," he writes to one of his cloistered correspondents, "I do not take it as a bad sign that you should be unable, as you tell me, to keep your mind fixed on some particular subject, which you have prepared in advance. I advise you not to pin yourself down to any specific topic, but to go to your prayers with the same freedom of heart, with which, in the past, you used to go to Mother d'Arrérac's room, to talk with her and help her to pass the time. To these meetings you did not bring an agenda of carefully studied subjects for discussion; for that would have put an end to the pleasure of your conversation. You went to her with a general disposition to foment and cultivate your friendship. Go to God in the same way."

"Love the dear God," he writes to another of his friends, "and permit Him to do as He likes. Where He works, the soul should give up its own coarse way of acting. Do this, and remain exposed to the will of Love, and to its power. Lay aside your busy practices, which are mingled with many imperfections that need to be purified."

And what is this divine Love, to whose will and power the soul is required to expose itself? "Love's work is to ravage, to destroy, to abolish, and then to make new, to set up again, to resuscitate. It is marvelously terrible and marvelously sweet; and the more terrible, the more desirable, the more attractive. To this Love we must resolutely give ourselves. I shall not be happy until I have seen it triumph over you, to the point of consuming and annihilating you."

In Surin's case the process of annihilation was only just beginning. During the greater part of 1637 and the first months of 1638 he was a sick man, but a sick man with intervals of health. His malady consisted of a series of departures from a state that was still tolerably normal.

"This obsession," he wrote twenty-five years later in *La Science Expérimentale des choses de l'autre vie*,* "was accompanied by extraordinary mental vigor and cheerfulness, which helped him to bear this burden not merely with patience, but with contentment." True, sustained concentration was already out of the question; he could not study. But he could make use of the fruits of earlier studies in astonishing improvisations. Inhibited, not knowing what he was going to say, or whether he would be able to open his mouth, he would climb up into the pulpit, with the feelings of a condemned criminal mounting the scaffold. Then, suddenly he would feel "a dilatation of the interior sense and the heat of so strong a grace that he would discharge his heart like a trumpet, with a mighty power

* For the only complete and authentic text of the autobiographical sections of this work, consult Vol. II of *Lettres Spirituelles du P. Jean-Joseph Surin*, edited by Michel and Cavalléra (Toulouse, 1928).

of voice and thought, as if he had been another man. . . . A pipe had been opened, disgorging into his mind an abundance of strength and knowledge."

Then came a sudden change. The pipe was stopped; the torrent of inspiration dried up. The sickness took a new form, and was no longer the spasmodic obsession of a relatively normal soul in touch with its God, but a total deprivation of light, accompanied by a diminution and degradation of the whole man into something less than himself. In a series of letters, written for the most part in 1638, and addressed to a nun who had passed through experiences similar to his own, Surin describes the first beginnings of that new phase of his malady.

In part, at least, his sufferings were physical. There were days and weeks when a low, but almost unremitting fever, kept him in a state of extreme weakness. At other times he suffered from a kind of partial paralysis. He still had some control over his limbs; but every movement cost him an enormous effort and was often accompanied by pain. The smallest actions were torturing ordeals, and every task, the most trifling and ordinary, was a labor of Hercules. It would take him two or three hours to unfasten the hooks on his cassock. As for completely undressing, it was a physical impossibility. For nearly twenty years, Surin slept in his clothes. Once a week, however, it was necessary (if he was to remain free of vermin, "for which I had a great aversion") to change his shirt. "I suffered so enormously from this change of linen that sometimes I would spend almost the whole of the night from Saturday to Sunday in taking off the soiled shirt and putting on the clean one. Such was the pain involved that, if ever I seemed to find some gleam of happiness, it was always before Thursday, whereas from Thursday onward I suffered the greatest anguish, thinking of my change of shirt; for this was a torture from which, if I could have had my choice, I would have ransomed myself by almost any other kind of suffering."

Eating was almost as bad as dressing and undressing. Shirts were changed only once a week. But these Sisyphean cuttings of meat, these raisings of forks to mouth, these laborious graspings and tiltings of the glass, were daily ordeals, all the more unbearable because of a total lack of appetite and the diner's knowledge that he would probably throw up everything he had eaten or, if he did not, would suffer from excruciating indigestion.

The doctors did their best for him. He was bled, he was purged, he was made to take warm baths. Nothing did any good. The symptoms were physical, no doubt; but their cause was to be sought, not in the patient's corrupted blood and peccant humors, but in his mind.

That mind had ceased to be possessed. The struggle was no longer between Leviathan and a soul that, in spite of him, was tranquilly conscious of the presence of God. It was between a certain notion of God and a certain notion of nature, with Surin's divided spirit fighting on both sides and getting the worst of every encounter.

That the infinite must include the finite and must therefore be totally present at every point of space, every instant of time, seems sufficiently evident. To avoid this obvious conclusion and to escape its practical consequences, the older and more rigorous Christian thinkers expended all their ingenuity, the severer Christian moralists all their persuasions and coercions.

This is a fallen world, proclaimed the thinkers, and nature, human and subhuman, is radically corrupt. Therefore, said the moralists, nature must be fought on every front—suppressed within, ignored and depreciated without.

But it is only through the *datum* of nature that we can hope to receive the *donum* of Grace. It is only by accepting the given, *as it is given*, that we may qualify for the Gift. It is only through the facts that we can come to the primordial Fact. "Do not hunt after the truth," advises one of the Zen masters, "only cease to cherish opinions." And the Christian mystics say substantially the same thing —with this difference, however, that they have to make an exception in favor of the opinions known as dogmas, articles of faith, pious traditions and the like. But at best these are but signposts; and if we "take the pointing finger for the Moon," we shall certainly go astray. The Fact must be approached through the facts; it cannot be known by means of words, or by means of phantasies inspired by words. The heavenly kingdom can be made to come *on earth*; it cannot be made to come in our imagination or in our discursive reasonings. And it cannot come even on earth, so long as we persist in living, not on the earth as it is actually given, but as it appears to an ego obsessed by the idea of separateness, by cravings and abhorrences, by compensatory phantasies and by ready-made propositions about the nature of things. Our kingdom must go before God's can come. There must be a mortification, not of nature, but of our fatal tendency to set up something of our own contriving in the place of nature. We have to get rid of our catalogue of likes and dislikes, of the verbal patterns to which we expect reality to conform, of the fancies into which we retire, when the facts do not come up to our expectation. This is the "holy indifference" of St. François de Sales; this is de Caussade's "abandonment," the conscious willing, moment by moment, of what actually happens; this is that "refusal to prefer" which, in Zen phraseology, is the mark of the Perfect Way.

On authority and because of certain experiences of his own, Surin believed that God could be known directly, in a transfiguring union of the soul with the divine Ground of its own and the world's being. But he also cherished the opinion that, because of our first parents' sin, nature is totally depraved, and that this depravity sets a great gulf between the Creator and the creature. Given these notions about God and the universe (notions idolatrously regarded as interchangeable with facts and the primordial Fact), Surin felt that it was only logical to attempt the eradication from his mind-body of every element of nature that could be uprooted without actually causing death. In his old age he recognized that he had made a mistake. "For it must be remarked that, several years before he went to Loudun, the Father [Surin is writing of himself in the third person] "had held himself exceedingly tight (*s'était extrèmement serré*) for reasons of mortification, and in an effort to remain unceasingly in the presence of God; and though there was in this some commendable zeal, there were also great excesses in the reserve and constraint of his mind. For this reason he was in a condition of cramped contraction (*rétrécissement*), which was assuredly blameworthy, though well meant." Because he cherished the opinion that the infinite is somehow outside the finite, that God is in some way opposed to his creation, Surin had tried to mortify, not his egotistic attitude toward nature, not the fancies and notions which he had set up in the place of nature, but nature itself, the given facts of embodied existence among human beings on this particular planet.

"Hate nature," is his advice, "and let it suffer the humiliations God wills for it." Nature has been "condemned and sentenced to death," and the sentence is just; that is why we must "allow God to flay and crucify us at His pleasure." That it *was* His pleasure, Surin knew by the bitterest experience. Cherishing the opinion of nature's total depravity, he had transformed the world-weariness, which is so common a symptom of neurosis, into a loathing for his own humanity, an abhorrence for his environment—a loathing and an abhorrence all the more intense because he still had cravings, because creatures, though disgusting, were still a source of temptation. In one of his letters he states that, for some days past, he has had some business to transact. To his sick nature the occupation brings a certain relief. He feels a little less miserable, until the moment comes when he realizes that the improvement was due to the fact that "every moment had been filled with infidelities." His misery returns, aggravated by a sense of guilt, a conviction of sin. He feels a chronic remorse. But it is a remorse which does not spur him to action; for he finds himself incapable of action, incapable even of confession, so that he has to "swallow his sins like water, to feed on them as though on bread." He lives in a paralysis of the will and the faculties, but not of the sensibilities. For though he cannot do anything, he can still suffer. "The more one is stripped, the more acutely does one feel the blows." He is in "the void of death." But this void is more than a mere absence; it is nothingness with a vengeance, "hideous and horrible, it is an abyss, where there can be no help or relief from any creature," and where the Creator is a tormentor, for whom the victim can feel only hatred. The new Master demands to reign alone; that is why He is making his servant's life utterly unlivable; that is why nature has been hunted down to its last retreat and is being slowly tortured to death. Nothing remains of the personality but its most repulsive elements. Surin can no longer think, or study, or pray, or do good works, or lift up his heart to his Maker in love and gratitude; but "the sensual and animal side of his nature" is still alive and "plunged in crime and abomination." And so are the criminally frivolous cravings for diversion, so are pride and self-love and ambition. Annihilated from within by neurosis and his rigorist opinions, he resolves to accelerate the destruction of nature by mortifying himself from without. There are still certain occupations that bring him a little relief from his miseries. He gives them up; for it is necessary, he feels, to "join outward emptiness to inward emptiness." By this means the very hope of external support will be removed, and nature will be left, utterly defenseless, to the mercy of God. Meanwhile the doctors have ordered him to eat plenty of meat; but he cannot bring himself to obey. God has sent him this sickness as a means of purgation. If he tries to get well prematurely, he will be thwarting the divine will.

Health is rejected, business and recreation are rejected. But there are still those flashy products of his talents and learning—the sermons, the theological treatises, the homilies, the devotional poems, at which he has worked so hard and of which he is still so wickedly vain. After long and torturing indecision, he feels a strong impulse to destroy everything he has ever written. The manuscripts of several books, together with many other papers, are torn up and burned. He is now "despoiled of everything and abandoned stark naked to his sufferings." He is "in the hands of the Workman who (I assure you) presses on with his work forcing me to travel by hard roads, which my nature revolts against taking."

A few months later the road had become so hard that Surin was physically and mentally incapable of describing it. From 1639 to 1657 there is a great gap in his correspondence, a total blank. During all this time he suffered from a kind of pathological illiteracy, and was incapable either of writing or reading. At moments it was difficult for him even to speak. He was in solitary confinement, cut off from all communication with the outside world. Exile from humanity was bad enough; but it was as nothing to that exile from God, to which he was now condemned. Not long after his return from Annecy, Surin came to be convinced (and the conviction endured for many years) that he was already damned. Nothing now remained for him but to wait, in utter despair, for a death which was predestined to be the passage from hell on earth to an infinitely more terrible hell in hell.

His confessor and his superiors assured him that God's mercy is boundless and that, so long as there is life, there can be no certainty of damnation. One learned theologian proved the point by syllogisms; another came to the infirmary loaded with folios and proved it by the authority of the Doctors of the Church. It was all in vain. Surin *knew* that he was lost and that the devils, over whom he had so recently triumphed, were gleefully preparing a place for him among the everlasting fires. Men might talk as they liked; but facts and his own deeds spoke louder than any words. Everything that happened, everything he felt and was inspired to do, confirmed him in his conviction. If he sat near the fire, a burning ember (the symbol of eternal damnation) was sure to jump out at him. If he entered a church, it was always at the moment when some phrase about God's justice, some denunciation of the wicked, was read or sung—for *him*. If he listened to a sermon, he would invariably hear the preacher affirm that there was a lost soul in the congregation—it was *his*. Once, when he had gone to pray at the bedside of a dying brother, the conviction came to him that, like Urbain Grandier, he was a sorcerer and had the power to command devils to enter the bodies of innocent persons. And that was what he was doing now—putting a spell upon the dying man. Ordering Leviathan, the demon of pride to enter into him. Summoning Isacaaron, the demon of lust, Balaam, the spirit of buffoonery, Behemoth, the lord of all blasphemies. A man was standing on the brink of eternity, ready to take the last, decisive step. If, when he took that step, his soul were full of love and faith, all would go well with him. If not . . . Surin could actually smell the sulphur, could hear the howling and the gnashing of teeth—and yet, against his will (or was he doing it voluntarily?) he kept calling on the devils, he kept hoping that they would show themselves. All at once the sick man stirred uneasily in his bed and began to talk—not as he had done before, of resignation to God's will, not of Christ and Mary, not of the divine mercy and the joys of paradise, but incoherently of the flapping of black wings, of assailing doubts and unspeakable terrors. With an overpowering sense of horror, Surin realized that it was perfectly true: he *was* a sorcerer.

To these external and inferential proofs of his damnation were added the inward assurances inspired in his mind by some alien and evidently supernatural power. "He who speaks of God," he wrote, "speaks of a sea of rigors and (if I dare say it) of severities, passing all measure." In those long hours of helplessness, while he lay pinned to his bed by a paralysis of the will, an alternate collapse and cramping of the muscles, he received "impressions of God's fury so great that there is no pain in the world to compare with it." Year followed year, and one kind of suffering was succeeded by another; but the sense of God's enmity never wavered within him. He knew it intellectually; he felt it as an enormous weight, pressing upon him— the weight of divine judgment. *Et pondus ejus ferre non potui.* He could not bear it, and yet there it always was.

To reinforce this felt conviction, there were repeated visions— so vivid, so substantial, that he was hard put to it to decide whether he had seen them with the eyes of the mind or with those of the body. They were visions, for the most part, of Christ. Not of Christ the Redeemer, but of Christ the Judge. Not of Christ teaching or Christ suffering, but of Christ on the Last Day, Christ as the unrepentant sinner sees him at the moment of death, Christ as he appears to the damned souls in the pit of hell, Christ wearing "an insupportable look" of anger, of abhorrence, of vengeful hatred. Sometimes Surin saw him as an armed man in a scarlet cloak. Sometimes, floating in the air at the height of a pike, the vision would stand guard at church doors, forbidding the sinner to enter. Sometimes, as a visible and tangible something, Christ seemed to radiate from the Sacrament and was experienced by the sick man as a current of loathing so powerful that, on one occasion, it actually knocked him off a ladder, from which he was watching a religious procession. (At other times—such is the intensity of the doubt which honest faith creates, by induction, in the minds of the believer—he *knew* for a certainty that Calvin was right and that Christ was not really present in the Sacrament. The dilemma admitted of no passage between its horns. When he knew, by direct experience, that Christ was in the consecrated wafer, he knew, by direct experience, that Christ had damned him. But he was no less certainly damned, when he knew with the heretics, that the doctrine of the real presence was untrue.)

Surin's visions were not of Christ alone. Sometimes he saw the Blessed Virgin, frowning at him with an expression of disgust and indignation. Raising her hand, she would discharge a bolt of avenging lightning, and his whole being, mental and physical, would feel the pain of it. Sometimes other saints rose up before him, each with his "insupportable look" and thunderbolt. Surin would see them in his dreams and wake up with a start and in agony, as the lightning struck him. The most unlikely saints made their appearance. One night, for example, he was transfixed by a bolt from the hand of "St. Edward, King of England." (Was this Edward the Martyr? Or can it have been poor Edward the Confessor? In any case, St. Edward displayed a "horrible anger against me; and I am convinced that this [throwing of thunderbolts by saints] is what happens in hell."

At the beginning of his long exile from heaven and the world of men, Surin was still capable, at least on his good days, of trying to re-establish contact with his surroundings. "I was always running after my superiors and the other Jesuits in order to pour into their ears an account of what was going on in my soul." In vain. (One of the chief horrors of mental derangement, as of extreme physical disability, consists in the fact that "between us and you there is a great gulf fixed." The state of the catatonic, for example, is incommensurable with the state of the normal man or woman. The universe inhabited by the paralyzed is radically different from the world known to those who have the full use of their bodies. Love may build a bridge, but cannot abolish the gulf; and where there is no love, there is not even a bridge.) Surin ran after his superiors and his colleagues; but they understood nothing of what he told them; they did not even wish to sympathize. "I recognized the truth of what St. Teresa said: that there is no pain more unbearable than that of falling into the hands of a confessor who is too prudent." Impatiently, they moved away from him. He caught them by the sleeve and tried, yet again, to explain what was happening to him. It was all so simple, so obvious, so unutterably terrible! They smiled contemptuously and tapped their foreheads. The man was mad and, what was more, he had brought his madness on himself. God, they assured him, was punishing him for his pride and his singularity—for wanting to be more spiritual than other people, for imagining that he could go to perfection by some eccentric, un-Jesuit road of his own choosing. Surin protested against their judgment. "That natural common sense, on which our faith is built, fortifies us so strongly against the objects of the other life that, so soon as a man asserts that he is damned, other people treat the idea as though it were an expression of madness." But the follies of the melancholy and the hypochondriacal are of quite another kind—to imagine, for example, that "one is a jug, or a cardinal," or (if one is actually a cardinal, like Alphonse de Richelieu) that one is God the Father. To believe that one is damned, Surin insisted, was never a sign of madness; and to prove his point, he cited the cases of Henry Suso, of St. Ignatius, of Blosius, of St. Teresa, of St. John of the Cross. At one time or another all of these had believed themselves to be damned; and all of them had been both sane and eminently holy. But the prudent ones either refused to listen, or if they did hear him out (with what an undisguised impatience!) were not convinced.

Their attitude deepened Surin's already enormous misery and drove him yet further along the road to despair. On the seventeenth of May, 1645, at the little Jesuit house at Saint-Macaire, near Bordeaux, he tried to commit suicide. All the preceding night he had wrestled with the temptation to self-murder and most of the morning was spent in prayer before the Holy Sacrament. "A little before dinner time he went up to his room. Entering it, he saw that the window was open, went to it and, after looking down at the precipice which had inspired this mad instinct in his mind [the house was built on a rocky eminence above the river], withdrew into the middle of the room, still facing the window. There he lost all consciousness and suddenly, as if he had been asleep, without any knowledge of what he was doing, he was hurled out of the window." The body fell, bounced on a projection of the rock and came to rest at the water's edge. The thigh bone was broken; but there were no internal injuries. Prompted by his inveterate passion for the miraculous, Surin rounds off the account of his tragedy with an almost comic postscript. "At the very moment of this accident, and at the very place where the fall took place, a Huguenot came down to the river, and while being ferried across he made jokes about the occurrence. Once over, he remounted and, in the meadow, on a perfectly smooth road, his horse threw him and he broke his arm, and he himself said that God had punished him because he had laughed at the Father for trying to fly, and he, from a much smaller height, had fallen into the same mishap. Now, the height from which the Father fell is great enough to be fatal; for less than a month since a cat, which was trying to catch a sparrow, fell from the same place, and was killed, though these animals, being light and adroit, ordinarily fall without hurting themselves."

Surin's leg was set and, after some months, he was able to walk, though always, thenceforward, with a limp. The mind, however, was not to be cured so easily as the body. The temptation to despair persisted for years. High places continued to hold a fearful fascination. He could not look at a knife or a rope without an intense desire to hang himself or cut his own throat.

And the urge to destruction was directed outward as well as inward. There were times when Surin found himself filled with an almost irresistible desire to set fire to the house in which he was living. The buildings and their human occupants, the library with all its treasures of wisdom and devotion, the chapel, the vestments, the crucifixes, the Blessed Sacrament itself—all should be reduced to ashes. Only a fiend could harbor such malice. But that precisely was what he was—a damned soul, a devil incarnate, hated by God and hating in return. For him, this kind of wickedness would be entirely in order. And yet, lost though he knew himself to be, there was still a part of him that rejected the evil which it was his duty, as one of the damned, to think and feel and do. The temptations to suicide and arson were strong; but he struggled against them. And meanwhile those all too prudent persons who surrounded him were taking no chances. After his first attempt at self-murder he was either watched by a lay brother, or actually tied with ropes to his bed. For the next three years Surin was subjected to that systematic inhumanity which our fathers reserved for the insane.

By those who get a kick out of this sort of thing (and they are very numerous) inhumanity is enjoyed for its own sake, but often, nonetheless, with a bad conscience. To allay their sense of guilt, the bullies and the sadists provide themselves with creditable excuses for their favorite sport. Thus, brutality toward children is rationalized as discipline, as obedience to the Word of God—"he that spareth the rod, hateth his son." Brutality toward criminals is a corollary of the Categorical Imperative. Brutality toward religious or political heretics is a blow for the True Faith. Brutality toward members of an alien race is justified by arguments drawn from what may once have passed for Science. Once universal, brutality toward the insane is not yet extinct—for the mad are horribly exasperating. But this brutality is no longer rationalized, as it was in the past, in theological terms. The people who tormented Surin and the other victims of hysteria or psychosis did so, first, because they enjoyed being brutal and, second, because they were convinced that they did well to be brutal. And they believed that they did well, because, *ex hypothesi*, the mad had always brought their troubles upon themselves. For some manifest or obscure sin, they were being punished by God, who permitted devils to besiege or obsess them. Both as God's enemies and as temporary incarnations of radical evil, they deserved to be maltreated. And maltreated they were—with a good conscience and a heart-warming sense that the divine will was being done on earth, as in heaven. The Bedlamite was beaten, starved, chained up in the filthiest of dungeons. If he was visited by a minister of religion, it was to be told that it was all his own fault and that God was angry with him. To the general public he was a mixture between a baboon and a mountebank, with some of the characteristics of a condemned criminal thrown in. On Sundays and holidays one took the children to see the insane, as one takes them now to the zoo or the circus. And there were no rules against teasing the animals. On the contrary, the animals being what they were, the enemies of God, tormenting them was not merely permissible; it was a duty. The sane person who is treated as a lunatic and subjected to every kind of insult and practical joke—this is a favorite theme of sixteenth- and seventeenth-century dramatists and storytellers. One thinks of Malvolio, one thinks of Lasca's Dr. Manente, one thinks of the wretched victim in Grimmelshausen's *Simplicissimus*. And the facts are even more unpleasant than the fictions.

Louise du Tronchay has left an account of her experiences in the great Parisian madhouse of the Salpêtrière, to which she was committed, in 1674, after being found in the streets, screaming and laughing to herself, and followed by large numbers of stray cats. These cats aroused a vehement suspicion that, as well as mad, she was a witch. At the hospital, she was chained up in a cage for the public amusement. Through the bars visitors would poke her with their walking sticks and make jokes about the cats and the punishment reserved for witches. That dirty straw she was lying on—what a fine blaze it would make when she was brought to execution! Every few weeks new straw was provided and the old was burned in the courtyard. Louise would be brought to look at the flames and hear the gleeful shouts of "Fire for the witch!" One Sunday she was made to listen to a sermon, of which she herself was the subject. The preacher exhibited her to his congregation as an awful example of the way in which God punishes sin. In this world it was a cage in the Salpêtrière; in the next it would be hell. And while the wretched victim sobbed and shuddered, he expatiated with relish on the flames, the stench, the draughts of boiling oil, the scourges of red-hot wire—forever and ever, Amen.

Under this regimen Louise, very naturally, grew worse and worse. That she finally recovered was due to the common decency of one man—a visiting priest who treated her kindly and had the charity to teach her to pray.

Surin's experiences were essentially similar. True, he was spared the mental and physical tortures of life in a public madhouse. But even in the infirmary of a Jesuit college, even among the highly educated scholars and dedicated Christians who were his colleagues, there were horrors enough. The lay brother, who acted as his attendant, beat him unmercifully. The schoolboys, if ever they caught a glimpse of the crazed Father, would hoot and jeer. Of such actors such actions were only to be expected. They were not to be expected of grave and learned priests, his brothers, his fellow apostles. And yet how crassly insensitive, how totally without the bowels of compassion they proved themselves to be! There were the bluff and hearty ones, the Muscular Christians, who assured him that there was nothing wrong with him, who forced him to do all the things it was impossible for him to do, and then laughed when he cried out in pain and told him it was all imagination. There were the malignant moralists who came and sat at his bedside and told him, at enormous length and with evident satisfaction, that he was only getting what he had so richly deserved. There were the priests who visited him out of curiosity and to be amused, who talked nonsense to him as though he were a child or a cretin, who showed off their wit, their priceless sense of humor, by being waggish at his expense, by making derisive jokes which they assumed, because he could not answer, that he could not understand. On one occasion "a Father of some importance came to the infirmary, where I was all alone, sitting on my bed, looked at me fixedly for a long time and then, though I had done him no harm and had no wish to do him any, gave me a well aimed slap in the face; after which he went out."

Surin did his best to turn these brutalities to the profit of his soul. God desired that he should be humiliated by being thought mad and treated as an outlaw, with no right to men's respect, no right even to their pity. He resigned himself to what was happening; he went further and actively willed his own humiliation. But this conscious effort to reconcile himself to his fate was not enough, of itself, to effect a cure. As in the case of Louise du Tronchay, the healing agent was another's kindness. In 1648 Father Bastide, the only one of his colleagues who had persistently argued that Surin was not irretrievably mad, was appointed to the rectorship of the college of Saintes. He asked for permission to take the invalid with him. It was granted. At Saintes, for the first time in ten years, Surin found himself treated with sympathy and consideration—as a sick man undergoing a spiritual ordeal, not as a kind of criminal undergoing punishment at the hands of God and therefore deserving of yet more punishment at the hands of men. It was still all but impossible for him to leave his prison and communicate with the world; but now the world was moving in and trying to communicate with him.

The patient's first responses to this new treatment were physical. For years, chronic anxiety had kept his breathing so shallow that he seemed to be living always on the brink of asphyxiation. Now, almost suddenly, his diaphragm started to move; he breathed deeply, he was able to fill his lungs with life-giving air. "All my muscles had been locked tight, as though with clasps, and now one clasp was opened, then another, with extraordinary relief." He was experiencing in his body an analogue of spiritual liberation. Those who have suffered from asthma or hay fever know the horror of being physically cut off from the cosmic environment, and the bliss, when they recover, of being restored to it. On the spiritual level most human beings suffer from the equivalent of asthma, but are only very obscurely and fitfully aware that they are living in a state of chronic asphyxiation. A few, however, know themselves for what they are —nonbreathers. Desperately they pant for air; and if at last they contrive to fill their lungs, what an unspeakable blessedness!

In the course of his strange career, Surin was alternately strangled and released, locked up in stifling darkness and transported to a mountain top in the sun. And his lungs reflected the state of his soul—cramped and rigid when the soul was stifled, dilated when it drew breath. The words *serré*, *bandé*, *retréci*, and their antithesis, *dilaté*, recur again and again in Surin's writings. They express the cardinal fact of his experience—a violent oscillation between the extremes of tension and release, of a contraction into less than self and a letting go into more abundant Life. It was an experience of the same kind as that which is so minutely described in Maine de Biran's diary, as that which finds its most powerfully beautiful expression in certain poems of George Herbert and Henry Vaughan— an experience made up of a succession of incommensurables.

In Surin's case psychological release was sometimes accompanied by an altogether extraordinary degree of thoracic dilation. During one period of ecstatic self-abandonment he found that his leather waistcoat, which was laced up the front, like a boot, had to be let out five or six inches. (As a young man, St. Philip Neri experienced an ecstatic dilatation so extreme that his heart became permanently enlarged and he broke two ribs. In spite, or because, of which, he lived to a ripe old age, working prodigiously to the very end.)

Surin was always conscious that there was an actual, as well as a merely etymological connection between breath and spirit. He lists four types of breathing—a breath of the devil, of nature, of grace and of glory—and assures us that he has had experience of each. Unfortunately he does not elaborate on his statement and we are left in ignorance of what he actually discovered in the field of *pranayana*.

Thanks to Father Bastide's kindness, Surin had recovered the sense of being a member of the human race. But Bastide could speak only for men and not for God—or, to be more accurate, for Surin's cherished notion of God. The invalid could breathe again; but it was still impossible for him to read or write or say Mass, to walk, or eat, or undress without discomfort or even acute pain. These disabilities were all related to Surin's enduring conviction that he was damned. It was a source of terror and despair, from which the only effective distractions were pain and acute illness. To feel better mentally he had to feel worse physically.*

The strangest feature of Surin's malady is the fact that there was a part of his mind which was never ill. Unable to read or write, unable to perform the simplest actions without excruciating and disabling pain, convinced of his own damnation, haunted by compulsions to suicide, to blasphemy, to impurity, to heresy (at one

* Surin's condition, it is interesting to remark, is described and specifically prescribed for on p. 215 of Dr. Léon Vannier's authoritative work, *La Pratique de l'Homéopathie* (Paris, 1950): "The Subject who is amenable to Actaea Racemosa has the impression that 'his head is surrounded by a thick cloud.' He sees badly, hears badly; around him and within him 'everything is confused.' 'The patient is afraid of going mad.' Oddly enough, if pains appear in any part of the organism (facial or uterine neuralgias, intercostal pains, or pains in the joints), he or she at once feels better. 'When the patient is in pain, the mental state improves.' "

moment he was a convinced Calvinist, at another a believing and practicing Manichee), Surin retained, during the whole of his long ordeal, an unimpaired capacity for literary composition. During the first ten years of his madness, he composed mainly in verse. Setting new words to popular tunes, he converted innumerable ballads and drinking songs into Christian canticles. Here are some lines about St. Teresa and St. Catherine of Genoa, from a ballad entitled *Les Saints enivrés d'Amour* to the tune of *J'ai rencontré un Allemand*.

> *J'aperçus d'un autre côté,*
> *Une vierge rare en beauté,*
>   *Qu'on appelle Thérèse;*
> *Son visage tout allumé*
> *Montrait bien qu'elle avait humé*
>   *De ce vin à son aise.*
> *Elle me dit: "Prends-en pour toi,*
> *Bois-en et chantes avec moi:*
> *Dieu, Dieu, Dieu, je ne veux que Dieu:*
>   *Tout le reste me pèse."*

> *Une Génoise, dont le cœur*
> *Etait plein de cette liqueur,*
>   *Semblait lui faire escorte:*
> *Elle aussi rouge qu'un charbon*
> *S'écriait: "Que ce vin est bon. . . ."*

That the verses are feeble and the taste atrocious was due to a want, not of health, but of talent. Surin's poetry was as poor when he was sane as when he was out of his wits. His gift (and it was considerable) was for the clear and exhaustive exposition of a subject in prose. And this precisely was what, during the second half of his illness, he actually undertook. Composing in his head and dictating every evening to an amanuensis, he produced, between 1651 and 1655, his greatest work, *Le Catéchisme Spirituel*. This is a treatise comparable in scope and in intrinsic merit to the *Holy Wisdom* of its author's English contemporary, Augustine Baker. In spite of its great length of more than a thousand duodecimo pages, the *Catechism* remains a very readable book. True, the surface texture of the writing is somewhat uninteresting; but this is not the fault of Surin, whose pleasantly old-fashioned style has been corrected, in the modern editions of the book, by what his nineteenth-century editor calls, with unconscious irony, "a friendly hand." Luckily, the friendly hand could not spoil the book's essential qualities of simplicity even in the subtlest analyses, of matter-of-factness even when it deals with the sublime.

At the time he composed his *Catechism*, Surin was incapable of consulting books of reference, or of going back over his own manuscript. And yet, in spite of this, the references to other authors are copious and apt, and the work itself is admirably well organized in a series of returns to the same themes, which are treated on each occasion from a different viewpoint, or with a graduated increase of elaboration. To compose such a book under such handicaps required a prodigious memory and exceptional powers of concentration. But Surin, though somewhat better than he had been at his worst, was still generally regarded (and not without reason) as a lunatic.

To be mad with lucidity and in complete possession of one's intellectual faculties—this, surely, must be one of the most terrible of experiences. Unimpaired, Surin's reason looked on helplessly, while his imagination, his emotions and his autonomic nervous system comported themselves like an alliance of criminal maniacs, bent on his destruction. It was a struggle, in the last analysis, between the active person and the victim of suggestion, between Surin the realist, doing his best to cope with actual facts, and Surin the verbalist, converting words into hideous pseudo-realities, in regard to which it was only logical to feel terror and despair.

Surin's was merely an extreme case of the universal human predicament. "In the beginning was the word." So far as human history is concerned, the statement is perfectly true. Language is the instrument of man's progress out of animality, and language is the cause of man's deviation from animal innocence and animal conformity to the nature of things into madness and diabolism. Words are at once indispensable and fatal. Treated as working hypotheses, propositions about the world are instruments, by means of which we are enabled progressively to understand the world. Treated as absolute truths, as dogmas to be swallowed, as idols to be worshiped, propositions about the world distort our vision of reality and lead us into all kinds of inappropriate behavior. "Wishing to entice the blind," says Dai-o Kokushi, "the Buddha playfully let words escape from his golden mouth. Heaven and earth have been filled, ever since, with entangling briars." And the briars have not been exclusively of Far Eastern manufacture. If Christ came "not to send peace on earth, but a sword," it was because he and his followers had no choice but to embody their insights in words. Like all other words, these Christian words were sometimes inadequate, sometimes too sweeping, and always imprecise—therefore always susceptible of being interpreted in many different ways. Treated as working hypotheses—as useful frames of reference, within which to organize and cope with the given facts of human existence—propositions made up of these words have been of inestimable value. Treated as dogmas and idols, they have been the cause of such enormous evils as theological hatred, religious wars and ecclesiastical imperialism, together with such minor horrors as the orgy at Loudun and Surin's self-suggested madness.

Moralists harp on the duty of controlling the passions; and of course they are quite right to do so. Unhappily most of them have failed to harp on the no less essential duty of controlling words and the reasoning based upon them. Crimes of passion are committed only in hot blood, and blood is only occasionally hot. But words are with us all the time, and words (owing, no doubt, to the conditioning of early childhood) are charged with a suggestive power so prodigious as to justify, in some sort, the belief in spells and magic formulas. Far more dangerous than crimes of passion are the crimes of idealism—the crimes which are instigated, fostered and moralized by hallowed words. Such crimes are planned when the pulse is normal and committed in cold blood and with unwavering perseverance over a long course of years. In the past, the words which dictated the crimes of idealism were predominantly religious; now they are predominantly political. The dogmas are no longer metaphysical, but positivistic and ideological. The only things that remain unchanged are the idolatrous superstition of those who swallow the dogmas, and the systematic madness, the diabolic ferocity, with which they act upon their beliefs.

Transferred from the laboratory and the study to the church, the parliament and the council chamber, the notion of working hypotheses might liberate mankind from its collective insanities, its chronic compulsions to wholesale murder and mass suicide. The fundamental human problem is ecological: men must learn how to live with the cosmos on all its levels, from the material to the spiritual. As a race, we have to discover how a huge and rapidly increasing population can go on existing satisfactorily on a planet of limited size and possessed of resources, many of which are wasting assets that can never be renewed. As individuals, we have to find out how to establish a satisfactory relationship with that infinite Mind, from which we habitually imagine ourselves to be isolated. By concentrating our attention on the *datum* and the *Donum* we shall develop, as a kind of byproduct, satisfactory methods of getting on with one another. "Seek ye first the Kingdom, and all the rest shall be added." But instead of that, we insist on first seeking all the rest—the all too human interests born of self-centered passion on the one hand and idolatrous word-worship on the other. The result of this is that our basic ecological problems remain unsolved and insoluble. Concentration on power politics makes it impossible for organized societies to improve their relationship with the planet. Concentration on idolatrously worshiped word-systems makes it impossible for individuals to improve their relations with the primordial Fact. Seeking first all the rest, we lose not only it, but the Kingdom as well, and the earth on which alone the Kingdom can come.

In Surin's case certain of the propositions he had been taught to worship as dogmas drove him out of his mind by creating occasions for terror and despair. But fortunately there were other propositions, more encouraging and equally dogmatic.

On October 12, 1655, one of the Fathers at the College of Bordeaux (to which, by this time, Surin had returned) came to his room to hear his confession and prepare him for communion. The only grave sin of which the sick man could accuse himself was that of not having behaved sufficiently wickedly; for, since God had already damned him, it was only right that he should live up to his damnation by wallowing in all the vices, whereas in fact he always tried to be virtuous. "To say that a Christian ought to feel scruples in regard to doing good will seem ridiculous to the reader, as it now does to me." These words were written in 1663. In 1655 Surin still felt that it was his duty, as a lost soul, to be wholly bad. But, in spite of this duty, he found it morally impossible to be anything but good. In this, he was convinced, he had committed a sin more enormous than that of premeditated murder. It was this sin which he now confessed, "not as a man living on the earth, for whom there is still hope, but as one of the damned." The confessor, who was evidently a kindly, sensible man, well acquainted with Surin's weakness for the extraordinary, assured his penitent that, though not at all prone to this kind of thing, he had often felt a strong impression, call it an inspiration, that all would finally be well. "You will recognize your mistake, you will be able to think and act like other men, you will die in peace." The words made a profound impression on Surin's mind, and from that moment the suffocating cloud of fear and misery began to lift. God had not rejected him; there was still hope. Hope for recovery in this world, hope for salvation in the next.

With hope came a slow return to health. One by one the physical inhibitions and paralyses disappeared. The first to go was the inability to write. One day, in 1657, after eighteen years of enforced illiteracy, he picked up a pen and was able to scrawl three pages of thoughts on the spiritual life. The characters were "so confused that they seemed scarcely human"; but that did not matter. What mattered was that his hand had at last been able to co-operate, however inadequately, with his mind.

Three years later he recovered the ability to walk. It happened while he was staying in the country, at the house of a friend. At the beginning of his stay, he had to be carried by two footmen from his bedroom to the dining room, "for I could not take a step without great pain. These pains were not like the pains of paralytics; they were pains which tended toward a shrinking and contraction of the stomach, and at the same time I used to feel a great violence in my bowels." On October 27, 1660, one of his relatives called to see him and, when the time came for him to go, Surin painfully dragged himself to the door to say good-by. Standing there, after the visitor's departure, he looked out into the garden "and began to study, with a certain distinctness, the objects that were in it, a thing which, on account of an extreme debility of the nerves, I had not been able to do for fifteen years." Feeling, instead of the familiar pains, "a certain suavity," he went down the five or six steps into the garden and looked about him for a little while longer. Looked at the black mold and the shiny green of the box hedges, looked at the lawns and the Michaelmas daisies and the alley of pleached hornbeams. Looked at the low hills in the distance with their autumnal woods, fox-brown under the pale sky, in the almost silvery sunlight. There was no wind, and the silence was like an enormous crystal, and everywhere was a living mystery of colors merging, of forms distinct and separate, of the innumerable and the one, of passing time and the presence of eternity.

Next day Surin ventured out again into the universe he had almost forgotten; and, the day after that, his voyage of rediscovery took him as far as the well—and it did not invite him to suicide. He even left the garden and walked, ankle-deep in the dead leaves, through the little wood that lay beyond the walls. He was cured.

Surin accounts for his unawareness of the external world by an "extreme debility of the nerves." But this debility never prevented him from concentrating his attention on theological notions and the phantasies to which those notions gave rise. Actually it was his obsession with these images and abstractions which so disastrously cut him off from the natural world. Long before the onset of his illness he had forced himself to live, at one remove from the given facts, in a world where words and reactions to words were more important than things and lives. With the sublime insanity of one who carries a faith to its logical conclusions, Lallemant had taught that "we ought not to see or wonder at anything on this earth except the Holy Sacrament. If God were capable of wonder, He would wonder only at this mystery, and that of the Incarnation. . . . After the Incarnation, we ought not to wonder at anything." In neither seeing nor wondering at anything in the given world, Surin was merely acting on his master's injunctions. Hoping to deserve the *Donum*, he ignored the *datum*. But the highest Gift is by means of the given. The Kingdom of God comes on earth and through the perception of earth as it is in itself, and not as it appears to a will distorted by self-centered cravings and revulsions, to an intellect distorted by ready-made beliefs.

As a rigorist theologian, convinced of the total depravity of a fallen world, Surin agreed with Lallemant that there was nothing in nature worth looking or wondering at. But his theories were not in accord with his immediate experience. "Sometimes," he writes in *Le Catéchisme Spirituel*, "the Holy Spirit enlightens the soul successively and by degrees; and then He takes advantage of everything that presents itself to consciousness—animals, trees, flowers or anything else in creation—in order to instruct the soul in the great truths and to teach her secretly what she must do for the service of God." And here is another passage in the same vein. "In a flower, in a tiny insect, God makes manifest to souls all the treasures of his wisdom and goodness; and there needs no more to provoke a new conflagration of love." Writing directly of himself, Surin records that "on a number of occasions my soul was invested with these states of glory, and the sunlight seemed to grow incomparably brighter than usual, and yet was so soft and bearable that it seemed to be of another kind than natural sunlight. Once when I was in this state, I went out into the garden of our college at Bordeaux; and so great was this light that I seemed to myself to be walking in paradise." Every color was more "intense and natural," every form more exquisitely distinct than at ordinary times. Spontaneously and by a kind of blessed accident, he had entered that infinite and eternal world, which we would all inhabit if only, in Blake's words, "the doors of perception were cleansed." But the glory departed and, through all the years of his illness, never returned. "Nothing remains to me but the memory of a very great thing, surpassing in beauty and grandeur all that I have experienced in this world."

That a man, for whom the Kingdom had actually manifested itself upon earth should yet subscribe to the rigorist's wholesale dismissal of all created things, is a melancholy tribute to the obsessive power of mere words and notions. He had had experiences of God in nature; but instead of making a systematic devotional use of these experiences, as Traherne was to do in his *Centuries of Meditations,* Surin chose to revert, after each theophany, to the old insane refusal to see or wonder at anything in creation. Instead, he concentrated all his attention on the more dismal propositions in his creed and on his own emotional and imaginative reactions to those propositions. No more certain way of shutting out the infinite goodness could possibly have been devised.

Each time Antaeus touched the earth, he received a new accession of strength. That was why Hercules had to lift him up and strangle him in mid-air. Simultaneously the giant and the hero, Surin both experienced the healing which comes from a contact with nature and, by sheer will power, raised himself from the ground and wrung his own neck. He had aspired to liberation; but because he conceived of union with the Son as a systematic denial of the essential divinity of nature, he had realized only the partial enlightenment of union with the Father apart from the manifested world, together with union with the Spirit in all kinds of psychic experiences. In its opening phase, Surin's cure was not a passage from darkness into that "sober certainty of waking bliss," which comes when mind permits Mind to know itself, through a finite consciousness, for what it really is; it was rather the exchange of a profoundly abnormal condition for another condition of opposite sign, in which "extraordinary graces" became as ordinary as extraordinary desolations had been before. It should be remarked that, even in the worst times of his malady, Surin had experienced brief flashes of joy, ephemeral convictions that, in spite of his damnation, God was eternally with him. These flashes were now multiplied, these convictions, from being momentary, became lasting. Psychic experience succeeded psychic experience, and every vision was luminous and encouraging, every feeling was one of bliss. But "to honor Our Lord as He deserves to be honored, you should disentangle your heart from all attachment to spiritual delights and perceptible graces. You should in no wise depend upon these things. Faith alone should be your support. It is faith which raises us to God in purity; for it leaves the soul in emptiness, and it is this emptiness which is filled by God." So Surin had written, more than twenty years before, to one of the nuns who asked him for advice. And it was in the same vein that Father Bastide—the man to whose charity he owed the first inception of his cure—now spoke to Surin. However elevated they may be, however consoling, psychic experiences are not enlightenment, nor even the means to enlightenment. And Bastide did not say these things on his own authority. He had all the accredited mystics of the Church behind him, he could quote St. John of the Cross. For some time Surin did his best to follow Bastide's advice. But his extraordinary graces came crowding in upon him, incessantly, insistently. And when he rejected them, they changed their sign once more, and turned into aridities and desolations. God seemed now to have withdrawn again and left him on the brink of the old despair. In spite of Bastide, in spite of St. John of the Cross, Surin went back to his visions, his locutions, his ecstasies, his inspirations. In the course of the ensuing controversy the two disputants and their Superior, Father Anginot, appealed to Jeanne des Anges. Would she kindly ask her Good Angel what *he* thought about extraordinary graces? The Good Angel began by favoring Bastide's cause. Surin protested, and after the exchange of many letters between Sœur Jeanne and the three Jesuits, the Angel announced that both disputants were in the right, inasmuch as each was doing his best to serve God in his own way. Surin was fully satisfied and so was Anginot. Bastide, however, stuck to his guns and even went so far as to suggest that it was time for Sœur Jeanne to break off communications with the heavenly counterpart of M. de Beaufort. Nor was he the only one to raise objections. In 1659, Surin informed the Prioress that an eminent ecclesiastic had complained "that you have set up a kind of shop for finding out from your Angel all the things people press you to ask of him, that you have a regular information bureau for marriages, lawsuits and other things of the kind." This sort of thing must be stopped immediately—not, as Father Bastide had suggested, by breaking off relations with the Angel, but by consulting him only for spiritual purposes.

Time passed. Surin was well enough now to visit the sick, to hear confessions, to preach, to write, to direct souls by word of mouth or by letter. His behavior was still somewhat odd, and his superiors thought it necessary to censor all his letters, incoming and outgoing, for fear that they might contain unorthodoxies or at least embarrassing extravagances. Their suspicions were groundless. The man who had dictated *Le Catéchisme Spirituel*, while (to all appearances) out of his mind, could be relied on to display an equal prudence now that he was well.

In 1663 he wrote the *Science Expérimentale*, with its history of the possession and its account of his own subsequent trials. Loius XIV was already well embarked on his disastrous career; but Surin was not interested in "public affairs and the schemes of the great." He had the sacraments, he had the gospels to read and ruminate, he had his experiences of God; these were enough. In certain respects, indeed, they were more than enough; for he was growing old, he was losing his strength, "and love does not go too well with weakness; for it requires a stout vessel to resist the pressure of its workings." The almost manic well-being of a few years before had gone; the regular and easy succession of extraordinary graces was a thing of the past. But he had something else, something better. To Sœur Jeanne he writes that "God has recently given me some slight knowledge of His love. But what a difference there is between the depth of the soul and its faculties! For in effect the soul is often rich in its depths and actually glutted with the supernatural treasures of grace, while its faculties are in a state of utter poverty. In her depths, as I say, the soul has a very high, very delicate, very fruitful sense of God, accompanied by a most comforting love and a wondrous dilatation of the heart, without, however, being able to communicate any of these things to other people. Outwardly, persons in this state give the impression of being without any taste (for the things of religion), devoid of all talent and reduced to an extremity of indigence. . . . There is an exceedingly great distress when the soul is unable, if the expression may be permitted, to disgorge herself through her faculties; the overplus within her causes an oppression more painful than can be imagined. What is happening in the soul's depths is like the banking up of great waters, whose mass, for lack of an issue by which to escape, overwhelms her with an unbearable weight and causes a deathly exhaustion." In some impossibly paradoxical way, a finite being contains the infinite and is almost annihilated by the experience. But Surin does not complain. It is a blessed anguish, a death devoutly to be desired.

In the midst of his ecstasies and visions, Surin had been on a track that led, no doubt, through very picturesque country, but toward a luminous dead end. Now that the extraordinary graces were over, now that he was free to be aware of the proximity of total Awareness, he had achieved the possibility of enlightenment. For now at last he was living "in faith," precisely as Bastide had urged him to do. Now at last he was standing in intellectual and imaginative nakedness before the given facts of the world and his own life— empty that he might be filled, poor that he might be made supremely rich. "I am told," he writes two years before his death, "that there are pearl fishers, who have a pipe that goes from the sea floor to the surface, where it is buoyed up with corks, and that through this pipe they breathe—and are yet at the bottom of the sea. I do not know if this be true; but in any case it expresses very well what I have to say; for the soul has a pipe that goes to heaven, a channel, says St. Catherine of Genoa, that leads to the very heart of God. Through it she breathes wisdom and love, and is sustained. While the soul is here, fishing for pearls at the bottom of the earth, she speaks with other souls, she preaches, she does God's business; and all the time there is a pipe that goes to heaven to draw down eternal life and consolation. . . . In this state the soul is at once happy and wretched. And yet I think she is really happy. . . . For without visions or ecstasies or suspensions of the senses, in the midst of the ordinary miseries of earthly life, in weakness and many-sided impotency, our Lord gives something that passes all understanding and all measure. . . . This something is a certain wound of love which, without any visible outward effect, pierces the soul and keeps it incessantly longing for God."

And so, fishing for pearls at the bottom of the earth, his pipe between his teeth, his lungs dilated by the air from another world, the old man advanced toward his consummation. A few months before he died, Surin finished the last of his devotional writings, *Questions sur l'Amour de Dieu.* Reading certain passages of this book, we divine that the last barrier had now gone down and that, for one more soul, the Kingdom had come on earth. Through that channel to the very heart of God had flowed "a peace that is not merely a calm, like the lull of the sea, or the tranquil flow of mighty rivers; but it enters into us, this divine peace and repose, like a flooding torrent; and the soul, after so many tempests, feels, as it were, an inundation of peace; and the relish of divine repose not only enters the soul, not only takes her captive, but comes upon her, like the onrush of a multitude of waters.

"We find that, in the Apocalypse, the Spirit of God makes mention of a music of harps and lutes that is like thunder. Such are the marvelous ways of God—to make a thunder like well-tuned lutes and a symphony of lutes like thunder. Likewise, who will ever believe or imagine that there can be torrents of peace, which sweep away the dykes, which breach the levees and shatter the sea walls? And yet this is what actually happens, and it is the nature of God to make assaults of peace and silences of love. . . . God's peace is like a river, whose course was in one country and has been diverted into another by the breaking of a dyke. This invading peace does things which do not seem proper to the nature of peace; for it comes with a rush, it comes with impetuosity; and this belongs only to the peace of God. Only the peace of God can march in such equipage, like the noise of the rising tide as it comes, not to ravage the land, but to fill the bed prepared for it by God. It comes as though fiercely, it comes with a roaring, even though the sea be calm. This roaring is caused only by the abundance of the waters, and not by their fury; for the moving of the waters is not by a tempest, but by the waters themselves, in all their native calm, when there is not a breath of wind. The sea in its fullness comes to visit the earth and to kiss the shores assigned for its limits. It comes in majesty and in magnificence. Even so it is in the soul when, after long suffering, the immensity of peace comes to visit her—and not a breath of wind to make a ripple on its surface. This is a divine peace, which brings with it the treasures of God and all the wealth of His Kingdom. It has its harbingers, the halcyons and heralding birds that announce its approach; these are the visits of angels which precede it. It comes like an element of the other life, with a sound of celestial harmony and with such swiftness that the soul is utterly overthrown, not because she has made any resistance to the blessing, but because of its very abundance. This abundance does no violence except to the obstacles in the way of its benediction; and all the animals that are not peaceable take flight before the onset of this peace. And with peace come all the treasures promised to Jerusalem—cassia and amber and the other rarities upon her shores. Even so comes this divine peace— comes with abundance, comes with a wealth of blessings, comes with all the precious treasures of grace."

More than thirty years before, at Marennes, Surin had often watched the calm, irresistible mounting of the Atlantic tides; and now the memory of that everyday marvel was the means by which this consummated soul was able, at last, to "disgorge herself" in a not inadequate expression of the experienced Fact. *Tel qu'en Lui-même enfin l'éternité le change*, he had come to the place where, without knowing it, he had always been; and when, in the spring of 1665 death overtook him, there was, as Jacob Boehme had said, "no necessity for him to go anywhere": he was already there.

EPILOGUE

(In amplification of material in Chapter Three)

Without an understanding of man's deep-seated urge to self-transcendence, of his very natural reluctance to take the hard, ascending way, and his search for some bogus liberation either below or to one side of his personality, we cannot hope to make sense of our own particular period of history or indeed of history in general, of life as it was lived in the past and as it is lived today. For this reason I propose to discuss some of the more common Grace-substitutes, into which and by means of which men and women have tried to escape from the tormenting consciousness of being merely themselves.

In France there is now one retailer of alcohol to every hundred inhabitants, more or less. In the United States there are probably at least a million desperate alcoholics, besides a much larger number of very heavy drinkers whose disease has not yet become mortal. Regarding the consumption of intoxicants in the past we have no precise or statistical knowledge. In Western Europe, among the Celts and Teutons, and throughout medieval and early modern times, the individual intake of alcohol was probably even greater than it is today. On the many occasions when we drink tea, or coffee, or soda pop, our ancestors refreshed themselves with wine, beer, mead and, in later centuries, with gin, brandy and usquebaugh. The regular drinking of water was a penance imposed on wrongdoers, or accepted by the religious, along with occasional vegetarianism, as a very severe mortification. Not to drink an intoxicant was an eccentricity sufficiently remarkable to call for comment and the using of a more or less disparaging nickname. Hence such patronymics as the Italian Bevilacqua, the French Boileau and the English Drinkwater.

Alcohol is but one of the many drugs employed by human beings as avenues of escape from the insulated self. Of the natural narcotics, stimulants and hallucinators there is, I believe, not a single one whose properties have not been known from time immemorial. Modern research has given us a host of brand new synthetics; but in regard to the natural poisons it has merely developed better methods of extracting, concentrating and recombining those already known. From poppy to curare, from Andean coca to Indian hemp and Siberian agaric, every plant or bush or fungus capable, when ingested, of stupefying or exciting or evoking visions, has long since been discovered and systematically employed. The fact is strangely significant; for it seems to prove that, always and everywhere, human beings have felt the radical inadequacy of their personal existence, the misery of being their insulated selves and not something else, something wider, something in Wordsworthian phrase, "far more deeply interfused." Exploring the world around him, primitive man evidently "tried all things and held fast to that which was good." For the purpose of self-preservation the good is every edible fruit and leaf, every wholesome seed, root and nut. But in another context—the context of self-dissatisfaction and the urge to self-transcendence—the good is everything in nature by means of which the quality of individual consciousness can be changed. Such drug-induced changes may be manifestly for the worse, may be at the price of present discomfort and future addiction, degeneration and premature death. All this is of no moment. What matters is the awareness, if only for an hour or two, if only for a few minutes, of being someone or, more often, something other than the insulated self. "I live, yet not I, but wine or opium or peyotl or hashish liveth in me." To go beyond the limits of the insulated ego is such a liberation that, even when self-transcendence is through nausea into frenzy, through cramps into hallucinations and coma, the drug-induced experience has been regarded by primitives and even by the highly civilized as intrinsically divine. Ecstasy through intoxication is still an essential part of the religion of many African, South American and Polynesian peoples. It was once, as the surviving documents clearly prove, a no less essential part of the religion of the Celts, the Teutons, the Greeks, the peoples of the Middle East and the Aryan conquerors of India. It is not merely that "beer does more than Milton can to justify God's ways to man." Beer *is* the god. Among the Celts, Sabazios was the divine name given to the felt alienation of being dead drunk on ale. Further to the south, Dionysos was, among other things, the supernatural objectification of the psychophysical effects of too much wine. In Vedic mythology, Indra was the god of that now unidentifiable drug called *soma*. Hero, slayer of dragons, he was the magnified projection upon heaven of the strange and glorious otherness experienced by the intoxicated. Made one with the drug, he becomes, as Soma-Indra, the source of immortality, the mediator between the human and the divine.

In modern times beer and the other toxic short cuts to self-transcendence are no longer officially worshiped as gods. Theory has undergone a change, but not practice; for in practice millions upon millions of civilized men and women continue to pay their devotions, not to the liberating and transfiguring Spirit, but to alcohol, to hashish, to opium and its derivatives, to the barbiturates, and the other synthetic additions to the age-old catalogue of poisons capable of causing self-transcendence. In every case, of course, what seems a god is actually a devil, what seems a liberation is in fact an enslavement. The self-transcendence is invariably downward into the less than human, the lower than personal.

Like intoxication, elementary sexuality, indulged in for its own sake and divorced from love, was once a god, worshiped not only as the principle of fecundity, but as a manifestation of the radical Otherness immanent in every human being. In theory, elementary sexuality has long since ceased to be a god. But in practice it can still boast of a countless host of sectaries.

There is an elementary sexuality which is innocent, and there is an elementary sexuality which is morally and aesthetically squalid. D. H. Lawrence has written very beautifully of the first; Jean Genêt, with horrifying power and in copious detail, of the second. The sexuality of Eden and the sexuality of the sewer—both of them have power to carry the individual beyond the limits of his or her insulated self. But the second and (one would sadly guess) the commoner variety takes those who indulge in it to a lower level of subhumanity, evokes the consciousness, and leaves the memory, of a completer alienation, than does the first. Hence, for all those who feel the urge to escape from their imprisoning identity, the perennial attraction of debauchery and of such strange equivalents of debauchery as have been described in the course of this narrative.

In most civilized communities public opinion condemns debauchery and drug addiction as being ethically wrong. And to moral disapproval is added fiscal discouragement and legal repression. Alcohol is heavily taxed, the sale of narcotics is everywhere prohibited and certain sexual practices are treated as crimes. But when we pass from drug-taking and elementary sexuality to the third main avenue of downward self-transcendence, we find, on the part of moralists and legislators, a very different and much more indulgent attitude. This seems all the more surprising since crowd-delirium, as we may call it, is more immediately dangerous to social order, more dramatically a menace to that thin crust of decency, reasonableness and mutual tolerance which constitutes a civilization, than either drink or debauchery. True, a generalized and long-continued habit of overindulgence in sexuality may result, as J. D. Unwin has argued,* in lowering the energy level of an entire society, thereby rendering it incapable of reaching or maintaining a high degree of civilization. Similarly drug addiction, if sufficiently widespread may lower the military, economic and political efficiency of the society in which it prevails. In the seventeenth and eighteenth centuries raw alcohol was the secret weapon of the European slave traders; heroin, in the twentieth, of the Japanese militarists. Dead drunk, the Negro was an easy prey. As for the Chinese drug addict, he could be relied upon to make no trouble for his conquerors. But

* J. D. Unwin, *Sex and Culture* (London, 1934).

316

these cases are exceptional. When left to itself, a society generally manages to come to terms with its favorite poison. The drug is a parasite on the body politic, but a parasite which its host (to speak metaphorically) has strength and sense enough to keep under control. And the same applies to sexuality. No society which based its sexual practices upon the theories of the Marquis de Sade could possibly survive; and in fact no society has ever come near to doing such a thing. Even the most easygoing of the Polynesian paradises have their rules and regulations, their categorical imperatives and commandments. Against excessive sexuality, as against excessive drug-taking, societies seem to be able to protect themselves with some degree of success. Their defense against crowd-delirium and its often disastrous consequences is, in all too many cases, far less adequate. The professional moralists who inveigh against drunkenness are strangely silent about the equally disgusting vice of herd-intoxication—of downward self-transcendence into subhumanity by the process of getting together in a mob.

"Where two or three are gathered together in my name, there am I in the midst of them." In the midst of two or three hundred, the divine presence becomes more problematical. And when the numbers run into the thousands, or tens of thousands, the likelihood of God being there, in the consciousness of each individual, declines almost to the vanishing point. For such is the nature of an excited crowd (and every crowd is automatically self-exciting) that, where two or three thousand are gathered together, there is an absence not merely of deity, but even of common humanity. The fact of being one of a multitude delivers a man from his consciousness of being an insulated self and carries him down into a less than personal realm, where there are no responsibilities, no right or wrong, no need for thought or judgment or discrimination —only a strong vague sense of togetherness, only a shared excitement, a collective alienation. And the alienation is at once more prolonged and less exhausting than that induced by debauchery; the morning after less depressing than that which follows self-poisoning by alcohol or morphine. Moreover, the crowd-delirium can be indulged in, not merely without a bad conscience, but actually, in many cases, with a positive glow of conscious virtue. For, so far from condemning the practice of downward self-transcendence through herd-intoxication, the leaders of church and state have actively encouraged the practice whenever it could be used for the furtherance of their own ends. Individually and in the co-ordinated and purposive groups which constitute a healthy society, men and women display a certain capacity for rational thought and free choice in the light of ethical principles. Herded into mobs, the same men and women behave as though they possessed neither reason nor free will. Crowd-intoxication reduces them to a condition of infra-personal and antisocial irresponsibility. Drugged by the mysterious poison which every excited herd secretes, they fall into a state of heightened suggestibility, resembling that which follows an injection of sodium amytal or the induction, by whatever means, of a light hypnotic trance. While in this state they will believe any nonsense that may be bawled at them, will act upon any command or exhortation, however senseless, mad or criminal. To men and women under the influence of herd-poison, "whatever I say three times is true"—and whatever I say three hundred times is Revelation, is the directly inspired Word of God. That is why men in authority—the priests and the rulers of peoples—have never unequivocally proclaimed the immorality of this form of downward self-transcendence. True, crowd-delirium evoked by members of the opposition and in the name of heretical principles has everywhere been denounced by those in power. But crowd-delirium aroused by government agents, crowd-delirium in the name of orthodoxy, is an entirely different matter. In all cases where it can be made to serve the interests of the men controlling church and state, downward self-transcendence by means of herd-intoxication is treated as something legitimate, and even highly desirable. Pilgrimages and political rallies, corybantic revivals and patriotic parades—these things are ethically right so long as they are *our* pilgrimages, *our* rallies, *our* revivals and *our* parades. The fact that most of those who take part in these affairs are temporarily dehumanized by herd-poison is of no account in comparison with the fact that their dehumanization may be used to consolidate the religious and political powers that be.

When crowd-delirium is exploited for the benefit of governments and orthodox churches, the exploiters are always very careful not to allow the intoxication to go too far. The ruling minorities make use of their subjects' craving for downward self-transcendence in order, first, to amuse and distract them and, second, to get them into a subpersonal state of heightened suggestibility. Religious and political ceremonials are welcomed by the masses as opportunities for getting drunk on herd-poison, and by their rulers as opportunities for planting suggestions in minds which have momentarily ceased to be capable of reason or free will.

The final symptom of herd-intoxication is a maniacal violence. Instances of crowd-delirium culminating in gratuitous destructiveness, in ferocious self-mutilation, in fratricidal savagery without purpose and against the elementary interests of all concerned, are to be met with on almost every page of the anthropologists' textbooks and—a little less frequently, but still with dismal regularity—in the histories of even the most highly civilized peoples. Except when they wish to liquidate an unpopular minority the official representatives of state and church are chary of evoking a frenzy which they cannot be sure of controlling. No such scruples restrain the revolutionary leader, who hates the *status quo* and has only one wish—to create a chaos on which, when he comes to power, he may impose a new kind of order. When the revolutionary exploits men's urge to downward self-transcendence, he exploits it to the frantic and demoniac limit. To men and women sick of being their insulated selves and weary of the responsibilities which go with membership in a purposive human group, he offers exciting opportunities for "getting away from it all" in parades and demonstrations and public meetings. The organs of the body politic are purposive groups. A crowd is the social equivalent of a cancer. The poison it secretes depersonalizes its constituent members to the point where they start to behave with a savage violence, of which, in their normal state, they would be completely incapable. The revolutionary encourages his followers to manifest this last and worst symptom of herd-intoxication and then proceeds to direct their frenzy against his enemies, the holders of political, economic and religious power.

In the course of the last forty years the techniques for exploiting man's urge toward this most dangerous form of downward self-transcendence have reached a pitch of perfection unmatched in all of history. To begin with, there are more people to the square mile than ever before, and the means of transporting vast herds of them from considerable distances, and of concentrating them in a single building or arena, are much more efficient than in the past. Meanwhile, new and previously undreamed-of devices for exciting mobs have been invented. There is the radio, which has enormously extended the range of the demagogue's raucous yelling. There is the loudspeaker, amplifying and indefinitely reduplicating the heady music of class-hatred and militant nationalism. There is the camera (of which it was once naïvely said that "it cannot lie") and its offspring, the movies and television; these three have made the objectification of tendentious phantasy absurdly easy. And finally there is that greatest of our social inventions, free, compulsory education. Everyone now knows how to read and everyone consequently is at the mercy of the propagandists, governmental or commercial, who own the pulp factories, the linotype machines and the rotary presses. Assemble a mob of men and women previously conditioned by a daily reading of newspapers; treat them to amplified band music, bright lights, and the oratory of a demagogue who (as demagogues always are) is simultaneously the exploiter and the victim of herd-intoxication, and in next to no time you can reduce them to a state of almost mindless subhumanity. Never before have so few been in a position to make fools, maniacs or criminals of so many.

In Communist Russia, in Fascist Italy, in Nazi Germany, the exploiters of humanity's fatal taste for herd-poison have followed an identical course. When in revolutionary opposition, they encouraged the mobs under their influence to become destructively violent. Later, when they had come to power, it was only in relation to foreigners and selected scapegoats that they permitted herd-intoxication to run its full course. Having acquired a vested interest in the *status quo*, they now checked the descent into subhumanity at a point well this side of frenzy. For these neo-conservatives, mass intoxication was chiefly valuable, henceforward, as a means for heightening their subjects' suggestibility and so rendering them more docile to the expressions of authoritarian will. Being in a crowd is the best known antidote to independent thought. Hence the dictators' rooted objection to "mere psychology" and a private life. "Intellectuals of the world, unite! You have nothing to lose but your brains."

Drugs, elementary sexuality and herd-intoxication—these are the three most popular avenues of downward self-transcendence. There are many others, not so well trodden as these great descending highways, but leading no less surely to the same infra-personal goal. Consider, for example, the way of rhythmic movement. In primitive religions prolonged rhythmic movement is very commonly resorted to for the purpose of inducing a state of infra-personal and subhuman ecstasy. The same technique for achieving the same end has been used by many civilized peoples—by the Greeks, for example, by the Hindus, by many of the orders of Dervishes in the Islamic world, by such Christian sects as the Shakers and the Holy Rollers. In all these cases rhythmic movement, long-drawn and repetitive, is a form of ritual deliberately practiced for the sake of the downward self-transcendence resulting from it. History also records many sporadic outbreaks of involuntary and uncontrollable jigging, swaying and head-wagging. These epidemics of what in one region is called Tarantism, in another St. Vitus's dance, have generally occurred in times of trouble following wars, pestilences and famines, and are most common where malaria is endemic. The unwitting purpose of the men and women who succumb to these collective manias is the same as that pursued by the sectaries who use the dance as a religious rite—namely, to escape from insulated selfhood into a state in which there are no responsibilities, no guilt-laden past or haunting future, but only the present, blissful consciousness of being someone else.

Intimately associated with the ecstasy-producing rite of rhythmic movement is the ecstasy-producing rite of rhythmic sound. Music is as vast as human nature and has something to say to men and women on every level of their being, from the self-regardingly sentimental to the abstractly intellectual, from the merely visceral to the spiritual. In one of its innumerable forms music is a powerful drug, partly stimulant and partly narcotic, but wholly alterative. No man, however highly civilized, can listen for very long to African drumming, or Indian chanting, or Welsh hymn-singing, and retain intact his critical and self-conscious personality. It would be interesting to take a group of the most eminent philosophers from the best universities, shut them up in a hot room with Moroccan dervishes or Haitian voodooists, and measure, with a stop watch, the strength of their psychological resistance to the effects of rhythmic sound. Would the Logical Positivists be able to hold out longer than the Subjective Idealists? Would the Marxists prove tougher than the Thomists or the Vedantists? What a fascinating, what a fruitful field for experiment! Meanwhile, all we can safely predict is that, if exposed long enough to the tom-toms and the singing, every one of our philosophers would end by capering and howling with the savages.

The ways of rhythmic movement and of rhythmic sound are generally superimposed, so to speak, upon the way of herd-intoxication. But there are also private roads, roads which can be taken by the solitary traveler who has no taste for crowds, or no strong faith in the principles, institutions and persons in whose name crowds are assembled. One of these private roads is the way of the *mantram*, the way of what Christ called "vain repetition." In public worship "vain repetition" is almost always associated with rhythmic sound. Litanies and the like are chanted, or at least intoned. It is as music that they produce their quasi-hypnotic effects. "Vain repetition," when practiced privately, acts upon the mind, not because of its association with rhythmic sound (for it works even when the words are merely imagined), but in virtue of a concentration of attention and memory. The constant reiteration of the same word or phrase frequently brings on a state of light or even profound trance. Once induced, this trance can either be enjoyed for its own sake, as a delicious sense of infra-personal otherness, or else deliberately used for the purpose of improving personal conduct by autosuggestion and of preparing the way for the ultimate achievement of upward self-transcendence. Of the second possibility more will be said in a later paragraph. Here our concern is with "vain repetition" as a descending road into an infra-personal alienation.

We must now consider a strictly physiological method of escape from insulated selfhood. The way of corporal penance. The destructive violence which is the final symptom of herd-intoxication is not invariably directed outward. The history of religion abounds in gruesome tales of gregarious self-whipping, self-gashing, self-gelding, even self-killing. These acts are the consequences of crowd-delirium, and are performed in a state of frenzy. Very different is the corporal penance undertaken privately and in cold blood. Here the self-torment is initiated by an act of the personal will; but its result (in some cases at least) is a temporary transformation of the insulated personality into something else. In itself, this something else is the consciousness, so intense as to be exclusive, of physical pain. The self-tortured person identifies himself with his pain and, in becoming merely the awareness of his suffering body, is delivered from that sense of past guilt and present frustration, that obsessive anxiety about the future, which constitute so large a part of the neurotic ego. There has been an escape from selfhood, a downward passage into a state of pure physiological excruciation. But the self-tormentor need not necessarily remain in this region of infra-personal consciousness. Like the man who makes use of "vain repetition" to go beyond himself, he may be able to use his temporary alienation from selfhood as the bridge, so to speak, leading upward into the life of the spirit.

This raises a very important and difficult question. To what extent, and in what circumstances, is it possible for a man to make use of the descending road as a way to spiritual self-transcendence? As first sight it would seem obvious that the way down is not and can never be the way up. But in the realm of existence matters are not quite so simple as they are in our beautifully tidy world of words. In actual life a downward movement may sometimes be made the beginning of an ascent. When the shell of the ego has been cracked and there begins to be a consciousness of the subliminal and physiological othernesses underlying personality, it sometimes happens that we catch a glimpse, fleeting but apocalyptic, of that other Otherness, which is the Ground of all being. So long as we are confined within our insulated selfhood, we remain unaware of the various not-selves with which we are associated—the organic not-self, the subconscious not-self, the collective not-self of the psychic medium in which all our thinking and feeling have their existence, and the immanent and transcendent not-self of the Spirit. Any escape, even by a descending road, out of insulated selfhood makes possible at least a momentary awareness of the not-self on every level, including the highest. William James, in his *Varieties of Religious Experience*, gives instances of "anaesthetic revelations," following the inhalation of laughing gas. Similar theophanies are sometimes experienced by alcoholics, and there are probably moments in the course of intoxication by almost any drug, when awareness of a not-self superior to the disintegrating ego becomes briefly possible. But these occasional flashes of revelation are bought at an enormous price. For the drug-taker, the moment of spiritual awareness (if it comes at all) gives place very soon to subhuman stupor, frenzy or hallucination, followed by dismal hangovers and, in the long run, by a permanent and fatal impairment of bodily health and mental power. Very occasionally a single "anaesthetic revelation" may act, like any other theophany, to incite its recipient to an effort of self-transformation and upward self-transcendence. But the fact that such a thing sometimes happens can never justify the employment of chemical methods of self-transcendence. This is a descending road and most of those who take it will come to a state of degradation, where periods of subhuman ecstasy alternate with periods of conscious selfhood so wretched that any escape, even if it be into the slow suicide of drug addiction, will seem preferable to being a person.

What is true of drugs is true, *mutatis mutandis*, of elementary sexuality. The road runs downhill; but on the way there may occasionally be theophanies. The Dark Gods, as Lawrence called them, may change their sign and become bright. In India there is a Tantric yoga, based upon an elaborate psychophysiological technique, whose purpose is to transform the downward self-transcendence of elementary sexuality into an upward self-transcendence. In the West the nearest equivalent to these Tantric practices was the sexual discipline devised by John Humphrey Noyes and practiced by the members of the Oneida Community. At Oneida elementary sexuality was not only successfully civilized; it was made compatible with, and subordinate to, a form of Protestant Christianity, sincerely preached and earnestly acted upon.

Herd-intoxication disintegrates the ego more thoroughly than does elementary sexuality. Its frenzies, its follies, its heightened suggestibility can be matched only in the intoxications induced by such drugs as alcohol, hashish and heroin. But even to the member of an excited mob there may come (at some relatively early stage of his downward self-transcendence) a genuine revelation of the Otherness that is above selfhood. This is one of the reasons why some good may sometimes come out of even the most corybantic of revival meetings. Some good as well as very great evil may also result from the fact that men and women in a crowd tend to become more than ordinarily suggestible. While in this state they are subjected to exhortations which have the force, when they come once again to their senses, of posthypnotic commands. Like the demagogue, the revivalist and the ritualist disintegrate the ego of their hearers by herding them together and dosing them with plenty of vain repetition and rhythmic sound. Then, unlike the demagogue, they give suggestions some of which may be genuinely Christian. These, if they "take," result in a reintegration of broken-down personalities on a somewhat higher level. There can also be reintegrations of personality under the influence of the posthypnotic commands issued by a rabble-rousing politician. But these commands are all incitements to hatred on the one hand and to blind obedience and compensatory illusion on the other. Initiated by a massive dose of herd-poison, confirmed and directed by the rhetoric of a maniac who is at the same time a Machiavellian exploiter of other men's weakness, political "conversion" results in the creation of a new personality worse than the old and much more dangerous because wholeheartedly devoted to a party whose first aim is the liquidation of its opponents.

I have distinguished between demagogues and religionists, on the ground that the latter may sometimes do some good, whereas the former can scarcely, in the very nature of things, do anything but harm. But it must not be imagined that the religious exploiters of herd-intoxication are wholly guiltless. On the contrary, they have been responsible in the past for mischiefs almost as enormous as those brought upon their victims (along with the victims of those victims) by the revolutionary demagogues of our own time. In the course of the last six or seven generations, the power of religious organizations to do evil has, throughout the Western world, considerably declined. Primarily this is due to the astounding progress of applied science and the consequent demand by the masses for compensatory illusions that have an air of being positivistic rather than metaphysical. The demagogues offer such pseudo-positivistic illusions and the churches do not. As the attractiveness of the churches declines, so also does their influence, so do their wealth, their political power and, along with these, their capacity for doing evil on a large scale. Circumstances have now delivered the churchmen from certain of the temptations, to which, in earlier centuries, their predecessors almost invariably succumbed. They would be well advised voluntarily to deliver themselves from such temptations as still remain. Conspicuous among these is the temptation to acquire power by pandering to men's insatiable craving for downward self-transcendence. Deliberately to induce herd-intoxication—even if it is done in the name of religion, even if it is all supposedly "for the good" of the intoxicated—cannot be morally justified.

On the subject of horizontal self-transcendence very little need be said—not because the phenomenon is unimportant (far from it), but because it is too obvious to require analysis and of occurrence too frequent to be readily classifiable.

In order to escape from the horrors of insulated selfhood most men and women choose, most of the time, to go neither up nor down, but sideways. They identify themselves with some cause wider than their own immediate interests, but not degradingly lower and, if higher, higher only within the range of current social values. This horizontal, or nearly horizontal, self-transcendence may be into something as trivial as a hobby, or as precious as married love. It can be brought about through self-identification with any human activity, from running a business to research in nuclear physics, from composing music to collecting stamps, from campaigning for political office to educating children or studying the mating habits of birds. Horizontal self-transcendence is of the utmost importance. Without it, there would be no art, no science, no law, no philosophy, indeed no civilization. And there would also be no war, no *odium theologicum* or *ideologicum*, no systematic intolerance, no persecution. These great goods and these enormous evils are the fruits of man's capacity for total and continuous self-identification with an idea, a feeling, a cause. How can we have the good without the evil, a high civilization without saturation bombing or the extermination of religious and political heretics? The answer is that we cannot have it so long as our self-transcendence remains merely horizontal. When we identify ourselves with an idea or a cause we are in fact worshiping something homemade, something partial and parochial, something that, however noble, is yet all too human. "Patriotism," as a great patriot concluded on the eve of her execution by her country's enemies, "is not enough." Neither is socialism, nor communism, nor capitalism; neither is art, nor science, nor public order, nor any given religion or church. All these are indispensable, but none of them is enough. Civilization demands from the individual devoted self-identification with the highest of human causes. But if this self-identification with what is human is not accompanied by a conscious and consistent effort to achieve upward self-transcendence into the universal life of the Spirit, the goods achieved will always be mingled with counterbalancing evils. "We make," wrote Pascal, "an idol of truth itself; for truth without charity is not God, but His image and idol, which we must neither love or worship." And it is not merely wrong to worship an idol; it is also exceedingly inexpedient. The worship of truth apart from charity—self-identification with science unaccompanied by self-identification with the Ground of all being—results in the kind of situation which now confronts us. Every idol, however exalted, turns out, in the long run, to be a Moloch, hungry for human sacrifice.

BIBLIOGRAPHY

In writing this history of Grandier, Surin, Sœur Jeanne and the devils I have made use of the following sources:

Histoire des Diables le Loudun (Amsterdam, 1693). This work, by the Protestant Pastor Aubin, is a very well-documented account of Grandier's trial and the subsequent possession. The author was an inhabitant of Loudun and acquainted with many of the actors in the diabolic drama.

Urbain Grandier in *La Sorcière*. By Jules Michelet. The great historian's essay is brief and inaccurate, but extremely lively.

Urbain Grandier et les Possédées de Loudun. By Dr. Gabriel Legué (Paris, 1880). A very thorough book. The same author's earlier work, *Documents pour servir à l'histoire médicale des possédées de Loudun* (Paris, 1876) is also valuable.

Relation. By Fr. Tranquille. First published in 1634. Reprinted in Vol. II of *Archives Curieuses de l'Histoire de France* (1838).

The History of the devils of Loudun. By de Nion. Published at Poitiers in 1634, and printed in translation at Edinburgh, 1887-88. Lauderdale's account of his visit to Loudun appears as a supplement to this narrative.

Letter. By Thomas Killigrew. Published in the *European Magazine* (February, 1803).

Bayle's *Historical Dictionary* (English edition, 1736). Article on Urbain Grandier.

Sœur Jeanne des Anges, Autobiographie d'une hystérique possédée. Edited, with introduction and notes, by Drs. Gabriel Legué and Gilles de la Tourette (Paris, 1886). This is the only edition of the narrative composed by the Prioress in 1644. The autobiography is followed by numerous letters addressed by Sœur Jeanne to Fr. Saint-Jure, S.J.

Science Expérimentale. By Jean-Joseph Surin (1828). This is a somewhat garbled edition of Surin's account of his stay at Loudun.

Lettres Spirituelles du P. Jean-Joseph Surin. Edited by L. Michel and F. Cavalléra (Toulouse, 1926). Vol. II contains a reliable text of what the editors call the Autobiography of Surin.

Dialogues Spirituels. By Jean-Joseph Surin (Lyon, 1831).

Le Catéchisme Spirituel. By Jean-Joseph Surin (Lyon, 1856).

Fondements de la Vie Spirituelle. By Jean-Joseph Surin (Paris, 1879).

Questions sur l'Amour de Dieu. By Jean-Joseph Surin. Edited, with valuable introduction, notes and appendices, by A. Pottier and L. Maries (Paris, 1930).

Le Père Louis Lallemant et les grands spirituels de son temps. By Aloys Pottier, S.J. (Paris, 1930. 2 vols.)

La Doctrine Spirituelle du P. Louis Lallemant. By Pierre Champion. First published in 1694. The best modern edition is that of 1924.

Histoire Littéraire du Sentiment Religieux en France. By Henri Bremond (Paris, 1916 and subsequent years). Contains excellent chapters on Lallemant and Surin.

INDEX

331